WHEN MILITARY WAGES PEACE

Military Bands in Diplomacy, War & Statecraft

WHEN MILITARY WAGES PEACE

Military Bands in Diplomacy, War & Statecraft

Saad S. Khan

PENTAGON PRESS LLP

WHEN MILITARY WAGES PEACE: Role of Military Bands in Diplomacy, War and Statecraft

Saad S Khan

ISBN 978-93-86618-72-6

First Published in 2019

Published by
PENTAGON PRESS LLP
206, Peacock Lane, Shahpur Jat,
New Delhi-110049
Phones: 011-64706243, 26491568
Telefax: 011-26490600
email: rajan@pentagonpress.in
website: www.pentagonpress.in

Printed at Aegean Offset Printers, Greater Noida, U.P.

Dedicated

To all men and women in this world

Who are

Whoever were

And whosoever will be

Musicians in a Band

From all past, present and future generations of humankind

Contents

PREFACE

Without music, life is a mistake

—Friedrich Nietzsche

Wittingly or unwittingly, most people believe in the above notion and wonder if life is possible without music. Music is so embedded into human life that it is just like the air we breathe—we rarely feel its inseparability and omnipresence.

We know that music affects the brain when we hear it, but especially when we play it. The maths involved in playing music keeps the brain active and growing. Music can uplift one's spirits when one is feeling down or depressed. And if one is happy, music buoys the mood.

There are religions and traditions that believe the universe was 'sung into being'. The aborigines of Australia held that it was done by their forefathers, while Hindu teachings describe the 'Word' in terms of the sound 'Om,' which is the vibratory essence of God and the creative energy used to bring the universe into existence. This understanding of 'Om', as the seed syllable for creation is clearly reflected in Buddhist religious thought as well. In the Islamic tradition, on the other hand, the universe will one day be 'trumpeted out' of existence. The end of the world, or doomsday, will come when angel *Israfil* blows a grand horn or trumpet (*Soor*) at the command of Allah, the Almighty.

The trumpet brings us to the issue of bands, which are—in their most basic form—combinations of wind and percussion instruments. If music is one of the defining components of our individual lives, the band has that role in our social, as well as national, lives. Imagine a world without music and without bands: imagine marriages, festivals, national days, university games, television shows and smart devices devoid of music. That kind of musical silence would be deafening!

This book is an endeavour to introduce the readership to the concept of bands, especially military and marching bands. It is also an attempt to foster an appreciation of the role that bands have been playing in our collective lives over centuries—from victories and defeats in the wars that our previous generations fought, in the peace they made, and up to the present day where bands shape, colour and enlighten our lives. The book also aims high at becoming a seminal treatise, suggesting more creative uses of military bands for making the world as harmonious as a musical symphony.

Despite this question being asked of me every so often, I do not know when, why or how my life got entangled with Bands—Military Bands, in particular, became my soul, my parallel existence! All I know is that my cognitive awareness of life and of band music developed together as I grew up. I never had any formal musical training, nor have I ever been a full-time member of a regular military band myself (participating in a private drum circle is another matter). But that does not dampen my passion for listening to military music, reading about military bands and amassing collections of videos, audios and pictures of military bands.

The more I waded into the affairs of military bands, the more I felt the need of a concise handbook for general information on military bands: one written for laymen. There are so many types of Bands nowadays, that the technically incorrect use of their labels lead to a lot of confusion about their roles, which discourages a layperson—even one learning to play *in* a band—gives up trying to learn *about* the band.

One fine day, I thought of compiling a simple, concise and easy-to-understand handbook of military bands myself. I thought a collection of my lectures and talks on military bands could run into a hundred pages, which could then be translated into the indigenous languages of South Asia, especially for use by military and police band members in the subcontinent. I wanted our bandsmen and women to become aware of the history of bands and to know their role enough to feel proud of being band members. As the work progressed, I realised that there were matters which might interest and influence people beyond band members—such as, for instance, policy makers. So the treatise started taking a shape that would target a broader potential readership. It has now expanded to a level beyond my imagination, and of course, much larger than a hundred odd pages. There are so many more things that came up as possible inclusions that if I try to incorporate all of them it will remain a work in progress for many more years. Plus, the purpose of a simple, crisp and easily-comprehendible volume may be lost in the process. Since this book is written by a layman, I believe it will serve the purpose of explaining the evolution, role and importance of bands in the simplest of terms. One does not require any prior musical knowledge to understand this work.

This book seeks to establish the undeniable linkages between musical bands, especially military Bands, and the promotion of world peace. It also introduces several innovative ideas on the peace building role of Bands that our website (www.marchingbands.band) has been advocating for quite some time. I must acknowledge three persons—a Frenchman, a Swiss man and an Englishman—who inspired me to toy with these outlandish ideas on peace with their courage of commitment. that I, at the very least, pretend to have. Even when I cannot clearly pinpoint an inspiration for my infatuation with the Bands, I can definitely cite these great men as my motivation for believing that the ideas propagated in this work will see the light of the day.

My first inspiration is from Switzerland, Henry Dunant who in the second half of the nineteenth century emerged as the ideological father of the Geneva Conventions on Humanitarian Laws for Warfare and the founder of the International Red Cross. He was later to have the honour of being the co-recipient of the first-ever Nobel Prize for Peace. My second inspiration is from France where Baron Pierre de Coubertin believed that sports could promote peace. He spearheaded the revival of the Olympics Games, after a long hiatus of two millennia, at the turn of the twentieth century. And finally, British singer and filmmaker, Jeremy Gilley, the founder of the Peace One Day movement who succeeded in getting September 21 declared as the Universal Day of Ceasefire and Non-violence by the United Nations. These three examples have left me with no doubt in my mind that the ideas being propounded through this book, especially its Chapter XV—outlandish as some of them may seem at the moment— may see their realisation sooner rather than later.

Let me conclude by recalling another personal experience. As I reached the fag end of my endeavour to write this book, I had the opportunity to attend the annual gathering of the International Military Music Society (IMMS) at Stockholm, Sweden. Among the activities planned for us was marching with the Mounted Band of the Royal Life Guard Dragoons from the Dragoon Barracks to the royal palace for their daily ceremony. We saw the band brace up at the barracks, trot through the city while playing on horseback, and ending up at the change of guard ceremony at the palace. In this journey of less than two miles, I tried to count the number of smiles that it brought on people's faces en route. I lost count after 8,000. And this was just one military band, in one city, for one hour! I believe that having military Bands is an inalienable right for humankind as it is rooted in two other basic rights: the right to happiness and the right to a cultural heritage. I, for one, would always consider it my duty to love, respect and defend the Bands.

At the end, I would be failing if I do not acknowledge the generous help I have received from family, friends and band-lovers for my venture. I must mention Bob Davis, the President of International Military Music Society (IMMS) for his interest, encouragement and support. I must also acknowledge the help of Lt. Col. Geoff Kingston, former Chair of the IMMS International Committee and Roger McGuire, head of the Canada Branch of IMMS, for having agreed to review my work on Brass Bands and Pipe Bands, respectively, in order to give valuable input. Special thanks are also due for Kris Schauvliege, head of the IMMS Belgium Branch, for generously sharing his photo collection with me. I am also indebted to my friend Ashok Behuria for his help in all stages of the present work.

And special gratitude is owed to Mr Rajan Aryaa for accepting the work for publication despite the reviewer warning him that this book had "limited market" and for his keen help at each stage of the publication process. Last but not the least, I owe it to my wife Sara, for all the support and help she gave me all along in this project, in all projects of my life and in my life itself, which has now become "her project".

I hope the present contribution will be a valuable addition to available knowledge on Bands. As US President Ronald Reagan once said: 'Life is one great sweet song, so start the music.' So let's start this book!

Saad S. Khan, PhD

Chairman, Marching Bands for Peace

Lahore, December 2018 Chair@marchingBands.band

CHAPTER I

Introduction to Military Bands

"Music hath charms to soothe a savage beast, to soften rocks or bend a twisted oak."

—William Congreve

There is no concept of a uniformed force without a Marching Band. The world over, the largest owners and patrons of Bands include all wings of the Armed Forces like the Army, Navy, and Air Force, as well as other security agencies such as the police, gendarmerie and the border security forces. In many countries, even fire, rescue and emergency services maintain Bands. All these military and non-military Bands have in them a pride in one's nation, aspirations of the citizenry and height of musical achievement.

It is not for nothing that uniformed forces have Bands. Being part of the Bands promotes discipline, teamwork and camaraderie that is of vital importance to the uniformed organizations. Long rehearsals, memorizing drills and remembering music makes one so professionally disciplined that it becomes a foundation for discipline in all other facets of life. Since every member of a team is important, and every person contributes, so teamwork gets imbibed into one's psyche through a Band. There is amazing satisfaction in coming together as a team and working hard alongside to perform a show. Hence, camaraderie becomes another important aspect of being part of the band of one's institution. Shared experiences over time build relationships and friendships. Being part of a band gives a mutual sense of ownership between the person and the organization.

What is a Band?

The most empirical definition of a Band is as an ensemble that performs musical duties. For an ensemble to be called a "Band," ordinarily it must have a combination of more than one type of instruments from amongst the percussion instruments (played by hand or sticks such as drums or cymbals), wind instruments (played by mouth such as pipes or bugles), string instruments (guitars, violins, etc.) and keyboard family (such as Piano). The Bands can, and often do, have a vocal component. In certain military and police Band traditions, the band is accompanied by a dance troupe too. So even if the ensemble does not rely on more than one family of instruments, it comfortably falls within the definition of "Band," if it performs more than one musical activity, such as music and song, music and march, song and dance, etc.

However, in modern days, as the types of Bands are increasing, it is not uncommon to see Bands that would defy virtually any form of stereotypical definition. Percussion-only Bands, sometimes called a Drum line, are popular with military and college drill teams while Wind-only ensemble such as the Bugle Corps with a military unit, say, for funeral ceremonies or the Palace Trumpeters to herald royal or presidential arrivals, are common sights nowadays. Larger Wind Bands are also common in military forces and civil institutions. One also finds Strings[-only] Bands worldwide playing rock or pop music.

The optional vocal component may mean an additional singer or vocalist, as is the case in many of the military Bands in the United States or a whole Choir such as the one with the famous Alexandrov Band of Russia. However, in several East and South European Bands, the band members sing together as chorus as part of the performance interspersing the instrumental component.

Likewise, for the dance troupe, it is customary to have one in the Bands of most Russian, East European and other former Soviet or ex-Communist Countries, Bandsas well as in many military Bands in South and East African States. Latin American States, such as Mexico, have military music and dance corps. The Bands in New Zealand conduct Maori war dances as part of their Band performance. This is closely replicated in several Pacific island nation Bands where Band performance includes ancient tribal dance manoeuvres.

What is a Military Band?

From the simple definition of Band being an ensemble entrusted with musical duties, it would follow that a "Military Band" could most conveniently be defined as an ensemble that performs musical duties *within the Armed Forces.*

However, a generalization can become misleading as in many countries "military band" can be a term used to signify the Wind-Brass Bands (all those Bands which use brass as well as woodwind instruments as opposed to simple fifes and drums), regardless of whether they are part of the Defence forces or otherwise. It is not uncommon to witness school and university Bands, across the

United States, having military-style uniforms, brass and woodwind instruments and army like marching drills. In another corner of the globe—across South Asia, that is—it is also common to find signboards of "*Private* Military Bands" that are available for hire, to march with the wedding processions. For most people in the West, however, such a term would appear as an oxymoron. Notwithstanding that even in the United States, a band called Virginia Grand Military Band (VGMB)—the winner of 2000 Sudler Silver Scroll—is a civilian concert band although it counts many retired members of US Army and Marine Bands in its current 80 members. Similar is the case of London Military—famous for Christmas concerts—which has nothing to do with the British Military.

Till the mid-nineteenth century, British military Bands were wholly composed of civilians, hired and paid for by the commanding officers of the units. Sweden tried to switch musicians of the military Bands from military personnel to civilians in the early 1970s but the policy did not work and was reversed. In the United States, Reserve Army Bands [Cf. Chap VI] are one of the three types of Military Bands and they consist of civilian musicians who perform for military divisions.

If military Bands, being totally civilian-based and civilian Bands calling themselves as military Bands was not confusing enough, Tom Dikon, an American Harmonica player from Hampton, has come up with something else; he has established a mix civil–military Band. Describing his Band album as "Bridge,", he aims at "bringing together" military and civilian musicians in performances. His Bandmates include civilians like him but also at least three active duty US Air Force musicians. Should his be called a military band or not, remains foggy.

In this work, which is mainly concerned with "military Bands," the term is used only to signify the Bands of the Armed Forces, regardless of the type of instrumentation, and whether or not the musicians are regular military personnel. This includes the Bands owned by the Army, Navy, Air Force and Marine corps of the world. It also includes Band of any other arm of the military which is treated as a separate branch of the Armed Forces such as the Corps of Air Defence of Saudi Arabia. In most countries, the Bands of the paramilitary forces such as the United States Coast Guards and India's Border Security Force are also counted amongst their military Bands.

The military band is almost ways a uniformed formation or at the least it has a thematic attire or appearance. Traditionally, for a variety of historical and ceremonial reasons, the uniforms of the military Bands and accoutrements are much more elegant than those of the military branch or unit they represent.

Even when many Bands are moving towards modern get-up, including

Western-style jacket-trousers-baseball-cap combo, there are some Bands in almost every country that still reflect the clothing and costume history of a nation, a region or an organization. That is to say, with the exceptions of reigning monarchs, the only group that dons the outfits traditionally used in the society centuries ago, are the military Bands. The Bands are also the legatees of the national musical heritage, including compositions, dances, drills and songs.

Difference between a Military Band and a Marching Band

When one is marching and a drum is beating, one will soon start marching in step with the rhythm. The Bands can be used in outdoor and indoor environment but not all Bands can perform in both the settings. For instance, the easiest to play while marching would be the Corps of Pipes (or Bugles) and Drums (see Chap VI). On the other end of the spectrum, philharmonic orchestra cannot be played while marching. Bands capable of playing while marching are ordinarily called the Marching Bands.

The Organization "Marching Bands for Peace" defines a *Marching Band* as "a uniformed ensemble of not less than eight members that performs musical duties, plays more than one type of instrumentation (wind, string, percussion, and keyboard), or more than one type of performance (instruments, songs, dance or drill), and is capable of performing while marching."

Since Bands originated within the military forces, more as a tactical necessity on the battlefields than anything else, the initial military music was mostly field music. It follows therefrom that traditional military Bands were marching Bands as they had to move with the marching forces into the battlefields. But today, it may not necessarily be so, although most of the world's military Bands would still fit into the above definition of marching Bands. And so do most of the school, college and university Bands, the South Asian wedding Bands as well as many Bands of the religious orders. In fact, the thousands of Marching Bands that belong to the colleges and universities today far outnumber the military marching Bands.

Today, institutions from the Armed Forces to Cathedrals also maintain philharmonic orchestras or other smaller variants of sit-in or *Chamber Bands*, but it is the *Marching Bands* that are most visible in a wide variety of settings like state ceremonials, public festivals and football games, etc. The focus of the present work remains mostly on military Bands, both marching and chamber ones, but references to other types of Bands also occur recurrently depending on the context of the discussion.

Bands Index

If one desires to know if a kingdom is well governed, if its morals are good or bad, the quality of the music will furnish the answer.

—Confucius (551 BC-479 BC)

What Confucius said over two and a half millennia ago, may well be true today. Observation and anecdotal evidence points to the likelihood that the Bands representing countries with greater per capita income, better quality of life or higher Human Development Index rankings, tend to excel over the ones from countries lower in these classifications, both in terms of their visual impression and musical performance. In other words, were the World Military Band Olympics [See Chapter XV] to be held today, we can expect the country-wise ranking in number of medals to closely follow their rankings in economic and governance related indicators.

Till then, Confucius' maxim, remains at best a hypothesis. If it is corroborated by evidence that the display, dressing and musical harmony of the Bands of the Armed Forces is a direct reflection of higher development, then the rise or decline of the quality of military Bands of a nation will help one guide towards the direction in which the State's governance and economy is moving.

However, it is clear that civilized nations take their national military Bands very seriously. Famous US Composer and founder of the US Marines Band, John Philip Sousa, in 1880, called it as the National Band of the United States. Sousa believed that the Band "should be as great among Bands as America is among nations" (Fettig 2016). The Military Band is also the first impression of a nation when a foreign head of state arrives for a state visit. As we shall see in this work, a poorly performing Band speaks a lot about the capabilities of the Armed Forces and about the status of material development in the nation it is representing.

Conclusion: Recognition of Military Bands

Development of Music, it is said, has been immensely influenced by the three institutions of Monarchy, Military and Marriage. This applies more so for the Band Music and the Bands. Monarchy needed the Bands for pomp and glory so the subjects remained impressed by the majesty of the rulers. The military required Bands for drill and discipline during peacetime and for enlivening of spirits and for signalling during wartime. And the institution of marriage adopted Bands since there could be no higher expression of happiness than through music, dance and songs. These three streams will be dealt with, respectively, in the Chapters III, IV and V.

The Military Bands have a long history spanning over several centuries. The Bands have represented the national pride, the national aspirations and, may be, the level of national development. The Military Bands have seldom been accorded their due share of prestige in the national and international scene. In fact, it is fairly recent that annual or bi-annual international military Bands tattoos have sprung up in some major cities of the world such as Edinburgh (UK), Moscow (Russia), Norfolk (Virginia, USA), Basel (Switzerland) and Oslo (Norway) among others. Many countries like Germany, Finland, India and Pakistan have started their national level Bands Tattoos.

It may take some time before recognition of Military Bands and Bandsmen matches the recognitions given to sports, television, opera and film celebrities in the world. Nevertheless, Military Bands and all sorts of Marching Bands are here to stay in this world, and gradually the global society may develop a better appreciation of the services the Bands have been providing over time.

CHAPTER II

Genesis of Military Bands: Regional Influences

The truest expression of a people is in its dance and music.

—Agnes de Mile (1905-93)

The genesis of Bands was a by-product of human disposition for sound recognition for pleasure, sorrow and to receive commands. Interestingly, Bands emerged as a war necessity since the need for audial communication was greatest in times of armed conflicts when the hazy environs of battlefields precluded the practicability of visual commands. As humankind started living in States around 3500 BC or thereabouts, the potential for intra and inter-State rivalry also emerged. This necessitated raising of armies by the monarchs both for offensive and defensive purposes. When the world population was small and troops had small strengths it was possible to shout commands. Gradually, larger military forces became the norm and in the din of battles, voice commands became ineffective means of communication.

Man found out that if he could blow wind in a hollow wooden tube or twig, or even a hollowed dried up fruit, a louder unidirectional sound could be produced. Further, refinement of this concept led to the development of fifes—the precursor of modern day pipes and bagpipes. On a parallel note, the beat of a stick on a hollow body such as a hollow piece of tree trunk, covered tautly by an animal hide, was also found to produce great sounds. Thus, drums got to be developed. And they became the pre-historic signalling instruments.

Countries like the China, Egypt, France, Russia, Pakistan and the United States are far removed from each other geographically, culturally and politically. Yet, in matters of war music, they have a great deal in common in the types of musical notes and instrumental combinations that developed, more often than not, independently over the course of the centuries. This chapter looks at the influence of such diverse regions in the development of military Bands

Influence of Roman and other Ancient Empires

Many of the earliest surviving pictorial, sculptured, and written records show musical instruments used by soldiers in battles in diverse corners of the world. Chronicles and pictorial remains from Egyptian, Greek, Roman, Indian, Arab-Oriental, and other cultures depict trumpets and drums of many varieties used in connection with military activities (e.g. signalling in combat, during parades, and in encampments).

The earliest known evidence of military Bands, from as early as 3000 BC, comes from stone art works that depict Assyrian and Babylonian musicians (in modern day Iraq) playing brass instruments while leading their armies in triumphal processions (Morris Jastrow 1915). Later day stone reliefs from the region, which is now known as the Middle East, provides the earliest known illustrations of ensemble music including the brass, reed, and percussion instruments (Music 2005).

Around 1000 BC, the Egyptians are known to have used music for ceremonies. Reliefs from this period show musicians playing harps, sistrums (instruments that used rattling rods to produce a percussive effect), and nays (whistle-like instruments) for dancers and listeners (Music 2005).

Jump another millennium and the Roman empire provides the first tangible evidence of organizational military musicians. Historical traces from around the time of Julius Caesar, circa 56 BC, indicate to the presence of Military Drummers in his Empire. Roman musicians, called Aenatores, performed duties often required of military musicians today. They signalled troop movements, performed for official functions and funerals, played on the march, and provided moral support for the troops. The Romans had three basic groups of signal musicians, namely, the tubicine, the cornicine and the bucinatore (Music 2005).

Another seven centuries passed when the first organized form of military Bands along with armies started appearing in what is now modern-day Turkey in the late 8th century A.D. This comes from their mention in the Orkhon Inscriptions, the oldest written source ofTurkish history. In the pre-Islamic times, these Bands were not able to play while marching. It was the Ottoman empire that raised the level of military music to full-fledged uniformed Marching Orchestras.

Influence of the Ottoman Empire up to the Modern Turkish State

Within the Islamic history, the introduction of the concept of strict discipline, drill and uniforms in the military—which is now the default outlook of any modern army—is sometimes attributed to the second Caliph of the Abbasside Dynasty Abu Jaffar Mansour (r. 754–776 AD). It is also well known that during the Crusade wars, the Muslim armies relied heavily on their Bands for signalling commands to their troops and as a psychological weapon against the European armies. However, it goes to the credit of the Ottoman empire to have fully developed Musical Corps of the Army. Records show that by the 13th century AD, the Turks had fully equipped large *Mehter* Bands accompanying their army into battles and wars. In fact, the first full *Mehter* Band might have been gifted to the founder of Ottoman dynasty, Osman Ghazi, by the Seljuk Sultan of Anatolia Alauddin Kaykubad III in 1289. The city of Bursa was the last major victory of Osman Ghazi before his death in 1323–24, although he did not physically participate in the campaign. His son and successor, Sultan Orhan Ghazi, made Bursa the capital of the Ottoman empire. A *Mehter* Band was established there in 1326. The *Mehter* Bands were the first organized, uniformed and disciplined military Bands not only amongst the Muslim armies but in the whole military world.

Even Turks themselves could find the military music overwhelming. The Bands "raise such a din that Venus begins to dance and the skies resound," famous Ottoman traveler and explorer Evliya Çelebi (1611-82) wrote of the *Mehter*, adding that when they passed by, "the noise of them presses men's brains out of their mouths" (Campbell 2012).

The importance of Military Bands for the Ottoman Caliphs had grown enormously by the 17th century. The Bands became part of the imperial household and its members were the highest paid servants in the imperial staff. So much so that when a dispute arose between the Chief Architect of the empire and Head (Aga) of Mehter band as to who was senior in terms of Court protocol, Caliph Murad VI, decided to give precedence to the Mehter chief in military and civil protocol. In fact, two of the Prime Ministers (Grand Viziers) of the empire, namely Zurnazen Mustafa Pasha and Daltaban Mustafa Pasha had risen from the ranks of the Mehter.

This status of Bandsmen was in sharp contrast to other leading European powers at the time. Take Sweden, for example, where the Band Members at the royal court consistently failed to raise their status from that of "servants" to that of "artists," what to speak of that of royal courtiers. Coming back to the Ottoman empire, a time came when all Turkish Viziers and Governors were obliged to maintain Mehter Bands in their regions and palaces as matter of prestige. Military Bands were eventually maintained by Swedish noblemen as well for their own prestige—a prestige not passed on to the Swedish musicians that has had implications to the sustainability of Swedish Military Bands to this day.

The Mehter Band marches behind the commander of the Band, known as *Corbacibasi*, who wears a headdress known as *üsküf.* After him to his left and right respectively march the bearers of the white, green and red standards, the latter with an armed guard. The White Flag is a sign of independence stands at the centre while to its right the Red Flag represents Turkish nation and to its left the Green flag represents Islam. Behind these nine plume bearers march three by three, with the "plume of attack" positioned behind the red standard. Then comes the Band master in the centre, and behind him the *Cevgâns* (jingling instruments in the form of a crescent), *Zurnas*, trumpets, *Nakkares* (small kettledrums beaten with the hands or two sticks), cymbals, *Davuls* (bass drums) and finally the *Kös* drums (giant kettledrums) played on horseback. The *Mehter* Band members form a crescent to perform, and play standing except for the *Nakkare* players, who sit cross-legged at the right-hand tip of the crescent, followed anticlockwise by the *Zurnas*, bass drums, cymbals and trumpets. When they march, the Band members pause every three steps and turn to right and left in salutation, in a rhythm set by the drums, chanting "*Rahim Allah, Kerim Allah*" (Merciful God, Gracious God). This marching style of looking at right and left was also part of the military caution during campaigns to ward off any sudden ambush from either side.

There are multiple traditions on the origin of the term "*Mehter.*" One is that it means Crescent which was the symbol of Islam and of the Ottoman Caliphate. The standard performance position was, as noted above, by standing in the shape of a crescent and this gave the name *Mehter* to the Bands. Another explanation is that *Mehter* means a single Piper and its plural *Mehteran* aptly describes the Buglers of the Ottoman military formations. In that case the term *Mehter* for the whole Band would be a misnomer. The two meanings do not necessarily exclude each other. Might be that since *Mehter* performance was crescent shaped, that led the individual pipers to be called *Mehter* too. But over the centuries *Mehter* has come to denote the whole Band.

Yet another version suggests that the word has origin in Persian language since the Band was gifted by Seljuk dynasty that had Persian origins. In the Ottoman era Persian, the word means "Imperial or great," and the Bands got to be known as such since they symbolized the glory of the Empire. On the other hand, Campbell argues the Persian root means "superior" and thus *Mehter* initially referred to all imperial servants of superior or high rank. Gradually, the term Mehter was confined to the Band members of the Court of Caliph. (Campbell 2012). Again, there is no great inconsistency in the latter two explanations of whether *Mehter* means "superior" or "great" in Persian.

The Ottoman *Mehter* Bands played at Caliph's coronations, assumption of office by a new Grand Vizier (Prime Minister of the Empire), change of the Raes ul Kuttap (President of the Assembly), weddings in the imperial household of the Caliph, arrival of dignitaries and at all State occasions. The *Mehter* Bands also played daily in the imperial court for the entertainment of the Caliph-Sultan of the Ottoman Empire.

The Ottomans empire extended well into the Eastern half of continental Europe. The centuries of warfare between the Ottomans and their rival powers had brought awareness about Ottoman military tactics, including but not limited to, the use of military Bands to the heart of Europe. The Ottoman Bands were used to march with expeditions, play during the heat of the pitched battles, were used in siege of Castles and also on board ships during maritime battles. The influence of the Ottomans on Europe catalyzed the development of modern Bands in almost all the European forces, as we shall see in the next section.

Meanwhile, back in Turkey, the Ottoman Caliph Mehmud II fell out with his Janissary regiments, dissolving and dispersing them in 1826. The fighting led to massacre of around 15,000 Janissary troops. Considering *Mehter* Bands as a symbol of Janissary regiments, the Caliph dissolved all the surviving Mehter Bands, exactly 500 years after the first full *Mehter* Band was established in Bursa.

But within five years, the need for an imperial Band was badly felt. At that time, Turks had started getting fascinated with European culture and style, just like the Europeans had a craze for everything Turkish in the preceding two centuries. The European style music shows were commonplace in Ottoman territories and as part of reformist efforts of the palace, the Caliph established a Western-style "Muzikia-e-Hümayun" (the royal Band) in place of traditional Mehter. The new Band had Western shirts trousers and peak caps as its uniform. From 1831, this was the Band of the palace as well as Band of the Armed Forces. Campbell aptly points out that in 1831, what had earlier "left Turkey as Eastern import to the West came back to Turkey as a Western import to the East" (Campbell 2012).

The *Mehter* genre remained in disarray and disfavour and continued to decline mirroring that of the Ottoman empire itself till the Young Turks revolution in

1908. Ferik Ahmed Muhtar Pasha founded the Imperial Military Museum in the same year. As its first Director, he attempted a somewhat successful revival of the *Mehter* tradition, but most of the musical repertoire of a century ago had been lost for good. By 1914, as the empire was beginning to collapse, Band was reestablished as the Mehterhane-i Hakani—Royal Mehter Band—attached to the museum as a reminder of former Ottoman glory. The Band revived its own distinctive marching step of turning to right and to left after every three step, with rhythm of the same words "*Rahim Allah, Kerim Allah*" noted earlier (Mehter Army Band n.d.).

Following the foundation of the Turkish Republic, Defence Minister Zekai Bey again banned the *Mehters* around 1935 considering them vestiges of past imperial rule which had "no place in modern Turkey." However, in 1952, the late President Celal Bayar got impressed by the historical Scottish military Band at the royal funeral of King Henry VI (father of present Queen Elizabeth) in London. President Bayar asked former Chief of General Staff Nuri Yamut to revive tradition military Bands in Turkey. So, by the next year, when 500th anniversary celebration of the conquest of Istanbul in 1953 was to take place, *Mehter* Bands were revived. Since most music pieces composed before 1826 were not found, so, new lyrics and melodies were added to the repertoire. The Ottoman Mehter Band plays twice daily at the Istanbul Military Museum and also at special ceremonies, both within Turkey and in friendly countries, with the players in historical costumes.

In the past three decades a number of private and civil *Mehter* Bands have emerged in Turkey. The Bursa *Mehter* is one such Band which claims to be the largest amongst civil *Mehter* Bands in modern Turkey. Established in 1991 in the historic North Eastern city of Bursa, it boasts of 75 musicians and is available for hire at weddings and other functions.

Influence on and of the European Kingdoms

Up to the early 18th century, proper military Bands in the modern sense, capable of playing patriotic tunes or performing at ceremonials, were unknown to Europe. However, utility of musical instruments for signalling was well known. For instance, the Side Drum, most closely associated with war, seems to have existed in Switzerland, perhaps as early as the 14th century. Eventually, it came to be seen and heard in the battlefields throughout Europe.

By the 16th century, trumpet also became widely used. Evidence comes from Niccoló Machiavelli's famous 1521 treatise *The Art of War* where he wrote that the commanding officer should issue orders by means of the trumpet because its piercing tone and great volume enabled it to be heard above the pandemonium of combat. Cavalry trumpets, Machiavelli suggested, ought to have a distinctly different timbre, so that their calls would not be mistaken for those pertaining to the infantry. Drums and flutes, he averred, were most useful as an adjunct to discipline on the march and during infantry manoeuvres on the battlefield itself. Because of, or perhaps regardless of, Machiavelli's pontifications, European armies of the time, would not assault the enemy unless urged by the sound of trumpets and kettledrums (Trotter 2005). They had learnt and absorbed the military signals through trumpets and drums from their Saracen adversaries during the Crusade wars.

Concept of proper Military Bands, as opposed to individual musicians accompanying the army, has undoubtedly come to Europe from the Ottoman Caliphate in Turkey. Thus, before dilating upon the European influence on Military Bands, it is important to study how Europe itself was influenced by the Ottoman Bands.

There are three theories as to how the Europeans got introduced to Ottoman Military Bands. One theory is about the siege of Vienna of 1683 where the Ottoman Army decisively failed to further enhance its territories into the heart of Europe. The legend goes that as the Ottoman army fled, the *Mehter* Bands had to leave their complete sets of instruments behind. These were seized by Polish and Austrian troops who self-learnt how to use them. Eventually, these Bands were adopted by newly established Bands in Europeans courts.

The second theory traces the adoption of Ottoman Bands by Europeans to the Treaty of Karlowitz in 1699. The Treaty marked the formal end of Austro-Ottoman War of 1683-97 and divided Europe into respective spheres of influence. To celebrate the peace, Ottoman delegation brought its military Band to the city of Karlovci (modern-day Serbia) where it played for many days. It so inspired the European Noblemen that they started adopting these musical traditions which spread to the whole of Europe.

The third theory links the introduction of *Mehter*-style military Bands to the Ottoman Caliph, Sultan Ahmed III, who in 1720, sent King Augustus II of Poland an entire *Mehter* Band as a gift. The Polish army thereafter adopted the Turkish Band style which was then transfused to other royal courts throughout Europe.

It is all the more probable that all three theories are equally correct, and each of these events must have had an impact on popularization of Military Bands in Europe. One cannot see these three incidents in isolation, as Europe had centuries of interaction with the Ottomans in diplomacy, wars and cultural intercourses.

All of that contributed to the mushrooming not only of modern military Bands in Europe but also various other Oriental traditions.

The Treaty of Karlowitz (1699) is important because after hundreds of years of Ottoman expansionism in Europe, it had ushered in a century-long era of peace, only to be upset by Napoleonic adventures in early 19th century. Thus the whole of 18th century is remarkable for across-the-board craze for Turkish culture in Europe, known as Turquerie, or Turkomania, and music was just one aspect of it. In fact, anything and everything Moorish, Islamic or Oriental appeared exotic to the European minds and became a fashion.

This was the time when the Europeans smoked Turkish tobacco in Turkish pipes, seated on Turkish carpets and drank Turkish coffee while wearing Turkish robes. Turkish baths opened everywhere and Turkish characters and interludes would appear in otherwise unrelated ballets and plays. Dozens of operas were written with Turkish scenarios. There were Turkish harem girls painted by European artists like Ingres and Delacroix. On top of it, the European aristocrats would get their own portraits painted in Turkish costume too. They decorated their private rooms with Turkish motifs and devoured the newly translated text of *A Thousand and One Nights* that, though not Turkish, was at least Oriental. So European militaries could not remain immune from the trend and developed a craze of their own for Ottoman-style military Bands.

The development of European Music took time to refine. For the first century of the three seminal events introducing Ottoman *Mehter* music to Europe noted above, the European Bands remained "a pale shadow" or a "clumsy imitation" of Ottoman *Mehter* music. But by 1831, the Ottomans had not only dissolved *Mehter* Bands but replaced them with, what they believed was, a *modern* Palace Band of European-style.

But this European-style was itself was an Ottoman legacy for the continent. The preceding four centuries of physical, territorial and cultural advance of the Turks westwards into Europe had profoundly influenced Western Music. For instance, "The pilgrim of Mecca" and "Ifigenia in Táuride" by Christopher Gluck (1714-87), "Goes Turkish" by Joseph Hayden (1732-1809) as well as his and Military Symphony, "March of the Janissaries", "The abduction in the Serrallo" by Wolfgang Mozart (1756-91), and "The Ruins of Athens" by Ludvig Van Beethoven (1770-1827) betrayed profound Ottoman-Oriental musical imprints. As late as in the 19th century, the Ottoman influence finally gave us Antonio Rossini's (1792-1868) "Italian Girl in Algiers" (*L'Italiana in Algeri*), and its sequel "The Turk in Italy" (*Il Turco in Italia*). The title of most influential Turk-influenced musical piece thus far in Europe, can safely be given to the finale of Beethoven's Ninth Symphony, the "Ode to Joy". Striking his use of the *Kös*, bass drum and *Zurna* in the last movement when the whole thing comes to a momentary halt, interrupted by the burps of a contrabassoon, followed by the Turkish marching music that sounds remarkably like the theme song to Hogan's Heroes (Saoud 2004).

Due to these greatest composers, who composed military music purposefully, the Ottoman music and instrumentation permeated the European armies. With the industrial revolution, the music got immensely refined over the next two centuries. The invention and addition of wind instruments, both brass and wooden, making way into the Bands was thus a *musical revolution* in its own right, parallel to the industrial revolution. Thence a new and beautiful genre of military music traditions started taking shape.

Another parallel factor that led to the development of Bands in Europe was the dynamics of the 17th-century warfare. War, by that time, had gradually become a stylized and highly formal business, as fierce charges gave way to the application of pressure by movement and massed firepower. Soldiers of the 1700s were required to function almost as automatons, to obey, smoothly and in formation, whatever commands were given by their superiors. With clouds of gun smoke added to the din of combat, oral commands or personal example were not always reliable means of giving direction to an army. An order that was not heard—or worse, not understood—could be as dangerous as the enemy. Musically transmitted signals, however, could be heard above the crash of gunfire. The voice of the trumpet and the cadence of the drums were clear and unambiguous, making them vital to command and control (Trotter 2005). This accelerated and catalyzed development of military music, invention of instrumentation and a focus on the personnel attached to it.

Over time, various national armies of Europe standardized their musically conveyed orders into a set of calls. Manuals from as early as the mid-16th century, list calls such as Marche, Approach, Assault, Retreat and Skirmish. Being able to identify those signals and translate them into specific actions was as basic a training skill as loading a musket (Trotter 2005).

Every nation eventually adopted its own signature march (tune)—the precursor of the modern national anthem—and its troops were required to memorize it as well. A column of troops on the move half a mile away could not be determined as friendly or hostile if their battle standard was obscured in the gin and smoke of battle. However, they could be identified by their march music

(Trotter 2005). Clever commanders could turn those conventions to their advantage. In one incident during the Thirty Years' War (1618-48), a German force deceived its opponent British force by manoeuvring to *The Scots Marche* instead of their own marching tunes.

Closely following the Germans and Austrians was the French imperial court. Jean Baptiste Lully (1632-87), chief court musician of King Louis XIV, composed for the reed Bands and expanded the instrumentation to include two *hautbois* (oboes), two clarinets, two horns, and two bassoons. Lully's marches are among the earliest examples of written Band music. This started the period of Band music known as "Harmoniemusick," lasting from the mid-18th to the 18th century.

Under Napoleon Bonaparte, French military Bands were equipped with Ottoman war musical instruments such as *Zil* (cymbal) and the kettledrums. He even employed them, following the Ottoman approach, at a precise moment before or during the battle to gain maximum advantage from their entry. The Napoleonic wars seem to have the greatest impact on development of military Bands in Europe. In fact, many of the oldest continuing military Bands in Europe trace their origin to the second decade of the 18th century.

Influence of Czarist and Communist Russia

Formal military Bands were instituted in the Russian Army by Czar Ivan the Terrible (r. 1547-1584). Right upon ascension to throne as Emperor of Russia, he created the Special Order of the Big Palace to manage the Russian military music. It took another century for military music to expand inescapably due to Russian engagement in the "Great Northern War" lasting almost the whole of the first quarter of the 18th century (1700–21). This name is given by Russian historians to the contest of a Russia-led alliance (along with the Kings of Denmark and Saxony-Poland) against the Swedish empire for influence over Northern, North Eastern and Baltic regions of Europe.

Peter I, having ruled jointly with elder brother Czar Ivan V since 1682, rose to have an undivided throne as Czar Peter the Great upon the death of his brother in 1696. Much of his independent reign (r. 1696-1725) was consumed in this war to neutralize the supremacy of the Swedes. This led inevitably to the development of Military as an institution, raising of new regiments, enlargement of Naval fleet and advancement in weapons and tactics. To this day, the Military Bands Service of the Russian Federation traces its origin to Czar Peter the Great's Ukaz no 2319 of 19 February 1711 that mandated the formation of military Bands and field music formations in the imperial army.

Czar Peter attributed a lot of importance to military music as a means of enhancing the discipline and the morale of the army. The Semyonovsky and Preobrazhensky regiments are the oldest surviving regiments in the Russian army which, along with their Bands, distinguished themselves in all Wars since the Great Northern War to the First World War.

The former regiment had been established by Czar Peter in 1683 and it took its name from a village called Semyonovskoe in eastern Moscow, part of the present-day Sokolniki District), where it was initially stationed. In 1700, the troops became the Semyonovsky Life Guards Regiment. From 1723 the regiment was quartered in St Petersburg, the new imperial capital that Peter the Great had founded.

The latter regiment raised a few years later, again from Peter's *poteshnye voiska*, (toy forces) during his military games in the village of Preobrazhenskoye (now a district in Moscow), was to distinguish itself in Great Northern War and became the elite lifeguard regiment of imperial Russia for the next two centuries. The first regular military Bands of the modern style appeared in Russia with these two regiments.

These Bands were played during the victory parades after the Great Northern War. "March of the Preobrazhensky Regiment" even became, after a while, the unofficial hymn of the Russian Empire. Following the death of Peter the Great, three Empresses took interest in military Bands one after the other. Czarina Anna (r. 1730-40) brought a Turkish Style *Mehter* Band into the imperial palace of St Petersburg to outdo her rival European Courts. The *Mehter* was soon dissolved but the fusion of its music with the existing Bands gave a new beauty to Russian military music.

In the seventh year of her reign Czarina Elizabeth Petrovna (r. 1741–62) instituted Silver Trumpet as the highest honour for any military regiment that had distinguished itself in valour and courage. Hence, a musical instrument was given a higher status than all the gallantry medals and banners. Some silver trumpets were inscribed with the Cross of St George the Martyr. These silver trumpets were considered higher than the ones without it. The Regiments kept the Silver Trumpets of St George to symbolize glory and military valour. These trumpets were played at rare special occasions. This tradition became firmly rooted in the Russian army (Rager 2013).

Czarina Elizabeth was succeeded by Czarina Catherine the Great (1762-96)—the longest ruling Empress of imperial Russia. She increased the staff of regimental Bands tremendously. The military, patriotic, social and cultural importance of the military music especially increased during the Turco–Russian wars during her reign.

Russian military music, created in the army and (at least, initially) for the army, became a unique phenomenon in the music culture of Russia. Works written for the military brass Bands reflect both the history of the Russian people and the constantly evolving levels of artistic culture. This institution of military Bands was the only vestige of the culture of Imperial Russia that was owned by the Communist Government after the October revolution of 1917 and taken pride in.

The Soviets who initially found imperial institutions as anathema. Even the Preobrazhensky and Semenovsky regiments as well as their Bands, that reflected the historic military legacy of Russian military, were disBanded by the new Communist Government following World War I only because of their association with the imperial past. Interestingly, the tunes of their Bands continued to rule Soviet military marches, although lyrics in many cases were changed to eulogize the revolution.

The Communist government had a change of heart with respect to the military Bands as early as 1920s when they started raising modern Bands since 1928 onwards. The next six decades (till 1986) of Soviet Military Music can be called the Alexandrov era, dominated by the, Alexander Vasilyevich Alexandrov, the composer of National Anthem of the Soviet Union[1] and later by his two sons.

Here a brief profile of Mr. Alexandrov is in order. He belonged to a poor rural family whose members used to perform folk songs and hymns at streets to earn bread. Young Alexandrov also sang at festivals from a young age. Singing at a village school, he caught the attention of a violinist Zaliyuhin of Kazan Cathedral who persuaded his parents to let the child go to St Petersburg to learn music. In 1898, the village boy became a pupil at St Petersburg Cathedral where, over the next two decades, he rose to the position of conductor and choirmaster. Soon on being noticed by Communist leadership, he was made the head of the Red Army Band created in 1928, a post he held till his death in 1946. His son Boris Alexandrov led the main Red Army Band for the next forty years till 1986 (Khan 2017).

In the post-Second World War years, brass music and popular songs were on the forefront of the Soviet-Russian culture. A lot of new military ceremonies appeared and the everyday performance practice of the Bands was broadened, covering the music for training of the troops, military manoeuvres and solemn parades. Music festivals and competitions also became part of the tradition in the next half of the century.

Starting from 1960s, army and navy Bands of Russia became permanent participants of international brass music festivals and began touring foreign countries. Due to a high level of performances coupled with Government patronage of artistic potential, Soviet military musicians played an important role in developing the Russian musical art. Quite uncharacteristic of Communist regimes, the Soviet one gave freehand to Military Bands to form their repertory. This freedom given to State-owned Bands was continued by otherwise autocratic governments of post-Soviet Russia. This allowed the military Bandmasters to successfully cooperate with composers of brass music from the private sector and to create fresh popular music (Khan 2017).

In 2013, Russian President Vladimir Putin revived both the historic Semyonovsky and Preobrazhensky regiments under a Presidential decree, renamed as the 1st Semyonovsky Independent Rifle Regiment and 154th Preobrazhensky Independent Commandant's Regiment, respectively.

In the contemporary Russia, military Bands actively participate in all the important social events, and engage in concerts and educational activities. Since 2007, the Russian Government has started an annual international military Bands tattoo at the famous Spasskaya Tower, the most recognizable landmark of Kremlin, Moscow. The Alexandrov Band, named after the great Alexander Alexandrov, is called modern Russia's "singing weapon".

Influence of the British Empire and its Colonies

French court music of King Louis XIV inspired England's King Charles II who studied the French Army and its music in France. Upon regaining the British crown in 1660, he began implementing French musical ideas in Britain which, by that time, had only known trumpets and kettledrums. The year 1678 saw the introduction of French instruments into the English military when six *hautbois* were authorized with the Band of the Horse Grenadiers. Although the cavalry still stuck to old instruments, all the infantry regiments had, by 1690, adopted the new instrumentation.

King Charles II also organized the British militia into a standing army. Field movements required steady rhythms; drum provided just that to keep soldiers in step, while the Bugle signals were needed to direct the movement of whole blocks of troops. Adding fifes or bagpipes to play martial melodies occurred after drummers became the standard timekeepers. The combined percussion-wind sounds became what was, and still is, called field music.

The English army employed the Bands as their Signals Arm even during peacetime. Drummers and Buglers were used for regimental discipline and for commands such as "assemble" in the early morning, call for "lunch" and "dinner" during meal times, and for "lights out" as the last call for the night. The British Officers during the imperial period were remunerated liberally but in return were also supposed to raise their own Bands, from their own purse. The Bandsmen so hired were almost always civilians.

The officers donned their Bands in ceremonial uniforms to represent their own high status. This concept of embellished unique uniforms for the Bands outlasted all other military traditions. The Bands became a symbol of prestige for the British aristocracy, in the same way, as for the Chinese and Ottoman aristocracies before them and the South Asian nobility subsequently.

The British army Bands became a regular feature of aristocratic functions and parties during the Victorian era. Over the period, there was a gradual shift towards playing tunes of folk songs like the "Lincolnshire Poacher," "The Girl I left behind me" and "The fly be on the Turnip". The British military music has preserved, promoted and immortalized the traditional English folk music.

The first Military School of Music in the British empire was opened at Kneller Hall in March 1857. For the first time, there was a proper training institution in place for the military Bands, so serving military men started being inducted into the Bands. Kneller Hall school's impact on development of military music, that went far beyond the Great Britain proper, can hardly be overstated.

Initially the Bands had Band Majors, Pipe Majors and Bugle Majors in this order of seniority. The bigger regiments started having a Band Master above them of the rank of the Warrant Officer (Class I). As the anecdotes goes, Queen Victoria (r. 1837-1901) was so exhilarated at the performance of massed pipes and drums at her Diamond Jubilee celebration pageantry that she ordered promotion of four Band Masters to Commissioned Ranks who were re-designated as Directors of Music. This distinction exists to this day that Band commanders of the rank of the King's commissioned officers are called Directors of Music and non-commissioned officers as Band Majors.

The Bands permeated into the civilian domain. Among the earliest Scottish civilian pipe Bands would include City of Brechin Band (1884) but it is not clear whether pipes were complemented with drums to make it a proper Band. However, two latter Bands Corps, namely Wallaceston & District, and Colinton & Currie (both raised around 1887), certainly used pipes and drums together.

However, the Military Bands of the United Kingdom, especially the corps of Pipes and Drums, permeated into all their colonies in East and South Asia, in different corners of Africa and in the Caribbean. The Bands also made their way to other branches of the Armed Forces such as the Navy and eventually the Air Force. The British colonies developed their own variants of Palace Bands, mounted Bands and wedding Bands. The Police and Law Enforcement Agencies started having Bands in the colonies first and many such concepts and innovations had reverse transfusion back into the United Kingdom proper which started having Police Bands itself decades later.

The following sections will illustrate what forms and shapes the modern Bands took in America, China and Indo-Pakistan subcontinent for instance.

Influence of the New World in the Americas

The first known Band in the new world was a Band in New Hampshire in 1653 comprising 15 *Hautbois* Oboe) and two drums. However, this was not a proper military Band in the modern sense. It took a whole century for the first recorded appearance of a proper military Band in America which is dated to 1756. This was a time when the Seven Years' War (1756–63) had already spread its tentacles into North America. An artillery regiment commanded by. Benjamin Franklin, later to become one of the founding fathers of the United States, marched that year with more than 1,000 men of his Pennsylvania Militia, of which he was an honorary Colonel. This march was accompanied by a primitive but proper fifes and drums Band.

Military Bands were used in the American War of Liberation (1775-83), also called the Revolutionary War, extensively. General George Washington was so sanguine about the defining role of Bands in victory and defeat that he ordered the Bands of his Continental Army to improve music or risk deduction in wages. "Yankee Doodle" was a satirical song from Dutch Middle Ages whose lyrics were adapted in America and by the end of the revolutionary war, it came out as a patriotic song. The eponymous famous Painting by Archibald M. Willard, typifies music's wartime role throughout the ages—both as a means of battlefield communication and as a way to generate patriotism and bravery.

Upon victory, George Washington made a triumphant tour of the northeastern United States. He was greeted at almost every village and town by the local militia Bands that he had so keenly supported. The regular militia, at that time, was not uniformed, but their Bands were always elaborately dressed, usually at the expense of the units they were attached. Noticeably absent from these military Bands were the brass instruments familiar to audiences today. At the time, only natural brass instruments, those without keys or valves, were available. Natural brasses could only play the notes of the overtone series and so were not as useful as woodwinds in ensemble playing.

George Washington served as the first President of the United States from 1789–97. He was succeeded by his Vice President John Adams as the second President. Adams had always been a strong proponent of pomp and prestige to ensure "dignity of the office of the President". Under his watch, the Congress voted on 11 July 1798 to establish the first Marines Band of the United States Armed Forces. This Band presented its first public concert in Washington on August 21, 1800. The Band made its White House debut on New Year's Day 1801 at a reception given by President and Mrs. John Adams and subsequently became permanently attached to this most recognizable House in the world. However, it goes to the credit of President Jefferson Jefferson, also referred to as the "godfather" of the Marine Band, for giving the Band the title "The President's Own" as it is known to this day (Fettig 2016).

Back in Europe around the turn of the century, a great flurry of invention had created brass instruments of all varieties, first with keys and later with valves and pistons. The biggest breakthrough was achieved in 1810, when Irishman John Halliday invented a keyed bugle that allowed a brass instrument to play all of the chromatic notes that previously had to be played on an oboe or clarinet. Although musicians in the United States were initially slower to adopt these new designs, European immigrants brought these newer instruments, along with their taste for brass Bands, to the United States in the decades before the Civil War. Eventually, it was the United States that adopted, developed and popularized the Brass Band concept.

The American Civil War necessitated the raising of thousands of Bands and contributed to changes and advancements in the instrumentation and their usage. There were 16,500 military Bandsmen in Unionist forces alone. Each Unit had at least a Bugler and a Drummer. However, there could be four to five musicians, at the most, with each moving company. Hence, the number of Bands in the military could be anywhere around a thousand during the civil war. Drums of each unit were embellished by unit names and became source of identity and pride of units along with flags and banners. There is also evidence that full-fledged pipe Bands were in existence at least in some military units at that time. For instance, there is a reference to the 79th New York Infantry having a pipe Band in 1861.

Brass Bands of all types were used during the Civil War, but a peculiar type of brass instrument, known as an over-the-shoulder horn, became associated with Bands of this era. The tubing on these instruments bent around, and featured a bell that pointed over the player's shoulder. This allowed the Band to march in front of the soldiers, and the sound would be directed behind the player towards the marching troops. Entire Bands of over-the-shoulder brass instruments, from tubas to cornets, were used during the Civil War. However, it was the President's Own Marine Band Marine Band that accompanied President Abraham Lincoln to Pennsylvania when he delivered his immortal Gettysburg Address. As the nation rebuilt from the war years, White House receptions resumed. Marine Band leader Francis Scala noted in his memoirs that both President and Mrs. Andrew Johnson supported and helped the organization immeasurably. Scala said, "Every time the Band played, Mrs. Johnson sent me a bouquet, and in return I dedicated a march to her" (Fettig 2016).

After the war, many veterans returned to their homes in both the North and South. Many others chose to settle in the great expanses of the West. In both cases, these former soldiers brought their love of military brass music with them, and organized Bands in communities large and small across the continent. Each city and community prided its Bands.

Another defining influence on the US Bands History was Military Conductor Patrick Gilmore (1829-92), probably the only person in the US military history to be titled as "Band Master General" of the Army. He composed the famous 22nd Regiment March and wrote the lyrics for *When Johnny comes marching home.* His great initiatives of linking Peace with Band Tattoos had an impact on US Band Culture that then got its own momentum, after successfully conducting the National Peace Jubilee Marching Bands Tattoo in 1869 and the International Peace Tattoo, three years later, both in the city of Boston. He led the Bands in the centennial celebrations of the city of Philadelphia in 1876 and the Bands' ceremonies marking the commissioning of Statue of Liberty near New York in 1886. It was in 1892 while composing music and leading practice sessions for the 400th anniversary celebrations of Christopher Columbus's voyage of discovery, that Gilmore collapsed and died. But his legacy of nearly half a century lives to this day.

By 1890s, there were already around ten thousand town and community Bands in the United States mainly led by demobilized soldiers or their descendants. The American Band movement, which would culminate with the great Bandleader John Philip Sousa (1854-1932) around the turn of the 20th century, had begun. Not to belittle the remarkable contribution of Mr Sousa, it is also a reality that when he emerged to dominate the Band music of USA, the legacy and momentum left behind by Gilmore and the presence of thousands of Bands created by demobilized civil war veterans, offered a propitious environment for his Band movement.

The number of Military Bands in the US Armed Forces have declined consistently over the decades due to conscious government policies of preferring the lethal wings of the Armed Forces over its music corps. As of the end of 2017, the US Armed Forces had 137 Military Bands with a combined strength of 6,500 musicians down to a tenth of the Civil War level, as shown in the following Table[2].

Table 2.1

Branch	*No of Bands*	*No of Musicians*
US Army	99	4350
US Air Force	15	800
US Marine Corps	12	750
US Navy	11	600
Total	137	6500

Apart from the United States, the other great country in the North American continent is Canada. It has strong British traditions of military music too. Despite having a much smaller army than the United States, it has a good number of military Bands. The Music Branch of the Canadian Armed Forces is composed of six full-time regular force Bands, 53 part-time reserve force Bands and 15 voluntary Bands.

Apart from the military, the first civilian pipe Band still in some sort of existence in the US appears to be the Holyoake Caledonian dating 1909–10. In the history of the Buffalo (NY) City Guard, which was formerly a militia unit, there is reference to the Buffalo St Andrews Society Pipes & Drums in the 1890s. The greatest contribution of the United States on the emergence and development of Bands, however, remains in the school, college and university Bands that will be dealt with in the next chapter.

The discussion on Americas will not be complete without mentioning the rich Military Bands tradition in South and Latin America. Some of the finest Bands exist in Latin America under various names such as *Banda de Guerra* (War Band) in Mexico, *Banda Militar* (Military Band) in Columbia, and *Banda Marcial* (Martial Band) in Brazil and Venezuela. These Bands manifest musical influences from a variety of European powers such as France, Spain, Germany and Turkey.

Influence on and by modern China

The Chinese adopted the Western-style Military Bands along with European instruments in the last years of the Qing dynasty (1644–1912). In fact, the defeat of the Qing imperial army at the hands of the Japanese during 1894–95 led to a strategic determination in China's power circles to modernize the army. And among other things, a need was felt to establish Western Style modern military Bands for better discipline and morale building. A person no other than Yuan Shikai accepted the responsibility to raise a new Band (Ching-chih 2010).

Shikai, who was to become the first President after the Xinhai revolution of 1911, converting China from a monarchy into a republic, raised the Xinjian (i.e. New) Army in December 1895 and spent next four years in their training at Xiaozhan, 35 km Southeast ofTianjin. It is believed that the first modern military Band in China was created under his watch, as early as mid-1896. Under instruction by his German military advisor Gao Sida and inspired by music from the Prussian *March of the Emperor Wilhelm II,* the Infantry arm was given 120 Bandsmen, the Artillery 24, the Cavalry 12 and the Engineers Regiment got 6 Bandsmen in the new aArmy. The revolution in military music had begun for China which had yet to see great political revolutions in the next half of the century (Ching-chih 2010).

The Infantry Bands corps was divided into 5 ensembles with 24 musicians each. The instrumentation for each ensemble consisted of 14 foreign brass instruments, 4 *foreign* European-style drums, and 2 each of the Chinese traditional watch drums, gongs and bugles. These military Bands received a setback during the Boxer rebellion (1898–1901) which witnessed a general disgust of everything Western including the Western music. Nationalist military commanders such as General Dong Fuxiang banned all Western tunes from the Chinese Army Bands.

In time, the 1911 Xinhai revolution led to overthrow of monarchy and Yuan Shikai, once the founder of New Army, became President in 1912 and briefly Emperor for 83 days at the end of 1915. Under his watch, there was a revival of military Band music of the modern style. The famous lyrics of the New Army known as the *Soldier's Training Song* had survived till the Xinhai Revolution despite challenges to it during the Boxer uprising. In post-1911 dispensation, the lyrics were changed but the tune continued to be used by the Chinese military. A well-known variant of the same tune was the *National Revolution Army Song* that the Chinese military continued to use. More variants of the tunes were adopted by the People's Liberation Army even prior to 1949 Communist Revolution.

The Communist government of China decided to raise a large military Band as early as in 1950 to mark the first anniversary of the Red Revolution. The Communist China's Military Bands also treaded the familiar trajectory of Bands elsewhere in the world, by starting with revolutionary and war music, moving on to folk music, and finally embracing the modern hip-hop music.

In 2016, for instance, in a bid to attract China's educated youth, People's Liberation Army started the release of hip-hop music videos to cater for the taste of modern generation. With the song titled "Battle Declaration" being posted on PLA Daily's website, the Chinese military betrays awareness that online medium is the correct path to reach the youngster target audience. Although lyric shows tilt towards the masculine gender, but that is to glamorize the military career for younger males. Otherwise, they are carefully worded to avoid sounding aggressive. The imagery is also cautiously chosen showing advanced weaponry that seems to be aimed at giving confidence to the nation that China is, or at least styles itself as, at par with the United States in military power.

The Chinese Military Bands today are the part of musical charm offensive of Beijing, playing the world over in military tattoos, State opening of National People's Congress, State Visits, Diplomatic events and the like.

Influence of modern South Asian powers (India-Pakistan)

South Asia has a very rich tradition of military Bands. Its Armed Forces, compared to those in any other region in the world, are the largest owners of marching Bands at their strength. There is a general perception that it was the British who brought modern style Military Bands into what is now India and Pakistan. This is only partly true since ancient India had a history of using musical instruments in warfare going back at least to thirty centuries. However, the local population was not acquainted with modern brass music until the British introduced them.

The British Officers raised Bands in India for military and political reasons. The Bands showed pomp and glory of the British empire as well as that of those individual officers. They were copied by the local nobility and aristocrats, especially the rulers of Princely States. Interestingly, the first modern military Band in South Asia was established neither in present day India nor in Pakistan. Credit goes to the unifier and founder of modern kingdom of Nepal, King Prithvi Narayan Shah (1723–75). Formerly, the ruler of Gurkha kingdom, Shah unified the Kingdom of Nepal in 1768 and laid foundation of a dynasty that ruled it till 2005. King Narayan Shah was so inspired by a modern Brass Band playing at the holy city of Varanasi (Banaras) that he established a modern military Band back in his own capital of Kathmandu around 1of the century, the Muslim Rulers (called Nawab or Nizam) and the Hindu and Sikh ones (called Maharajas) of Princely States of India developed a craze for having Palace Bands with modern instrumentation. The Maharaja of Baroda and Mysore as well as the Nawab of Jaora and Rampur raised very fine Bands as did the Nizam of Hyderabad Deccan.

As of 1838, the Sikh Kingdom of Maharaja Ranjit Singh is known to have a modern Band that played at the visit of the Duke of Auckland to Lahore, present day Pakistan, that year.

Hence, we can say that to the extent of South, West and Midlands of the Indo-Pakistan subcontinent it is correct that Bands were introduced by the British. But this may not be correct as far as the North Western part of the British India (present day Tribal Areas of Pakistan bordering its Khyber Pakhtunkhwa province) where British military campaigns were countered by tribal forces who were adept at battlefield musical instruments.

Sir Winston Churchill had served in India in late 19th century when he was a Captain. His accounts of the Malakand campaign (26th July to 22nd August 1897) detailed in his book *The Malakand Field Force* gives repeated hints of presence of Bands in the tribal forces. Two of his excerpts are reproduced here:

[T]he tribesmen rushed down .... piquet of the 24th Punjab Regiment on the road was driven back and the tribesmen flooded into the bazaar. Others ... climbed the hills on either side ... and began a fire into the camp which would continue for several days until the assault on Malakand ended. The noise was overwhelming *with drums beating and pipes playing. A bugler was heard in the ranks of the tribesmen playing all the calls of the British Army in turn.* The bugler was part way through the "Officers' Mess call" when he abruptly ceased, presumably shot. [Emphasis added] (Churchill 1916)

About another battle, Churchill writes:

> *... tribesmen fought on foot.... were in possession of firearms [but had...] no artillery or machine guns.... Flags representing villages, clans and tribes were carried in battle as rallying points.* Drums of many sorts were beaten; pipes and trumpets played. *[Emphasis added} (Churchill 1916)*

Thus, North Western tribes were not only familiar with military drums and trumpets but routinely used them in warfare However, it was the British colonial administration that introduced brass Bands into the rest of South Asia where they then got a life of its own.

The British Colonial Army had officers mostly from the Great Britain but the rank and file was almost all indigenous. The regiments, especially the Infantry ones, had a Pipe Band as an essential component. In August 1947, British suzerainty ended and two newly born nations, namely, India and Pakistan, inherited the military legacies of the British. In fact, the early Pakistani and Indian army consisted of officers and troops from the Colonial army who had opted for either country.

The regiments under the Indian or Pakistani army retained Bands for the same purposes as the British, i.e. for ceremonial parades, official functions, officers' mess parties, regimental dinner nights, unit celebrations and drill parades.

After the British left India, the Indian and Pakistani military commands realized that there were no schools to carry on their tradition of marching Bands. Pakistan established the Army School of Music on April 17, 1952, at the frontier town of Cherat under Capt. D Keeling, Director of Music from UK. It was shifted to Lahore in 1952 under new Director Capt. A N Baker and finally to its present permanent location of Abbotabad in 1956. For nine years, it remained a constituent of the Frontier Force Regimental Centre. In 1965, its operational control was transferred to the Baluch Regimental Centre. In 2004, it was upgraded as an autonomous School with its own Commandant.

In India, Field Marshal. K. M. Cariappa, the first Indian Commander in chief of the Indian army, retained the services of a British military Bandmaster and founded the headquarters for a music school, on Oct 23, 1950, in Pachmarhi. The town is almost at the centre of India, in the Satpura Range of hills in Madhya Pradesh state, about 80 miles southeast of Bhopal, the state capital. At an altitude of 3,500 feet, this hill town of barely 10,000 population has a special character with cottages of brick and wood and red-tiled roofs.

The Indianization of martial music actually began with Dr Harold Joseph who was an Officer on Special Duty (Military Music) at the Defence Ministry for more than a decade. He broke new ground by composing a number of quick march tunes based on Indian folk melodies. Later, some tunes were composed based on *Raags* (Indian folk melodies). Indian musical instruments such as *Santoor*, *Sitar*, Bamboo flute, *Tabla*, *Dholak*, *Dilruba*, and Violin got included to the standard Band instrumentation of the Indian Armed Forces.

The Military Bands in India and Pakistan are disciplined, polished and talented enough to deliver a Mozart composition as comfortably as a Movie song within minutes of each other. Over the years, the South Asian military Bands diversified their repertory. Now Indian military Bands can play pieces ranging from Handel's "Wedding March" to "Colonel Bogie's March," "Never on Sunday" and "Charge of the Light Brigade" amongst the world's most popular marching tunes as comfortably as they can play tunes of Bollywood songs of Rafi, Asha Bhonsle and Lata Mangeshkar. The Pakistani military Bands play tunes such as "Hundred Pipers," "Ode to Joy," "Ides of March," "Sound of Sylhet" and "Forward Christian Soldier" as efficiently and flawlessly as they play Pakistani classical music. Pakistani forces have developed several indigenous marching tunes such as *Naveed e Shifa* an *Tariq ki Dua* for Pipe Bands and *Dushmano tum ne kis qaum ko lalkara hai* and *Istaqlal March* that are played by Brass and Concert Bands.

Since the Military Bands of both countries now also play classical music of their countries—which in India translate into tunes of popular songs from heartthrob movies—at State occasions, it has sometimes raised eyebrows. In India, the trend of military Bands following Bollywood musical lead appeals to the popular taste but at times draws criticism from familiar circles. A former vice chief of the Indian Amy, Lt Gen Vijay Oberoi, a veteran of 1965 Indo-Pakistan War where he lost one of his legs, is a strong critic of, what he calls "mixing the *Beating the Retreat* ceremony with Bollywood circus." Writing for a web portal called *thecitizen.in*, Gen Oberoi lashed out at military command saying he was "disillusioned and devastated" that "our Bandsmen, besides playing martial music, are also adept at playing symphonies (both western and Indian), but there is a place and occasion to play them. By all accounts, a *Beating the Retreat* ceremony is not one of them!"

Due to a history of Indo-Pak warfare, however, playing of each other's classical or movie music by the military Bands, is considered a total taboo, bordering on act of treason. The playing of their own military music to commemorate war victories is also interesting. For instance, in Sept 2015, Pakistani Military announced three *days* of military Band parades to commemorate the 50th anniversary of Pakistani *victory* in the Second Indo-Pakistan War of 1965. They were in for a surprise when the Indian Defence Forces announced three *weeks* of military Bands pageantry to celebrate the Golden Jubilee of Indian *victory* in the same war. Among the smaller conflicts, the two nations clashed for control over the town of Kargil in 1999. The fighting lasting 10 weeks remained confined to the Northern mountainous area of Kashmir mostly in Kargil and Siachen sectors. Each year, Bands from both sides play a medley of tunes in their garrisons to celebrate *their* victory [claimed by both sides] in the Kargil conflict of 1999.

Today, military Bands in Pakistan and India, far outnumber all military Bands of UK and continental Europe put together. India with 576 Bands in its Armed Forces and Pakistan with 242 are, respectively, the number one and number two country in the world in terms of the number of Military Bands.

There is also a history of "*private* Military Bands" (though for Western audience it may appear as an oxymoron), especially for leading the procession of the groom called *Barat*, which became a feature of South Asian weddings, not only in India and Pakistan but in their smaller neighbours too. This is South Asia's singular contribution to the world of marching Bands but more of it in Chapter V.

Conclusion: Regional Musical Integration

The musical instruments and ensembles emerged in almost all regions of the world, sometimes independently and under extra regional influences at other times. The Turkish and other Islamic empires, the Western and Eastern parts of Europe, the East Asian regions especially the Sino-Korean-Japanese civilizations as well as the New World (United States), all had their part in growth of military Bands. The regions not covered above in greater detail for reasons of space and scope, such as Africa or Latin America, also had a lot to contribute in the growth of Bands. As the State became powerful, the various institutions of the State got involved in the development of Bands. For the military, the Bands marked an operational necessity, but gradually the Bands permeated the civilian space too. The civil branches of the State embraced Bands for identity and glory of the institution.

The military music made strangest of journeys sometimes into or across enemy lines or unfamiliar territories. For example, Germany's famous march *Alte Kamaraden Marchetan* (Old Comrade March) got adopted not only by their sworn rivals, the US forces, but also by Argentinian Army, in the far distant corner of the globe. On its part Argentinians gave the Germans *Marcha de San Lorenzo* (the March tune of Argentina's Battle of Independence won at San Lorenzo on 3rd February 1813) that the Germans adopted and played upon their victory over France in 1940 during the Second World War. The musical influences became more pronounced during the Cold War when Taiwanese military adopted US tunes and Cuban Army adapted to Soviet style of Military Bands, all tunes, marching styles and dress uniforms.

Over the past century, parallel to the phenomenon of fusion, the military music of all the above regions moved in the familiar trajectory of playing regimental tunes, moving on to mix and play local folk tunes, and eventually making debut into the evolving pop music of the respective countries. This makes any function where a military Band were present, more colourful and enjoyable. It is a bit hard to synchronize in a military Band but hard labour and interest of musicians has brought success in the history of music.

NOTES

1 In the year 2000, the same composition was adopted by the Russian government as its national anthem although the lyrics were changed.

2 Data taken from official website of US Military Corps of Music www.music.army.mil (accessed on 16 Dec 2017)

CHAPTER III

Growth of Bands: Influence of the State Institutions (Civil)

Music Gives a soul to universe
Wings to the mind,
Flight to imagination,
And life to everything

—Plato

The highest institution of the State is the Head of State. The royal palace—or Presidential Mansion in modern Republics—symbolizes the sovereignty of the State and supremacy of its government. It was indeed the first civil institution where Bands made a debut. The Bands in such civil institutions mostly reflect a vertical growth of Bands, that is from military formations in the field moving upwards to the Palace of the Head of State. This phenomenon was quite distinct from the horizontal growth within various arms of the military. There was no operational requirement for a palace to have a Band. But the sooner it dawned that the Bands reflected prestige and glory of the office, and of the State, they proliferated into civil domain.

As autocratic dispensations gave way to representative democracies, the power and glory gradually shifted from the Palaces to the Parliaments. Parliament buildings became the centre stage for national day and other functions. More and more Bands started appearing in the lawns of legislative buildings worldwide.

In the law enforcement or security services, such as the police, the need for Band was akin to that in the military, i.e. training, parade, discipline, etc. Hence, as a parallel development, the Bands in civil institutions other than the parliament, found their way in the Police Forces. From the law enforcement and armed agencies of the State, the Bands have permeated into other civilian institutions such as the fire or prison services or other uniformed and disciplined agencies. We shall explore the emergence of Bands in these civil institutions of the State further in the present chapter.

Bands in the Palaces of Emperors, Caliphs, Sultans and Kings

Amongst the oldest known Bands in an imperial palace are the ones in imperial capital of the Tang Dynasty (618-907 AD) in China. The historic city of Chang'an (now called Xi'an)—930 km South West of present capital Beijing—used to be the seat of Tang Emperors. The ancient orchestras of bells, stone chimes, flutes, drums, and zithers, plus court dancers, were an essential part of all imperial court ceremonies from the early 7th century. There was a clear distinction between court music (*yayue*) and common music (*suyue*). The former included style of Music for every royal occasion including concert music, banquet music and even "Imperial birthday music". On the occasion of Emperor's birthday dancers moved into a formation representing the Chinese characters meaning "Long Live the Emperor" in the modern marching-Bands tradition.

The imperial guard in China was so intertwined with imperial music that imperial Band musicians were chosen from the troops tasked with protection of the Emperor. In fact, the purpose of routine inspection of emperor's personal guard was to choose musicians from them. The imperial guard during Tang dynasty used to comprise bodyguards, chariot troops, instrumentalists and vocal singers.

To look after the Imperial Palace Bands, there was a full-fledged musical bureaucracy that organized Palace music into ten performing Band divisions or *Shibu ji*. Of these ten, two groups represented China proper one for the Formal Court Music and other for the Chinese folk music. The remaining eight Bands in attendance at the Court represented foreign Music (*Huyue*) through musical ensembles, one each from neighbouring Kingdoms of India, Samarkand, Bukhara, Kashgar, Kuch and Turfan while the last two Bands came from the defeated kingdoms of Baekje and Goguryeo from the Korean peninsula.

Steadily, the imperial court music spread to rest of Asia. In Vietnam for instance, the Tran Dynasty (1225–1400) instituted the Court Music called *Nhã nh c*. This tradition outlasted the dynasty and continued in the royal courts of the last royal dynasty–the Nguy n Dynasty (1802–1945). The theme of the royal dances, mostly to wish the king longevity and the country wealth, survives even today when Kingship has become history.

In the Islamic world, the Ottoman rulers maintained personal *Mehter* Bands consisting of 90 musicians with 12 types of instruments in the Palace. They not only played at formal royal ceremonies but also for personal pleasure of the Caliph. So much so that the *Mehter* Bands would provide background music even when the Royal Barbers were shaving the Sultan. The Bands led the Caliphal procession when he toured the city and at ceremonies such as the birthday of the Prophet or that of the Caliph.

There were some instruments reserved for the Ottoman Caliph, such as *Kös* Drums, having the size of a bathhouse dome (and the "sound like thunder"). The *Kös* were only played by royal *Mehter* Bands when Caliph himself was leading a campaign or, sometimes, a commander-in-chief leading the army in lieu of the Sultan. Palace Bands were not restricted to the Caliph alone but Governors and Noblemen across the Ottoman empire patronized *Mehter* Bands in their palaces as a symbol of their status.

The Bands in the Ottoman Caliphate were not only distinguished by Drum sounds but there was a defined protocol for the number of Ceremonial Crescents (*Cevgen*) that the Band was entitled to carry. The Turkish Crescent or *Cevgen* in Turkish was an 8-feet high pole topped with a conical brass ornament and crescent-shaped Brass crosspieces. Numerous bells were attached to the Crescent, with two red plumes hanging on both sides to depict war. It was basically a percussion instrument played either by shaking up and down or by twisting to create sounds. But it was a symbol of honour also. The personal Band of the Ottoman Caliph was entitled to seven *Cevgen*-bearers. The Grand Vizier (Prime Minister) of the empire's own Band had five *Cevgens*, the Viziers (Ministers or Advisors of the Court) were entitled to three *Cevgens* in their personal Bands. The Commander in Chief (*Bererbeyi*) and Senior Governors were entitled to two Turkish Crescents in their Bands. The lowest rank entitled to *Cevgen* in their Band was *Mirliva* in the Ottoman Army and Navy (a rough equivalent of Major General/Rear Admiral in modern Armed Forces) who could have one *Cevgen* in his personal Band.

Along the same time, Bands became a regular feature of the Courts of the imperial courts in Delhi. The famous Moroccan traveller Ibne Batuta recalls his travels across India and gives the account of the Drummers, Fifers and Buglers in court of Sultan Mohammad Tughlaq (1334–41). The Drummers would beat drums at the arrival of the Sultan as well as for the noblemen and knights of the Court. The number of drum beats symbolized the status of the person. A hundred or so drummers would together beat the drum, with a loud chant of *Allah o Akbar* (God is Great), to herald the arrival of the King or to announce any decision or announcement by him in the court. The fifers would play when rebels would be executed or punished publicly.

The greatest patron of music in Indian history was the Mogul empire. The emperors from Babur to Shah Jahan had a great fondness for music. Emperor Humayun had fixed Mondays and Wednesdays for music in the imperial court. Emperor Akbar was another great lover of music. According to Abul Fazal, his court musicians are arranged in seven divisions, one for each day of the week. Abul Fazal[1] gives us a list of 36 singers and performers on various instruments. His famous historical treatise *Ain-i-Akbari* contains details of the daily routine of performances by the palace Band. Some of the Band Musicians were given the highest ranks of 10,000 *Mansab*.[2]

In France, Louis XIV ascended the throne in 1643, making him a contemporary of Mogul Emperor Shah Jahan, one of the greatest patrons of art and culture in India. Jean Baptiste Lully, chief court musician of Louis XIV, composed a new form of Court music known as Harmoniemusick, as noted in the previous chapter. This music trickled down from the Palace to the French imperial military units which adopted them. Imperial France is thus another example where Music travelled downwards from Palace to the Garrisons.

In time, the British Kings got impressed by the French Court Music and started depending on trumpets as part of trappings of Royalty. Proclamations of the English kings were not considered legal unless accompanied by a trumpet flourish. The trumpet became as important as the seal of the king when putting forth a royal decree. From royal palaces in London, the trumpets made their way into the mansions of the nobility becoming important in depicting the rank of the knights.

One of the most prominent continuous surviving Royal Palace Bands in Europe is the Guides Band of Belgium. King Leopold I, the founding monarch of modern Belgium, asked the Conductor of the 1st Guides Regiment of the Cavalry, Jean-Valentin Bender, to raise a Band of the regiment: The King's Own, attached to his personal Guard. This was the year 1832. It marked the King's accession as a constitutional monarch before the National Congress, the previous year. Over the period of nearly two centuries, this royal Band has got an international recognition. With 84-member Symphonic Orchestra and a 19-strong Trumpet Corps, it is one of the premier Wind Bands of the World. The Band of Belgian Guides has almost the same role in Defence of Belgian Music as the Belgian Army has for the defence of Belgium itself.

Another unique royal palace Band is the *Hans Majestet Kongens Garde* (HMKG). Translated as His Majesty, the King's Guard is a regiment of the Norwegian Army that has the twin tasks of personal protection of the Monarch and the Defence of Oslo. The Regiment has four rifle companies, a logistic company and a Band & Drill Company. This last Company is the Band of the Royal Palace. The strangest thing about this Regiment is that its Mascot is an actual King Penguin living in Edinburgh Zoo in Scotland, UK. Thus, it is the only regiment whose Colonel-in-Chief is an actual animal. The Penguin named Nils Olav III holds the title of "Sir" and the military rank of a Brigadier

Monarchy still survives in around one-eighth of the countries of the world, in all but few of them, it is merely in a ceremonial role. Royal Palace Bands from Norway to Nepal, from Britain to Bahrain and from Morocco to Malaysia are known to perform the most beautiful melodies. However, as Kingdoms become Republics—Nepal being the latest example—the Bands also move from the Royal to the Presidential Palaces.

Appearance of Bands in the modern Presidential Palaces

The first elected, albeit indirectly, office of the President is that of the United States. The first-ever Presidential Band was also the White House Marine Band—the only musical organization whose primary mission is to provide music for the President of the United States. When the nation's capital moved from Philadelphia to Washington, the Marine Band came with the President and made camp "on a hill overlooking the Potomac" near the present site of the Lincoln Memorial.

In the initial years of US History, the difference between a King and a President was not all that clear then, except that the latter was an "elected monarch". In the constitutional debates amongst the Founding Fathers in Philadelphia, the titles "commensurate with the dignity of the office of President" of the United States, such as "His Elective Majesty," "His Highness the President and the Defender of the Liberties," and many others were seriously considered and debated. The proponents of such proposals included persons no less than the first Vice President and the second President of the US, John Adams (1735–1826) and the President of the Continental Congress, Richard Henry Lee (1732–94).

Another idea that was critical in the earliest debates among American constitutionalists that created the Union, was about civilian control over the military. One of the Declaration of Independence's grievances against King George III was that his government had rendered "the military independent of, and superior to, the civil power." Earlier, on May 15, 1776, the Virginia Convention had asserted the primacy of civilian control through these words in the Virginia Declaration of Rights: "In all cases the military should be under strict subordination to, and governed by, the civil power." The federal president was thus envisaged not as a part of the military but an elected civilian with supreme power over it.

It is in this context that the pomp of the Presidential Palace of the United States, aptly called the White House, has to be seen. In 1800, the then US President John Adams, ordered the Marines Band created two years earlier to perform at his Executive Mansion at State functions. The following year, the third US President Thomas Jefferson called the Band to perform at his 1801 inauguration—a tradition that is continuing to date. Better known as the author of the Declaration of Independence, the Presidential Band is one of Jefferson's lesser known legacies. The military Band performing at the Civil institution of the Head of State was the pinnacle of civilian superiority that the founding fathers, including Jefferson, had envisaged.

After the Civil War, all type of State and social activities resumed in the White House and under President Ulysses S. Grant (1869-77), the President's Own Marine Band became more visible than ever before. President Harry Truman, whose love of music and the piano are well known, called the President's Band "[a] most attractive ceremonial institution...musically eloquent...[and] a source of comfort and pleasure to [every] occupant of the White House." President Calvin Coolidge had a great affiliation with the Band and once he was unable to attend a special Marine Band concert in 1924, he sent flowers and a personal note to them.

About the administration of the Franklin Delino Roosevelt, Elise Kirk, author of *Music at the White House*, calls the Presidential Band as "the real unsung hero of the FDR White House" that played for "every important State Dinner, reception, birthday, debut, anniversary, and holiday celebration at the White House and for numerous ceremonies within the capital and beyond." President John F. Kennedy's personal affection is reflected by his words that "...the only forces that cannot be transferred from Washington, without my express permission, are members of the Marine Band. They are the only forces I have, ... to hold the White House against all odds."[3] President Nixon remarked that during his service as Vice President and President, he had "never failed to be proud" of this "splendid musical organization." His successor President Ford recalled memories of the Marine Band during his 28 years of public service in Washington. He wrote, "The excellence of their performance makes them a welcome and important part of State functions" (Fettig 2016).

The Presidential Band performed at private functions of the Presidents such as the wedding of President Grover Cleveland to Frances Folsom (1886)—the only President ever to be married in the White House—and that of three First Daughters including Nellie Grant (1874), Alice Roosevelt (1906) and Lynda

Johnson (1967). Many of the US Presidents had immense fondness for Band music such as President Warren G. Harding who had played every Band instrument except Trombone and E-flat and President Clinton who had himself been a University Band Member. President Harding organized the "Citizen's Cornet Band" of Marion, OH, which played for both Democratic and Republican campaign rallies. President Bush became the first President of the United States to conduct "The President's Own" United States Marine Band on April 26, 2008, at the annual White House Correspondents Dinner (Fettig 2016). The President's Own Marine Band is an inseparable part of the White House ceremonies doing up to 500 performances a year at State functions.

This trend of Military Bands at civilian Presidential mansions permeated the whole of American continent. In 1845, the President Jose Ballivian of Bolivia, commissioned an anthem which, from then on, was played at the Presidential palace by military Bands. Close to follow was Argentina where the all-Brass *Alto Peru Mounted Fanfare Band* of the Argentine Regiment of Mounted Grenadiers, donned in the ceremonial uniform design dating from 1813, serves as the Band of the Presidential Palace at Buenos Aires. Likewise, the *Mounted Fanfare Band Company* of the Presidential Life Guard Dragoons Regiment acts as the Presidential Palace Band of the Republic of Peru. Thus, most President Houses have military Bands regularly attached to them for all civil and State functions.

In 1882, the Russian Government also attached Military Bands with the Imperial Palace to play at official state ceremonies including for receptions of foreign ambassadors and at the events with the highest presence. After the Communist revolution in Soviet Union, the Kremlin Music Team of the Moscow Kremlin Garrison was created, that eventually became the equivalent of President's Own Band of Kremlin. Since 2005, performances of brass Bands by the President's Band of Russia, take place at the Alexandrovsky garden cavern in summer. This initiative was supported by the Moscow Government as well as a lot of public culture organizations. So now almost all the military music groups known in Moscow perform at the Alexandrovsky garden cavern.

Among other dedicated Presidential Palace Bands include the Band of the President's Guard Battalion of Brazil and the *Alto Peru Fanfare Band* of the Regiment of Mounted Grenadiers in Argentina. Known as the President's Own, the Regiment has one of the few surviving mounted Bands in Argentina. Today, Bands are a regular feature at the State ceremonies in all residences of the heads of state across Asia, Africa and the Americas. The Bands play at State receptions, welcome ceremonies for State visits and receiving of credentials from Ambassadors in what is called State House in Kenya, Blue House in Korea, *Aiwan-e-Sadr* in Pakistan, *Rashtrapati Bhavan* in India, *Qasr el Ittihadia* (Federation Palace) in Egypt and scores of other Mansions.

One major difference in the Bands attached with Presidential palaces is that the Music travelled bottom up from Military formations to the Presidential Houses, rather than the other way round as in case of Royal Palaces where movement, in many cases, was top down.

Emergence of Bands in Parliaments and elected Houses

Dedicated Bands for the Parliament Houses or Legislative buildings of a country are rare but do exist in republican tradition; Uruguay is a conspicuous example. The Army's 1st Infantry Brigade Band, sporting dress uniforms worn during the Argentina-Brazil War, is the dedicated official honours Band of the General Assembly of Uruguay.

The United States never had a dedicated Congress Band for the Congress Building, called the Capitol Hill. However, there is reference from 1854 that President Franklin Pierce approved legislation allowing the President's Own Band extra pay for "playing on the grounds of the President *and the Capitol*" [emphasis added], meaning thereby that the Band did play at the lawns of the Congress-House (Fettig 2016).

As there is a general trend amongst the governments worldwide of slashing the numbers of Bands and a funding cut for existing ones, few States have totally dedicated Bands for the Legislative Bodies. However, for ceremonial occasions such as the Constitution Day or beginning of the parliamentary year, the Military Bands remain readily available at the opposite ends of the governance spectrum. Bands are as likely to be seen at new parliamentary years in the Great Hall of the People in Beijing as at the Westminster Palace (the seat of British House of Commons) in London.

Introduction of Bands in Para Military Guards and Militias

There is no uniform definition or understanding of the term "Paramilitary Forces." Generally speaking, a paramilitary would be a force raised, trained and deployed in a military style but still not part of the regular Armed Forces.

The paramilitaries usually are well trained but lightly armed land forces, with no heavy weapons like tanks and artillery. Ordinarily, they are commanded by civilian authorities like the Home or Interior Ministry of a country, although in case of war, they can be placed under the command of the regular Armed Forces. The Governments use the paramilitary forces for presidential security, border patrol, protection of sensitive establishments and are called on duty to deal with major riots or national emergencies that the Police alone is unable to cope with.

Among the examples of the state paramilitary include military auxiliary forces such as the France's Republican Guard or Argentina's Presidential Guard; Gendarmeries, such as Egyptian Central Security Forces; and Russia's National Guards, Border Guards, such as Pakistan Rangers and India's Border Security Force, and sometimes even Foreign volunteers, youth-based Scouts, cadet organizations and the like.

Not all paramilitary are land-based, for instance, the Federal Protective Forces of the US include Air National Guards, while Pakistan and India have sea-borne Coast Guards which are defined as Para Military.[4] Sometimes the term "paramilitary has been used to denote militant, insurgent or guerilla movements fighting against the State. That usage is outside the scope of this section.

When were the first Bands in State-controlled Paramilitary forces formed remains hazy for want of a universal definition of the term. As far back as 1633, in North America, drummers performed for marching practice during militia drills in the colony of Virginia. However, it was in 1687, when Virginia State voted to purchase musical instruments for its militia. All free white males were required to serve in these militia units. Interestingly, while militiamen were required to supply their own rifles, this was not the case with Drummers whose instruments were procured by public funds and they received money for their service. In a way, these continental militias were precursors of various paramilitary forces that the United States has today.

There can be many conflicting claims about the oldest continuing Paramilitary Band. If French Foreign Legion is accepted as a paramilitary force of France, separate from the French army, then the Legion's Band based in *Aubagne* can make this claim. This Band has been an integral part as well as the icon of the Foreign Legion, since as early as 1832. Otherwise, another close claimant of being the oldest continuing Paramilitary Band can again be traced back to France. The Orchestra of the French Republican Guard founded in 1848 by Jean-George Paulus is by all definitions a Para-military Band.

But around the same time as the Band of French Foreign Legion was raised, or probably a year earlier, the Turkish Gendarmerie has established full-fledged military Bands to replace the Mehter Bands that the Ottoman Sultan had abolished five years earlier in 1826. But the question remains whether that was a military or a para-military Band. This same conundrum is faced by a large number of other Bands that emerged in the 19th century in the uniformed forces of Latin and South American countries. Which ones of them were military Bands and which ones the paramilitary, shall remain a subject of historical inquiry as much as of technical and definitional scrutiny.

Today, Bands of the paramilitary forces complement the Forces they represent. The United States Coast Guards and Air National Guards, the Saudi National Guard, the Argentinian Presidential Guard, the Indian BSF, the Russian Border Guard Service, the Pakistani Frontier Corps, the Iranian Revolutionary Guards, all can boast a rich tradition of ceremonial and marching Bands.

Evolution of Bands in Police Departments

Some sources point to the fact that the first proper Police Band sprang up in the Caribbean Islands, east of the mainland of American continent. The Royal Barbados Police Band (RBPB) founded in 1835 is probably the oldest police Band in the world. Police Bands are common throughout the Anglophone Caribbean, and are known for playing a wide variety of Caribbean music, as well as marches and popular songs.

When the RBPB was first established, it was with a complement of 19 serving Policemen selected on the basis of musical knowledge and interest. At that time, they wore regular police uniforms. The first Bandmaster was Mr. Willocks who came to the Island with the 2nd Battalion of the West Riding Regiment, as its Bandmaster. Another famous Bandmaster in its history was Major Emmanuel Bennernagel of the British Guiana Militia Band who was appointed to lead RBPB in 1914.

The first civilian pipe Band in the United Kingdom proper is recognized as the Burgh of Govan Police (later Glasgow Police, now Strathclyde Police) raised in 1883. In fact, there are other claimants to be the oldest Police Bands in the United Kingdom or its overseas territories such as the Kent Police Band in UK or the Victoria Police Band in Australia raised around 1891. Early police and fire brigade pipe Bands mostly played military-type field music.

Milwaukee Police Band in Wisconsin State, USA, boasts to be the oldest Police Band in the United States. It must have been raised around the same time when the Milwaukee police force was established in circa 1897. In continental Europe, city of Antwerp Police Band, founded in 1901, was an initiative of Antwerp Police Association founded the year before. Consisting of Police personnel only, playing on voluntary basis, it was entitled as Representative Band of Antwerp

City during the visit of Crown Prince Leopold in 1926. It got its royal title in 1991 and is now a prominent presence at Belgian Palace and at national day parades.

In Asia, the oldest Police Band is the one at Kolkata (India) raised in 1858. The Eastwards expanse of Police Bands within Asia also took time, with Malay Police Band being raised in 1905, the Singapore Police Band in 1925, and finally, a Police Band being raised in the British colony of Hong Kong, as late as in 1954, almost a century after the Kolkata Police Band.

In fact, the evolution of police Bands in Indo-Pakistan subcontinent appears to be accidental. After the war of 1857, when the East India Company troops defeated, dethroned and banished the last Mogul Emperor Bahadur Shah Zafar from the Indian empire, the British government decided to take direct control of India as its crown colony. Kolkata city (then called Calcutta) used to be the seat of the Governor General appointed by the East India Company. On November 1, 1858, the formal change of guard from Company Bahadur to the British Crown was to take place.

The British officers were not comfortable with the change of guard without certain amount of pomp and splendour which would have been incomplete without a big liveried musical accompaniment. An ensemble of 248 Englishmen and Indian *Darogas* [head watchmen—the predecessors of regular police] were hurriedly mobilised from the city of Calcutta and organised into a "Pipe-Band" to play at the British Governor General's grand mansion.

With a training of merely one week, these men in full regalia marched to the tunes the assorted musicians played. Shortly thereafter, they were inducted into the Calcutta Police to form the Police Band. Today, a well-trained group of seventy men proficient in both Brass and Pipe instruments carries the legacy as being the oldest Police Band in South Asia. The Police Bands were quick to reach the North of British India, such as Lahore where Police Band was raised in 1861. Lahore Police Band was capably led by British conductors for three quarters of a century from Captain Ryan (1861–96), Captain Waan (1896–1921) and DSP Chapman (1921–48) when it started being led by Pakistani Band Masters starting from SP Fazal Ilahi who led it from 1948 to 1980. The Police Bands reached the Western coasts of India fairly late, hardly eleven years before independence and partition, with Bombay Police Band being raised as late as in 1936.

The British India was rich in military-style palace Bands that the princely rulers, Nabobs and Maharajas patronized. As India and Pakistan became independent, the princely states were dissolved and most of the jobless musicians of the palace Bands formed wedding marching Bands. However, quite a few of them were hired in toto by local police forces to form the Police Bands. A very prominent example is that of the Police Band of Mysuru which remained the capital of princely state of Mysore from 1399 to 1947.

The state of Mysore rose to fame when its de *facto* ruler Hayder Ali and later his son Tipu Sultan fought four wars with the British East India Company between 1761 and 1799. The end of fourth Anglo-Mysore War was brought about by the death and defeat of Tipu Sultan in the Battle of Sirangapatam (4 May 1799). The British restored the kingdom to the Widayar dynasty.

The Mysuru Palace Band originated during the early years of the reign of Widayar ruler, Maharaja Sri Krishnaraja Wadiyar Bhaddur IV (r. 1894–1940). In the years following the independence in 1947, all princely states were abolished both in India and Pakistan. So Mysore hereditary monarchy was also dissolved and the domains got merged into the Indian State of Karnataka. The historic city of Mysuru also lost its status as the capital which is now the city of Bengaluru (earlier Bangalore) 93 km away. In 1951, both the Mysuru palace Bands (Indian Orchestra of 56 musicians and English Band of 34 Bandsmen) were integrated to the Mysuru Police Department. The Mysuru Police Band has since been renamed as Mysuru Government Orchestra.

Among other notable police Bands we can name the Italy Polizia Band, the Band of Indonesian National Police, Royal Mounted Police Pipe Band of Canada, the three Bands of the Columbia Police (that of the National Police, the Civil Guard and the Investigation Police, not to mention the Russian MVD (Ministry of Interior) Central Band—the one of the only two Bands still entitled to use the term Red Army Choirs—which is, in effect, the Central Band of the Russian Police.

Arguably, sifting Police Bands from Paramilitary Forces Band is never an easy task. In many countries, forces such as Carabineers in Latin America, are military-style forces under civilian control, mostly doing policing and patrolling functions. On the other hand, China's People's Armed Police (PAP) is anything but a Police. It performs all functions of militia or border guards, akin to what its counterparts, the Indian BSF and Pakistan Rangers, do in China's two Western neighbours which are military powers in their own right. Hence, PAP Band, in this work, is counted as a Para Military Force Band while, for instance, the Band of now-defunct Civil Guard of Peru (lately merged with Peru National Police) is counted in Police Bands, though, the word "Police" does not appear in its name. Another similar example is that of the Carabinero of Chile that, since 1927, consisted of a

Fiscal Police and Rural Police. Although the Force sent mounted contingents in national parades but their Band, not a horse-mounted Band, marched on foot. Since 1973 coup, the Carabinero was given under the control of the army, hence, in our definition became a para-military force.

Extension of Bands in non-Police Civil uniformed agencies

From the 1980s and onwards, the Bands have started popping up in State institutions and organizations other than those related to law enforcement and security. These Bands are raised to give pride to the institution, to boost spirits of the employees and to provide entertainment and a healthy activity to the human resource of the institution.

Among the earliest unique Bands in non-Police civil agencies includes the Band of the Tax and Customs (NAV for short) of the Hungarian government. The NAV Department was set up in 1867 following a "compromise" agreement which established the dual monarchy of Austria-Hungary. By 1890, Choral societies and large and small instrumental ensembles of the Tax and Customs Department were already giving concerts for the public. In 1925, several of these ensembles came together within the organization to form an Orchestra of Vamszaki (Customs Officials) whose conductor was Bela Marco and later Joszef Zaborsky.

In 1942, Hungary has another first, at the occasion of 75th anniversary of the Department, since the 1867 compromise, that Ministry of Finance ordered the raising of "National Finance Wind Band" to celebrate the anniversary and to focus public attention to the Finance Service. From 1956, all Band members were required to be Finance Department officers. In 2017, the Finance Ministry Band celebrated the 150th anniversary of the Department and 75th anniversary of the Band.

The Fire Services Bands are also a notable presence in United Kingdom, Australia, Hungary and several other countries. A famous example is the Band of the Paris Fire Brigade (*Musique de la Brigade de Sapeurs-Pompiers de Paris)* which performs with distinction along with the Bands of French Armed Forces and the Foreign Legion at the annual Bastille Day Parade in Paris, France.

Among the non-Police civil government Bands, many have represented their countries by performing or competing at international military Band tattoos. The case of the Band of the Ministry of Emergency Services (Russian Federation), the Prison Department Bands (India), the Railways Headquarter Brass Band (Pakistan) and the Band of New South Wales Fire Department (Australia) are cases in point.

Conclusion: Power as Patron of Bands

State is composed of its civil and military establishments. Like all forms of art and architecture, the Military Bands could not have seen growth unless patronised by the State. People like Michelangelo, Firdousi, Leonardo Da Vinci and Ibn e Khaldun might have faded to oblivion but for the support of noble or religious patrons they, and therefore their arts, enjoyed. The Court, the Church, the Nobility or anyone that represented the State needed visual and audible elements to demonstrate prestige and superiority. The Military Bands embodied that political statement and hence the uniforms, the formations, the musical content and occasions for display were dictated by the powers. One who pays the piper, calls the tunes!

It is usually the military Bands that perform for State ceremonials including events at the Palaces and the Parliaments. However, sometimes the palaces did have their own Civil Bands. Rarer still, the Palaces had both civil and military Bands. Vietnam, during the long reign of monarchies, is a case in point. The Dance ensembles of chamber music for the entertainment of the King were defined as either *Van vu* (civil servants' Band) or *Vo vu* (military Band).

From the 19th century, even private and community Bands started to pop up in the civilian domain, outside the influence of the State. The Allentown Concert Band in Pennsylvania, has a continuous existence from its first recorded performance on Independence Day (July 4) 1828 to this day. It is a non-official civilian Band that has performed before ten US Presidents from Abraham Lincoln to Jimmy Carter. The origin of unofficial civilian Bands took place in the United Kingdom and many of its overseas dominions and former colonies. For instance, in Canada, the Sons of Scotland Pipe Band, formed on Burn's night in 1896, claims to be its oldest continuing civilian pipe Band in the country. It is based in the capital city of Ottawa. There were, no doubt, Canadian pipe Bands (that is, organised pipes and drums ensembles) before this time, but no other has a continuous existence to this day.

When was the first-ever civilian Band commissioned, outside the palace but within the State apparatus, is a question open to further inquiry. Within the regions of British influence, the Milwaukee Police Band in USA, Victoria Police Band in Australia, Kolkata Police Band in India and Lahore Police Band in Pakistan, not to mention the Strathclyde Police Band within the United Kingdom, are amongst the old, if not the oldest, civilian Bands in the respective countries. All of them were raised during the second half of the 19th century. Over the past century and a half, the Bands proliferated into the civil institutions other than Police too, from town hall to the Fire Services.

NOTES

1 Abu al-Fazal ibn Mubarak (1551–1602) was the Grand Vizier (Prime Minister) of Mogul empire during the reign of Emperor Akbar, and author of the *Akbarnama*, the official history of Akbar's reign in three volumes, (the third volume is known as the *Ain-i-Akbari*). He was also one of the so-called "Nine Jewels" (senior most noblemen) of Akbar's imperial court along with his brother Faizi, the poet laureate of empire at that time.

2 The Rank *(Mansb)* system in Mogul empire entitled the rank holder to raise, maintain and command the number of troops for the imperial army for which he was adequately rewarded by the Emperor. Thus, a rank of 10,000—a fairly high rank—would entitle the holder to cash reward enough to maintain a body of 10,000 troops that could be called to service as and when the emperor required for any military expedition.

3 In fact, the express permission of the White House was required for any tour of the President's Own Band outside Washington DC till as recently as 1986 when it was delegated to Defense Secretary and eventually Secretary of the Navy (Fettig 2016).

4 The United States Coast Guard, on the other hand, is one of the five branches of the Armed Forces along with Army, Navy, Air Force and Marines. The Army National Guard (ARNG) and the Air National Guard (ANG), however, are treated as militia forces or the military reserve forces of the United States.

CHAPTER IV

Growth of Bands: Influence of the State Institutions (Military)

An Army Without a Band, is not a Real Army

—American Saying

There is no concept of a military force in the world today without Bands. Their origin in the military was not for entertainment but as a necessary and, many-a-times the only, means to usher commands to the troops in hazy battlefields. After the age of industrialisation, environs of the battlefields have become noisier and messier. But the aptly called Revolution in Military Affairs (RMA) as well as the telecommunication and information technology revolution has made the communication role of the Bands redundant. But utility of Bands has risen in so many other ways that could not have been conceived in the past.

For instance, for the troops deployed to a forward operating base, the loud, dull roar of diesel generators, the incessant tapping metal from pistons deep inside armour vehicles, the clanking of mine rollers, the occasional thumping of helicopter rotors beating the air or a chest pounding boom from artillery, are some of the unpleasant sounds that they have to get accustomed to, even when no fighting is taking place. To neutralize these annoyances, the troops serving the nation, any nation for that matter, deserve some pleasant sounds. Hence, sending Military Bands to perform at their bases, is an operational and ethical necessity nowadays. And this is just one example!

A fortiori, it is not for nothing that over the past two centuries the Bands have seen momentous vertical (towards higher institutions of the State such as Palaces and Parliaments) and horizontal (towards sister branches of the military) expansion. Traditionally, the term "military Band" signified a Band attached with an infantry unit. Over the time, the mounted cavalry regiments started having buglers and ultimately full-fledged Bands. Then, the maritime forces of the State felt the need for Bands. From 1903 onwards, each British Navy ship started having a Band aboard. After the First World War, the Air Force started emerging as a separate arm of the military force. From 1920s onwards, Air Forces of the world are the latest entrants into the stream of military Bands although it took scores of years for Bands to be firmly established in Air Corps traditions.

Thus, we see the Band traditions continue to advance horizontally within different branches and arms of the Military. The present chapter will review the mushrooming of Bands in the military institutions of the State.

Army Bands of the Infantry and Dragoon Regiments

Although the regular Military Band corps was introduced by the Ottoman Turks. For centuries, all Military Bands were Infantry Bands. They marched with the infantry troops and provided necessary support to the commanders for transmitting the commands. The friendly ranks found the Bands inspiring for their morale while the Turk Ottoman Bands, with their thunderous drum beats, instilled fear in the opposite numbers.

It was not until the British Army adopted the Bands that the institution witnessed unprecedented growth, horizontally into other arms of the military as well as spatially in other regions of the world. The Royal Artillery Band was raised in the British Army in 1762, towards the end of the Seven Years War (1756–63), which is the oldest continuing Band in British army. The British also introduced the concept where Band musicians would double as Medics and vice versa. In fact, most Band members with British Infantry used to be civilians and their equally vital battle-time role was that of stretcher-bearers. They were tasked to evacuate the wounded from the battlefield back towards medical help.

The officer corps of the British Army was drawn from aristocratic families and they had to foot the costs of their Bands. So the Bands represented their owner and were given most embellished badges and accruements to reflect status and wealth of the Commander. This concept of the military Bands being elaborately dressed also continues to this day. The two institutions still donning ceremonial outfits in the world are that of Monarchy and that of Infantry Pipes and Drum Bands.

In the late 18th, and 19th centuries, the advent of mass armies gave rise to the patriotic war songs, of which "La Marseillaise" of revolutionary France was the prototype. In the American Civil War, songs such as "The Battle Cry of Freedom" lifted the spirit of Union soldiers on the march and in combat. In Germany and Japan in particular, military authorities made sure that singing was a regular part of army life as a means of improving the martial order of their conscripts.

During the British and other European colonial administrations in Asia and Africa, modern brass and pipe Bands spread in these continents as a contagion. Australia, New Zealand and the British dominions in the Pacific region also developed a tradition of military Bands which fused the British and local tunes and dances into a new genre of military music. The North- South transfusion of Dutch military music in East Indies, the German and Belgian military music in their overseas territories in Africa, and Spanish music in most of Latin America, led to a true musical globalization.

Hence, most of the military brass music of today, is to a large measure, Western in origin, though international in practice and appreciation. Hence, it is interesting to see that music in the Armed Forces of the world have striking resemblances and common features. The instruments that are in use by the Bands of different countries are fairly similar. The kind of music that is played by these Bands has a great deal of resemblance too.

Here, the Bands of Dragoon regiments or Dragoon guards also merits mention. The term Dragoon, though has varying connotations across regions, is generally applied to units that were expert in riding on horseback (for rapid commute to the battlefield) but were trained to fight on foot. Thus, they fall between infantry and cavalry in terms of their fighting mode. The Dragoon regiments may have foot Bands or mounted Bands. The Royal Dragoon Body Guard Regiment of Sweden has a famous mounted Band that plays at the royal palace daily during summer season, at the royal palace at Stockholm. It is one of the three surviving Bands with the Swedish Armed Forces.

Introduction of Mounted Bands in Cavalry

For centuries, as noted earlier, the term military Band was synonymous with an Infantry Band. This started changing from the 17th century onwards when the tradition of mounted Bands started firmly taking root. Since it is difficult to ride while playing or play while riding, the mounted Bands are difficult to train and maintain. Animal-mounted Bands suffered from another challenge—the panic sometimes created amongst animals due to music sounds—that might spur them to run amok throwing off the Musician.

In any case, mounted Bands did emerge and are part of the global Bands tradition. The four main types include horse-mounted military Bands, camel-mounted military Bands, elephant-mounted military Bands and the bicycle-mounted military Bands.

Horse-mounted Military Bands

The European contribution to the development of Military Bands includes the evolution of horse-mounted Bands. In 1797, the British raised the Royal Horse Artillery regiment, as a mounted arm of their old and glorious Artillery regiment. Although it was a mounted regiment but its Royal Horse Artillery Band was not a mounted Band. It took almost a century when in 1886, the mounted counterpart, the Royal Artillery Mounted Band was raised. In the meantime, other Cavalry regiments also started raising mounted Bands. Eventually there was a mounted Band with each horse regiment. The practice lasted till 1930s when all cavalry regiments were disBanded, except the Royal Household Cavalry for ceremonial purposes at the Buckingham Palace and the Windsor Castle. As the cavalry regiments were dissolved so all the mounted Bands started vanishing. In 1984, the historic mounted Band of Royal Artillery was disBanded too. Ultimately, two mounted Bands were left in the British army: Mounted Band of the Life Guards and Mounted Band of the Royal and Blues. In 2014, these last two mounted Bands were merged into a single mounted Band. This last remaining vestige of mounted music is called the Royal Household Cavalry mounted Band. The mounted Bands continued to spread to continental Europe through the mounted Bands of the Republic Guard of France, to those of the Royal Guard and Civil Guard of Spain, northwards into Scandinavia such as the Swedish Life Guard Mounted Band, the regiment that protects the person of the King of Sweden to this day, and further Eastward into the Russian empire.

The mounted fanfare Bands were in vogue in most kingdoms in continental Europe before the World War I. Most of them have disappeared except a few still in place in Russia and Scandinavia. The Fanfare tradition is continuing in some countries of Latin America, including Brazil, Chile, Argentina and Peru, where at least one mounted Band each exists with their Armed Forces, mostly for the State ceremonial.

The first mounted Band in the United States army was raised by General George Armstrong Custer who commanded his Bands into combat repeatedly. A mounted Band spearheaded his famous cavalry charge at Columbia Furnace in 1864. Two years later, when he organised the Seventh Cavalry for the Indian Wars, Custer insisted on a mounted Band. This Band led the charge at the Battle of Washita in 1868 and again on the north bank of the Yellowstone river, below the mouth of the Bighorn in 1873. In the decades, that followed, the mechanisation of warfare led to the end of mounted soldiers. The US cavalry lost its last mounted combat unit in the 1940s. With this, the horse-mounted Bands also vanished from the US military scene. There is no mounted Band on the strength of United States Armed Forces today. In fact, the whole world is left with twenty or so horse-mounted Bands attached to the Military Forces, down from hundreds of them with each army, as recently as the 19th century.

Modern day mounted Military Bands are different from the Military Infantry Bands in a number of ways. First of all, the mounted Bands are usually Brass Bands with no Woodwind instruments. Secondly, unlike other Brass, Wind and Concert Bands, the Band Major carries a mace or a staff which is otherwise the characteristic of the leaders of Pipe Bands. Thirdly, it is the Bugle Major, not the Drum Major, who is the Band Major of a mounted Band. At best, most European mounted Bands have just one (Kettle) Drummer. Other than the Military, there are mounted Police Bands as well in Canada and several Latin American nations, in particular.

Camel-mounted Military Bands

The practice of mounted Bands also influenced Asia. The British Administration raised a Jordanian Camel mounted Mobile Force, under Gen John Glub, in 1920, with a hundred troopers. It grew to a 1000-strong Arab Legion by 1923. Although the Camel regiment did have a small Band but there is no evidence that it was a camel-mounted Band. The German colonial administration, however, did have a camel-mounted Band (*Schutztruppe*) in South West Africa (presently Namibia), around the time of World War I.

In the British India, a few of the princely rulers seem to have had horse-mounted Bands. The British colonial administration also had toyed with having a mounted Band with 17th Cavalry Regiment of Bengal Lancers. Raised in 1895, the same was disBanded soon afterwards in 1902. The Regiment was eventually merged into Pakistan Army where it still exists as 37th Baluch Horse Regiment. The horse-mounted Band, however, was never revived since 1902.

However, camel-mounted Bands are there to symbolise the military competition between India and Pakistan. Presently, the Indian Border Security Force (BSF) has the largest Camel-Mounted Band which is a star item in the Republic Day Parade in New Delhi on January 26 each year. In a tit-for-tat, the traditional rival, Pakistan Rangers, the border security agency of Pakistan, also raised a Camel-mounted Bands which is used for ceremonial purposes at the

Pakistan's Republic Day Parade on March 23 and at other occasions. The Indian BSF Camel Band is a Brass Band while Pakistan Rangers Camel Band is a Bagpipe Band. They are the only living camel mounted-military Bands in the world at present.

Elephant-mounted Military Bands

The first historical reference to Pipers mounted on elephants is during the reign of the Sassanid imperial dynasty (r. 224–651 AD) in Persia (modern-day Iran). Elephants continued to be used in War to intimidate the enemy in Persia and ancient India. However, when modern percussion instruments were formed, elephant-mounted Band became an unattractive proposition. This was because sometimes the elephants became terrified by the sounds of drumbeat and tried to flee in panic trampling their own soldiers to death.

However, during the British period amongst the more than five hundred or so Princely States in united India, at least one Prince maintained an elephant-mounted Bands. This was by the Maharaja of Orchha. This elephant-mounted Band also performed in the coronation ceremony of King Henry V, at the Delhi Darbar of 1903. There is no elephant-mounted Band in the world at present.

Bicycle-mounted Military Band

Band of the Netherlands Mounted Arms Regiment is one of the two professional orchestras within the Royal Netherlands Army and the only full-time professional mounted fanfare orchestra in the world. The Band continues the traditions of the Bicycle Music Corps, sporting uniforms issued in 1914, playing bent instruments while riding bicycles. This is the only known bicycle-mounted military Band in the world.

Bands of the Dragoon Regiments

There is a difficulty to place the Dragoon Guard regiments, or mounted Infantry so to speak, in many countries as Infantry or as Cavalry. Just like Marine forces (*See below*) fall somewhere between Army and Navy performing both functions, the Dragoon regiments were basically mounted regiments skilled at fighting on foot. Thus, they were mounted on horses only for quicker mobility towards the battlefields where they were supposed to dismount and fight on foot along with infantry. Their name originates from a type of firearm, called *Dragon*—a type of rifle used by French Dragoons, similar to blunderbuss. Besides France, Dragoon regiments existed in Iberian nations (Portugal and Spain), Russia, Switzerland, various Latin American countries, including Chile, Peru and Brazil, and all the

Nordic States. By the early 18th century, some countries started using them as light cavalry to fight with swords from horseback.

As the history of Infantry regiments has shown that many-a-times they may have a mounted Band and likewise there is no certainty that each of the Cavalry regiments will maintain a mounted Band. Hence, Dragoon regiments also have varying traditions of having a foot marching Band or a mounted Band. The King's Own Life Guards Dragoon Regiment of Sweden has a very famous mounted Band which is one of the two Bands left with the Swedish army. Otherwise, many Dragoon regiments have non-mounted Bands and have been considered as Infantry Bands.

Origin of Bands in the Navy and Sea-borne Forces

Just like Army and Police Bands, it is next to impossible to determine exactly when the first Navy Band was formed. The Ottoman Navy had sent their army *Mehter* Bands aboard their fleet at some point in time in history where they might have played during sea battles. The British Marines also had drum corps at their fixed establishments as early as the end of 17th century but there is no evidence they played on sea. A few littoral states in Europe like Venice and Portugal might have Drummers associated with their Naval Infantry. But none fits into our definition of a proper Navy Band.

About the first Naval Band on a ship, the website of Navy musicians tells an interesting story from Italy. One of the early recollections of a Band on a ship dates back to 1802 in the Italian port of Messina. A local group of musicians was invited to play aboard a visiting Navy ship. The sailors were so mesmerised by their music that they forgot to tell the musicians that the ship was lifting its anchors and setting to sail. When it was realized, the ship was already far into the Sea and the poor musicians had no choice to stay aboard. The Band remained on the ship till it returned to the same shore a year or so later.

The origin of Naval Bands in the United States is similarly fortuitous. In 1812, the American Frigate eponymously named *United States* acquired an eight-piece Band of French–Italian musicians purely by accident. The story begins when the Band had enlisted aboard a French ship, but were captured by the Portuguese and taken to Lisbon as captives. Here they were signed on a British warship named *HMS Macedonian* which, as fate would have it, was captured by the Americans. The Band ended up playing on the decks of the American Naval vessel *United States* and the men became the Ship Band for the US Navy personnel aboard.

Later, many American ships, such as the warship *Cyane*, organised various types of musical units as early as 1820. William Raymond enlisted as a Musician in 1820 at the Naval dockyard of Norfolk, Virginia; musician James F. Draper signed aboard the frigate *USS Brandywine* in July 1825; John Page had his rating changed from Seaman to Master of the Band aboard *USS Constellation* in 1826 and took Ordinary Seaman William Tuton as his fellow Musician. The crew of *Constitution* formed a 20-piece Band in 1825. By 1827 this unit became the first known Navy Band to be formally shipped aboard an American warship.

Navy Bandsmen were first recognized officially in 1838, when the pay tables of the US Navy Register listed the grades of Bandmaster, First and Second Class Musicians. The number of Navy Bands fluctuated initially but gradually increased in succeeding years through the American Civil War until the turn of the century, although it appears that no particular method of procurement or training of musicians was practiced.

The first of a series of fleet musician schools was established in 1903 at St. Helena, Virginia ,in an effort to improve the training and performance of Bands in the Navy. The Washington Navy Yard Band was formed in 1916 from the Ship Bands of USS *Mayflower* and USS *Kansas*. It was re-designated the United States Navy Band in 1925. A group photo on board USS *Henderson* shows the 35-man contingent from the Navy Band that accompanied the then US President Warren Harding on his visit to Alaska that started on 5 July 1923. Harding was the first President of United States to visit Alaska. He died in office the following month, on the second day of August 1923.

In 1935, Lt. Charles Benter, Leader of the Navy Band, Washington, D.C., established a Band School there. In 1941 the school was detached from the Navy Band, and became the United States Navy School of Music with Boatswain (later Lieutenant) James Thurmond as the first officer in charge.

However, it is the Admiralty Band of Russia that claims to be the world's oldest Naval Band. The first Band of the Admiralty in Russia was established at St. Petersburg by Czar Peter the Great. He had moved his capital from Moscow to the Baltic port of St. Petersburg in 1703. An Admiralty building was built (completed in 1706) for ship manufacturing. The Admiralty Band was raised in the Autumn of 1704 to provide entertainment to the ship workers. The music of oboes and drums mixed with the sounds of hammers and creak of capstan engines accompanied the construction of the Russian Fleet. The idea was that ship workers should not become bored while building ships that the Czar needed in pursuit of his maritime ambitions.

Although, it cannot be claimed with historical certainty, but in all likelihood this first Admiralty Band consisted of the same twenty-nine musicians that were drafted in February 1703 in Moscow to form the first Moscow Choir. If so, the birthplace of the first Naval Band is Moscow which paradoxically is not a port city.

It seems that initially the new Navy music was rather poorly received, because the Czar ordered daily noontime practice sessions for the Band to improve their performance. Practice makes one perfect, the idiom goes, and this is what might have happened to the Admiralty Band because seven years later, in February 1711, Peter the Great gave official status as "The Chorus of the Admiralty Battalion" to the Band. The Admiralty Tower was completed in 1719 and the Band used the place for its concerts till the middle of the century. Under the short reign of Czar Paul I (r. 1796–1801), the Admiralty Battalion was disBanded and so was its Band in 1798. The concerts were gone too.

But was the Admiralty Band a Naval Band? It was not meant to perform on board the ships. In fact, it was meant for the Naval ship building factory. In any case, it is not a continuing Naval Band as it was dissolved in 1798. However, the story of Russian Navy Bands did not end. The head of the defunct Admiralty Battalion, Adrian Zakharov convinced Czar Paul I to establish a Naval College of Ship Architecture that same year (1798). In the middle of the 19th century the College moved to Kronstadt—a citadel of the Russian Navy. It was here that the legendary Nikolay A. Rimsky-Korsakov, acting as the first Inspector of the Musical Corps of Russian Navy, revived the Admiralty Band as well as other Bands at the Kronstadt port and became their Conductor. So after a hiatus of nearly half a century, Russian Naval music was back on stage, Korsakov organized a massed Band of the Kronstadt port and conducted concerts for the benefit of the sick and injured. The tunes that Korsakov had developed in mid-19th century influenced the development of military Band music for the Russian Navy for times to come. Transformations that he was introducing in the military Bands on the fleet and the organization of their training were a great example for imitation during similar reforms in the Russian Army.

After the 1917 revolution, the College was restructured and moved back to Saint-Petersburg. Soviet Union took keen interest in patronizing the Naval Bands. Before World War II, the Naval College's Band was renowned as one of the best in the Soviet Union Navy. The Central Band of the Russian Navy is still named after Nikolay Korsakov.

The Naval Bands of China, Korea, Indonesia, South Africa, Italy, Argentina, Australia, New Zealand, India, UAE, Japan, Pakistan and many other nations have made their niche in world Naval Music. Whenever a Naval Ship visits the port of a friendly nation, the host nation's Naval Band welcomes it. More often than not, the States send their Navy Bands aboard their ships to friendly countries. The Naval Bands uniforms mostly have White colour in Summers and Navy Blue (or Black) in Winters in line with Naval uniforms, although, the Band uniforms are much more embellished. In many States, the Naval Bands still have swords in their scabbards as part of the ceremonial outfits.

Origin of Bands in Marine Corps

The tradition of Naval Bands got firmly institutionalised and was extended to Marine forces and coast guards all over the world. *Marines* are a branch of Armed Forces that are capable of fighting both on land and at sea. In ancient times there was no difference between soldiers and sailors. In close naval contests, hand to hand sword fight could ensue if one side tried to board other's battleships. As warfare became a more technical affair, many countries tried to raise a separate force capable both of land and sea warfare. The first organised corps of marines was created by Spanish King Carlos I, named Mediterranean Galley Squadrons in 1537. It was followed, in 1550, by the Naval Infantry the Republic of Venice (presently in modern day Italy), while the third oldest Marine Corps is the Portuguese one founded in 1618.

Marines, mostly called Naval Infantry, were used for helping maintain discipline and order aboard the ship (reflecting the pressed nature of the ships' company and the risk of mutiny), the boarding of vessels during combat or capture of prize ships, and providing manpower for raiding ashore in support of the naval objectives. In military operations, the role of marine troops was mainly in the littoral zone. Operating from ships, they are trained to land on and secure key points to around 50 miles inland, or as far as ship borne logistics can provide.

Today, there are Marine Forces or Naval Infantry, under various names in as many as 50 states out of a total of 200 countries and territories across the globe. In a few countries, they are a separate fourth arm of the Military Forces, equal in status to the other three, as in the United States. In most other states, they form a wing of the Navy, or rarely, as in France or Israel, of the army. Of the half a million marine force personnel in the world, around 260,000 personnel are in the US Marines Corps while the remaining half are divided into fifty states, with even UK having just 7,200 Marines.

Although there is a probability that the Spanish or Italian Marines may have had drummers for drill of the Naval Infantry, but proper Marines Band is another matter. Likewise, in the United Kingdom, the companies of the Duke of York and Albany's Regiment of Foot—the forerunners of the Royal Marines—were raised in 1664. Their "Colour and the Drum" provided a rallying point in close battle. In 1767, Royal Marines Divisional Bands were formed at Chatham, Plymouth, Portsmouth and Deal. The development of music in the Royal Marines is linked to British Military Bands. But most of their duties were in camps and training fields rather than on the ships or during the combat.

In the United Kingdom, a Naval School of Music was established in 1903 at Portsmouth, nearly half a century after the establishment of Kneller Hall Music School. The task of training the Naval musicians was given to the Royal Marines. This gave way to the creation of Royal Marine Band Service which became the musical arm of the British Navy and till recently was the only arm of the Marines where women were inducted. The Band Service moved to Malvern just after the Second World War, relocated to Burford a year later, and finally to Deal in 1950 where it suffered the IRA terrorist attack in the later part of the century. Ultimately, the Royal Marine Bands Service returned to Portsmouth where it exists to date.

Upon relocation to Deal in 1950, the School was renamed as the Royal Marines School of Music and all Naval and Marines Bands were merged into the Marines Band Service. However, it was anything but. Rather than strictly a Marine Bands Service, the new Service was and is the British Naval Band Service. The word Marine in the name indicates a choice of terminology because of the origin of Marines being tasked to train naval musicians. This terminology of Marine Bands to be used as a substitute for Naval Bands permeated in many countries of Europe. Technically speaking, they are not Marines Bands except the Bands of certain Amphibious units of Sweden's Territorial Guard or Bands of Naval Infantry of Spain which are in essence Marine Bands.

First proper exclusive Marines Band is undoubtedly the United States Marines Band established through an Act of Congress on 11 July 1798. This was the first regular military Band within the four arms of the military in the United States. From the year 1800 onwards, US President Adams associated it with the ceremonies in the White House. Even today, centuries later, it is called "President's Own" Marine Band and remains the official Marine Band of the White House.

Origin of Bands in the Air Forces

The Bands of the Air Force are newest amongst the Military Bands since the Air Force itself is the youngest arm of the Military. The oldest Air Force of the world is the Royal Air Force (RAF) of the United Kingdom, founded in the final months of the First World War. On 1 April 1918, that is, the British Army's Royal Flying Corps and the Royal Naval Air Service were amalgamated to form the RAF commanded by a Chief of the Air Staff (with the rank of Major-General). This new Corps comprised over 20,000 aircraft and was governed by its own government ministry (the Air Ministry). And it is this Air Ministry that decided that Air Force must have its own Bands for training, discipline and morale of the Air Force personnel.

Dr Walford Davies, who later became Master of the King's Music, was invited to become the first Organising Director of Music for the Royal Air Force. He quickly established the RAF School of Music to train Band instructors and trumpet majors. The World War I ended in November 1918, and following the armistice, many of the musicians returned to civilian life. The remainder were formed into a Band at the RAF School of Music to await further developments.

Davies left the Service in 1919, taking up the newly created Chair of Music at the University College of Wales, Aberystwyth, but not before composing the Royal Air Force "March Past" tunes. It was his successor Major Dyson who, in 1920, reorganised RAF Music Services on a proper footing. The School of Music was disestablished and the Central Band of the RAF and the Band of the RAF College were formed at RAF Uxbridge and RAF Cranwell, respectively.

By the 1930s, Royal Air Force had become well established and the rank of Air Chief was elevated to be at par with Chiefs of the other arms, i.e. Army and Navy. The two Bands of the Air Force also got their prestige raised, making a reputation for innovation and musical excellence. In the lead up to World War II, there was a large expansion of RAF Music Services. Additional military Bands were provided on a Command basis, with the RAF Symphony Orchestra and the famous "Squadronaires" Dance Band being established. The Central Band of the RAF included some of Britain's finest musicians such as Dennis Brain, Norman Del Mar and Gareth Morris.

In the meantime, more and more countries started treating their Air personnel as a separate arm of their Defence establishments. First, the South African Air Corps (SAAC) was converted into South African Air Force in 1920; Australia formed its Air Force in 1921; New Zealand in 1923; Finland in 1928; Egypt in 1937 and Brazil in 1941. The raising of Air Force Bands in these countries, except in South Africa, closely followed the separation of the Force itself from the other military branches. Interestingly, Canadians who had raised their Air Force at the end of the World War I dissolved it for operational reasons shortly thereafter. On the other hand, the United States and Japan, the two major belligerent states of

World War II did not have a separate Air Force till 1947 and 1954, respectively. Their air fighting units during the World War II were either under army or naval commands. Today, only Mexican Air Force remains an integral part of the Mexican army rather than being a separate force.

The creation of separate Air Forces did not mean creation of Air Force Bands simultaneously as happened in the United Kingdom. For instance, though South African Air Force (SAAF) is the second oldest Air Force in the world, its first Band was established decades later. In fact, at the end of the World War, the Union Defense Forces Band (UDFB), was disBanded due to financial constraints. The late Capt. Harry Philips, former UDFB Musician, founded the SAAF Band as its first Bandmaster in 1946.

The case with the United States of America is entirely the opposite where Air Force Bands predate the establishment of its Air Force. The first "Air Force Band" was raised after the USA had joined the Second World War. On 6 October 1941, the first USAF Band had its humble beginnings with just three musicians. Over the next four years till the end of the second World War in 1945, fifty-nine Air Bands had been raised. Musicians were selected after country-wide auditions from thousands of applicants from 32 major symphony orchestras and 38 famous Dance Bands. Earlier in 1944, Col George S. Howard was named as the Commander and Conductor of Air Force Bands, a position he held for the next 20 years.[1]

Gradually the Band at the US military Headquarters grew to a strength of 179 and earned the designation as "The Official Band of the *Army's Air* Forces" [emphasis added]. With the separation of the Air Force in 1947, this Band got renamed as "The United States Air Force Band." It is the US Air Force's premier musical squadron which includes the Concert Band, Singing Sergeants, the Airmen of Note, the USAF Strings, Ceremonial Brass, Max Impact, Chamber Players, and a myriad of other ensemble combinations, including rock, pop, country, and dedicated show units.

In January 1951, Col. Howard organised the 543rd Air Force Band made up of 19 female airmen from the Women in the Air Force (WAF) program. He expanded this group to some 50 members. In June 1955, they were officially designated "United States WAF Band," acknowledging their de facto status as USAF representatives rather than their original status as a simple base Band. Their official mission became to "assist, within their capabilities, in promoting Air Force objectives and enhancing the prestige of the Air Force and the United States." This meant there were now two Bands serving as ambassadors of the USAF: the all-male Air Force Band and the all-female WAF Band. The WAF Band was dissolved in 1961 following its commander's contravention of a directive from Col George Howard restricting performances at civilian schools and county fairs.

By 1950, under the direction of Wing Commander George Sims, the United States Air Force Bands were reorganised on a geographical basis. Their number also started dwindling from 59 during the World War to only 14 by the beginning of Donald Trump presidency.

Since 1960, their counterparts in the UK Royal Air Force Music Services have also been gradually reduced in size. The 10 established Air Force Bands in UK, include the "Central Band of the Women's Royal Air Force," numerous voluntary Bands and a School of Music. The British female personnel did not meet a similar fate as that of the WAF Band in USA. In 1990, the Royal Air Force became the first Service in the United Kingdom to recruit women into mixed Bands. Now, females are recruited on the same basis as their male colleagues. The personnel with some RAF Bands are nearly half females.

Interestingly, the claimant to being the oldest Band with the Air Force (not the oldest Air Force Band) is the Band of the Norwegian Air Force, which traces its history to 1817–18. At that time, the Norwegian military established five Bands for its five brigades that eventually became Division Bands. In 2006, the Air Force adopted the Fifth Division Band as the Air Force Band, based in Trondheim. After being organised under the Royal Air Force, the Band has transformed from being a Central Norway-based Band, to serve the whole country, playing for both military and civilian audiences (Military Music 2015).

Today, Air Force Bands of France, Iran, China, India, Philippines, Pakistan, Chile, Ukraine, Egypt, Kenya and several other countries are prominent musical organisations on the international stage. The Air Force Music has evolved into a separate genre and is distinguishable in uniforms, tunes and repertoire from Army and Navy Bands.

Conclusion: Musical and non-Musical Role of Military Bands

The military Bands had initially immortalised war music and war songs. The playlist of military music faced worldwide progressive shifts from war music to patriotic music and then folk and traditional music. Thus the Military Bands became the repositories of whole treasure of the national musical heritage from folk to classical. The Bands led the development of new forms of music and saved the musical heritage from extinction.

As public fad moved towards modern rock music, the military Bands also got finesse in playing opera, rock music and other popular songs of their nations.

Today, the military Bands are an inalienable part of national life all over the world. As the Bands become increasingly visible for all State and private occasions, so far from fading away, the need for maintaining military Bands is getting greater

Here, it is important to underline that there is no time or place that the Military Bands remain idle. Whenever they are not playing music, there are a wide range of non-musical duties that each country assigns to them. For example, in November 1981, the US Army published, what it called the TRADOC Pamphlet 525-13. Titled "US Army Operational Concepts Use of Army Bands in Combat Areas", this policy paper identified the requirement of musical support before, during, and after a combat. This publication also deleinated the secondary missions for Army Bands. Bands assume the secondary mission when combat reaches an intensity that makes the primary music mission impractical. The secondary mission includes four areas: (1) Command post security; (2) Perimeter defence; (3) Traffic control (4) Prisoner of war security. As we shall see in the coming chapters that such like duties are increasingly being assigned to military Bands in recent years in wartime and peacetime.

A fairly recent example from the British Military History where Bands are given certain secondary roles comes from Cyprus expedition. The first time in the history of the Royal Marines Band Service that Musicians and Buglers had been deployed in company strength as an independent military unit to perform their secondary role was on 1 April 2007. This marked a significant milestone for the Band Service as 90 of their deployed ranks took over the duties as the Cyprus Reinforcement Unit for two months.

NOTES

1 The John Philip Sousa Foundation awards the Col George S Howard Citation to the best military concert band in recognition of the memory of Col Howard. More of this in Chapter XIV.

CHAPTER V

Evolution of Bands: Substate, Parastate and Non-State Institutions

Music is the voice that tell us that the human race is greater than it knows

—Napoleon

The State traditionally was resourceful enough to be able to maintain all trappings of glory, Bands being one of them. For the Civil arms of the State, Band was an instrument of prestige. For the military arms of the State, however, Band was a necessity. The military Bands had spilt over the other institutions in Parastate and Substate institutions as well as within those institutions of the society where State has no direct interference, such as a family.

This chapter aims at exploring the Bands existing outside the government-owned or controlled institutions, both civil and military. Here the Church is considered as an institution parallel to the State. The educational establishments like Universities, Colleges and Schools are categorised here as Substate institutions. The Bands also sprang up outside the formal State structure such as the towns, villages and families, which for our purpose, are non-state institutions. In recent times, Bands also became available as commercial service providers to provide music to wedding, funerals and parties. Such Bands are commercial enterprises in their own right. What follows is an attempt to explore all four classifications one by one.

Bands in Parastate Institutions: The Religious Orders

Next to the Word of God, noble art of music is the greatest treasure of the world

—Martin Luther

Music has generated theological debate in all major religions. Some sort of oral music like singing, reciting or chanting has been a part of religious worship universally. However, it is the use of instrumentation that has evoked many a doctrinal controversy in all major religions. The instrumental music has been considered by some as being too worldly to have anything to do with religion while others saw musical expression as a way to praise God. At the end of the day, musical Bands do exist in virtually all major religious traditions today. And the Religious Orders have had immense influence on the development of Bands worldwide.

The question of what is Islamic or Christian or Jewish music and what makes music religious, continues to be explored in academic and artistic circles alike. For our purpose religious music refers to the content and context of the music that may have liturgical or implicit references to the Divine, that which is played at a religious service or place of worship of a particular religion, or a type of music that is generally associated with one religion or its followers.

Religious music is sort of a triangle of lexical, vocal and instrumental components as its three corners. The lexical or verbal component refers to the verses, the poetry, the lyrics or any content that is chanted or sung. The vocal component of music is the actual singing or chanting of the content. The instrumental means the tunes provided for the musical service. The present section on religious Bands includes marching Bands, the pop and rock Bands, or any other sort of Bands. Since enough has been written in the world about religious music in general, this section looks at the emergence or presence of Bands in five influential religious streams, namely Christianity, Islam, Judaism, Hinduism and Buddhism.

Marching Bands in Christian Religious Practice

> *Music is the art of the prophets and the Gift of God*
>
> —Martin Luther

Christian music is prevalent in the church services or other religious gatherings. Most Christian music involves singing, whether by the whole congregation (assembly), or by a specialised subgroup—such as a soloist, duet, trio, choir, or a worship Band. Frequently, the music is accompanied by instruments like an organ, piano, electronic keyboard, or guitar. In richer and larger Churches, a full Band or Orchestra provides the music. Taking the example of Sweden alone, there are more than 100 Bands within the Salvation Army, the Alliance Mission and the Pentecostal Movement, nearly all of them British-styled brass Bands. The

Missionary Church has about 60 Bands, both with and without woodwind. The Evangelical National Missionary Society of Stockholm, the Church of Sweden and the Swedish YMCA maintain about 30 Bands (Jansson 2018).

The Bible does not condemn the use of instruments of music in worship, but neither does it command their use. Some Christian denominations such as the Free Church of Scotland, the Churches of Christ, the Primitive Baptists and some Exclusive Brethren avoid any instrumental music in religious practice, citing their absence from the New Testament. Eastern Orthodox and some denominations that vehemently oppose instruments argue that many other things we know to be wrong are not condemned by name in the Bible. Thus, we can never assume having God's approval for an act only because there is no explicit prohibition in scriptures. The opponents of Bands also argue that in the New Testament, Paul says that faith comes by hearing the word of God and that whatsoever is not of faith is sin. This is another way of saying that if you cannot find command or example for an act of worship in the will of Christ (the New Testament), you should not do that act (Romans 10:17 and 14:23).

Nevertheless, the Christian religious tradition has many supporters of Bands, so Bands have a conspicuous presence in the Christian history. As the Bands become more ubiquitous several of the Christian sects and groups that have traditionally considered Bands as being prohibited in religion have revised their stance. Just like acceptance of female ordainment and greater tolerance towards LGBT communities, a more welcoming attitude towards Bands is a sign of reformation that the religion is undergoing. Our discussion on Christian Bands starts with the institution of the Roman Catholic Pope.

Papal Bands of the Vatican City State: The Pope enjoys the status of a Head of State of the Holy See. In this capacity, his personal protection is the responsibility of the Pontifical Swiss Guards. In fact, the Pope also happens to be the second most protected person in the world after the US President. The Swiss Guards act as the military unit of the Holy See as well as the Body Guard battalion for the Pope. Established in 1506, they wear four coloured elaborate uniforms. The persons recruited must be unmarried Roman Catholics with Swiss nationality aged between 19 and 30. They must at least have a diploma, and must have completed military service with the Swiss Armed Forces and must be ready to serve for a minimum of two years.

On the day the new recruits are sworn in at the Vatican, that is 6 May every year, a promise is taken from them that they would die for the Pope. What they are not required to pledge is to play music for him. But that comes later and it is important all the same. Like all other armies, they have a Marching Band with a long and glorious history.

There is also a second Marching Band at the disposal of the Papal Basilica which has somewhat secular origins. As Head of State of the Vatican City State, the security force of the Pope is the State Gendarmerie. Unlike the Swiss Guards, who are responsible to the Holy See, the Gendarmeries are employees of the Vatican State. The Gendarmeries have policing and internal security duties in Vatican. The Band of the Gendarmerie also acts as Marching Band of the Vatican City State. Founded in 2007, the Band is made up of 100 volunteer conservatory graduates who come from Italian military Bands across the country.

Bands of Northern Ireland/Bands of the Orange Order: Many Churches of different denominations have marching Bands which are highly visible during Saint Patrick's Day parade and other religious events. In fact, Belfast, the capital of Northern Ireland, used to become a battle ground between the Catholics and the Protestants when one side's religious procession, consisting of up to twenty Marching Bands, passed through the areas populated by the other side. The Bands of the Orange Order are most prominent amongst the Protestant religious marching Bands, although they may not match the much longer history for the Catholic (Swiss Guards and Gendarmerie) Bands at the Vatican.

Military Bands of the Sovereign Order of Malta: From times immemorial, various religious orders have used military power to propagate the religion. Before the rise of State and ethnic nationalism starting mid-18th century onwards, the bulk of warfare in humankind had religious and sectarian origins. Several military denominations of various religious orders exist in the world, though, most of the still-surviving regimented religious organizations claim to work for peace and harmony these days.

The most prominent continuous example of a militarised religious formation is the Sovereign Military Order of Malta founded in 1099. It is a Roman Catholic religio–military order, now mostly concerned with humanitarian aid. It is a *sui generis* sovereign entity in the world today. It also enjoys Observer Status in the United Nations as a sovereign entity. It still has an army corps, with its three Brigades, operating under the general command of the Italian Defence Forces. The Grand Commander of the Order still dons military outfits and is entitled to all pomp of a Prince of the Military Order including, of course, the military salutes in ceremonial parades. No military style organization can have its drills without Bands. The Military Order of Malta is no exception.

The Salvation Army Brass Bands: The Salvation Army is another example of a religious movement modelled on army. Founded in 1865 in London, it is a Protestant movement. It had military uniforms, ranks, salute, emblem and flags but initially did not have military Bands. It tried to convert people to the Salvation cause through proselytising.

As the popularity of the organization grew and Salvationists worked their way through the streets of London attempting to convert individuals, they were sometimes confronted with unruly crowds. A family of musicians from Alderbury—the Frys—began working with the Salvation Army preachers as their "bodyguards" and played music to distract the crowds.

The tradition of having musicians with the preachers continued eventually growing into standard brass Bands. These are still seen in public at Salvation Army campaigns, as well as at other festivals, parades and at Christmas. Across the world, the brass Band has been an integral part of this Army's ministry and an immediately recognisable symbol of the Salvation Army.

The Salvation Army also has choirs; these are known as Songster Brigades, normally comprising the traditional soprano, alto, tenor and bass singers. The premier Songster Brigade in the Salvation Army is the International Staff Songsters (ISS).

Biblical Rock Bands: The rise of Jazz and Rock Bands in the past one century also saw a challenge to Christian values from the Atheist thought. As Rock Bands with themes ridiculing the Divine or mocking Christian beliefs emerged, other Rock Bands with purely religious litany and lyrics sprung up in response. These Bands may not have the Christian label but biblical themes and their Christian faith remain at the root of much of their music.

Military Bands playing religious music: In many Christian majority countries, regular Bands of the Armed Forces can be found playing Christmas Carols not only at State Functions or royal palaces, but also for the general populace in some public park, etc. But this is not a general rule as some Military formations take their secular heritage very seriously. Times are different in the United States since the annual Easter Egg Roll moved to the White House grounds during President Rutherford B Hayes (1877-81), when as with all other official events, music was provided by the US Marines Band. As recently as 2015, one of the US Army Quartet Choir Bands declined an invitation to perform at Fox Radio Christmas Show saying they were not supposed to perform at religious events. This decision was fiercely criticised by the Fox media network. But the Military stood by its decision. In fact, the Army Quartet played it safe, as only two years later an inquiry was opened against US Army Pershing's Own Band, for its appearance at a Mormon temple in Washington, DC for their annual Festival of Lights, an event billed as a celebration of the birth of Christ. The complaint, which came from active duty military personnel, spelled out the specific violation of Army regulations that this appearance entailed: "*Public affairs activities will not support any event involving (or appearing to involve) the promotion, endorsement, or sponsorship of any individual, civilian enterprise, religious or sectarian movement, ...*" (Brayton 2017).

One also finds military Bands not controlled by the Military. The London Military Band, for instance, is a unique wind ensemble consisting of off-duty professional serving military musicians and even retired musicians trained at the Royal College of Music. Led by a former musician from the Grenadier Guards, Alan Shellard, the Band performs spectacular traditional Christmas concerts for the public.

Marching Bands in Islamic Tradition

> Rahim Allah Karim Allah {God the Merciful, God the Kind]
>
> —Chant of the *Mehter* Bands

The Islamic religion is also sharply divided on the issue of instrumental music. There are divergent jurisprudential deductions from, and interpretations of, the two occasions when songs were sung and *Daff* (Tambourine) was played to welcome the Prophet Mohammad at Medina. Once upon his arrival after *Hijra* (migration) and secondly upon return from the Tabuk expedition (630 AD), *Daff* (which is drum like instrument) was played and Prophet did not object. Hence, a school of thought interprets it as a permission for Percussion instruments. But many of the same scholars vehemently disallow wind instruments. The only reference to a wind instrument in original Islamic teachings is the Trumpet (*Soor*) that Angel Israfel is supposed to have that he will blow to usher in the Doom's Day.

Islamic scholars who consider Instrumental Music (Wind instruments) as *Haraam* (forbidden), include all four leaders of Sunni jurisprudence (Imam Abu Hanifa, Imam Shafi'i, Imam Malik and Imam Ahmad) as well as Hasan Basri, Tabari, Imam Bokhari, Imam Tirmizi, Al Bahayqi and Al Qurtubi. On the other hand, those who see the permissibility of music include some of the towering jurists in Islamic scholarship such as Imam Ghazali, philosophers like Ibne Rushd and Ibn Hazm, Sufi poets of the stature of Maulana Rumi and scientists that include Bu Ali Ibne Sina, known as Avicenna outside the Muslim world.

In spite of this great debate between the supporters of music and those who think that Music is impermissible (*Haraam*) for Muslims, the Islamic Civilization made big contributions to the development of instrumental and Band music. However, the integration between religion and music, as exists in the Christian and Hindu religious traditions, is mostly missing in Islam.

Religious Duties of Ottoman Bands: At least in the Muslim military circles, a pro-Music view seems to have prevailed since the first two centuries of the dawn of Islam. Proper Bands were well entrenched into the Muslim army formations during the Crusade Wars, well before the mantle of spiritual leadership of the Islamic world was assumed by the Ottoman Caliphate.

The Ottoman Caliphs started using Military Bands for various religious functions centuries before the Band of Swiss Guards was raised by the Papal authorities. The *Mehter* Bands not only represented the religious and temporal authority of the Caliph but were a manifestation of the prestige of the empire. The Bands played at the assumption of the mantle of Caliphate by each new Ottoman Sultan. The tradition of Military Bands leading the coronation march of a Caliph lasted till the abolition of Caliphate in early 20th century. Once Mehter Bands had been disBanded, modern Military Bands of Turkey led the public welcome of the coronation of the three Ottoman Caliphs Mehmet V, Mehmet VI and Abdel Majeed II who ascended to the seat in the last century

Over the previous centuries, the Mehter Bands had several other religious duties. They awakened people before the dawn call to prayer. The Bands played at nights during the fasting month of Ramadan from castles and towers to awaken the people to start their fast. Mehter groups also performed religious songs for pilgrims leaving for the Hajj to Makkah and again to welcome the people who returned back after the Pilgrimage.

Bands and Kos Drums in Sufi Orders: Sufism closely identified with music. Hafiz, the famous Persian poet of the 14th century, closely related song with soul. "People say that the soul, on hearing the song of creation, entered the body" Hafiz says, "but in reality, the soul itself was the song".

Sufi brotherhoods also played Mehter-style music, using cymbals and the *kuddum* (a kettledrum larger than the *nekkare*). The Ottoman Caliph Sultan Selim III (1796–1808) lent his personal set of *Kös* to the Istanbul Mevlevi Lodge, of which he was a member. The Lodge was famous for the Dancing *Derweshes* (*Sufi* mystics) who did a whirling dance to praise the Divine.

The ascetic and mystic system of Sufism spread far beyond the Ottoman domains. The mystical musical choirs in South Asian tradition (Pakistan, India, Bangladesh) called *Qawwalis* are matched by religious choirs in other Islamic traditions from Indonesia to Egypt.

Marching Bands in the Sunni Religious Order: Attachment of the Bands with a Sunni religious seminary or religious institution is rare but not absent. The scarlet-clad marching Bands attached to various *Dar ul Quran*s (Koranic schools) in Indonesia and elsewhere in Sunni-dominated regions of the Far East are a novelty. That these religious Islamic Bands have a mixed male–female composition is another first—as till half a century ago, it was impossible for men and women to pray together in a single-mixed formation, what to speak of playing military-style music together, if at all.

Bands in the Shiite (Ismaili) Religious Orders: The Shia tradition in Islam traditionally had a slightly more liberal view towards all kind of fine arts. The Ismaili tradition within the *Shite* school has developed a very fine tradition of Bands in the past 150 years.

The Agha Khani Ismailis have their major concentration is in Northern Pakistan, Afghanistan, Tajikistan, West India, and East Africa, but they have pockets in Europe too. They have a uniformed marching Band with almost every big *Jamatkhana* (Mosque-cum-community centre). A large number of Bands were raised to mark the Platinum Jubilee of the accession of their spiritual leader (*Hazir Imam)* His Highness Prince Sultan Mohammad Khan Aga Khan III in 1954. Another stream of Bands was raised on the occasion of Golden Jubilee of the accession of his grandson and successor—the present Imam Prince Karim Aga Khan III in 2007. The former are known as the Aga Khan Platinum Jubilee Bands while the latter are called the Aga Khan Golden Jubilee Bands.

The other branch of Ismaili tradition—called the *Bohra* Ismailis—also have followed suit and raised Bands for their communities. The seat of *Bohra* religious leadership is in Mumbai in Western India. The community has over 40 Bands attached to their Mosques in the city of Mumbai alone. The uniformed marching Bands play on the accession day of their present spiritual leader *Mufaddal Saifuddin*, on his birthday celebrations, on both Eid festivals and other religious and temporal occasions.

Bands in Regimented Religious Movements: Among the two great religious traditions in South Asia—the Muslims and the Hindus—several semi military-style religious organizations were born during the British rule. The *Khaksaar* movement among the Muslims was the Muslim version of Salvation Army. The *Khaksaar* volunteers donned uniforms and marched on the beat of drums like the military. Their Drum Bands wore military-like uniforms and displayed military finesse in their drills. The *Khaksaar* movement has almost faded into history.

Religious repertoire of Wedding Marching Bands in Pakistan: The military-style Marching Bands leading wedding processions are a feature of South Asian cultural landscape. While certain religious denominations are hell bent against Music being un-Islamic, the religious bent of the repertoire of such Bands is itself striking. The musical repertoire at wedding functions starts nearly universally with the tune of a *Na'at* (song praising Prophet Muhammad) entitled *Shah-e-Madina* being played. Then, of course, the repertoire moves to more temporal and largely romantic tunes while leading the wedding procession. In rare cases, the above *Naat* is preceded by a tune of *Hamd* (song praising Almighty God) entitled *Teri Unchi Shan he Maula* sung by a famous Pakistani singer Adnan Sami Khan who later moved to India and acquired its citizenship. Surprisingly, in come cases, Wedding Bands in India, both Hindu and Muslim, start their wedding repertoire with these or other religious passages as a way to invoke divine blessing for the couple being wedded.

Military and Police Bands at Islamic festivals: During the past one century, military and police Bands in Muslim countries have started featuring in religious festivities such as *Eid Milad-un-Nabi* [festival of the birth of Prophet] which falls on the twelfth day of the third month of the Islamic *Hijrah* lunar calendar. Likewise on the annual Muslim festival of *Eid-ul-Fitr* marking the end of the fasting month of Ramadan, one has seen Police Bands playing in Police headquarters or Police colonies in Pakistan. Marching Band shows from private Bands take place on the Holy Prophet's birthday, called in Jerusalem, Palestine, India and amongst some Muslim communities in Europe.

Marching Bands in the Hindu Religious Movement

Our soul is composed of harmony

—Leonardo DaVinci

Music is an integral part of Hindu religion. The religious services in all temples have music and songs as the dominant element. However, in the ideal structure laid out in Hindu texts, the first stage of life is that of a student (*Chela*) given to the care of a teacher (*guru*), whom he lives with and serves for many years while studying the sacred Vedas under the teacher's guidance. The lifestyle assigned to this stage of life is one of austerity, asceticism, and discipline. The chaste student should restrain from small worldly pleasures like honey, meat, perfume, and garlands, and also from more obvious ones such as dancing, singing, and playing musical instruments (*Manu:*2.175–80). Hence, despite music being an essential Temple worship (*puja*), paradoxically a chaste religious holy man has to be a man who shuns music, especially instrumental one. In this respect, the Hindu holy men appear closer to their devout peers of other religions who similarly shunned music. But like all other religions, Hinduism eventually failed to keep its distance from Band Music or, for that matter, any music.

During the 19thand early 20th centuries, the emergence of military-style religious movement in Hindu religion had more to do with anti-colonial struggle against the British than spiritual advancement of the followers of Hinduism. Around 1915, the *Rashtriya Swayamsevak* Sangh (RSS) was raised in a military style among the Hindus in the British India. It follows army-like marching and discipline. Having anti-imperialist undertones, it is a strong political force in modern India.

The RSS Marching Band: The Band of the RSS was raised to develop essential qualities of martial music that have been described in great detail by the sage Bharata Muni. Dating back to around 3rd century BC, he wrote his Sanskrit treatise on music titled "Natyashastra." He described music as God's creation, capable of touching the heart and soul, thus, arousing emotions. The holy texts proclaimed that the music aided by beats and sounds is one of the many forms of music particularly composed to create *Veer Rasa* (the spirit of courage).

The RSS is still very much there and thriving in subcontinent as a potent political force. The Band was an essential component of its formation right from its inception in 1927. The RSS Bands are a regular feature of the organisation's assemblies and marches.

Bands in Jewish Religious History

Music is the Speech of Angels

—Thomas Carlyle

Despite the holy Judaic scriptures having several descriptions of orchestras and Levites making music, the Orthodox Jews have traditionally considered instrumental music a sin. The Old Testament (*Torah*) explicitly permitted instrumental music (2 Chr. 29:25; Ps. 33:2). Yet after the exodus from Jerusalem in 70 AD when Hebrew nation got banished from the holy land, there was a near theological consensus among the Jewish religious leadership that Music was against religion. For a long time, the Rabbis took pains to eradicate all types of choral and instrumental music. Famous scholar Werner finds it paradoxical that even modern day Rabbis continue to praise the instrumental music of the Temple but prohibit any and all instrumental music in their synagogues today (Werner 1984).

Religious Jewish music is about the Temple and Synagogal music from Biblical to Modern times. The earliest Synagogue music was based on the same system as that used in the Temple in Jerusalem. According to the Mishnah, the regular Temple orchestra consisted of twelve instruments, and the choir of twelve male singers. After the destruction of The Temple, Rabbis totally outlawed Music for the Jewish people. However, the social need of merrymaking at weddings could not diminish, and musicians filled the vacuum.

Klezmer is a musical tradition of the Ashkenazi Jews of Eastern Europe. The term comes from a combination of Hebrew words: *kli*, meaning "tool, or utensil" and *zemer*, meaning "to make music". This leads to Klezmer, literally "vessels of song," that is musical instrument. Hence, by definition it was instrumental music for Jewry. Played by professional musicians called *klezmorim*, the genre originally consisted of instrumental tunes for weddings and other celebrations. Thus, for all purposes Klezmer music was a Band Music. The first known Klezmer musician's name was Yakobius ben Yakobius, in Samaria in the 2nd century AD. However, the earliest written record of the *Klezmorim*, as the Klezmer musicians are known, is from the 15th century.

From the time of the Renaissance, Jewish communities in western Europe have shown some interest in modernising the service by introducing composed music on the European model. Salamone Rossi (1570–1630), a composer of Jewish lineage at the court of Mantua, present-day Italy, published a volume of Psalm settings in a Baroque style similar to the Catholic composer Claudio Monteverdi (1567–1643), but this did not become widely popular in the Synagogue until much later.

Already in 1603, the keyboard-style instrument Harpsichords were used in the Spanish and Portuguese synagogues in Hamburg for religious ceremonies. In due course, the Jewish community of Venice commissioned a number of works from non-Jewish composers such as Carlo Grossi and Benedetto Marcello for use in religious ceremonies by the mid-1700s. Particularly in the Amsterdam community, there was a flourishing of classical music in the synagogues in the 18th century. The style and structure of Klezmer as we know it today is thought to have come largely from the bulk of traditional repertoire that was written in the second half of the 19th century.

The Klezmorim based much of their secular instrumental music upon the devotional vocal music of the synagogue, in particular cantorial music. Even so, Klezmorim—along with other entertainers—were typically looked down on by Rabbis because of their secular travelling lifestyle. Klezmorim often travelled and played with Romani musicians, because they occupied a similar social strata. They had a great influence on each other musically and linguistically. Klezmorim sometimes played for Christian churches and local aristocracy, and taught some Italian classical violin artists too. The Klezmer music, though secular in nature, is a reality of the Jewish history. Present music of Jewish society and Diaspora has borrowed heavily from Klezmer.

Jewish School Bands in United States: In the United States, Klezmer genre evolved considerably as Yiddish-speaking Jewish immigrants from Eastern Europe, arrived between 1880 and 1924. This music mingled with and assimilated American jazz. Today, at least two Orthodox Jewish Schools have Marching Bands in United States which would have been unthinkable just two decades ago.

Jewish Rock Bands: Influence of the rock world came to the Orthodox world with Bands like the Diaspora Yeshiva Band, founded in 1975 by American-born student-musicians in Jerusalem. The Band infused rock and bluegrass with Jewish lyrics, creating a style of music it called "Hasidic rock" or "Country and Eastern." The Band was very popular on college campuses in the early to mid-1980s, and was famous in Jerusalem for its Saturday-night concerts at David's Tomb. It inspired later Bands such as Blue Fringer. Even Sh'siyah, Reva l'sheva, Soulfarm, the Moshav Band and Shlock Rock.

Israeli Army Military Bands: The inclusion of Jews into the Czarist army Bands of Russia during the 19th century led to the introduction of typical military Band instruments into Klezmer. Brass instruments—such as the French valved Cornet and keyed German trumpet— eventually inherited a counter-voice role. Modern klezmer instrumentation is more commonly influenced by the instruments of the 19th-century military Bands than the earlier orchestras. The European immigrants into Israel laid the foundations of the military Bands of the Israeli Armed Forces. In spite of being secular in orientation, unlike their counterpart militaries in Muslim and Christian countries, the Israeli military Bands do not perform on Yom Kippur or other religious events due to Orthodox prohibition of playing music on religious days.

Bands in Buddhist Religious Context

Music in the Soul can be heard by the Universe

—Lao Tzu

Buddhist music is *music* created for or inspired by *Buddhism* and forms part of the *Buddhist* art. The relationship between Buddhism and music is as complicated as with other major religions. Association of music with earthly desires led early Buddhist religious leadership to proscribe musical practice of all kinds. At the end of the day, instrumental music ended up intruding into religious practice: Drums in the Tibetan Buddhism and Flutes in the Zen Buddhism.

Drum Music of Tibetan Buddhism: The Tibetan Buddhism is the most widespread religion in Tibet. Musical chanting, most often in Tibetan or Sanskrit, is an integral part of this religious tradition. These chants, often recitations of sacred texts or in celebration of various festivals, are complex. Yang chanting is accompanied by sustained syllables and resonant drums.

Flute Music of Zen Buddhism: Zen Buddhism is another variant of the religion. *Honkyoku* are the pieces of Shakruhachi or Hocchiku (both types of end-blown Japanese flutes) music played by wandering Japanese Zen monks called Kumosu. Although Komuso temples were abolished in 1871, but their music, *Honkyoku* (literally: Original Pieces), is one of the most popular contemporary music styles in Japan, which was played as early as in 13th century for enlightenment and alms. Around the mid-1700s, a Komuso named Kinko Kurosawa of the Fuke sect of Zen Buddhism was commissioned to travel throughout Japan and collect these musical pieces. The results of several years of travel and compilation were 36 pieces known as the Kinko-Ryu Honkyoku.

Bands in Chinese Buddhist Monasteries and Palaces: In mainland China, we have a different variant of Buddhism. Historical novels and stories also fantasise about military Bands in palaces and monasteries. For instance, Shansky in his fictional work titled *Trio of Zen Buddhist Stories* writes about courtiers assuring "His Majesty" that two military Bands would be there to welcome him (Shansky 2011). A non-fiction historical work such as Hsüan-chih Yang's Record of Buddhist Monasteries in Lo-Yang also mentions about two marching Bands with a monastery (Yang 2014).

Military Band of Dalai Lama Army: If military Bands could reach the Basilica of the Pope and Palace of the Caliph, there was no historical reason that Military Bands would not find their place under the patronage of Dalai Lama too. The Tibetan Army was the military force of Tibet after its *de facto* independence in

1912 until the 1950s. As a land army, modernised with the assistance of British training and equipment, it served as the *de facto* military force of the Dalai Lama government. The Tibetan Army had Japanese, Chinese, and British influences. The British influence, in particular, was of such an extent that the Tibetan officers gave their commands in English and the Tibetan Army Band played tunes that included "God Save the King" and Auld Lang Syne.

Modern Band of the Tiantai Temple: In modern times, Tiantai temple located in central China's Hubei province, became famous for its Buddhist music. Young Buddhist monks and nuns play beautiful "Buddhist music" with violins, cellos, pianos and other instruments which is their way of self-cultivation. In 2008, Tiantai Temple made it official by forming its own Band—Guangxuan Art Troupe. It now has over 40 members, tasked to "spread Buddhism outside the temple". Little wonder, it performs spiritual music at functions outside the temple.

Buddhist School Bands: In 1995, Lely Marching Band performed Dance Routine featuring Buddha and the Blessed Child in the United States. At least a handful of Buddhist schools and colleges in Myanmar, Thailand, Cambodia and Hong Kong do have marching Bands.

Buddhist Punk Band: *Ruin* calls itself the "first Buddhist punk Band," creating a fusion between theatricality, musicianship and Buddhism. Founded by one Glenn Wallis, the Band was meant to be an antidote to sitting around and getting wasted. Wallis is an Associate Professor of Buddhism and Indian Religions at the University of Georgia, and a translator of the Buddha's teachings. Wallis and his Bandmates took some time to talk about the life, death, and rebirth of what most certainly was the world's first punk Band comprising all practicing Buddhists.

Bands in Substate Institutions: Schools to Universities

> *If I can survive marching Band, I can survive anything.*
>
> —Nellie McKay

The school, college and university Bands—and we can include the Bands of the Boy Scouts and the Girl guides in this category—are now a global phenomenon. The greatest mushrooming of the school and college Bands can be seen in the United States where they number in tens of thousands, more than the combined total of school Bands in the rest of the world. Their appearance in the United States is traced back to mid-19th century. Over time, by the advent of the 20th century, they became embedded in the popular culture. Beginning 1907, use of

Bands in inter-university games had a seminal impact on the phenomenon of Bands.

University Bands

During the pre-World War I football (and baseball) craze in the United States, inter-university sports competitions saw the emergence of university Bands as a by-product. They were to provide entertainment to the audience in order to keep them engaged during the half-time breaks. Iowa State University (ISU)- Cyclone Football "Varsity" Marching Band, established in 1881, was the first such university Band.

The first recorded Band performance in a sports competition was during a football match between the University of Chicago and the University of Illinois in 1907. The half-time performance provided an activity to the audience that helped not only in retaining their interest to keep them seated till the next half was played, but also helped in avoiding other nuisances such as fans throwing cocktails at each other or picking up fights. Many university Bands adopted the slogan of *Half Time Is Our Time.*

As time passed, universities and colleges raised their Bands as their institutional identity in order to perform at events within the institution and without. Sometimes one's identification with the Band of his institution is as strong than with the institution itself. Or sometimes, both identities become synonymous. Legend has it that during the 1970s President of the celebrated Stanford University Band, Richard Lyman, was presented a cheque of 1million dollars to denounce his Band but he tore down the cheque and emphatically declared that he loved the Band.

At present, the biggest university Band in the United States is the Texas A&M University. It has 800 musicians and includes the nationally famous Fightin' Texas Aggie Band, four concert Bands (the Wind Symphony, Symphonic Winds, Symphonic Band and Concert Band), two jazz Bands, the Aggieland Dance Orchestra and the University Orchestras (the Philharmonic Orchestra and the Chamber Orchestra).

The John Philip Sousa Foundation, established in 1980 to replace the Sousa Memorial Committee, is named after the most famous prominent composer of American Band music. The organization has instituted a number of highly coveted awards for excellence in Band Music. All these Awards are named after Louis Sudler, a Chicago real estate developer and arts patron, whose generous support instituted these awards.

In order to promote healthy competition between University and College Bands, the John Philip Sousa Foundation has instituted a *Sudler Trophy* since 1982. Since 2007, it is awarded biannually to a University or College Band that has shown performance excellence consistently over a number of years. As per the Foundation website, the Trophy is aimed at "honoring the close historical relationship and outstanding contribution of College Marching Bands to the American way of life." The travelling trophy, weighing 80 pounds and measuring exactly 22½ inches from the base to the tip of the drum major's mace; precisely the size of standard 8 to 5 step in marching, was designed by the same artist, Ed Blackwell, who made the Heisman Trophy (the annual trophy for the best Football player in the USA).

The ISU Cyclone Marching Band, the oldest in the United States, was the winner of the 2017–19 Sudler Trophy. It was presented at a 2017 home football game by the chairman of the Foundation's selection committee. This was ISU's second win of the most coveted trophy that it had once won earlier in 1990 too. The 362 members of ISU Varsity Football Band include musicians, a featured twirler and colour guard who perform at all home football games as well as other university events throughout the year.

College Bands

The oldest American college marching Band, the Notre Dame Marching Band, was founded in 1845. In the United States, modern College marching Bands are most commonly associated with performances during American Football games. The Notre Dame Band first performed at a football game in 1887, forty-two years after its establishment. Gradually, Marching Bands became inextricably intertwined with the game of Football between the College teams. The Band Performances have become so popular that one may wonder if Soccer Games would ever become the HalfTime Shows between Marching Bands performances.

The John Philip Sousa Foundation, as noted above, instituted the Sudler Trophy for the best University or College Marching Band in the United States. Its purpose, as per Foundation website, is:

> *"to identify and recognize collegiate marching Bands of particular excellence who have made outstanding contributions to the American way of life. ... Trophy is awarded ... to a college or university marching Band which has demonstrated the highest musical standards and innovative marching routines and ideas, and which has made important contributions to the advancement of the performance standards of college marching Bands."*

To date, none of the College Marching Bands has won the trophy. All the winners have been universities so far. Still College Marching Bands are an inalienable part of American Marching Bands tradition. The annual Rose bowl parade in California, continuing for over a century, consists of a sizeable number of Marching Bands performing after the New Year Football games in California.

The total number of universities, colleges and degree awarding institutes in the United States was 4,140 in the year 2010. More than half of them had full-fledged marching Bands.

School Bands

The discussion on school Bands can be started with the formation of one of the most recognisable faces of school-aged boys and girls playing in Bands: the Tivoli Youth Guard Band from Denmark. The tradition dates back to 1843. Tivoli Garden opened successfully in Copenhagen in 1843. At first anniversary of the Garden the following year, its founder Georg Carstensen decided to raise Tivoli Boys Guard as a gift to himself. The Guard was opened for girls in 2015. The 100-strong Youth Guard comprises boys and girls aged between 8 and 16, and consists of a Colour Guard, a 50-strong Guard Band (mainly Brass) and a 24-strong Fifes and Drums. The Bands march in the Tivoli gardens on weekends and represent Denmark in tattoos worldwide.

Obviously Tivoli Youth Guard Band is not a Band belonging to a specific school, yet it is a year-long Music School in itself consisting of school-aged children. Every year, 15-20 young boys and girls are inducted after an entrance exam and musical audition, equalling the number of the older ones who leave. The red jacket-white trousers combination reflects the colours of the Danish flag while bearskin hats resemble those of the royal guards at palaces in Copenhagen and the United Kingdom. The experience in Tivoli Guard Bands forms part of the schooling and upbringing of the members.

The most spectacular school Bands movement is probably that of Norway which peaked in early 1980s. It boasted of 2,230 School Bands across Norway with roughly 92,000 members. The May 17 celebrations in Norway, feature hundreds of school Bands in parades all over the country. There is no greater assortment or variety of parades of School Bands anywhere in the world, than the ones held all across Norway on their Constitution Day annually (Dahle 2017).

The leader in terms of School Marching Bands is, undoubtedly, the United States. The first high school Band in the US was the Boston Farm and Trade School Band, founded in 1859. However, it was disBanded before the turn of the century; the exact date is not known. The oldest school Band having a continuous existence to date is The Christian Brothers Band of Tennessee. It was established at Christian Brothers High School (Memphis, Tennessee) in the Fall of 1872. Br. Maurelian served as the first Band director.

As the economy of the United States grew, and concomitantly the awareness on the benefits of music for human life, it became possible for the US Government to fund Bands in public schools as well. Today, each child can learn at least one musical instrument before his or her graduation. Each school Band roughly costs the taxpayer between $80,000 to $150,000 per annum, on average, depending on the strength, size and instrumentation of the Band. These annual costs sometimes have a prohibitive impact on the decision to raise and retain a Band by municipality or the ministry funding the concerned school. It is a separate debate altogether that the benefits provided by the Bands far outweigh the costs.

As per the US Department of Education website under the title High Schools at a glance, there are 26,407 public high schools and 10,693 private high schools in the United States. Four-fifths of the public high schools and slightly above half of the private high schools have marching Bands. Each Band has anywhere between 80 to 300 members, though bigger sized Bands do exist. At any given time, around three million students in the United States are members of a Marching Band.

The John Philip Sousa Foundation has established three types of Prizes for best school Bands, which according to the official website of the Foundation are:

> *"Bestowed to identify, recognize and honor high school Band programs internationally that have demonstrated particularly significant high standards of excellence in concert activities over a period of several years."*

Sudler *Flag of Honor* is an award to recognize the best High School Band anywhere in the world. Bands receiving The Sudler Flag of Honor, four by six feet in size, is a unique and colourful nylon flag executed in red, white, and blue, trimmed with gold fringe. The music director receives an engraved plaque and each of the members of the Band receives an individualized diploma in addition to the Flag.

The *Sudler Shield* recognizes the most outstanding high school marching Bands within the United States, rather than internationally. The *Sudler Cup* is a similar award for junior and middle schools' Band programs. None of these three awards, Sudler Flag, Sudler Shield and Sudler Cup, are awarded for a winning a particular competition but the Bands must have demonstrated significant high standards of excellence in concert activities over a period of several years, at least, more than seven.

The Sousa Foundation also recognises the individual Band Director of a School or institution through a *Legion of Honor*. Sponsored by the Band World magazine, eight Awards are given each year for life long services (more than 20 years of Service to Bands) to any Band Leader who distinguishes himself in leading, training and conducting a Band.

The Foundation also administers *Dr Robert Hawkins Memorial Scholarship* for students interested in pursuing a degree in instrumental Band music.

Founded in 1981, the Sousa National High School Honors Band is an ensemble made up of roughly 100 high school junior and senior musicians, selected from the top applicants worldwide. The Band performs biennially in New Orleans, Louisiana, and is conducted by former United States Marine Band conductor Col. John R. Bourgeois.

As noted above, the Bands at school and college level were mostly military-style Bands and in many counties they are indeed called as such, as long as they use brass or woodwind instruments. In fact, many of the school and university Bands in the United States often use military-like formations, marches and discipline during their public displays. Most US school/college Bands till the Vietnam war used military-like uniforms as well. That trend is gradually shifting towards athletic-style uniforms for Bands in the past four decades. This, some critics argue, is because the military prestige was affected by their failure to subdue the irregular Viet Cong fighters in the Vietnam war.

There are other school Bands in the world that follow different ways. For instance, in Germany the Marching Band is not carried out as a school-related activity. In fact, almost all extra-curricular activity like music and sports of school-age kids is in non-school-affiliated associations where kids begin in the youth program and ideally later move up to the adult groups. In Ireland, rather than Marching Bands, Schools may have indoor orchestras. In Sweden, there are Municipal Schools of Music, separate from the ordinary schools, which impart musical education. There are up to 500 Bands in the country with the municipal music schools (Jansson 2018).

Although the influence of British pipe and drum marching Bands on the US cannot be denied but the latter had its own trajectory where School Bands use brass instruments not pipes and drums. In the United Kingdom, what survived to the present day is 12-15 strong "Juvenile Jazz Bands" that pale before American School Bands with 200 or so members. Usually organised by a local church or social club, these juvenile Bands consist of kids with a few drums and a few Kazoos (a type of hollow pipe) along with five or six baton-twirlers. In some countries in Africa, South Asia (India and Pakistan), and East Asia, many of the prestigious large schools continuing since the colonial era boast of marching Bands as recognisable symbols of the pride of the School. In all fairness, the United States remains the leader of School Bands in the world.

Bands in Non-state Institutions: Community, Village and Family Bands

> *Band is not proud because it performs well; it performs well because it is proud.*
>
> —George Parks

The Marching Bands have gradually got embedded into the social fabrics in all parts of the world. Apart from the State, it is the society which has now embraced the Bands. The form of music may be different and the type of Band may not be similar either, but Bands have permeated into the human society all over the globe.

Bands are seen at the town or community level where private persons and volunteers come together to have Bands to represent the whole community. Then comes the village or neighbourhood level which may have a drum circle of its own. And finally, the family is the smallest and most basic unit of the society, and one can witness mushrooming of family Bands too.

Community Bands and Factory Bands

A Community Band is a concert Band or a brass Band ensemble, generally sponsored by the town or city in which it is located and consists primarily of amateur performers. Bowen defines a community Band as, "A community-based ensemble of wind and percussion players, composed primarily of adults who do not receive the majority of their livelihood from participation in the ensemble, which regularly holds rehearsals and performs at least one time per year" (Bowen 1995).

The Bands culture became so pervasive in the United States during the Civil War (1861–63) that Bands became part of a community's identity. As the demobilised soldiers returned to their native villages when the Civil War ended, they not only brought back their instruments but also their pride in them. Wartime patriotism is not limited to the Civil War. Even the World Wars I and II, Korean and Vietnam Wars and more recent US military engagements in Afghanistan and Iraq have added to the popularity and number of community Bands.

As per one estimate there are about 2,500 community Bands across the United States today. They are down from 10,000 town and community Bands in the

United States that were there in 1889. Of those, close to 100 Bands have an uninterrupted and continued existence till date.

In 1921, famous Band composer Karl King was influential in establishing the Iowa Band Law, which allowed cities to levy a local tax "for the maintenance and employment of a Band for musical purposes." This law was eventually adopted by 28 other states. During the United States Bicentennial celebrations of 1976, having a community Band was one of the criteria for being designated a "Bicentennial City."

Some of the community Bands are also marching Bands that participate in parades or other outdoor events. Community Bands are also referred to as "town," "citizen" or "civic"Bands. Sometimes, their names may end with the words "wind orchestra," "wind symphony" and "wind ensemble" instead of the word "Band." The name is usually preceded by the name of the community or organization that sponsors the Band or the town or county where they are based. It may occasionally be preceded by the name of a local geographical landmark or regional term. Sometimes the name just contains a place name followed by the word"Band."

Community Band concerts are most frequently given during holidays and patriotic events, such as the Fourth of July, Memorial Day, Father's Day, and the lighting of community Christmas trees. During the summer, most community concerts are given outdoors. The size of a community Band varies from a few tens of musicians to over one hundred.

The John Philip Sousa Foundation has an annual award called Sudler Silver Scroll that recognises and honours those community Bands that have demonstrated particularly high standards of excellence in concert activities over a period of several years, and which have played a significant and leading role in the cultural and musical environment in their respective cities, towns or communities.

The community concert Bands which have won the award include Lawrence City Band, Lawrence, Kansas (1988), Kiel Municipal Band, Kiel, Wisconsin (1990), Tacoma Concert Band, Tacoma, Washington (1990), Allentown Band, Allentown, Pennsylvania (1990), Racine Municipal Band, Racine, Wisconsin (1994), Coastal Communities Concert Band, San Diego, California, and Twin City Concert Band, West Monroe, Louisiana (both in 1997), Community Band of Brevard, Brevard County, Florida (1999), Lafayette Citizens Band, Lafayette, Indiana (2001), City of Fairfax Band, Fairfax, Virginia (2004), South Jersey Area Wind Ensemble, Egg Harbor Township, New Jersey (2006), Lake Oswego Millennium Concert Band, Lake Oswego, Oregon (2013), East Texas Symphonic

Band, Longview, Texas (2014), Metropolitan Wind Symphony, Boston, Massachusetts (2015), among many others.

The John Philip Sousa Foundation also assembles and organises a National Community Band biennially at some location within United States. Composed of volunteers who are part of community Band in their own community or town, the Band performs multiple concerts at the host city for four or five days and then dissolves itself. After two years a new National Band is raised again by the Foundation and performs at the pre-announced host city for a few days. This cycle goes on.

The nearest equivalent of Community Bands in the United States were the Factory Bands in the United Kingdom that emerged along with evolution of industrial revolution in factories, steel works, collieries and other such places of mass employment. They are comparable to US School Bands in terms of involvement and community pride, but in comparison to the US Bands, the British was on solid musicianship than crowd-pleasing showmanship. There was intense rivalry between the Bands, and national competitions were hotly contested. Sadly, these Bands could not survive the twin transformations of the early 1980s with the rise of television and mass electronic media and the closure of so many of the traditional industries.

Village Bands

Much as the town or community Band is a phenomenon most popular in the United States, the concept of Bands in rural areas has its roots in England and Scotland. In former times, the watchmen who patrolled during the night were called the *waits* (sometimes spelt as *Waites*). These city or town waits used a musical instrument to mark the hours and to show they were on duty. Their duties varied from time to time and place to place, but included playing their instruments through the town at night, waking the townsfolk on dark winter mornings by playing under their windows, welcoming royal visitors by playing at the town gates, and leading the Mayor's procession on civic occasions.

These musical Bands were often attired in colourful liveries and in some cases wore silver chains. They added dignity to ceremonial occasions. From the Middle Ages to the 18th century, town records include transactions concerning waits, upon their appointment and on the provision of cloaks, ribbons, badges, etc. Payments were also made for their instruments, such as hautbois, bass viols and fiddles.

From the medieval times up to the early 19th century, every British town and city of any note had a Band of Waites. As a result of the Municipal Corporations Act of 1835, Waites were abolished. About the same time, village Bands started emerging across Great Britain. They were a 19th-century British phenomenon akin to the contemporaneous community Bands phenomenon in the United States. Unlike the Waites who were pipers, these village Bands used brass instrumentation and performed at various social functions. These ensembles provided an important base for the eventual establishment of the brass Band. The village Bands gradually disappeared from the United Kingdom by the first quarter of the 20th century.

But they were replaced by factory Bands around the same time as noted in the previous section. The popularity of factory Bands was so much that if a factory did not sponsor a Band, the same were formed by villages, counties, or even just a street. Since, at that time, most people were poor enough to afford expensive brass instruments, they would play whatever they already had or could scrape together. With the advent of television and radio, these Bands have mostly disappeared at the village levels.

Family Bands

Family Bands have come from the musical families—the families whose traditional profession had been musical performances. Even amongst families where music was not their vocation, some where "music ran in their blood."

Today, family Bands are found in the United States, Australia, Ireland, Israel and many other countries. In the United States, some like Gruber Family Band are as old as 1920 and continuing is the fourth generation, while some made beginnings fairly recently. For instance, as late as in 2002, Walker Family Band started when Scott, his daughter Jennie, his brother Landon and close friend and musical associate Scott Manring began playing and then recording together to make Albums.

Krause family Band started in 1970s at Los Taconazos, USA. Initially known as the Polka Family, it mostly played Mexican Style music at backyard parties, weddings, baptisms, fiesta's and many Mexican occasions. Lately, the father and children practiced and learned to play a few Polish polkas to be equally adept at Polish music. Savoy Family Cajun Band in California comprise a husBand, wife and their two daughters. George Rea family Band consists of three real sisters, their mother and a cousin. Robert Randolph and the Family Band is another prominent name through availability of their videos in social media.

In Australia, the Kelly Family Band consisted of a mother (Kristin), a father (Alan) and their three kids who were then aged 14, 11 and 10. It mostly plays

Irish music. Another popular folk plus rock Band, from Brisbane, Australia, is *The Fergies* formed by the five Ferguson siblings, Kahlia, Daniel, Joel, Nathan, and Shani. Their performances on Queen Street Mall, uploaded to YouTube fetched 1.3 million views. A famous Family Band from Israel is named *Havaiia* consisting of nine members—seven siblings and their parents—of a musical family touring the globe to practice music and explore musical frontiers. The tradition of emergence of more and more family Bands is new but is growing impressively.

Bands as a Commercial Institution

Music Makes Us Want to Live

—Mary J Blige

In the world, almost every thirtieth person, i.e. around three per cent of the humankind is directly or indirectly attached to the musical profession. As technology grows, it becomes easy to disseminate music. People engaged with this vocation also explore avenues of earning income from it.

Music is form of emotional expression, and happiness and sorrow have always been expressed through arithmetic sounds. This has created a niche for Bands to perform at occasions such as weddings, partying and mourning. Traditionally, people would like to sing and dance themselves at a family festivity but hiring the services of a Band commercially is also becoming a social norm.

Wedding Bands

Marriage is one of the institutions which had the greatest impact on the development of music. Music is a signature activity for any kind of joy or festivity amongst human beings. The wedding ceremony, being the most conspicuous social custom, is marked by instrumental music since ages in many civilisations.

For example, the Jewish religious prohibition of music could not stop the development of secular religious music *Klezmer* amongst the Jews within the first 50 years of Exodus in 70 AD, primarily because of need for music at the weddings. Christianity was a later religion. Its wedding customs too, across the times included song, dance and music to celebrate the union between two persons. Finally, within the Islamic civilisation too, Bands became an essential part of the weddings far and wide. One Turkish folk song goes, "I don't care what happens as long as the *Mehter* plays and the wedding goes on." Historical records point to the fact that smaller, unofficial Mehter Bands played folk songs at weddings throughout the centuries. There are many such commercial private *Mehters* today as well. The

Mehter or Ottoman music had strong influence over European Wedding music, especially since segments of the *Ode to Joy*, the fourth movement of Ludwig van Beethoven's Ninth Symphony is played at weddings.

The culture of "For Hire" Wedding Bands exists both in the West and in the Orient. In the Western countries, modern Jazz Bands, Blue Bands, Hip Hop Bands and even Rock Bands are hired to perform at wedding functions. The music that is played by the Western Wedding Bands in Europe includes various works for trumpet and organ, arguably the most famous of which include the Prince of Denmark's March by Jeremiah Clarke as a processional, the "Trumpet Tune" by Henry Purcell and the "Trumpet Voluntary" by John Stanley as recessionals. In the United States, selections by George Frideric Handel, perhaps most notably the "Air" from his Water Music as processional and the "Alla Hornpipe" as recessional are fairly common.

The "Bridal Chorus" from Lohengrin by Richard Wagner, commonly known as "Here Comes the Bride," was used often as the processional. But due to allegations of Wagner being anti-Semitic, his Bridal Chorus is avoided at the American Jewish weddings who replace it by Johann Pachelbel's Canon as an alternative processional. In this case, the "Wedding March" from Felix Mendelssohn's incidental music for the Shakespeare play *A Midsummer Night's Dream* is used as a recessional.

Now coming to the Asian weddings, it must be emphasised at the outset that the role and context of Bands within weddings is quite different between the Orient and the Occident. The singular most important contribution of South Asia for the Band Music is in embedding the marching Bands into the social fabric of the region (Booth 2006). The concept of a wedding, without a marching (military-style) Band leading the procession, remained alien to modern South Asia for a considerable time. The anecdote goes to the British colonial times when the Imperial [later Indian] Civil Service, the ICS for short, used to be the steel frame of the empire. Each administrative unit of the British India, called district, used to be headed by a British officer called the Deputy Commissioner (DC), who lived in palatial DC Houses. Once, as the story goes, a British Officer, went back to England to get married and came back with his bride. He hosted a garden party in honour of notables of the district to introduce his bride. As the party ended, and the DC and his bride withdrew to their bedroom, to the pleasant surprise of the couple, a Police Band hidden behind the trees in the vast lawns of the Deputy Commissioner's mansion started playing melodious romantic tunes. The local revenue officer (called *Tehsildar*) had requisitioned the Band and concealed them during the dinner party behind the shrubs in order to give a surprise welcome serenade to the newly married couple. The tradition spread to other British officers in British India, then to the local Indian gentry and finally to the broader community in Indo-Pakistan subcontinent to have uniformed Bands to perform at wedding related functions,

In all countries of South Asia, there is a proliferation of private wedding Bands, called *Barat* Bands. In wedding functions, *Barat* is one of the most festive parts of a ceremony. It is actually the procession of the groom and his family who go to the bride's family to bring her to the groom's house. For those who can afford to hire one, the *Barat* procession is led by a uniformed marching Band. These Bands are mostly privately owned and commercially hired. They are self-labeled as military Bands only because of their instrumentation and marching styles. These private military Bands are sometimes staffed by retired military or police Band musicians.

Apart from these private Bands, the actual military Bands do offer their services at weddings of young military officers in India and Pakistan. The civil government officers have the option to hire the Police Bands at their own or for any wedding in the immediate family.

The Indo-Pakistan subcontinent had a musical history spanning over millennia. However, the culture of modern military Bands was introduced into South Asia by the military officers of the British colonial army. British officers and aristocrats raised Bands by hiring local musicians and training them for regimental and field music.

The British imperial administration at the zenith of its glory ruled only two-thirds of the area of subcontinent directly. The remaining one-third area was spanned by 562 hereditary princely states that were largely left untouched. The local rulers imitated the British aristocracy and military elite by raising Bands at their palaces as symbols of grandeur and prestige.

As hereditary states were disBanded both in India and Pakistan after the independence from Britain in 1947, their palace Bands were mostly dissolved. In rare cases though, they were merged with local police forces in India to act as police Bands. However, most of the palace Band musicians became jobless and bankrupt.

Many of these musicians struggled to keep their profession alive and their Bands intact. In order to do so, they rebranded them as Wedding Bands and became available for hire on weddings and other festive occasions. Such later occasions may even include winning a seat in the Local Council during municipal elections or the birth of a son to the landlord. The people were simply exhilarated at the prospect of hiring a Band at their house for a function which they had hitherto seen only at Royal houses and royal functions of the princely rulers. The independence from Britain had brought them an independence to hire liveried marching Bands at their disposal.

No proper census has ever been done but an estimated 7,000 such private marching Bands exist in India, a thousand of which are based in the Greater Delhi area alone. Pakistan also has anywhere between 1,200 to 1,400 marching Bands, of which around 350 are based in or around the cultural capital of Lahore. Bangladesh, Nepal and Sri Lanka also have this concept of wedding Bands at a smaller scale but no reliable estimate of the number of such Bands in these countries could be traced.

As modernity creeps into cultural norms, people are adopting and adapting cultural ideas from across the world. Thus, richer people have started imitating Western weddings where instead of marching Bands they have started hiring rock and pop-style small Bands that play and sing on stage at a wedding reception.

Party Bands

The type of Bands that can be invited to parties also varies according to the region and the context. If it is an official reception at a Government House, a military garrison or a formal occasion, it may not be uncommon to find a Wind Ensemble of a State institution performing the musical backdrop for the event.

For ordinary citizens and their private parties, the affordable Band range would be a trio, a quartet or a quintet of musicians, at least one of whom would be a singer. As seen in the previous section, that many small family Bands, for example, are available for hire to perform at a town concert or a small courtyard party in a home, to entertain the guests. The smaller party Bands can play rock, pop, blue or jazz music depending on the requirements of the hosts.

Then we have the category of party marching Bands in the United States. These are big marching Bands that are difficult to be placed in Carnival or Scramble category as they mix elements from various traditions. The Detroit Party Marching Band, for example, carries the spirit of entertainment embraced by modern marching Bands, but without the formalities. Jamming to arrangements of popular music, members openly groove and dance as they play. Less attention is placed on the precision of visual style and more is placed on the creation of fun, lighthearted atmosphere. These party Bands cannot be hired for a small party but may be for a City, town or at least a university level function or festivity.

Funeral Bands

Dedicated Funeral Bands available for hire are a recent phenomenon. In the past, the Bands of the royal courts from Ottoman Caliphate to the Chinese Emperors would play somber tunes to mark the death of the sovereign or at his funeral, as part of their duties. The regular Military Bands play at royal or presidential funerals even today, at the military funerals of their fallen comrades and at the War memorials. But that falls outside the scope of the section about commercially available funeral Bands only.

Just two centuries ago, there were hardly any dedicated commercial Bands for funerals and mourning, except in parts of Africa where Drum Ensembles had developed cadences that were only to be played at the death of the tribal chief. Nevertheless, for ordinary mortals, there was no concept of availability of a funeral Band upon payment or otherwise.

Today, the Bands specialized for Funeral Music are available in all of America and Western Europe. The Funeral Bands are heavy metal Bands which may or may not use funeral *Dirge*. A *Dirge* is a somber song or lament expressing mourning or grief, such as would be appropriate for performance at a funeral. *Doom Metal*, meanwhile, is an extreme style of heavy metal music that typically uses slower tempos, low-tuned guitars and a much "thicker" sound than other metal genres. Both the music and the lyrics intend to evoke a sense of despair, dread, and impending doom.

During the 1980s, a number of Bands from England (*Witchfinder General* and *Pagan Altar*), the United States (*Pentagram, Saint Vitus* and *Trouble*) and Sweden (*Candle Mass* and *Court Raven*) contributed to Doom Metal being defined as a distinct musical genre. This genre is strongly influenced by the early work of Black Sabbath, who formed a prototype for doom metal with songs such as "Black Sabbath, Children of the Grave," "Electric Funeral" and "Into the Void.

Funeral is the name of a modern Norwegian Funeral Doom Band, formed in 1991, by Thomas Angell and Anders Eek, and later joined by Einar Frederiksen as Bassist and Christian Loos as Guitarist. This Band is known as one of the pioneers of the funeral genre in Northern Europe.

Funeral rites and, therefore, funeral music has had fusion due to globalization. Offering a prominent example is Chinatown in San Francisco (USA) that is a cultural mélange where Eastern and Western traditions often overlap. Few places show the contrasts more than the funerals. A typical Chinese funeral procession may look like a parade, starting with a full-size marching Band playing Christian hymns and banging cymbals followed by participants tossing spirit money and paid mourners wailing.

While marching tradition and hymns music descends from the military marching Bands that the British started in the 19th-century Hong Kong, the spirit money is a Chinese tradition to distract malicious ghosts that might prevent the spirit of the deceased from staying close to the body. One such Band, the Green Street Mortuary Band, is successor to the Cathay Boys Band started in 1911 that has had several names since then. The group was originally composed of Chinatown residents who worked at other jobs during the week and performed for funeral occasions to earn some extra cash. A hundred years down, this group has a cultural legacy that needs to be preserved and cherished.

The funeral music is an evolving genre and may take time to settle down.

Conclusion

As resources, awareness and knowledge grew, the Bands ceased to remain a preserve of the State. The institutions of Church, School, and Town Hall raised their Bands. Bands grew in the cities, the communities, the villages and the hamlets. People bought instruments and started playing along with family members, friends, and neighbours. Millions of people worldwide made Band music their vocation. Bands are there for every event and every occasion. They are accessible to everyone.

Like all other arts, from poetry, painting and architecture, music has moved down from palaces to the homes of common people. In other words, now the Band Music has become communalised and commercialised. They are either owned by the community or its individuals or are part of the economic machine where capital, labor and entrepreneurship are involved.

There is no denying the role of the State for the patronage of Bands but State is no longer the only, or even the most dominant, stake holder. The United States Military has been left with 137 Bands while 2,500 cities have formal Bands and so do more than 20,000 schools and institutions within the country. Much as politicians try to roll back or cut down on Government and military-controlled Bands, it would be difficult for any one State or one institution to do away with Bands. In any case, ordinary people's Bands are there to stay. And in all probability, the growth is an irreversible phenomenon. The great Band revolution has already occurred in the human race.

CHAPTER VI

Types and Classifications of Military Bands

Music doubles and triplicates the Army.

—Alexander Suvorov (Russian General)

The traditional concept of Military Bands was a Corps of Marching Fifer and Drummers. As Fife was replaced with Pipe and later with Bugle, we had Bugle and Drum Corps in the United States, Bagpipe and Drum Bands in England and Scotland, the Bagad Bands in France and simple Pipe [and Drum] Bands in India and Pakistan. As more and more Brass instruments were invented, the military Brass Bands started appearing with multiple brass instruments (instead of Bugles only) and a few percussions. In the modern jargon, however, the stand-alone term "military Band" usually signifies a combination of woodwind, brass and percussion instruments blended together according to certain internationally accepted conventions. A more appropriate term would be a "Concert Band" for such a Band.

There are a number of ways in which military Bands can be classified according to the branch of military they are associated with or the functional duties they perform. There are other types of classification too, such as the types of instrumentation they use, the type of music they play, the type of uniforms they wear or the nature of duties they perform. On a closer look, this is not as complex as may appear on first sight. The type of instrumentation determines the type of music, which in turn, defines the nature of duties. On top of it, there are some broad customs about the uniforms a military Band with particular instrumentation would wear.

Types of Military Bands (Classification by Military Branches)

There are military Bands attached with each branch of the Armed Forces which may be known by the Branch they represent. Armed Forces are usually divided into three arms or branches: the land forces called Army, the maritime forces called Navy and aerial defence corps called the Air Force. So Army Bands, Navy Bands and Air Force Bands can be called the general types of Military Bands. In some countries, the Marine Corps, also called the Naval Infantry, capable of undertaking amphibious operations and fighting both at land and sea, can be a fourth arm of the military. This is the case with the United States where the Armed Forces is divided into five branches: Army, Navy, Air Force, Marines, and the United States Coast Guards. Hence, from the US perspective, the Bands with these five branches will be categorised as Military Bands.

In Saudi Arabia, the Air Defense Corps is a separate fourth arm so has its own Central Band. In Iran, the *Pasdaran-e-Inqilab* (the Revolutionary Guards) also have their own land, naval and air forces just like the same three forces with the Iranian regular army. All three wings of the Armed Forces and all three of the Revolutionary Guards have their own Bands. (Their category-wise origin and history has been described in detail in previous chapters)

Army Bands

The Bands attached with the Army are called Army Bands. The first full-fledged uniformed army Band was raised by the Turkish Sultan in the town of Bursa in North West Turkey in the year 1326. At present, there are an estimated two thousand army Bands in the world ranging from just one army Band in New Zealand to 576 army Bands in India which is the highest number for any army.

Navy Bands

The Bands attached with the Naval Forces are called the Navy Bands. They usually don white uniforms in summers and Navy Blue colour in Winter in line with the customary colours of the Navy all over the world. The oldest recognized full-fledged Band of the Navy appears to be the Central Band of the Russian Admiralty, formed by Czar Peter the Great in Russia around 1704. At present, there are an estimated 600-700 Naval Bands in the World.

Marine Bands

The Bands which are part of dedicated Marines Corps or Naval Infantry of a country are called Marine Bands. The first-ever recognized Marine Band in the world was established by an Act of US Congress on 11 July 1798 in the United States. It is now called the "President's own Marine Band" and performs at all major functions at the White House. There may be around 50 to 60 dedicated Marine Bands in the world including the ten Concert Bands of the US Marine Corps. The United Kingdom has six very famous Royal Marine Bands which are, technically speaking, Bands of the Royal Navy. Hence, they have been counted above in the Naval Bands.

Air Force Bands

The Bands associated with the separate air arm of the military varyingly known as the Air Force or the Air Corps are called the Air Force Bands. There may be around 300-400 Air Force Bands in the world today. The first Air Force Band was established in United Kingdom in the final days of the First World War in 1918. Generally, a shade of Blue, called Ultramarine Blue, is universally being used as Air Force uniforms. The Air Force Bands also follow a darker hue of this colour with epaulettes and lanyards in fancy stuff.

Types of Military Bands (Functional Classification)

As per the United States Army website <goarmy.com>, its Bands are presently divided into three types (History of Army Music n.d.). This functional classification may not be applicable elsewhere. Here the US classification is being presented as a general guideline who the military authorities may classify their military Bands, within a given branch of the Armed Forces.

Special Army Bands

Out of the 137 Military Bands in the United States Armed Forces, only four have been specially designated for performing at State and official functions at the White House and for international dignitaries. These four, called the Special Bands, are also used for high level ceremonial functions within the United States and in friendly States abroad. Only the best and most qualified musicians are accepted into these four Bands, namely, the Pershing's Own Central Army Band (Washington DC), the US Old Guard Fife and Drums (Washington DC), the US Military Academy Band (West Point, NY) and the US Army Field Band (Fort Meade, Maryland). Other than the Army, the President's Own Marine Band and the Central Band of the United States Air Force are also, for all purposes, Special Bands.

Active Army Bands

The traditional Army Bands play an integral role in the Army, from strengthening the pride of Americans to enhancing Soldiers' morale to providing support for local troops and their communities. The Active Army Bands consist of regular military personnel as members. At the moment, of the 95 Active Army Bands, four are permanently stationed overseas—one each in Germany (US Army Europe Band) and Japan (296th Army Band) and two in South Korea—(2nd Infantry Division Band and the 8th Army Band) and the rest within United States, mostly as Division Bands.

Reserve Army Bands

Army reserve Bands consist of civilians who are engaged part time with US Military Bands while keeping the civilian career or continuing to pursue higher education. This is a popular choice for college students and professional musicians alike.

Types of Military Bands (Classification by Instrumentation)

By instrumentation, there are four basic kinds of military Bands, simplest of which is the pipe and drum Bands. If, for the wind component, Brass instruments are used instead of Pipes, it is called a Brass Band. If woodwinds are added, it will be called a Concert Band. In case, string and keyboard instruments are also added to brass and woodwind, the same will become an Orchestra. In the latter three Bands, there is likely to be a percussion component also.

Pipes and Drum Bands

The oldest form of military Bands, by instrumentation, are called Fifes and Drums Bands. It is also called Corps of Pipes and Drums or the Band of Pipes and Drums in many countries. In South Asia, they are simply called Pipe Bands but the name should not mislead the fact that they are always accompanied by Drums.

The *fife* is a small flute usually made of a single piece of wood, with six finger holes that could provide for a diatonic scale. The *drum* most associated with this Band was a Snare Drum. Known also as a side drum because it hangs on a sling at the player's side. The cylindrical instrument has two skin heads: the batter head (top), which the drummer beats with two sticks, and the snare head (bottom), so named for the gut twine that when placed against the head gives the instrument its characteristic "buzzy" sound (Dobney 2004). In European art depictions, the side drum is often depicted with other military equipment, as a symbol of war.

Although the Swiss side drum could and was played alone for a long time but eventually started being used with fife that provided melodic tunes to accompany the rhythmic cadences and tempo of the drum. The traditional pairing of the drum and fife developed from the medieval practice of a single player performing on a tabor (small drum) and pipe to accompany dance (Dobney 2004). Fife and Drum played together by separate musicians was the most rudimentary form of military Band and is the precursor of present day Pipe Bands.

Whether Fife is used or a Pipe, the same is reflected in the label of the Band too. The Scottish version of Pipe and Drum Bands used Bagpipes, which are actually Pipes with multiple reeds. Hence this type of simple marching Band is called Bagpipe Band in Scotland. In the United States, after the Anglo-US war of 1812, pipes got replaced by brass bugles and the pipe and drums corps were gradually replaced by Bugle and Drum Corps.

While the Americans concentrated on Brass, the British saw a growth of Pipe Bands, primarily due to the love of Queen Victoria for pipes, pipe music and the pipers. While pipes were used for a long time to issue peacetime commands in the British tradition, their combination with drums, to produce unique sounds was a later phenomenon. The proper Pipe Bands in the modern sense with Pipers and Drummers playing as an integrated unit, started around the Crimean War (1850–53). There were acrimonious debates over their composition, dressing and marching styles at that time. The "great debate" over whether the Pipers or Drummers are to be at the front while marching could neither be decided by the parliament not by the military top brass. It was the Queen herself who directed that Pipers were to lead the marching formations of pipe Bands. The Pipe Bands are known as *Bagad* Bands in the Brittany area of France.

In larger South Asian armies, almost every Infantry Unit has a Pipe Band attached to it. The ordinary composition of Pipe Bands in South Asian military and police formations is given in Annex B (1) on page 290. The Indian army and police used a smaller version of pipe and drums consisting of a Band master and 17 musicians. This still follows the Victorian era guidelines not to have more than eight pipers. The remaining 9 to 13 at that time used to be Drummers, thus drummers used to have a majority. In the European, mainly Scottish, Bagpipe Bands the only instruments used are the drums and bagpipes. Meaning thereby that Maracas, flute or tambourine are not used.

Traditionally, these Bands are identified by the Band Major carrying a Staff or a Mace, unlike the next three types of Bands, where the Leader only has a conductor stick. Some Bands have a Turkish Crescent or a Jingling Johnny in the hands of the Band Major while New Zealand Army Band Major is more likely to carry a *Tewhatewha* which is also staff-like weapon of Maori tribal chiefs by which he would give commands during battles. The practice of such staff or a mace is on the decline in the Western Pipe and Drum Bands but not so in Asian Bands, as yet.

Brass Bands

The Brass Bands are the ones using the Brass family of instruments that became prevalent in past two hundred years. Brass instruments have a higher and unidirectional sound and can play more accurate tunes. Although Brass Bands are preferably used in field, but can also be used indoors as Chamber Music. In United Kingdom, the Oxford University and Cambridge University Brass Bands have the same prominence among academic institution Bands as the two universities have over all other academic institutions.

The origin of various brass instruments has a long history. Many changes occurred in Europe during the 17th and 18th centuries. The clarinet was improved, or probably invented, by J.C. Denner (1655–1707) of Nuremberg and was in commonly used by 1720. The clarinet changed the basic sound of the traditional oboe-bassoon Band. The Royal Kent Keyed Bugle was patented in 1810 by Irishman Joseph Haliday, who was the Bandmaster of Cavan Militia, in Dublin. The bugle was made of brass but used a key mechanism similar to the saxophone. The keys enabled the bugle to play the full chromatic range and melodies. Brass instruments were no longer delegated to playing only harmonic parts. By 1814, Hanoverian Bugle had become the symbol of British Light Infantry. (Music 2005)

Valves were patented in 1818 by Heinrich Stoelzel (1777-1844) and Friedrich Bluhmel (1777-1845) in Berlin. The early valved brass instruments had only two valves. Shortly afterwards, a third valve was added and valve instruments could play the entire chromatic range. In 1842, Belgian conductor and inventor, Adolphe Sax (1814–94) invented the saxophone and developed the saxhorn. Saxhorns are conical bore instruments with a perfected valve system to correct intonation problems (Music 2005).

Prussia (modern day Germany) produced the first Bandmaster to take advantage of the new brass instruments. He was named William Weiprecht (1802–72), appointed as Instructor of military Bands in Berlin in 1838. Standardization of military Bands instrumentations started with him. Through his invention of Tuba, Weiprecht proved the advantage of using trumpets and horns with valves. Players could now produce all notes of the chromatic scale without inserting crooks (Music 2005). Under his watch, each military arm of the Prussian army such as the infantry, cavalry, artillery and guard had Bands with their own instrumentation. Spanish Military Bands may have a Tuba player as the Band Sergeant Major which is not the case in other European nations.

The royal trumpet troupes to play fanfare at royal arrivals are also a type of Brass Bands. So are the Bugle Bands of the Spanish Legion and the Bands of Paratrooper Brigade of Spain.

In European tradition, the usual composition of a Brass Band is given in Annex B (2) at the end (Kingston 2016). In the South Asian context, the term "Brass Band" is erroneously used for Concert Bands which have both Brass and Woodwind instruments. Hence, an ensemble calling itself a Brass Band of Pakistani or Indian army must ordinarily be deemed as being a concert Band.

Concert Bands

When the Woodwind instruments are also added to the Brass instruments, it is called Wind Band, Woodwind Band or simply Concert Band. They are best for Chamber music but since the instruments are portable so they can also play outdoors both in sitting or marching positions. In South Asia, they are generally called Brass Bands or more commonly as Military Bands. In Indo-Pakistani Armed Forces, each regimental centre or military training academy has this Band. Although the term "concert Band" is a technically correct description, yet it is unheard of in Pakistani Indian military circles.

Concert Band Composition in South Asian tradition, generally followed in Pakistan is given in Annex B (3)(a). The Indian Army considers a proper balanced military Band to consist of a Bandmaster and 33 musicians, which is slightly smaller than the strength followed by Pakistani military Bands. Concert Bands Composition in European Tradition is given at Annex B(3)(b) at the end of this volume (Kingston 2016). The concert Bands are the most widely conspicuous amongst the military Bands and are an essential part of State ceremonials.

Symphony Orchestra

The fourth type of Military Band, by instrumentation, is the symphony orchestra, also known as Philharmonic Orchestra. In this one, string instruments are added on top of percussion, brass and woodwind instruments.

The precursor of modern Orchestra is the Fanfare Band. The modern fanfare Band first appeared during the 19th century. Founded in 1806, in Belgium, the *Koninklijke Stadsfanfaren Izegem* is the oldest and still performing Fanfare Band and Orchestra in the world. At the same time, similar formations were also raised in the Netherlands.

And by the late 19th century, fanfare Bands became the official field music formation within the French, Dutch and Belgian armies, with the bugle replacing the fife in the infantry and other arms.

The likely instrumental composition of a small classical orchestra is given at Annex B(4)(a). Modern Philharmonic Orchestra are a much larger formation. The standard instrumentation is given at Annex B(4)(b.)

It is purely a Chamber Music and cannot be played in a marching formation. It is employed to play national anthems, patriotic songs and other instrumental and vocal symphonies at national occasions or purely for entertainment at festivals, etc. As required by the compositions in the programme, various electrical or electronic instruments may be used in the orchestra. The performers are not typically permanent orchestra members. They are typically freelancers hired on contract for one or more concerts.

Types of Military Bands (Classification by Music)

The genesis of Military Music owed to its indispensability in the field—in the battlefield to be precise. This was for the wartime. Over the period, peacetime uses of field music were also discovered, for instance, in the parade grounds. Both were outdoor, and hence called Field Music. The knights, noblemen and officers who commanded the units had to hire, clothes and equip Bandsmen through their own purse. Hence, Bands were instructed to play at their mansions at parties and other occasions. This gave birth to another genre of Band music called the Chamber Music that was played indoors. Gradually, multiple categories of Bands emerged that could fall in between the two, depending upon the instrumentation used. These Bands which could pay both in indoor and outdoor settings are called Mixed Music Bands. Hence, in terms of Music the military Bands can be classified into three categories.

Field Music Bands

The Bands that were used outdoors for issuing cautions and commands to the military both during peace or war time, initially consisted of drums and fifes (a particular type of pipe) alone. The drum beat could be heard from a distance and the marching steps could be synchronised with it. Fifes could however be heard from close range only and had limited tactical utility. But of course no tune could be played without a wind instrument so fifes ended up becoming part of the Band ensemble. However, the Drum Major was to have precedence in the Band even if his military rank was lower to Pipe Major of the Band. In fact, the position of Pipe Major or Chief Piper was introduced by Queen Victoria in the field Bands hierarchy, although even she would not raise their status above the well-established Drum Majors. In time, many Brass instruments were developed which could produce unidirectional sound audible from afar. The rank of Bugle Major also remained below that of Drum Major until the Drum Corps, along with its Majors and minors, all but vanished from the modern Brass Bands. The only exception is the mounted Bands where the Bugle Major is usually the Band Major. The Fifes saw themselves on the way out, while Bugles became the default choice for Wind component in the field music.

The Pipe Bands, Bagpipe Bands, the Corps of Pipes and Drums or the Corps of Bugles and Drums are the different names used in Military traditions in various parts of the world to denote the Bands which are used for Field Music. They can only be played outdoor and usually in marching formation. With the demise of their use in real-life battles, field music is employed for parades and other ceremonial purposes.

Mixed Music Bands

The introduction of Brass instruments into military Bands was a gradual process spanning over two centuries. They were embraced because their sound could be heard in noisy environments. As the brass instruments grew in sophistication, nicer and delicate tunes could be played with the brass instruments than with the bagpipes or fifes. Slowly the latter started replacing the former as the main genre of military Bands.

With the passage of time, popularity of Indoor or Chamber music increased for ball room and dinner parties. The brass instruments were found to be too loud for a closed space. The woodwind instruments were introduced which, as the name indicates, were wind instruments made of wood (and sometimes, wood and metal combined). The advantage of woodwind is that they can be heard all over—front, back and sides with the same ease. Unlike brass instruments which can be heard from a distance, but in the front direction only, woodwinds are not suitable for stadiums and open grounds. Hence, the term Concert Band for the woodwind Bands.

The Concert Bands and the Military Bands are the terms used interchangeably to denote Bands with instrumentation that is equally good for both chamber music and the field music. Hence, they are called Mixed Music Bands.

Chamber Music Bands

Finally, the Bands started having String instruments then Keyboard instruments and finally electrical and electronic instruments. This new equation brought the world towards symphony orchestras. Orchestras, of course, cannot be played while marching as many of the instruments are too big to carry. Hence, the Military Orchestras, Symphony Orchestras and Philharmonic Orchestras can only be played as Chamber Music.

Types of Military Bands (Classification by Placement)

In terms of placement, there can be three obvious types—those placed with military headquarters or Command centres, those placed with fixed military establishments such as the training centres and those with field formations or mobile units such as the Infantry regiments.

In South Asian tradition, the Headquarters have Orchestras, the establishments have Brass/ Concert Bands and the field formations have Pipe Bands. India has 576 military Bands out of which three are Orchestras, around 50 are brass Bands and the remaining are pipe Bands. Pakistan has 242 Bands out of which one is Orchestra, 22 are Brass Bands and the rest are Pipe Bands. During the World War, a close approximation of Band-type by placement, were respectively called Organization Bands, Separate Bands and Special Bands (History of Army Music n.d.).

Regiment Bands/Organization Bands

In South Asian tradition, each military/infantry unit has a Pipe Band. Hence they are called Unit Bands, Battalion Bands or Regiment Bands. Thus, they are Bands of the mobile formations. The Regiments are invariably from the category called Pipe Bands, although they consist of Pipes and Drums.

What are called Regimental Bands in Asia, were known as Organization Bands in the United States army till the final years of the Second World War. Organization Bands were part of the US infantry units. They were attached to combat commands to provide music for the unit's combat and support troops. These Regimental Bands were abolished in 1943 as individual units and consolidated to form Division Bands. This practices continue to this day when Bands are attached with Army Divisions in the United States instead of individual units.

Bands of the Military Centres/Separate Bands

The large fixed establishments such as the Corps Centres, Divisional HQs, Regimental Centres and Training Academies, Schools and Centres of the Armed Forces of South Asia (mainly India and Pakistan) have bigger Military Bands.

The term used for these Bands is "Brass Bands" but are not restricted to Brass instruments only. They have all modern woodwind and percussion instruments and in the Western understanding, they might be called Concert Bands. Hence, it is the Brass and Concert Bands in South Asia that are with the fixed military establishments.

In the United States military tradition, such Bands were known as Separate Bands. They were controlled by the Adjutant General and supported the administrative, technical, and training centres to which they were attached. The United States Corps of Music is well resourced to the tune of nearly half a billion dollars a year. The budget of the US Army Bands is more than the Defence Budget of four of the smallest NATO Allies. Hence, unlike South Asia, where the training establishments may not have full-fledged Orchestras, it is possible to find a US Academy or fixed establishment to have a Military Orchestra, a Wind Ensemble, a Choir and Gun Drill team as part of the Band of the Center.

Headquarter Bands/Special Bands

The Military Orchestras are large and expensive and for poor South Asian countries, they can be kept with the General Headquarters of the Armed Forces. Pakistan has one with the Army School of Music while India has three in all.

The nearest equivalent in the United States used to be the US Army Band (Pershing's Own);the US Military Academy Band and the US Army Air Corps Band, were the designated special Bands. As special Bands, they performed at special ceremonies, concerts, parades, and recruiting drives. Today, the number of Special Bands has risen to four as was noted above in this chapter.

Types of Military Bands (Classification by Uniforms)

The concept of Band having military uniformed also came from the Ottoman military Bands. The clothing of the *Mehter* has a distinct beauty. The leading player of each instrument wore a red broadcloth bonnet and "çaksir" (a type of baggy trousers), yellow morocco leather shoes and red headgear. The other players had dark blue broadcloth, red çakþýr, green headwear and red shoes. Over time, fancy uniforms became the norm for military Bandsmen.

The British military officers came from aristocracy and donned their Bandsmen with elaborate uniforms. Military uniforms were a practical way of protection, needed to be convenient enough to be worn with armour and were necessary for identification with a Kingdom to avoid deaths by friendly troops in the confusion and mayhem of battlefields. For the last foregoing purpose, the soldiers would wear a fig from a local plant, a feather from a local bird or a local flower, to identify them with their region. These figs, feathers and flowers became the precursors of present-day insignias of military formations. The uniforms of the Military Bands accentuated all these features and were more distinctive than the army they represented.

The United States followed suit where Bands wore distinctive uniforms; one of the reasons, apart from aesthetics, was to make them distinguishable from a distance. The idea was that fighting armies were expected not to shoot at each other's Bandsmen who were unarmed. In any case, the military origin of most Band uniforms, even in the civilian domain, is hard to miss.

The Military Bands are also distinguished by the paradoxical element of uniformity and dis-uniformity in their uniforms. On the one hand, a whole army of a country may have the same basic colour theme and scheme of the military uniform, while the uniform of the military Bands may differ from unit to unit, depending upon the historical context. On the other hands, the level of uniformity required in the appearance of a single Band may be so rigorous that until recently the Band Members of Spanish Grenadiers and Spanish Fusilier regiments were not allowed to wear glasses or sport beards—something that might be unheard of, for the uniforms of their non-Band comrades in the same regiments. Going a step ahead, North Korean leader wanted the height of each member of his favourite all-female military Band to be 165 cm. Anyway, the types of Bands by instrumentation, by placement and by type of music have been discussed above. The Bands can also be classified based on the type of uniforms they don.

Military Bands with Ceremonial Uniforms

The Pipe Bands of South Asian military, the Bagpipe Bands of British and Scottish regiments, the Fanfare Bands of continental Europe and the single surviving Old Guard Corps of Fife and Drums of the US Army don ceremonial uniforms.

The Pipe Band uniforms are a bit more elaborate than other types of Bands. In the British Bands tradition, which is carried in part of Africa, all of South Asia, parts of Australia-Pacific and the Caribbean, the uniforms of Pipers include an ornamental Piper's cloak and those of drummers by a lanyard on the front with two hanging drumsticks. Thus, the wind component of these Bands (The Pipers) are distinguished by Cloaks behind, while the percussion component (the Drummers) are recognisable from the front of their uniforms through elaborately embroidered lanyards and drumsticks hanging in front.

The Band Major of the Pipe or Bagpipe Bands usually carries a long staff or

Mace, although this tradition is waning from all parts of the world except South Asia. He also wears a sash embroidered with insignias of the unit and the army he is representing.

Military Bands with Modern or Traditional Uniforms

The modern military, brass and concert Bands usually have modern uniforms with Western-style jackets and trousers, with a Peaked Cap/Service Cap. In South Asian Military traditions where ordinarily, peaked cap is only authorised to officers while the Soldiers and Non-Commissioned Officers usually don berets, Military Brass Bands are the only groups where the soldiers also wears ceremonial Peaked Service Caps. In the Bands where beret is part of the Band uniform, a plume of some other decorative addition is made for the headgear to make it more impressive and distinctive from other soldiers.

In many cases, even if the Brass and Concert Band is wearing the Western Dress, the headgear is likely to be local or traditional. For examples, most of the Military Brass Bands in the subcontinent wear the Turban or *Pagri* which is the traditional headgear of the region. There is a piece of cloth left hanging once the turban is wrapped around the head, which is called *Shimla.* The Muslim Band regiments have a *Shimla* rising above the head of the Turban, the Hindu majority regiments had a *Shimla* facing downwards from the Turban and the Sikh Regiments did not have a *Shimla* attached to their Turbans.

Likewise, the Arab Military and Police Bands wear Arab Headdress called Kiffeyeh (the head scarf) along with the otherwise Western uniform. The British Bands also wear traditional Bearskin Caps; the Australian, Canadian, Kenyan and most Latin American military Bands compliment distinctive historic headdresses with their Western-style uniforms.

However, some Military Bands wear totally traditional uniforms such as the *Mehter* Band of Turkey, the Traditional Army Band of South Korea, the Central Band of Egyptian Military (Pharaoh era uniforms). Thus, some armies retain at least one Concert or Brass Band that dons the traditional dress.

Military Bands with Opera-style Uniforms

Orchestras do not necessarily wear the uniform of the branch they represent. It is customary for them to wear black or dark-coloured lounge suit with plain white shirt and a bow tie. In some cases, the colour of the lounge suit may follow the colour theme of the regiment or the colour of the ceremonial dress of the branch of military the Band represents.

Single-Bands & non-Instrumental (components of) Military Bands

The term "Band" originated for the combination of percussion and wind instruments, initially drums and fifes. The mushrooming of Band types resulted in Bands using either type of instrumentation, i.e. wind-only as well as percussion-only Bands. They can still be called Bands within our operative definition for this work. Most of the wind Bands include a percussion element now. Likewise, Battery Drumlines usually combine military drills, so multiple Musical performance justifies the term Band. The two non-instrumental musical performances are the Songs and Dances. Martial songs and battle dances have a long history, and today choirs and dance troupes have made their entry in many military musical organizations. Although both song and dance can be performed without instrumental accompaniment but that is rare in Military Bands where sound and beats always perform cadences for the choir or the dance, or for both (McNeill 1995).

Military Percussion Bands

Percussion Band consists of various types of percussion instruments including drums, cymbals and tambourines. There are two popular types of percussion formations: Drumline and Drum Circle. Within the Military, the Drumlines may exist independently or as part of military drill teams, sometimes called "Drum and Drill Corps". In High School and College Marching Bands, however, Drumline is one component of a bigger Band. This may ordinarily be called Battery Drumline that marches in the field with Tenor, Snare and Bass Drums as well as, occasionally, Cymbals. Likewise, the Drum and Bugle Corps, which is a type of military-style Band, used both by military and non-military institutions, have a Drumline included in it.

Percussion or Drum Bands may also be part of rock and roll music, such as the music for some of Michael Jackson's hit songs includes cadence provided by scores of drummers beating drums together. A typical example may be provided through video of this song by Jackson:

> *All I wanna say is that*
> *they don't really care about us.*

Percussion Bands may also be religious Bands such as the "Flourish of Hundred Drums" that the Chinese community in Malaya and elsewhere in South East Asia uses to observe religious rituals associated with harvest season. Groups of hundreds of drummers beat 24 drums representing the 24 terms in Chinese lunar calendar.

Indoor percussion Bands include many Funeral Bands that play heavy metal beats to create a sombre ambience of mourning.

A *Drum Circle* is any group of people playing (usually) hand-drums and percussions in a circle. They are distinct from a drum troupe in that the drum circle is an end in itself, rather than preparation for a performance. They can range in size from a handful of players to circles with thousands of participants. Drum circles are related to other community-based music gatherings. Typically, people of all ages gather to drum in "drum circles" with others from the surrounding community. The drum circle offers equality because there is no head or tail. The main objective is to share rhythm and get in tune with each other and themselves in order to resonate, to entertain and to form a group consciousness.

One recent, yet famous, example of a military-style Drum Band is the Top Secret Drum Corps from the city of Basel in Switzerland. This 25-member Drum Corps became famous because of its demanding six minutes' routine performed at its debut appearance at the Edinburgh Tattoo of Military Bands 2003, becoming the first non-Commonwealth non-military Band to be invited to the Esplanade of the Edinburgh Castle. Basel has a drumming tradition dating back to the Middle Ages and at any time the city can count thousands of active drummers among its residents. Mainly composed of College students, the Drum Corps had adopted patterns of drumming drills from the military traditions of Swiss Army dating back several centuries. The Drum Corps has not only returned to Edinburgh tattoo multiple times but can also be credited with the founding of Basel Tattoo of Military Bands.

In case, the Drummers are not part of a bigger and broader Band (such as one having a Wind component) or a Drill team (with marching battery), then the term Percussion *Band* becomes a misnomer. A more appropriate labelling for such groups is *Percussion Ensemble*. Unlike elsewhere, where this term can be used to describe *any* such group of drummers without other accompaniment, *Percussion Ensemble* has a definite connotation as far as North America is concerned. There it refers to professionally trained percussionists performing primarily classical music, most commonly found at conservatories. George Anteil's Ballet Mécanique (1923), written originally as a film score, is one of the earliest examples of composition for percussion.

Military Wind Bands

Wind Band typically used to refer to a musical group playing wind instruments only (without a percussion supplement). Such Wind Bands started as Military

Ensembles in the 18th century, doing double duty as entertainment at the royal courts, either alone or combined with orchestral strings. Composers such as Mozart were writing music for these groups, called Harmonie, which evolved to a standard eight-piece Wind-only instrumentation of two oboes, two clarinets, two horns and two bassoons.

In time, not only more Wind Instruments were developed and included into such Bands but, under Turkish influence, percussion component became part of such Chamber music. Thus today Wind Band has become a second name for standard Concert Bands of the Military. The term is interchangeably used with Wind Band, Symphonic Band, Wind Symphony or Symphonic Wind, or Wind Orchestra. Whatever the label, these military musical ensembles perform instruments from the woodwind, brass and percussion families of instruments, along with the double bass. Thus, today a Wind Band must not be confused with Wind-Only-Band. At best, a Military Band without percussion may be called a Wind Ensemble to avoid confusion. Today, the repertoires of the Military Wind Bands include original wind compositions, transcriptions/arrangements of orchestral compositions, light music, and popular tunes.

Professional Wind Band not associated with the military are rare. Examples of non-military Wind Bands include Dallas Wind Symphony, led by Jerry Junkin and Tokyo Kosei Wind Orchestra, led for many years by Frederick Fennel. Another name that comes to mind is the Osaka Municipal Symphonic Band. The Royal Hawaiian Band, created by royal decree in 1836 by King Kamehameha III is yet another example of civilian Wind Band.

Military Choirs

A Military Choir is a music ensemble of singers. Choral music, in turn, is the music written specifically for such an ensemble to perform. Choirs may perform music from the classical music repertoire, which spans from the Medieval era to the present, and/or popular music repertoire. Most choirs are led by a conductor, who leads the performances with arm and face gestures. *Choirs* seem to have originated from Church services from the time of Pope Gregory I. Similar groups who performed in opera halls or theatres are usually called *Chorus*, but this distinction is far from rigid.

Amongst the most famous Military Choirs was the Choir of the Alexandrov Band of Russia before its tragic end in a Christmas Day military plane crash in the Black Sea in 2016. The Alexandrov Band had an instrumental accompaniment, a Choir and a Dance troupe. In fact, almost all military Bands that have a Choir, this is as an additional component to the the core of the Band that is always the instrumental ensemble. Alexandrov Band was unique where it had been the other way round; its Choir overshadowed the accompanying military orchestra as the most recognizable and popular face of this Band. The "Singing Sergeants" in the United States Air Force Band provide another prominent example of a Choir. Formed as an all-male Chorus in 1945, it started inducting women in 1971. With 24 members, and up to 200 performances annually, it the most recognisable image of the United States Air Force Band.

It is pertinent to mention here that the term "Choir" has the secondary definition, that of an (instrumental) subset of an ensemble; thus one speaks of the "woodwind choir" of an orchestra. There can also be different "choirs" of voices and/or instruments in a poly-choral composition.

Military Dance Troupes

Military Dance Troupes originated from the traditional war dances of the ancient battles. Dance is basically a performance of art form consisting of purposefully selected sequences of human movement. Usually accompanied by music, even unaccompanied dance is rhythmic enough to qualify being a musical performance itself (McNeill 1995). Just like other forms of music, the institutions of Monarchy, Marriage and the Military contributed immensely to the development of Dance. Dances were part of Royal Court ceremonies from ancient China to ancient Ghana, Dances were a part of wedding festivities from Celtic regions to Arabian Peninsula, and from Indo-Pakistan subcontinent to Latin America.

Most importantly, Military Dances became the opening shot of the battle in areas so far geographically detached from each other that one could not have been historically influenced by the other. Maori Dances in New Zealand, Kwazulu Dances in South Africa and tribal dances in Nordic and Baltic regions were employed to enliven a spirit of gallantry in own troops and terrifying the opponent combatants. Today, dance-like movements are done by Military Bands as part of the performance in hundreds of military and military-like Bands worldwide. For instance, the Band of the Russian Emergency Services, the Band of Ukraine Air Force, the Band of Mexican Land Forces, and in countless others, the Dance Troupe moves and performs as a separate component of the Military Band.

The standalone Dance Bands exist for the Russian National Guard, Flag-thrower Band of Tuscany (Italy) and the Armed Forces Dance Band of Kenya, all three of which performed at the Tripoli Festival of Military Bands (2009) that Libyan President Moammar Qaddafi had organised to mark 40 years of his ascension to power. The Dance remains part of some other military Bands' traditions, such as the New Zealand Army Bands start their performance with Maori War dances while the Fiji Police Band and many other Bands in Pacific region also open up their performance with indigenous tribal dance manoeuvres. Military Drill and Gun teams almost always perform along with a Drumline, so Dance remains part of the Military Bands in a large number of military traditions.

Dance troupe itself can hardly be labelled as a "Dance Band," but since Dance is almost always performed accompanied by Music, so Dance Bands do exist in military traditions. The United Service Organizations (USO) during World War II regularly sent Dance Bands to perform for the US troops fighting at forward locations in Europe. The British War Ministry also used to send Dance Bands to entertain British and allied troops in war theatres even up to the time of Korean War.

Conclusion: Battles between drums and pipes

The War has remained a serious business but its depiction in popular culture has only recently been studied (Adams 2002). The military Bands remain a significant cultural aspect of warfare. The list of types of Military Bands is not exhaustive. In fact, many of them overlap not only with each other but also with the types of civil Bands, which is the topic of the next chapter. Every region and within the region, every country may have peculiarities in classification. The militaries usually remain secretive about their affairs, which includes the military Bands and their nomenclature, as well. Hence, it remains a herculean task to dig out information as to how most of the military forces characterise their Bands.

One important facet of military Bands is the conflict between drums and other percussion instruments on the one hand and wind instruments from pipes to bugles on the other. The British Bands have Pipers in the front while in most Bands in France and Latin America (such as Ecuador and Peru) the Drummers march in the front. Unlike the seniority of Drum Major over Pipe Majors in the British system, several types of Bands such as the Bugle Bands, mounted Bands and Fanfare Bands are led by Bugle Majors.

CHAPTER VII

Types and Classifications of Non-Military Bands

Music can change the world because it can change people.

—Bono

In the context of the present work, an ensemble of two persons as a Band is not recognized as a Band. Except the Percussion or Wind Bands of the Institutions such as the Armed Forces, the Police or the Universities and Colleges, an ensemble is not accepted to be a Band unless it has more than one type of musical expression, that is wind and percussion instruments, percussion and strings, keyboard and song, drum and dance, and so on.

There can be a large number of possible classification of Musical Bands. Every book and website has classified the Bands in a variety of ways and, depending on the criterion and definitions, the total types easily exceed a 120. The most obvious Band classifications, not covered in the preceding chapter on military classifications, are on the basis of size, gender, marching style and musical repertoire of the Bands.

Types of Bands by Size

In terms of the number of musicians, the Bands can be divided into three categories of small, medium and big Bands, explained as follows:

Small Bands

The Bands in which the number of musicians is less than eight—anywhere between three to seven—are deemed as Small Bands. Thus, as per the opening definition in this chapter, a duo is not recognized as a Band. Likewise, the small Bands must have at least two types of instruments or more than one type of musical expression, say a keyboard and a vocalist. All kinds of trios, quartets and quintets, will be thus small Bands.

The Jazz Bands in the United States have usually up to seven members, many of the modern pop Bands in India and Pakistan (see next section Boy Bands) had up to five members, four instrumentalists plus a vocalist. Many of the funeral Bands, the rock and roll Bands, the Blue Bands and the like are all examples of Small Bands.

Medium Bands

The Bands having a membership between eight and eighty members are called medium-sized Bands. Almost all Pipe, Brass and Concert Bands of the Armed Forces are medium-sized Bands. Obviously, there are exceptions such as the President's Own Marine Band of United States has 130 members while Alexandrov Band of the Russian Federation has 186. Thus, they are big-sized military Bands.

Big Bands

Any Band with a strength of 81 or above will be called a Big Band. Orchestras are generally big Bands and so are most of the School and College Bands all across the United States.

Types of Bands by Marching Styles

The Ottomans gave the idea of the Band having a definite style of Marching. The members of the Mehter had a special style of walking. They walked slowly and chanted, "Generous God, merciful God." At every three steps they would stop and turn both right and then left. Their style of walking represents the Ottoman's dignity and caution. While the Mehter has retained its style over the centuries, but none of the modern Bands emulates its marching style. However, a number of marching styles have arisen and Bands can be classified in terms of their marching styles.

Military-style Marching Bands

The modern marching Bands originate from the military Band tradition. Military-style marching is characterized by straight, organized ranks that move in the forward direction. Music is played continuously with the tune and rhythm to aid the marching, thus putting a heavy emphasis on the uniformity of their visual style. Military Bands have military-style costumes as uniforms, instruments like brass and percussion, and often play national or patriotic tunes.

Such marching Bands are believed to have come into existence because of nomadic musicians who showed their talent at celebrations and festivals in the olden times. When the warfare ripped apart the states, these musicians were roped in to become part of armies. This phenomenon then culminated into the creation of "Military Bands." This style then proliferated into all sorts of marching Bands including those of schools and colleges.

Marching Show Bands

Performances of Show Bands, also called the traditional-style Bands, are mainly for sports events and generally on the field, particularly seen before, after and during middle time at football events. The instrumentation may depend upon the show. If it is a sporting event, the focus will be mainly on crowd entertainment and sometimes scripted storytelling. Since these Show Bands are probably the most prolific in popular culture in the United States, so a lot of school and college competitions are held where the emphasis is on showing their visual and musical talent and abilities to the panel of judges. They rarely perform on solemn occasions or at parades on national occasions.

Carnival Marching Bands

Carnival Bands are a European variant of American Marching Show Bands. Carnival Bands typically contain brass instruments with a few percussions, but may generally not use the woodwinds. They march in time to the music but not in military style of strict discipline but more so in entertainment mode. The Carnival Bands participate in parades, mainly those of festive nature like Rose bowl parade, St Patrick's Day parade or in carnivals. They do sometimes take part in competitions as well. Their performance will be usually to march with the tune of the music.

Scramble Marching Bands

Also known as "Scatter" Bands, these Bands do not march in tune with the music, but often incorporate comedic elements into their performances. They, as their name implies, scramble from design to design in order to include humour in their performances. Except the Cornell University, all Ivy League Universities use the Scramble style, while the majority of American Universities go for Show Band style.

The Drum and Bugle Corps

The Drum and Bugle Corps borrow marching elements from the military Band, but add their own unique flair. For example, they have more ceremonial and colourful flair than an ordinary military-style marching Bands. They use elements of the regimented nature but make formations that can be more organic and even pictorial.

Drum and Bugle Corps do not have a unidirectional forward march, but freely move forwards, backwards and side-wards. Band members often make forms that may be linear, curvilinear, or scatter while ensuring that their upper bodies consistently face the front of the field, making a constant wall of sound no matter what direction they move. Music selections can include anything from symphonic music, film scores, to world music, jazz, rock, or pop music.

The Drum and Bugle Corps can be employed both for formal national occasions or for sports events or celebrations. Their style will depend upon the occasion, situation and the circumstances. If it is a national event, the Band may include a "color guard" that spin flags or a rifles party. On the other hand, if it is a celebration, the Band may also incorporate dance.

Unlike the military Band style, where Band Major twirls the batons and the size of step of the marchers is uniform and constant, the drum corps style does not use baton or mace and step sizes are constantly changing to accommodate the differing forms the Band is creating on the field. Visual elements unique to the corps style is the usage of props, backdrops, and even costuming—with the purpose of adding more theatrical elements to the show.

Fanfare Bands

Fanfare Bands are a unique type of marching Band that plays for entertainment, public occasions and gatherings as well as competing in various competitions. Particular to Europe, they are the nearest equivalent of America's Drum and Bugle Corps. Their instrumentation includes percussion, bugles, natural horns and natural trumpets (although lately some have started using modern brass instruments as well). Fanfare Bands exist both in military and civilian traditions in Germany, France, Netherlands and Belgium as descendants of the old medieval trumpet and drum (usually snares and tenors) teams that sounded fanfares on important holidays or ceremonial events and also serve as timekeepers in various towns. From the medieval times, they were also employed to motivate mounted troops in battle as well as on parade.

Types of Bands by Gender composition

With rare exceptions, in most parts of the globe, there is a greater gender integration today in social life than was the case as recently as half a century ago, even in countries such as the United States and Great Britain. Not only school or college Bands, but even many military Bands now have mixed composition. However, for a considerable time, there were Bands whose musicians were always of the same sex, basically for cultural, historical or religious reasons. This section explains such male and female Bands.

Boy Bands

A boy Band (or boyBand) is loosely defined as a vocal group consisting of young male singers, usually in their teenage years or in their twenties at the time of formation. The first earliest boy Bands such as the *Beatles*, the *Monkees* and the *Jackson 5*, sang love songs centred towards young females.

Since, they were initially vocal-only groups, so the term "Band" appeared something of a misnomer. However, in time, instrumentation was added and so was the dance in highly choreographed performances. In the United States, some Boy Bands formed on their own, some evolved out of church or gospel music groups, while others were created by talent managers or record producers after holding auditions. Moving into the 2010s, Boy Bands were popular especially in the United Kingdom and the rest of Europe due to the continued commercial presence and longevity of nineties Boy Bands such as *Backstreet Boys* and (before it dissolved in 2012) *West Life.*

American and British groups like *Dream Street, 98 Degrees, O-Town* and *Blue Busted* gained wide popularity both domestically and internationally so Boy Bands started springing up elsewhere. From late 1980s, Boy Bands spread into Asia. *Pearl Avengers, Strings* and *Vital Signs* appeared in Pakistan and became heartthrobs all over South Asia. In 1999, Japanese Boy Band *Arashi* made their first release and has sold over 30 million copies of their records since. From 2001, Taiwanese boy Band *F4* (called *JVKV* since 2007) became a huge success throughout Asia.

As a solution to the Jewish law against men hearing women singing, Jewish boys choirs became popular in the 1970s. Among the more notable of these groups are *Pirchei London*, the *Toronto Boys Choir*, and the *Yeshiva Boys Choir*. Probably the most popular is *Miami Boys Choir* led by Yerachmiel Begun, with a number of albums amongst the top record sales in Orthodox Jewish circles.

There are also Marching Boy Bands. For example, the Boys' Brigade (BB)—an interdenominational Christian youth organization, conceived by Sir William Alexander Smith in 1893—to combine drill and fun activities with Christian values—maintains a number of Boys' Brigade marching Bands in many countries.

The Ismaili Muslim community also has a number of Marching Boy Bands mainly in Northern mountainous region of Hunza in Pakistan. Inspired by such marching Bands, a group of poor boys from slum areas of a town called Hyderabad in Hunza valley raised a Boy Band named "*Josh*" (tr. Enthusiasm) Band in 2012. For drums they scavenged for empty cooking oil vessels, for drumsticks they use tree twigs and have devised pipes from hollow tree trunk pieces.

Girls Bands and All-Female Bands

An all-female Band and the Girls Bands are two different genres. For many decades, popular music as rock, blues, jazz and related genres remained exclusively a male preserve, and it is only in recent decades that women-only Bands have started evolving. So all Rock, Jazz or Pop Band exclusively composed of female musicians started being called Female Bands although they are not as common as male Bands in these genres. The Benjamin Sisters of Pakistan and Tetseo Sisters of India are obvious examples.

The Female Band is distinct from a girl group or a girl Band, in which the female members are usually in their teens or early twenties and traditionally consisted solely of vocalists. A Girl Group is a music act featuring several female singers who generally harmonise together. The term "Girl Group" is also used in a narrower sense in the United States to denote the wave of American female pop music singing groups which flourished in the late 1950s and early 1960s.

As these musical groups started playing instruments, the term "Girl Groups" came to be replaced by "Girl Bands." But the two terms get sometimes interchangeably used. For instance, instrumentalists *Girlschool* are termed a "girl group" while vocalist groups like *Sugababes* and *Girls Aloud* are referred to as "girl Bands."

In the modern Jewish communities, female Orthodox musical Bands like *Tofa'ah*, *Ashira* and *Bulletproof Stockings*, have emerged, survived and found success as "Girl Bands" though they perform at female-only audiences. Likewise, in a conservative society like Afghanistan, which has only recently come out of Taliban rule, *Zohra Orchestra* of 35 young girls between ages 13 to 20 has become an internationally acclaimed Girls Band. Despite life threats from conservative clergy back home the Band has performed at World Economic Forum at Davos in Switzerland in January 2017.

The Girls-only Marching Bands emerged from the Girls Brigade amongst Christians in many European countries and the Ismaili Girl Bands from the Muslims in India and Pakistan.

Types of Bands by Musical Repertoire

Unlike the Military Bands, which develop expertise in a wide variety of musical repertoires, the non-military ones try to focus on a particular genre of music. The Small Bands may concentrate on folk music, classical music, popular (pop) music, Jazz music, blues or the modern rock and roll. Four of famous types of Bands, by musical litany, are the Folk Bands, the Jazz Bands, the Rock Bands and the Pop Bands shall be discussed here.

Folk Bands

Folk Bands exist all over the world and play folk songs, dance and instruments. The term Folk music originated in the 19th century but is often applied to music that was older. The 20th century saw an interest in all the traditional and classical music that nations had as part of their cultural heritage which led to a great folk revival.

The term. Folk music has been defined in several ways: as music transmitted orally, music with unknown composers and hence no copyright, or music performed by custom over a long period of time. The music was often related to national culture and history and was identified with a particular region, especially if it had been performed over a long period of time, usually several generations. The term has been contrasted with modern commercial styles of music.

Musical and Dance ensembles that perform folk music are called Folk Bands. They commemorate historical and personal events. Particular songs celebrate certain days of the year, such as religious or cultural festivals. Traditional weddings and funerals may also be have a component of songs, dances and special costumes. Birthdays may often have a folk music component for which folk Bands may be hired.

In the context of immigrant groups, folk music acquires an extra dimension for social cohesion. It is particularly conspicuous in immigrant societies, where Greek Australians, Somali Americans, Punjabi Canadians and others strive to emphasise their differences from the mainstream. They learn songs and dances that originate in the countries their grandparents came from.

Jazz Bands

Jazz Music is African–American in origin, when the African music got fused with American music. Varying in strength and style, jazz Bands are usually made up of a rhythm section and a horn section. Some Bands use vocalists, while others are purely instrumental groups. Jazz Bands usually have a Bandleader.

The size of a jazz Band is closely related to the style of jazz they play as well as the type of venues in which they play. Smaller jazz Bands, also known as combos, are common in nightclubs and other small venues and will be made up of three to seven musicians; whereas those found in dance halls and other larger venues may have many more members.

The term jazz trio can refer to a three-piece Band with a pianist, double bass player and a drummer. But of course, they can play as a quartet, a quintet or in bigger sizes where there can be more than one player for a type of instrument.

Jazz Bands and their composition have changed many times throughout the years. The music itself changes with each performer's personal interpretation and improvisation which is one of the greatest appeals of going to see a jazz Band.

Rock Bands

A rock Band is a small musical ensemble which performs rock and roll music or a related genre. The four-piece Band is the most common configuration in rock and roll music. Before the development of the electronic keyboard, the configuration was typically two guitarists (a lead guitarist and a rhythm guitarist, with one of them singing lead vocals), a bassist, and a drummer (e.g. *Avenged Sevenfold, KISS, Franz Ferdinand*). Another common formation is a vocalist who does not play an instrument, electric guitarist, bass guitarist, and a drummer (e.g. *The Who, The Monkees, Led Zeppelin, Queen*, and *U2*). Instrumentally, these Bands can be considered as trios.

The smallest ensemble that is commonly used in rock music is the trio format. In a hard rock or heavy metal rock group, a "power trio" format is often used, which consists of an electric guitar player, an electric bass guitar player and a drummer, and typically one or more of these musicians also sing (sometimes all three members will sing).

Pop Bands

As the Rock and Roll music was fast, loud and heavy, small Bands with lighter music started appearing. Pop, short for popular, concentrated on latest popular music including classical and modern.

The pop Bands may have the same composition of anywhere between three to seven, and may not have a heavy drum.

Conclusion

This chapter furnishes only an indicative guide to the type of Bands which may exist outside the military Bands category. This list has no pretension of being exhaustive or all-inclusive. The larger Military Bands may consist of multiple component units such as an Orchestra, a Rock Band, a Singing Troupe, a Jazz Band and a Marching Colour Guard, etc. A Military Band may be a Men-Only or Women-Only Band. The connotation for a Big Band might be different for civilian and military Bands. For the latter, a 35-strong Band might be a Medium Band while for Rock, Blue or Jazz Bands, anything above 20 (sometimes even above 12) shall be a Big Band.

Privately, the Bands are used for a wide variety of reasons. Sifting through Band News one finds a Shop having failed to stem shoplifting by any other means, hired a Band that would follow a shoplifter to embarrass him or her. A School Band would assemble at the lawns of their teacher undergoing Cancer treatment to welcome him to his home, once he was discharged from hospital. One finds a Marching Band taking to streets to play in order to attract attention towards a lost pet dog of one of their members. One may see Marching Bands playing as an act of defiance, leading the way in street demonstrations against a Government or against many Governments, say, at the G-20 Summit.

CHAPTER VIII

First World War & Bands in Pre- and Early Modern Warfare

Pride, pomp, and circumstance of glorious war!
The spirit-stirring drum, the ear-piercing fife,

—William Shakespeare, *Othello*

Music has been an integral part of warfare since the dawn of history. Typically, drums and horns were shown as symbols of War, along with swords, spears and arrows, in ancient art depictions. In imperial Russia, the highest award for valour for a regiment used to be, neither a flag nor a medal, but a Silver Trumpet. Even today "Summons of the Trumpet" is the name of a book on Vietnam war. Likewise, "following the drum" is an idiom signifying enlistment in the Armed Forces. Especially, in Infantry formations all over the world, drums traditionally had the same significance as its flags and colours that were the pride of a regiment.

The standard function of music in war has been as a means of communication. But, this was during warfare up to the 19th century when no other reliable means of communication with the fighting troops existed. Although several other means like shouting an order, firing cannon shots or shooting a firework in the sky could and did substitute for drum and bugle commands. Nevertheless, as the famous but doomed "Charge of the Light Brigade" during the Crimean war had shown, one command misunderstood from another signal could spell death for the troops.

Over time, beginning with the Ottoman forces who brought modern marching orchestras with them in battlefields, the signalling role was eclipsed as a "Band" was the new weapon in its own right. Ottoman Bands were brought to the battlefield with more important duties: to raise spirits of one's own army on the one hand and to terrify, annoy or confuse the enemy, on the other. The examples of all three roles are galore, some of them have been mentioned in this chapter. Napoleon used Bands to terrify the Russians in the Battle of Austerlitz (1805) while British military tunes annoyed the enemy during the US War of Independence (*See* Col Reed incident below). As for confusing the enemy, the most obvious example is provided by the Battle of Oudenarde (1708), a key fight in the War of the Spanish Succession. The Allied (Anglo-Dutch-Austrian) drummers played *The French Retreate* so convincingly that part of the French army believed that it was their drummers who had conveyed the command to retreat and they did, in fact, withdraw from the field.

In the battlefields, with death and destruction raining from all sides, the way unarmed Bandsmen have shown exceptional valour and fearlessness all through human history, must itself be a separate subject of historical inquiry. Military Historian Cousins rightly point out that:

> *War, it would seem, spawns its special genus of musical influence spurring on men to deeds of valor and its peoples to endure. Instances are legion. (Cousins 1981)*

The study of the role of Bands seems to corroborate the above assertion. This chapter focuses on the role of Military Bands in the ancient warfare—the First Generation or the pre-modern warfare (period from Treaty of Westphalia to the Napoleonic wars) and the Second Generation or the early modern warfare (from Napoleon to the end of the First World War).

Musical instruments in ancient Palestinian, Roman & Indian warfare

> *Have seven priests carry trumpets of rams' horns in front of the ark. On the seventh day, march around the city seven times, with the priests blowing the trumpets.*
>
> —Verse 6:4 Book of Joshua, Old Testament

Ancient Middle Eastern Armies

The first recorded uses of Bands in a war victory appears in the Book of Joshua (Chapter 6) of the Old Testament. There is an exceptionally detailed description of the deployment of a ram's horns by Johsua's army in the siege of Jericho, the oldest fortified human settlement known to archaeology, in present-day Palestinian Authority. This Battle might have taken place nearly 4,000 years ago. Although a ram's horns do indeed make a powerful sound, but the blowing of horns can hardly be deemed sufficient in itself to level 20 feet high stone wall of Jericho. Hence, the Biblical story of the collapse of Jericho walls by the sound of horns is most likely allegorical (Trotter 2005). So the exact use of Horns by Joshua,[1] played in unison by his priests, whether they were used for signalling, for raising spirits of his troops or to harass the defenders of Jericho, remains conjectural. However, it appears the he was an intelligent general who used hit-and-run tactics against the enemy, relied on espionage and was adept at using musical instruments to the advantage of his army.

Another example of use of musical instruments in the ancient Middle East is from Egypt. Since olden times, close relationship of music and war is evidenced through prehistoric battle reliefs that prove the use of trumpeters in the times of Pharaohs. Such reliefs date back to around 1000 BC. It appears that the trumpets of Pharaohs were there to issue commands to the troops.

Ancient European Armies

Similarly, in ancient Greece armies on campaign employed musicians to accompany poetic recitations of odes designed to remind soldier and citizen alike of the valour of past heroes (Trotter 2005). The known records point to the musicians' presence in warfare during old City States of Greece as early as 7th century BC.

In the immediate two centuries before the Christ, armies in the Roman Empire are known to have employed large number of marching military musicians who used wind and percussion instruments—including the ancestors of the modern Cornet and Tuba—to convey information in camp, on the march and in the field. After the collapse of Rome in the West, its tradition of martial music was preserved and refined by the Byzantine empire in the East.

There was a time when present-day England had been a Roman colony. There was no shortage of such practices among Rome's Celtic enemies,[2] who for centuries charged—and later marched—into battle accompanied by their own array of horns, drums and bagpipes (Trotter 2005). The Celtic region more or less coincides with the present-day England and Scotland.

Ancient South and East Asian Armies

The ancient Indian continent seems to have known military Bands in warfare since ancient times. The religious book *Mahabharata* talks about *the war drums of gods sounded in the heavens,* meaning that even heavens knew of the drumbeat in warfare. Even during times of the Vedic Kings, drums along with the banners, were counted as Insignia of the monarchs. Indian military scholar P. C. Chakravarti, in his work on the art of war in ancient India writes about military marches:

Behind the travelling army was an entire host of rabble, retainers, servants, prostitutes, all led by the marching drum and the clamour of the masses (Chakravarti 2011).

About the Army in battlefield, he notes:

Great importance was given to positioning the army in the field according to the harmony of the ground. .... [T]here are many descriptions of the numerous battle formations used in the era. War drums thundered, music was played (drum, tambourine, trumpet, conch shell, horn, and lyre) (Chakravarti 2011).

Likewise, in olden China, the Tang dynasty which ruled during 7th to 10th centuries AD used Musical ensembles for signalling, imperial and military activities and ceremonies, raising fighting spirit in the troops before the battles and celebrating victory afterwards.

Use of Bands by Muslim and Arab Armies during Crusades

Sound of Saracens' kettledrums so disconcerted the Christians that they were compelled to cover the eyes and stop the ears of their horses.

—Henry G. Farmer

During the Crusade wars (1096–1272 A.D) the Arab and Islamic armies utilised a wide range of instruments such as reeds, shawms (a double reed instrument), pipes (bagpipes), bells, cymbals, and an entire family of drums. This gave them the capability of sounding complex signals to communicate tactical objectives and troop positions, provide a rallying point for dispersing troops, and inspired fear in the enemy (Farmer 1949).

First Two Crusades

Framer confirmed that the Christian armies were equipped with no more than trumpets and horns. Impressed by the Arabs' use of military Bands as both a means of instantly transmitting orders to distant formations and as a weapon of fear and affray, as Bartholomaeus Anglicus expressed it in the 13th century, the Christian knights soon emulated them. Before Crusades, Bands were not part of the battlefields, though music [not full-fledged Bands] was used both in Churches and in Courts (Farmer 1949).

Third Crusade and Beyond

As the Europeans were often embroiled in various feudal or religious conflicts, the use of martial music spread rapidly. Such music also acquired new modifications, as different soldiers, including those in the mercenary armies, adapted it to their local tastes and practical needs. In time for the third Crusade (1188–92), the European armies had got some finesse in using Bands music in combat against the Arab armies the concepts they had borrowed from the Muslims in the first place.

The earliest mention of instruments borrowed from Arabs against them in combat appears in *Itinerarum Regis Anglorum Ricardi*, which is a history of the reign of King Richard the Lionheart of England and his exploits in the Third Crusade. This work was published in 1648. In the *Itenerarum*, there is reference to trumpet calls being used to signal the start and recall of a Christian cavalry charge. (Trotter 2005) There were two famous battles fought between the Syrian King Salahuddin Ayubi (popularly known as Saladin to the West) and King Richard-I. It is not clear whether this reference was to the Battle of Asruf (1191) or the Battle of Jaffa (1192), both in present-day Syria, or both, where the European side made a debut in instrumental signalling for its cavalry.

Deployment of Bands by Ottoman Sultans during Warfare

> *Ottoman military Bands music is "so warlike, that even cowardly souls throw out their chests"*
>
> —Christian Schubart (German poet)

In the initial centuries, the fundamental role of Ottoman Bands remained as signalling. The Mehter marching Bands were brought to battlefield to issue commands to the fighting formations. The various drumbeats and bugle calls were deployed to command the troops to "march," "charge," or "halt." As more and more musical instruments were developed, louder and finer tunes could be played by the Bands. That led to another "first" of the Ottoman methodology of warfare: the Bands were deployed to boost the morale of the army by playing patriotic tunes. A parallel military use of the Ottoman Bands was that they were specifically brought to the battlefields to play loudly and instil fear in enemy troops.

Era of the Ottoman Sultanate (1289-1517)[3]

The *Mehter* were brought in the middle of the battle to inspire troops to give a final push to the enemy. A collective drum beat by 300 or so drummers together scared the opposite forces during the heat of the battle. The timing of bringing *Mehter* Bands into the battle was very important and used to be a carefully considered tactical decision in order to confuse, confound or terrify the enemy.

In addition, the *Mehter* Band used to play even at night on the battlefield to prevent the camp guards from falling asleep and as intimation to the enemy that the Ottoman military camp was vigilant.

In due course, the number of *Mehter* players rose to ten thousand, and some sources says, tens of thousands. There was a Military Bands Headquarter in the imperial capital of Constantinople, conquered by Sultan Mehmet the Conqueror in 1453. The *Mehterhane*, i.e. the House of *Mehter*, was a twelve-storey building and was the equivalent of the headquarters of a Corps of Music in a modern army.

During the seminal Battle of Chaldiran (1514) which brought a decisive victory of the Ottomans against the Safavid Empire, Sultan Selim I added the *Kös* (a giant timpani or kettledrum) to frighten the enemy Iranian troops. The Janissaries shouted, "God is one!" in unison along with beat of the Drums. The Safavid King Ismail was wounded and defeated. This started an era of Ottoman supremacy, which through a serious of subsequent wars and treaties, continued till the dissolution of the Ottoman Caliphate in early 20th century.

Another epoch making Battle of the time of Sultan Selim, where Bands were central to strategy, was the Battle of Marj Dabiq in 1516, North of the present city of Aleppo, in modern Syria. This was the decisive defeat of the Mamluk dynasty of Egypt. The following year, Sultan Selim-I forced the last Abbasid Caliph, who lived in Cairo as a puppet of the Mamluk dynasty, to transfer the mantle of Caliphate to him. This founded the Ottoman Caliphate which lasted till 1924. In the Battle of Mar Dabiq, the Sultan had brought 200 *Mehter* Bands in the war theatre. This Battle ushered in the era of Caliphate for the Turks where Bands continued to be pivotal in the tactics and strategy for war (BMB 2017).

Era of the Ottoman Caliphate (1517-1924)

The military *Mehter* Bands symbolised the sovereignty of the Ottoman state. When German poet Christian Schubart heard a *Mehter* group playing in Europe in the mid-1700s, he wrote the comment, given in the beginning of this section, that their music was so warlike and terrifying (Campbell 2012). The powerful stirring music of Mehter has a spirit which one can appreciate even today when listening to it.

How much these Bands contributed to each Ottoman victory is not known. However, the very fact that the Ottomans continued to bring their Bands into the battlefields for several centuries is a testimony to the fact that reliance was placed on their efficacy in warfare. The Ottoman Caliph, Sultan Sulaiman the

Magnificent, brought Bands in to the siege of Vienna in 1529 (BMB 2017). One and a half century later, another of his descendant, Ottoman Caliph, Sultan Mehmet IV, brought the Bands to the same city in the last abortive attempt by Ottomans to capture it in 1683. After their failure to take Vienna again, the withdrawing Ottoman forces could not take heavier and bigger Band instruments back home, which were seized by Austro-Hungarian troops. This is one of the incidents that is believed to have contributed to the advent of full-fledged Bands in Western royal courts.

During this latter period, the concept of playing in the layers also emerged. The Band team would perform in 3, 5, 7 or 9 layers. A layer of three would mean there are three instruments of each kind, while a layer of five would mean that there are five instruments of each kind, and so on. Discipline is the main rule of their practice. Gait and march was conducted by *Amir e Azam* (Seargeant Major) while *Mehterbasi* (Master of the Band) would conduct the sounds and music (BMB 2017). He was assisted by *Aga* for each type of instruments. In other words, every layer would have a Chief who would be responsible to the Bandmaster.

Role of Bands during British Imperial Wars

Beat them in their own damned tune.

—Order of Duke of York to the British Army
in the Battle of Famars (1793)

Bands have been used during British imperial wars both by the British themselves as well as their rivals for at least three centuries. The British military Bandsmen, like their peers from the opposite forces, have shown exceptional valour during the battles. In some parts of the world, a customary practice had developed of not deliberately targeting each other's Bandsmen, especially when both sides had brought Bands into the battlefield. However, Bandsmen were mercilessly slaughtered where one side did not rely on Bands and the other side's music offended or scared them. Thus, British army can note the enormous sacrifices its military Bands have made over time.

British Imperial Wars in Scotland and America

Till the 18th century, the English troops were not well versed with the use of military Bands. In fact, they learnt this art from their adversaries, such as the Bagpipe music from the Scots during Anglo–Scottish wars. Bagpipes formed an integral part of Prince Charles Edward Stuart's Scottish army against the British. Following his defeat in 1746, the English were so incensed with the Scottish

Bagpipes, that all Scottish Band instruments were outlawed in England (Trotter 2005). However, it did not take the English army long to realise their need for their own Infantry Regiments. The ban was soon reversed and these instruments made their way into British army, especially the Scottish regiments of the British empire.

Thirty years later, during the American war of independence (1775-83), the British regiments were regularly using Military Bands against the continental army in the New World. The British music was found offensive and insulting by the Americans who were first introduced to the bugle horn (forerunner to the modern bugle) during the Battle of Harlem Heights (1776), near the present day Manhattan (New York). The Adjutant General of the continental army, Col Joseph Reed would, in a letter to his wife, later recall, "the enemy appeared in open view, and sounded their bugles in a most insulting manner, as is usual after a fox chase. I never felt such a sensation before—it seemed to crown our disgrace" (Reed 1776).

British Imperial Wars in Africa

Almost a century later, and in another continent Africa, the British found themselves embroiled in a number of armed conflicts where Bands found themselves in action as an essential component of warfare. Take the Anglo-Ashanti Wars, in West Africa, for instance, which were a series of five conflicts. They were fought during the 19th century between the Ashanti Empire, in the interior of the Gold Coast (now Ghana) and the invading British Empire and their-allied African chieftains. During the third Anglo-Ashanti War, the Black Watch regiment led the attack on the imperial capital of Kumasi (1874). The regimental Band played *The Campbells Are Coming,* rousing the fury of the Scotsmen to charge into the bushes with bayonets, making the shocked Ashantis flee. The capital Kumasi was then destroyed by British troops (Watson 1915).

Five years later and in another corner of Africa, the British empire's expansionism dragged them into the Anglo Zulu war. The Battle of Isandlwana that took place on 22 January 1879 was the first major encounter of the war between the British Empire and the Zulu Kingdom. Eleven days after the British commenced their invasion of Zululand in South Africa, a Zulu force of some 20,000 warriors attacked a portion of the British main column consisting of about 1,800 British, colonial and native troops. It was one of the worst defeats of the British forces in Africa with 1,300 of them were slaughtered. Among those to be ruthlessly killed were the non-combatant drummer boys, some as young as 16, of the Bands of first and second 24th Regiment whose bodies were reportedly mutilated and "then hooked and opened like sheep" (Knight 2004).

The British Bands were there in South Africa to stay for a long time. A couple of decades later, come the Boer war, and Bands were in action again. Out of the Boer War came such fabulous tunes as *Goodbye Dolly Gray* and *Marching to Pretoria.*

British Imperial Wars in Asia

The stories of valour by Bandsmen, of course, were not limited to the British side. During the colonisation of Indian subcontinent, instances of the bravery by the Pakhtoon Bandsmen (North Western tribal frontiers, now in Pakistan) have been well recorded by British writers in their reports and books. British Officers Captain YounghusBand and Colonel Sir Francis write in their recollections of the expedition as follows:

> *"Of the enemy's bravery it is difficult to speak too highly, and individual cases were conspicuous. More desperate courage than this is difficult to imagine. Again, one of the enemy's drummers, not content with taking his fair share of risks, perished in mounting on to the roof of a hut, where he showed up clear and conspicuous against the sky line, and hence cheered on his comrades. Every now and again, a bullet would find him out and he would drop to dress his wounds, and then again mounting re-commenced beating his drum. At last a bullet got him through the heart, and he fell headlong a hundred yards down the cliff, and there lay stark dead, but with his drum round his neck, and his arms ready raised to strike it. (YounghusBand 1910)*

Likewise, during the Boxer rebellion in China at the turn of the 20th century, the locals had attacked anyone and anything European or Christian. The famous Kansu Braves, an almost exclusive Muslim Army from the central province of Kansu (now Gansu) that was defending the imperial capital of Peking (now Beijing) was known to have modern Western-style military Bands. But during the war frenzy hatred towards the Westerners was so pathological that their Commander General Dong Fuxiang had outlawed using any British or British sounding tune.

Bands taking part in European Continental Wars

Let the Thunder of Victory Sound!

From the middle of the 18th century well into the start of the second half of the 19th century, the Military Bands were used in almost all the continental wars in Europe including the Turco Russian Wars, the Anglo French Wars, the Napoleonic wars and others. In the latter period, the technique and armament became more advanced. Due to denser fire and quicker manoeuvrability of the army in the late 19th century, bringing of military Bands directly into the Battlefields perforce became limited all over Europe.

Turco-Russian Wars

I seized the Ismail fortress with unfolded banners and loud music

—General Suvorov

The Count of the Holy Roman Empire and one of the most prominent Russian war heroes, Alexander Suvorov (1730–1800), referred to his 1791 victory over the Ottoman Fortress of Ismail (on River Danube, in present day Western Ukraine) by emphasising the important role of Russian military Bands in the conquest. He said, "Music doubles and triplicates the army. I seized the Ismail fortress with unfolded banners and loud music". The Battle for Ismail was an important turning point during the Russo–Turkish War of 1787–1792. Although the fortress was returned to the Ottomans under the peace treaty at the end of the war, but at that time the victory was so important for Russia that it was glorified in the country's first national anthem, "Let the thunder of victory sound!"

Anglo-French Wars

If ye shall want music, they'll have my soul.

—Dying British Bandsman in the Battle of Vimiera (1808)

In this regard, an incident from the Anglo–French War 1793 is revealing as far as the importance of Bands in the battlefields is concerned. In the Battle of Famars (1793), the French Band was playing revolutionary tune "*Ca Ira*" while the troops were fighting. British Commander-in-Chief, the then Duke of York, was so incensed by this that he ordered his Band to "beat them in their own Band tune". The Band of the 14th Royal Lincolnshire Regiment complied and started playing *Ca Ira* as good as their French rivals were playing. Eventually, the British won the battle. The Duke of York ordered *Ca Ira* to be the quick march tune for the Yorkshire regiment which continues to this day.

Just 15 years down the road, in the Battle of Vimiera (21 August 1808), military Bands performed in the heat of the battle. The village of Vimeiro near Lisbon, Portugal, was the site of a fierce clash between the British and the French during the Peninsula War. The British Force commanded by General Arthur Wellesley (later known as the Duke of Wellington) defeated the French under Major-General Jean-Andoche Junot. This battle put an end to the first French invasion of Portugal. The stories of valour of Bandsmen in the battle resound to this day. British Piper George Clark, badly wounded in the groin while playing his company forward, continued his tune while stretched bleeding on the battleground. He continued to play till his last breath remarking, "If ye shall want music, they'll have my soul."

Napoleonic Wars

> *In Russia, I have two enemies: the cold frost and the Russian military Bands.*
>
> —Napoleon Bonaparte

It is said that the battle of Austerlitz (1805) in which Napoleon was victorious over the combined armies of Austria and Russia, was due in part to the psychological impact of the noise of his military fanfare Bands in the battlefield. Russians took this defeat seriously and within seven years when Napoleon miscalculated by invading Russia, the latter employed military music to the fullest potential against France.

In fact, development of Russian military music in early 19th century was mostly defined by this resistance to the invasion of Napoleon I of France in 1812. In Russian history, this is known as the "Patriotic War" and the tunes Bands played during military marches became the symbols of the courage of the Russian army. The patriotic impulse and increasing sense of national identity due to the war against Napoleon were brightly manifested in military music. A variety of patriotic music works appeared, such as the marches of Kozlovsky, Titov, Kavos, Antonolini, Derfeld and others. During the second quarter of the 19th century, the music of Dargomyzhsky, Glinka, Alyabyev and some others reached full blossom It was then that the first steps towards creating original music works for brass Bands were made. Russian government military websites attribute the statement to Napoleon, mentioned above, that his defeat owed, at least in part, to the Russian military music.

Usage of Bands in warfare on the American continent

> *Play gayest tunes in your books, play them loud and keep playing them, never mind if a bullet goes through a Trombone or Trombonist now and then.*
>
> —Order by Union Gen Philip Sheriden during Civil War (1865)

The Bands were used in all the wars in the new world, i.e. the American continent from the War of Independence (1775–83), Anglo-US War (1812–14), American Civil War (1861–65) right up to the later Indian Wars (1870s to 1890s) in the final decades of the century and the America–Spain War (1898) just before the turn of the 20th century. During this century and a half, the Bands gradually moved into a trajectory towards Brass music—tradition that was borrowed from their counterparts in Europe. That is to say that in the independence war, the Bands were almost exclusively Pipe Bands while by the time of the Civil war, brass instruments had become universally adopted by all sides.

The Military Bandsmen gave their share of suffering and sacrifices in the War. For instance, by the beginning of the First World War, the Military Musicians in the United States Army had already earned no less than 32 Medals of Honor, also called the Congressional Medal of Honor, which is the highest Award for individual acts of gallantry in US Army to date.

The American War of Independence (1775-83)

During the revolutionary war, the drummers and fifers were used in battle to signal the soldiers to fire as visual command was not practicable in the hazy battle fog. Over all, these Military Bands did play an important role in military victories. In the Battle of Bennington (1777), the American commander, Colonel John Stark, had his fifers and drummers play into the very teeth of the enemy. His troops, inspired and stimulated, proceeded to defeat British General Burgoyne's forces so decisively that this battle became an important turning point in the war.

The US Maj. Gen. Wilhelm von Steuben compiled the first American Soldiers' Manual that was issued to the Continental Army in 1778; it contained a list of beats and signals modelled on those used in European armies. Each company had its own field musicians, one fifer and one drummer, to provide the daily signals telling the soldiers to wake up, eat, and go to bed. For more formal occasions such as visit by a General, all the drummers and fifers of a regiment gathered to create the larger fife and drum corps. The Drummers were also used to summon people from rural areas to take up arms against the British.

The Anglo-US War (1812-14)

The movement towards Brass started during the Anglo-US War of 1812, when Bugles were introduced as the third compliment to the Fifes and Drums within the United States army. Bugles, first used in England around 1800s, are brass instruments characterised by a conical bore tubing, usually wound once around wide bells. Cavalry units in the United States were the first to adopt the bugle for their field signals but Infantry units followed suit by the end of the century. Many of the calls originally performed on drums were adopted as bugle calls. This is why these Bugle calls are still called "Taps"; originally named for the action of the drummer playing on his drum. By the end of the Anglo–American War (1812–14), Bugle sounding had replaced the fifes and drums for signals. The bugler was always positioned by the side of his commander to convey his commands promptly.

The first military Band of New York City was organised in 1810 and offered its services to the 11th Regiment of the New York Militia. It was stationed at Bledsoe's Island in the New York Harbor, near the present site of the Statue of Liberty. Militia Bands became a common sight during the Anglo–American war and the Pipes and Drum Corps got replaced by Bugle and Drum Corps in America, which exist to this day.

In 1830, General Winfield Scott headed a board to prepare a manual of infantry tactics for the Army. Drummers and Bands were given a place in the regimental order of battle. For example, the Manual required the drummers to be "ten paces in the rear of the left center company." The pay for enlisted Bandsmen was now $17.00 per month for the chief musician and $8.00 per month for each Bandsman.

The American Civil War (1861-65)

By the start of the Civil War, many towns and villages had already got their own Bands, and often sent them along with their militia units. The Bands, like the young fighting soldiers, were a symbol of pride for communities large and small across the North and the South.

As soon as the War broke out there was an urgent need for a much greater number of Military Bands than what were existing. Frantic Band recruitment drives were initiated which were so successful that within 1861, the number of Bands with the Union Army alone had touched 618 with more than 16,500 musicians. If the Confederate Bands are conservatively estimated at between 300 and 350, they might have had over 10,000Band members. The total might be a thousand Bands with around 27,000 soldiers performing musical duties.

The first Band to suffer casualties during the Civil War was the 6th Massachusetts Regiment Band. On April 19, 1861, the Band arrived by train in Baltimore, Maryland. As the Band left the station, a mob marching through the street attacked the Band. The Band fled, aBandoning all equipment, as local Union sympathisers took Band members into their houses. The Band suffered 4 deaths and 30 injured in the melee.

How important were the Bands for the soldiers can be gauged from the letter of a young South Carolina private. After an especially rousing concert in 1861, at the outset of the American Civil War, he wrote: "I have never heard or seen such a time before. The noise of the men was deafening. I felt at the time that I could whip a whole brigade of the enemy myself!" (Trotter 2005).

During the war, the duties of Union Bands varied. They performed concerts, parades, reviews, and guard mount ceremonies for encamped troops. They also drummed soldiers out of the Army and performed for funerals and executions. The Bands played for troops marching into battle, actually performing concerts in forward positions during the fighting. The martial and patriotic music the Bands performed frightened the enemy and rallied soldiers to victory. Bands were stationed at major military hospitals lifting the morale of suffering soldiers.

Bandsmen's days were busy. Buglers sounded calls throughout the day. The musicians sounded the call for guard mounting at eight in the morning each day. Some regiments held dress parades twice a day, but most staged these events in conjunction with retreat ceremonies when regimental or brigade Bands provided the music.

Performing under fire became commonplace for Bands under the command of General Philip H. Sheridan. Sheridan loved music and took a personal interest in his Bands. This was shown in the equipment, mounts, and uniforms he accorded his Bandsmen. Army Bandsmen's pay was substantially higher during the Civil War than previous years. The chief musician received $45.00 per month while senior most Bandsmen received $35.00, which compared favourably than what their seniors got a generation ago, in 1830s as noted above. To pay for these privileges, the Bands performed at the front. On an occasion, General Horace Porter once "encountered one of Sheridan's Bands, under heavy fire, playing Nellie Bly as cheerily as if it were furnishing music for a country picnic."

Despite these salaries, the musicians were by no means overpaid when their high casualty rate is taken into account. A reference to the record of the 125th Ohio Regimental Band (known as the Tiger Band) shows that only 10 of the original 36 members of this organization could still be accounted for at the end of the war in 1865. General Sheridan paid tribute to Army Bands when he remarked, "Music has done its share, and more than its share, in winning this war."

From the American Civil War we gained such endearing songs as *Marching Through Georgia*; *John Brown's Body*; and *When Johnny Comes Marching Home*, which have been immortalized by the Military Bands of the United States to this day. For acts of valour during the civil war, 20 musicians of military Bands got the highest gallantry award Congressional Medal of Honor.

One of the impacts of the American Civil War on the Military Bands was that the bugle had replaced the fife and drum ensemble in the American ranks, much more quickly than in Europe. Shortly after the end of the Civil War, in 1867, "bugle calls" for the U.S. Armed Forces, mostly patterned after French models, were codified and standardised into a form that largely survives today.

The final stage of American Indian Wars (1875-90)

The American Indian Wars is the name given to a series of campaigns against native American population—called the Indians—throughout US history up to the 1924. The Bands were part of many expeditions and showed exemplary courage. Ten of their 32 Medals of Honor were won by the Bandsmen during the Indian Wars. For instance, Trumpeter John E. Clancy, Light Battery E, First Artillery, received the Medal of Honor for his actions at Wounded Knee Creek massacre on 29 December 1890.

The American Spanish War (1898)

Spanish American War was triggered after the explosion in *USS Maine* at the harbour in Havana. The US Constitution gives the Congress the sole power to declare War which it has exercised five time in history against eleven sovereign states. This war with Spain was one of them, the other four being the Anglo-US War of 1812, the Mexico–US War of 1846 and the two World Wars.

The Spanish war was the first time when field musicians were taken at the war front, away from the US mainland. Although every infantry regiment maintained a Band at that time, most of the duties the Bandsmen performed in this war were non-musical. Yet, quite a few Bandsmen displayed bravery enough to be recommended for the Medal of Honor. For instance, while at the front at Santiago, Musician Herman Phisterer, from H-Company of the 21st Infantry Regiment, earned the Medal of Honor for assisting in the rescue of wounded in front of the lines while under heavy fire. Musician Oscar N. Oden, Troop 1, 10th Colored Cavalry, was also recommended for the Medal of Honor, but received a Certificate of Merit, for his actions at San Juan. He continually exposed himself to heavy fire to obtain the exact range of the Spanish position.

Military Bands and the First World War

The World War I (1914-18) had enormous influence on military and war music and the Military Bands culture in general. The lyrics and the tunes of *It's a Long Way to Tipperary, Pack Up Your Troubles* and *Keep the Home-fires Burning*, to name but a few, have been indelible gifts of the brutal war to human senses, culture and memory. All these historic songs, and especially their tunes, have become immortalized by the military Bands of the participating nations. The section below is divided into the role of the Military Bands and the Pop Bands during the World War I.

Military Bands in World War I

The military Bands played a great role during the war effort and some writers have gone to the extent of claiming that their role in defeat of Germany was pivotal (Dean 2016). Still, the role of military Bands has remained unnoticed, unappreciated and unrecognised in most historical accounts of the World War. In this section, we will discuss the role of US, Russian, British, French and Italian Military Bands during the First World War.

American Military Bands: The World War I is credited with triggering an irreversible popularity of African-American Music within the United States in general and in its Armed Forces in particular, as well as for introducing Jazz Music to Europe—all because of Military Bands.

The United States remained aloof from the World War in the initial years while it continued to boost its military capacity, in the event it was dragged into war. Bands were considered a necessary component of military capacity to the extent that in 1916, the US Congress passed a bill to establish Bands for the headquarters companies of infantry, cavalry, and artillery regiments, as well as the Corps of Engineers. After the US entered World War I in 1917, General Pershing was appointed as Commander of Allied Expeditionary Forces (AEF). He believed that military Bands were a key element in maintaining the morale of his soldiers. After he arrived in Europe, he convinced Congress to authorise 20 additional Bands. He also increased the strength of each Band from 28 members to 48. In order to train Bandsmen who were sent to Europe in haste, and could not be trained in US proper, he established a Band school in Chaumont, France, to train Bandmasters and musicians.

The United States entered the First World War on April 6, 1917. As General Pershing led two million US troops to fight in Europe, there were over 50 Bands that were sent on duty to the war theatre with him. This US entry into European theatres led to, among other things, mobilisation of 27 African-American regiments to augment the US Army's existing four black regiments. To create Regimental

Bands of these Units, the US Armed Forces experienced a great influx of professional civilian musicians from the Clubs of New York and Chicago. Experienced Jazz and Blues musicians, from African-American community, were the pioneer Bandmasters of the newly formed regimental Bands.

The greatest name among such Band Masters was James Reese, who was a Lieutenant in the all-Black 369th Infantry Regiment. This great Jazz leader and composer was tasked to head the Band of the regiment, also called the "Harlem Hell-fighters." This name was given to the regiment by the German adversaries since the Regiment "never lost a soldier to capture or a foot to the trench." The success of the regiment led to change of public perception about African-American units in the army and laid the foundation of racial equality in the US Armed Forces. What is less appreciated, however, is the role of the Harlem Hell-Fighters' Band. This Band is credited with introducing jazz to Europe. The Hell Fighters Band performed at forward locations for the US and allied troops and is credited with boosting the morale of the Allied Forces.

Lieut. James Reese, much before joining the military, had founded an organization for African-American musicians, called the Clef Club, back in 1910 in New York. Barely 20 years old and a civilian at that time, Reese was a prominent figure on American music scene of the time. His Clef Club graduated into a 125-strong Orchestra that would eventually perform for all-White audiences at Carnegie Hall. Unlike smaller Jazz Bands at the time where musicians improvised their own music, James Reese's Orchestra performed music strictly composed by him with no room for improvisation. When the First World War started and the US involvement became increasingly imminent, he was amongst those to volunteer for the army. He then led the musical initiative into the war theatre. The Band of 369th Regiment moved with troops closer to the fighting and played to boost the morale.

The 369th Regiment returned to America after the war and led the victory parade on the streets of New York on 12 February 1919. The Band then made a national tour of the country holding concerts for the public till their last concert in Boston on May 9 of the same year. Tragically, the same night a heated argument with a Drummer of his Band led to Reese being stabbed to death, at the age of 29. Lieut. James Reese became the first African-American to be given a ceremonial public funeral in New York. The legacy of 369th Regiment Band outlives him to this day.

Russian Military Bands: On the Russian side, their military Bands, with experience from their role in Russio-Japan war, actively participated in the military operations during the First World War. According to the Russian military website, many Russian military musicians perished in battles. Many distinguished military units were often awarded Silver Trumpets of St George. After the October revolution of 1917, the Soviet government withdrew from the world war, During the peace that followed, the Russian military Bands concentrated on military training and the numerous parades honouring the Red revolution.

British, French and Italian Military Bands: On 4 August 1914, the Band of the Coldstream Guards was playing at Wakefield, UK, when its Director of Music was informed that the declaration of War was due by 11 pm that night. Band Director Capt John Rogan addressed the people gathered around Bandstand appealing them to enlist in army. All joined in singing *Rule Britannia* and *God Save the King.*

When the First World War started, there were four regiments of Foot Guards and three regiments of Household Cavalry within the British Military force, that already had Bands. When Welsh Guards were raised in 1915, the raising of its Band was considered a wartime priority, which demonstrated the value placed on musical contribution to war effort.

A few months into the war, in early 1915, the Guards Bands volunteered to go to the warfront to play for troops. After some procrastination, the British Government ordered the Band of Grenadier Guards to proceed to France to play for the troops. The Bands would meet the battalions returning from trenches with patriotic tunes and then play marching tunes for battalions replacing them. Capt. Rogan's Band saw a battalion returning from the warfront with soldiers wearing haggard looks due to fatigue, and each bent by the weight of carrying 80 pound kits. Hardly anyone was expecting a Band to welcome them. With the first tap of Bass Drum, there were cheers from the soldiers which could be heard miles away. It appeared that their fatigue had vanished in the air. The morale was lifted by the pleasant surprise. The Band continued to play until they settled in their barracks.

Likewise, for units moving towards the forward trenches the Bands would march with them up to five miles to raise their morale and spirits. The Welsh regiment, for example, reached the ruined village of Méaulte in France when they were amazed to see Welsh Regiment Band waiting for them at the roadside to play them in. Since the Band was raised and trained after the Regiment had already left for the war front, this was the first occasion for the troops to see their own regimental Band play for them.

In Paris, four Bands of British Guard regiments were augmented by the Guard Bands from France and Italy. All these Bands played for the citizens, throughout much of 1916, to lift their morale. The following year, the King of Italy requested allied countries to send military Bands to play at Milan, Florence and Rome. Since, the US had also joined World War I by 1917, so the American military Band joined the French and British Bands in the odyssey across cities in Italy where the host countries' army Bands joined them. It was a feat of public diplomacy never seen before. The Pope expressed the desire to meet all Roman Catholic musicians in the military Bands of the four nations at Vatican (Dean 2016). The Bandsmen were elated to be given audience by the Pope.

The military Bands continued to perform near the fronts placing themselves in harm's way in order to enliven their fellow soldiers in the fighting units. Even in the final months of the war, Bands continued to face casualties. In one of the incidents in France, on 21 August 1918, a shell fired by the German forces pierced through the ceiling of the shed in which the Band was about to perform, resulting in losses for the British Band.

Pop Bands in World War I

As far as Europe was concerned, Great Britain is a typical example of the musical legacy of the great war. At the outbreak of war, pop Bands produced songs which called for young men to join up. Examples included *We Don't Want to Lose You, but We Think You Ought to Go*, *Now You've Got the Khaki On* or *Kitchener's Boys*. It was a matter of months when death toll rose astronomically that the recruitment music all but disappeared. By the 1915 "Greatest Hits" collection published by Francis & Day did not have a single recruitment song. Rather the Music Hall pop songs which mentioned the war (about a third of the total produced) were more and more dreams about the end of the war—*Keep the Home Fires Burning* and *When the Boys Come Home* are two well-known examples.

Since it was almost impossible in the United Kingdom and its colonies for any pop Band to sing anti-war songs on the stage for fear of prosecution for treason, the managers of music halls were in a quandary. Rising death tolls had brought a general war weariness among the public. The stage managers needed pop songs which would be instant hit with the audience but feared license cancellation in case an anti-war performance was presented. So dissent about the war drive was expressed through sarcastic songs such as *Oh It's a Lovely War* or bitter complaints about conscription like in the lyrics of *The Military Representative*.

However, this must not give an impression that all non-Military music of

World War I was anti-War. Popular, patriotic music was composed in bulk that served to raise the morale of soldiers and civilians alike. The Pop Bands sang a variety of themes, such as separation of loved ones, adventures in war as well as humorous songs about the military life.

The United States had not been in the war in the initial years so it was more tolerant of anti-war Music. Pop Bands sang the likes of *I Didn't Raise My Boy to be a Soldier* at public meetings but Opera owners did not risk allowing Pop Bands to sing such-like lyrics on Music Hall Stage. Despite the public sentiment about War and pacifist disposition of President Wilson himself, the United States did eventually get dragged into war in 1917. From that day on, the mood of Pop songs changed and the tolerance of the Government towards any Band that would play anti-war songs reached its limits.

Since there were no radios or televisions that reported the conditions of the battlefields, Americans had a romantic view of war. Not only were many of the songs patriotic, but they were also romantic. These songs portrayed soldiers, who were mostly men, as brave and noble, while the women stereotypes of being weak and loyal as they waited for their loved ones, were also reinforced. This would all change in the Second World War as we will discuss in the next Chapter.

The German side also ordered composition of popular music in support of the war effort. The German Government did not show any leniency towards a music that did not go well with the State's narrative. On top of patriotic music promoting love for Germany, some of the songs contained pathological hatred for their rivals, such as the hymn by Ernst Lissauer:

> *We will never forgo our hate*
> *We have but one single hate*
> *We love as one, we hate as one,*
> *We have one foe, and one alone*
> *England!*

Conclusion

History is rich in instance of singing soldiers, marching bagpipers and military Bands colouring the morale of troops and implanting dismay in their enemy. During the peacetimes, the main objective of martial tunes for the infantry is to promote orderly marching, enliven the spirit, and minimise fatigue and boredom. They also inspire the troops to fight and carry out orders and commands. This role is continuing to this day at a larger scale.

However, due to the advent of internet, smartphones and modern telecommunication the world has changed so much today that it is difficult to imagine how a song like *Over There* could, to quote just one example, become such a powerful motivator of patriotism during the World War I. This underscores the point that in addition to the Military Bands, performing for troops on the war front, the pop music back home had its role in keeping the population motivated. Most historians of popular culture agree that World War II's pop songs were curiously inferior to those of World War I—few outlived their brief moment, and most have become dated to the point of embarrassment—which is scarcely the case with pop music of the First World War (Trotter 2005).

However, the greater role of military music as "an effective means by which states could manipulate the morale, energies and attitudes of armies and indeed entire populations" remained important till the middle of the 20th century, well beyond the end of the Second World War (Trotter 2005). Future conventional wars will no doubt give birth to more enduring melody. This role of Military Music may never end.

NOTES

1 Joshua is a central figure in the Hebrew Bible (Book of Yohua) who was a trusted lieutenant of Prophet Moses and became the leader of Israelite tribes after the prophet's death. Joshua is a highly respected figure in the Islamic thought. Most believe him to be a Prophet and is known as Hazrat Yush'e Ibn Noon. Many Muslims also believe him to be the "attendant" of Moses mentioned in the Qur'an, before Moses meets the legendary saint—named in Quran as—Khidr.

2 The Celtic nations are territories in western Europe where Celtic languages or cultural traits have survived. The six territories widely considered Celtic nations are Brittany (Breizh), Cornwall (Kernow), Wales (Cymru), Scotland (Alba), Ireland (Éire) and the Isle of Man (Mannin or Ellan Vannin). In each of the six nations a Celtic language is spoken.

3 The starting date of the period (1289) marks the first major victory of founder of Ottoman dynasty Osman Ghazi over the Seljuk Sultan Keykubad III. The latter is said to have gifted a Band to his Victor. The Ottomans may have founded the first band of their own in the year 1326 in the city of Bursa [*See* Chapter II} During this period, the Ottoman empire had not laid claim to Caliphate [the spiritual and temporal leadership of the Muslim World], which Sultan Selim I did in 1517. The Ottoman Caliphate lasted till the fall of dynasty after the First World War.

CHAPTER IX

Second World War & Bands in Modern Warfare

I do not believe that any nation that would go to war without a Band would stand a chance of winning.

—John Philip Sousa

John Philip Sousa, composer of USA's most famous marches, including the unofficial theme song of Independence Day *The Stars and Stripes Forever*, underscored music's power in warfare by saying that every great army since ancient times had relied on it. "You want something to put pep in a man, to make him fight," he said, adding the above quote about the impossibility of winning a war without a Band (Philipps 2016). The quote was obviously in reference to the signalling role of Military Bands in the battlefields up to the 19th century. But as telecommunication technology was revolutionized, their role in warfare did not diminish. Regular Military Bands were in action in the First World War as they were in the Second. Yet, by the latter war, cinema had been invented and so was Radio; both the media were relied upon heavily to motivate the citizenry. Radio would broadcast military music and songs to the soldiers on the front lines far, far away.

The pep that Sousa talks about became all the more essential as the firepower of modern weaponry became deadlier than earlier generations. The Second World War, which is considered as the first major example of the Third Generation Warfare, saw the revival of the tradition of bringing back the Military Bands close to the front lines, to motivate the troops. In fact, what we now understand as the Third Generation Warfare, is rooted in the German manoeuvres of the final months of the World War I, though most of that war was fought on Second Generation tactics. The importance of Bands continued as long as the third generation warfare continued. Band Music, both military and popular, remained important during the Cold War and both the Western and Eastern blocs relied on it, as a weapon in different ways.

Regional conflict zones had their input in the world of Military Music in different ways. South Asia has long witnessed a military standoff between two nuclear powers India and Pakistan while the Middle East has been the theatre of Arab Israeli conflict. How the State and the Military has used and created music for, and due to, the wars is interesting study. While Military forces lost men and material in the warfare, the military Bands got enriched by the music created by the adversity of war and sacrifice. Some of the music so created owes to the silver screen. From the theatres of the Cold War, like Korea, Vietnam and Afghanistan, to the regional conflicts, including the aforementioned ones, Cinemas glorified and romanticized the wars but also helped create a lot of music that was eventually immortalized by military Bands.

In this chapter, we will explore the military Bands of the Second World War, the role of Military Bands, during and owing to, the Cold War and its ancillary wars such as Korean and the Vietnam Wars, and finally, the Military Music generated by the regional conflicts in two conflict-afflicted regions of the Middle East and the Indo-Pakistan subcontinent.

Bands in the Second World War

During World War II, both military and non-military Bands were used by all sides as part of the war effort: allied powers including United States and the Soviet Union and the Axis powers including Nazi Germany and Japan. Unlike the World War I, we have some written accounts of the role of Military Bands in the World War II written by the Bandleaders. Major James Howe of Scots Guards wrote *A Conductor's Journey*, Lt Col Andrew Brown of Argyll & Sutherland Highlanders was the author of *From Music to War* and to the credit of Band Sergeant-Major Bill Grainger is *The Life and Times of the Bands of the King's Own Yorkshire Light Infantry*. These works helped the world understand the impact of Band Music during the Second World War.

The Second World War brought a number of innovations in the culture and composition of Bands. The first Air Bands (even though Air Force had not been established as a separate arm), the first Women-only Bands, and the Civilian Orchestra Bands for war-related musical duties, are some of the important impacts of the War on the Bands culture. This reliance on civilian Bands and orchestras is important from the Allied side, since the American and British governments could, for the most part, count on popular music reflecting much of the same war aims that the government wanted. Never mind, popular music had its downside too that needs to be noted: there was anti-war music available, some sarcastic music ridiculing government position as well as certain hate music about the enemy, all of which was in bad taste.

We shall review the role of Bands in the Second World War in three areas, namely, the Military Bands at or near the front lines (including their non-Musical duties), the Orchestra Bands back home for the civilians, the Pop Bands of various kinds, and finally, transmission of War Music through radio broadcasting.

Military Bands in World War II

During the World Wars II, the Military Bands that earned fame for wartime duties included the 82nd Airborne Division Band, the 101st Airborne Division Band and the 1st Infantry Division Band. All these Bands got decorations for meritorious services. From the US side, the tunes which made history, include *Ev'ry Times We Say Goodbye* composed by Cole Peter (1944); *I'll Be Seeing You,* music by Sammy Fain; *I'll Walk Alone* by Martha Tilton, and many others. The tune of *Colonel Bogey's March* became marching tunes for 50 different armies of the World.

The Bandsmen from all fighting nations offered their blood in the war. For example, for the Military Bands Service of the British Armed Forces, by the end of the World War II, 225 of their ranks had been killed in action, which was a quarter of their strength. Ratio-wise, after the Bomber Command, this was the highest percentage of losses for any branch of any Service in the Royal Armed Forces. We will look at the American, British and Soviet Military Bands one by one.

The US Military Bands: The United States alone utilized the services of approximately 500 military Bands. They were categorized into three types: special Bands, separate Bands, and organization Bands, which has already been discussed above in the chapter on classification of Bands. The Bands performed musical and non-musical duties with distinction. It may be noted that funding constraints had forced the closure of the only Army Band School in 1928, and till 1941, when the Pearl Harbor attack dragged the United States into the World War, there was no Band School for the army in the whole country.

In order to meet the musical requirements of a large army, the United States War Department established an emergency Army Music School which started crash courses of three months duration to train maximum number of Bandsmen to be sent to war duty. In June 1941, the Department of the Army established a separate school for Bandmasters at the Army War College. Soon after, the school was relocated to Fort Myer, Virginia (Music 2005).

On July 20, 1942, the first contingent of women was inducted into the Women's Army Auxiliary Corps (WAAC) at Fort Des Moines, Iowa. By early 1943, five Bands, the 400th Army Band, 401st Army Band, 402nd Army Band, 403rd Army Band, and the 404th Army Band were composed entirely of women. On January 21, 1944, WAAC Bands were later re-designated and officially activated in the Women's Army Corps (WAC) (Music 2005).

The women's participation in War and their exclusive representation, at least, in some of the Military Bands companies, brought about a sea change in military and public perception of women. Unlike the image of a fragile, docile woman during the First World War, this time an equality of sexes was becoming a reality in the military and popular cultures. Just like WW-I Military Bands brought Blacks and Whites on equal footing, the WW-II made the men and women equal in public perception. And in both instances, military Bands had played a role in this perception transformation

The Military Bands took part in the D-Day landing. Both British and American troops were complemented by the Bands. Cornetist Jimmy McPartland figures prominently amongst the military musicians who landed on D-Day with the US infantry. The 28th Infantry Division Band made history during the Battle of Bulge in the Second World War. The Battle of Bulge, was the last major German offensive against the allies in the forested Ardennes region of Belgium, France and Luxembourg. As this offensive had taken the Allies completely by surprise, the American forces met their highest losses of the World War. Although the Germans officially called it *Unternehmen Wacht am Rhein* (Operation Watch on the Rhine) but the contemporary press described it as Battle of Bulge to indicate the bulge in Allied front lines on wartime news maps. This was the name that became famous (Music 2005).

During the battle, the divisional command post at Wiltz, Luxembourg, came under severe German attack. Members of the 28th Infantry Division Band took up arms and fought as part of holding line around Wiltz to stop the German advance. The Band put away their instruments, dug foxholes and picked up carbines (rifles). A Clarinetist, PFC Collins, of the Band manned a small rocket launcher called *Bazooka*. After the Battle, in order to save the Band instruments, PFC Collins drove away a truck loaded with all the Band's stuff. Unluckily, ten miles out of Bastogne, the convoy was ambushed and destroyed, all the music burned. Only 16 of the Band's 60 men survived the fighting in the Ardennes.

The 28th Infantry Division Band was not the only Band involved in the Battle of the Bulge. The Band of the 101st Airborne Division helped hold on to Bastogne preventing it from falling to the Germans. The 82nd Airborne Division Band was sent for rescue and rehabilitation to Ardennes, but was caught in the battle. The front line being manned by their Division (the 82nd Airborne) was stretched thin. The 82nd Airborne Band joined the depleted front line to hold off the German spearhead. The Bandsmen fought gallantly and helped hold off two German Infantry Divisions and a Panzer Division (Music 2005).

Because the demand for music units exceeded the number of available Bands and ensembles, many Allied commanders organized Field Music Units, composed of drums and bugles played by the soldiers on the fronts. These troops spent their mornings on military duties, and their evenings in rehearsals. These amateur units became so popular they performed extensively until the end of the World War.

The war in Europe was not limited to just regimental (called: organization) Bands. The Special Bands had their role too. The Pershing's Own Army Band embarked on a wartime tour in 1943 to entertain and enliven troops at the battlefronts. The tour was sanctioned for two weeks but lasted two years. The Band performed near Metz, not far from combat, to lift morale during the Battle of the Bulge. Of all the premier Bands in Washington DC, the Pershing's Own Special Band is the only one to ever perform in a theatre of foreign combat operations during the Second World War (Music 2005).

The Pershing's Own Army Band played concerts for civilians and performed at countless Red Cross events. The Band also gave music for the dances organized by United Service Organization for National Defense—commonly called USO—established by Presidential Order in 1941 for welfare and support to servicemen and women.

Through various initiatives by the USO, it was also a time when Dance Bands of the Army emerged. Due to their mobility, entertainment value, and the positive morale factor, Dance Bands became important. This was a reflection of the large dance Bands that popped up in America proper. Many soldiers who would have thirsted for the music they left behind in America were gladdened by USO Dance Bands near the front lines.

The British Military Bands: The Military Bands were part of the earliest expeditionary force to Europe in Sept 1939. The Bands suffered heavy casualties although some survived and were evacuated from Dunkirk. Prime Minister Winston Churchill ordered that Bands were to be re-formed at Regimental Depots to keep up the morale of the troops there. The Bands did just that throughout the war (Curtis 2016).

The Band of Coldstream Guards was amongst the earliest Band deployed to war duty. At the outbreak of the Second World War in 1939 its familiar uniform of scarlet tunics got replaced by khaki outfits. During the war, this Band did important work encouraging the morale of troops and civilians throughout the country. It was on Sunday, June 18, 1944, that the greatest tragedy in the history of the Band occurred. The Band was playing in the Guards Chapel, Wellington Barracks when it was struck by a German VI Flying bomb. Over 120 people were killed including the Director of Music, Major Windram, and five musicians. Despite this disaster the Band continued to function until the new director of Music, Captain Douglas Alexander Pope was appointed. One of his first duties was to follow the Allied forces to Europe after D-Day.[1]

The D-day is the greatest day in World War II history turning the tide of the War in favour of the allies. The military musicians accompanied the troops in their great amphibious attack. A historic picture in British War Museum of Operation Epsom dated 26 June 1944 shows advance of the 7th Battalion of the British army into enemy, i.e. German-occupied French territory, led by a Bagpiper.

The Band of the Royal Artillery was ordered to proceed to North Africa where its 250 musicians travelled 14,000 miles in an exhausting eight months' tour performing for troops and civilians alike. No sooner had the extended African tour come to an end that the Band was sent to Europe where it performed for many months in Rome, Vienna, Berlin and Gibraltar before returning home after the end of the War. The Band of Life Guards was sent to Palestine, early in the war, where it lost its Band leader in a terrorist attack. Later, this Band was ordered to perform in France and Belgium over the years.

Philip Howard, in his history of The Black Watch regiment, vividly describes the airborne invasion of Crete in 1942 where the Highlanders had to go in with bayonets. The pipers played the Battalion in with "Highland Laddie"—their Regimental march—and "The Black Bear." This last tune has a pause for a yell at intervals, and is traditionally played when a final effort is needed from tired men (Howard 1968).

The Soviet Military Bands: The Nazi attack on Russia and the siege of Leningrad (now St Petersburg) is an important epoch of the World War. The period of 1941 till the end of the war, is known as the Great Patriotic War in Russia. Throughout the period, the Russian military Bands made concerts on the radio and at the front, raising the morale of the soldiers. Their repertories, based on military march tunes, mostly consisted of the works of Russian composers and folk music.

During World War II, the famous Red Army Band (now called the Alexandrov Band) created one of its most famous works: the song "The Sacred War." The Band accompanied the Red Army as it set off for the front on June 26, 1941 to fight back the Nazi Army. In the course of the Second World War, the Alexandrov Ensemble alone gave some 1,500 performances at military units and field camps on Soviet territory.[2]

From the Soviet side, the famous songs born out of the Second World War include Smuglyanka, Blue Scarf, Ogonyok, Katyusha, Lili Marleen, and the like. Traditionally, these WW-II tunes are played by Soviet military Bands at all important functions. Even after the fall of the Soviet Union, many of these became theme songs of the annual Spasskaya Tower Military Bands Festival at Moscow.

Orchestra Bands in World War II

In 1942, a diary was found in the pocket of a dead German soldier on the Russian Front. One of the last entries in the diary said, "Last night I heard a performance of Bruckner's Ninth Symphony, and now I know what we are fighting for!" Apparently, the dead soldier had just returned from leave in Berlin and had attended a concert there (Trotter 2005). This incident is enough to gauge the power of Orchestra music that was employed both by the Allied Powers and the Axis Powers. We will confine the section to the Orchestra Bands of the United States, the USSR and Germany.

American Orchestra Music: In the United States, all the noted music artists, from Frank Sinatra to Leopold Stokowski, gave War Bond concerts and made recordings exclusively for the Armed Forces. Among the songs that made history include. *It's Been A Long, Long Time* by Harry James & His Orchestra; *Waitin' For The Train To Come In* by Peggy Lee; and *What a Diff'rence a Day Made* by Andy Russell with Paul Weston & His Orchestra (1944). On top of all these *When The Lights Go On Again (All Over The World)* by Vaughn Monroe & His Orchestra (1943) had a notably non-aggressive and hopeful tone(Fauser 2013).

After successful incorporation of music into the war efforts, more was needed in order to keep hopes alive and stable, both back in the US and on the home front. Various times music was used as a tool for battle in the war, whether it was to entertain or to recuperate the soldiers during the war. American music composed during the 1940s was unlike music of any other time because of its emphasis on making the listener feel like they are part of the war even if they were physically somewhere else (Fauser 2013).

More important is the impact that the music of the 1940s had on the people then and the effect that it continues to have now. Fauser (2013) argues that that songs from World War II continue to be used today in order to remember those harsh times of war. Some examples of this would include Aaron Copland's *Fanfare for the Common Man* (1942) and *Lincoln's Portrait* (1942). These are still being played for presidential inaugurations and continue to remind everyone of the cost of liberty and freedom.

Soviet Orchestra Music: The iconic Soviet composer and Bandleader, Dmitri Shostakovich, was commissioned to compose tunes for military marches in 1939 but soon the war broke out. As the Germans advanced towards Leningrad, Shostakovich tried to enlist for the Soviet Army but was turned away due to his poor eyesight. He then decided to enlist as a volunteer in the firefighter brigade. Under heavy aerial bombardment, he would try to compose his seventh Symphony in shifts between his firefighting duties (Trotter 2005).

In October 1941, Kremlin ordered him to be flown out of Leningrad to the wartime capital of Kuybyshev on the Volga River. He was told that his greatest service to Russian war effort would be in creating music rather than fighting as part of Red Army or putting himself in harm's way in rescue operations under heavy fire. He composed his Symphony No. 7, subtitled Leningrad, dedicated to his beloved native city which was undergoing the most protracted and frightful siege of modern history. Its opening movement, featuring a "hypnotic 13-minute crescendo depicting the relentless Nazi advance, is a gripping musical impression of mechanized warfare, and its concluding movement is a thrilling paean to victory" (Trotter 2005). This Orchestral score was microfilmed and smuggled dramatically to the United States after top secret stops at Cairo and Tehran. The Symphony was received ecstatically in America generating financial, political and emotional support for the Soviet war effort.

German Orchestra Bands: The German Government took Music very seriously as a propaganda tool and as an instrument in War effort. The Propaganda Ministry took control over press, cinemas, theatres and Opera houses. The soldiers being sent to the Russian front were rewarded with Orchestra passes. And so were the wounded soldiers returning from the Front who were granted not only the Iron Crosses but also free passes to Orchestra performances at Wagner Festival at Bayreuth (Trotter 2005).

The works of "impure artists" and Jewish composers vanished overnight. Rather, there were Composers, with Aryan blood, that the Government promoted. Nazi Protocol demanded that every Conductor begin his Orchestra with a raised arm salute. Germany's greatest living composer, Richard Strauss, accommodated himself easily to the new regime in his old age. Another young conductor Herbert von Karajan, took advantage of the Reich's cultural peculiarities to advance his career in a manner that he and his likes have since defended as apolitical. Pianist Walter Gieseking promoted German *Kultur* by means of tours in neutral countries. Orchestras were also tasked to give performance to Krupp Ammunition Plants to give solace and encouragement to the exhausted Tank assemblers (Trotter 2005).

While any political dissent with Hitler Regime by an ordinary mortal could invite serious trouble, composers could be a different matter. Famous Orchestra Conductor Wilhelm Furtwangler was so influential that he ensured that the Nazi Government Order of 1939 to dissolve Vienna Philharmonic Orchestra was withdrawn due to his intercession.

The third Reich heavily relied on Beethoven's Symphony no. 5 and operas of Richard Wagner. Metaphors and symbols from the latter's operas were used to lend prestige to Nazi ideology, such as Hitler was equated with the Wagnerian hero Siegfried.[3] In spite of Beethoven's Fifth Symphony being the signature music for German Military, as noted above, the Allied forces adopted the opening notes of this Symphony—three Gs and an E-flat, corresponding to three dots and one dash in Morse code—to signify V for Victory. This musical signature became a recurring motif for Allied propaganda including their Operas, Orchestras and even Films much to the chagrin of Nazi regime. Goebbels failed to have thought about this use first (Trotter 2005).

Pop Bands during World War II

With the war brewing through the 1940s, initiatives to help the soldiers continue fighting arose. With drafting numbers in the United States reaching close to 500,000, the Army along with other Defense institutions began to sponsor music which would serve the purpose of boosting morale in the home front, while at the same time keeping patriotism and nationalism at an all-time high. This section is restricted to the Pop Bands in the United States alone.

The type of Pop Band music, whether officially sponsored or privately produced, can be clubbed in three categories. First category had religious overtones, especially prayers to God for victory, such as *Praise the Lord and Pass the Ammunition* by Composer Frank Loesser (1942) and *Comin' in on a Wing and a Prayer* by the Song Spinners.

The second category of military songs included those about military marches such as *Col Bogey's March* or sarcasm of the enemy such as the soldiers' song *Hitler has one got one ball.* The *Col Bogey March* is another famous marching tune which not only became the title tune for famous Hollywood movie "The Bridge on River Kwai" but remains a popular marching tune in scores of countries which were allied with the Allied Powers.

The final and the largest category was about the loneliness felt by soldiers on the fronts and their families back home. The themes of saying goodbye to soldiers leaving for the front, wishing them safe return and thinking about the loved ones far away. These themes include *Long Ago And Far Away* composed by Ira Gershwin and Jerome Kern (1944); *Kiss the Boys Goodbye* composed by Frank Loesser and Victor Schertzinger from eponymous movie (1941); and *You'd be so Nice to Come Home* to composed by Cole Porter (1942).

To comprehend the wartime role of the Pop Bands, the officially sanctioned and the unofficial reactionary music may need to be studied with equal vigour. The unofficial music produced during war years could be lively but sometimes rude to the extent of being unprintable. Of boisterous or unruly military music, the examples are legion such as *Washing On the Siegfried Line, Lili Marlene, Beer Beer Glorious Beer, Roll Out the Barrel,* and others equally carefree lyrics.

World War II was the first time that pop music was mobilised as a weapon of war. Frauser (2013) argues that the music composed during the Second World War had various purposes. He particularly mentions the tension that grew between institutions in order to find the right way to use music for overall US interests. Examples can be seen throughout the different types of songs being produced and publicised during the time. Songs like *I'll be Seeing You* (1938) and *Praise the Lord and Pass the Ammunition* (1942) were songs that kept the citizens back in the US calm and hopeful for the return of their loved ones. On the other hand, the same songs had very different effects on the soldiers fighting abroad. For them songs like these brought nostalgia and homesickness

Despite these differences, the United States had a definite musical advantage over the Axis rivals. The US, for one, did not need a Propaganda Minister, like the Goebbels of the Nazi regime. This was because the Allied Powers could count on big Bands producing music that reflected the primary interest of the leadership which were in line with the desires of the population.

Impact of Radio in World War II Tele-distribution of War Music

The Second World War was the first conflict to take place in the age of electronically mass distributed information and music. Many people in the war listened to radio and long playing records *en masse*. By 1940, 96.2 per cent of Northeastern American urban households had radio. The lowest American demographic to embrace mass distributed music, Southern rural families, still had one radio for every two households.

Similar to the United States, high adoption rates of electronically mass distributed music occurred in Europe too. During the Nazi rule, radio ownership in Germany rose fourfold from 4 to 16 million households. As the major powers entered the war, millions of citizens had home radio devices that did not exist in the First World War. Also during the pre-war period, sound was introduced to cinema and Musicals (whole movies where parts are played singing and dancing) started becoming very popular (Akkus 2015).

Therefore, World War II was a unique situation for music and its relationship to warfare. Never before was it possible for not only single songs, but also single recordings of songs to be so widely distributed to the population. Never before had the number of listeners to a single performance (a recording or broadcast production) been so high. Also, never before had States so much power to determine what songs were performed, recorded and listened to. Though local people still sang and produced songs, this form of music faced serious new competition from centralised electronic distributed music (Akkus 2015).

Radio Music by Allied Powers: Luckily for the allied governments of USA and UK, the war aims of the government were aligned with those of the populace. The people of these wanted a quick final victory over the Axis Powers without compromise, and so did the governments. Hence, the songs about a World-after-the-War, at peace with itself and with the boys coming home, not only met the personal desires of people but also reflected the goals of the Allied governments. Due to radio, the information was more readily available and war ceased to remain romantic for people living away from active theatres.

The selective draft had brought many outstanding musicians into the Army and the Army Air Corps. In 1943, the famous American Bandleader and Composer of Band Music, Glenn Miller's 45-piece orchestra began a weekly series of half-hour radio programmes called "I Sustain the Wings." This program included a dramatic skit to recruit men into the service and selling war bonds. In 1944, the Band, now named the *American Band of the Allied Expeditionary Force*, began a weekly radio program broadcasted to Europe and later to the continent. Miller lost his life in 1944 *en route* to play for troops in the European theatre. The US Air Force military aircraft bringing him from Bedford in UK to France disappeared over the English Channel, probably hit by a bomb jettisoned by returning Allied Bombers from a foray over Germany, never to be found again.

American troops had regular access to radio in all but the most difficult combat situations, and not only did soldiers know specific songs, but specific recordings. This gave a nature to American troops music during WWII, not as much songs sung around a fire or while marching, but listened to between combat on Armed Forces Radio.

Radio Music by Axis Powers: Radio was used by the German government round the clock for playing military music interspersed with special announcements (*Sondermeldung*). *Les Préludes* by Hungarian composer and father-in-law of Richard Wagner—Franz Liszt—used to be a signature theme before such announcement of Victory. After the announcement, a contemporary military march tune used to be played. *Les Préludes* would also accompany film footage of dive bombers (Trotter 2005).

The *Sturmabteilung*, literally Storm Detachment, were the original paramilitary wing of the Nazi Party. Owing to the Brown colour of their uniform, they were also known as "Brownshirts" (*Braunhemden*). The march tunes of the Brownshirts also remained a continuous musical theme on the German Radio throughout the war, although, occasional corrections used to be made. For instance, *We're Marching Against England* was played ad nauseam in the initial years of the War. When the Russian front was opened, anti-Bolshevik themes dominated the military music played on Radio. In the final days of war when heavy Allied Bombing was razing cities to the ground, Mozart's Requiem was banned as too depressing, while *Dancing Together Into Heaven* had to be dropped from playlists as it appeared ironic to what was happening around (Trotter 2005).

Round the clock playing of famous composer tunes on Radio was a consistent and conscious policy by German government. In order to broadcast the lengthy symphonies of Anton Bruckner, German technicians succeeded in discovering the first significant use of magnetic tape as a recording medium. Allied intelligence personnel, unaware of the new tape technology, monitoring those broadcasts in the wee hours of the morning assumed that the entire Berlin Philharmonic Orchestra was ordered out of bed before dawn to play live Radio concerts (Trotter 2005).

Military Music of the Cold War

By the second half of the 20th century, the world had become wiser. The experience of the two world wars and the development of nuclear arsenal had made the costs of a direct conflict prohibitive. Hence, despite the political conflicts of more serious nature and dimensions, the half a century following the Second World War, saw only a "Cold" War. The era of 1945 to around 1990–91 was known as such because, unlike the two World Wars preceding it, one, active hostilities between the main actors were largely replaced by proxy wars, and two, the two main belligerent blocs competed with each other through arms buildup and psychological warfare.

The Cold War saw music, especially Band music, used by all sides not only within the battlefields but also as an instrument of psychological warfare that the Cold War was largely about. Let us begin with the active combat zones. There were no less than forty active war theatres during the nearly half a century of the Cold War. Three of the most brutal Cold War-related conflicts that resulted in fatalities of a million-plus each included the Korean War (1950–53), the Vietnam War (1967–74) and the Afghanistan War (1979–88). None of these conflicts saw US troops and the Soviet troops directly facing each other. If in the Vietnam war, US troops were directly involved, the Vietcong militias fought as proxies for the Communist world. In Afghanistan, the Soviet Union intervened directly, so *Mujahideen* militias fought vicariously for the US and Western interests.

For the militias and guerilla groups (Vietcong in Vietnam and *Mujahideen* in Afghanistan), which rely on hit-and-run operations, it is neither feasible nor practicable to have Bands. It was the side whose regular Armed Forces were fighting that was likely to have Bands in the War theatres. And they did. The allied forces in Korean War, the US troops in the Vietnam war and the Soviet contingents in the Afghanistan were augmented by military Bands to boost their morale and lift the fighting spirits.

Both the biggest Communist giants, Soviet Union and China, had invested in modern military Bands as part of modernisation of the military since the early days of the Red revolutions in 1917 and 1949, respectively. It was their communication wing that was still lagging behind their adversary Western militaries. Hence, in the Korean War, the Chinese army and their North Korean allied militias were still using bugle, trumpet and drum calls for war signalling. Same was the case in the Vietnam War where Viet Cong used Bandsmen with Band instruments for communication.

The Bands of the Western Powers

The Military Bands were deployed by the Western powers wherever they sent their boots on ground. Korean and Vietnam wars offer interesting case studies:

Military Music of the Korean War (1950–53)

In the Korean war, US military Bands accompanied combat units into action many a times. Bands travelled many miles to perform several concerts a day for units close to the frontlines. One report read, "The closer we play to the front line, and recently we have been within a half-mile of it, the more enthusiastic has been the response to our music." (History of Army Music n.d.) Of the ten US Army Bands serving in Korea, one received the Distinguished Unit Citation and six received Meritorious Unit Commendations from the US Military. In addition, the Blue House, as the Presidential Palace in Seoul is known, granted Presidential Unit Citations to six of the Military Bands from allied forces, on behalf of the Republic of Korea.

However, due to the constant infiltration, sabotage, and behind-the-line attacks by Communist troops, Bandsmen in the UN-backed allied troops were forced to participate in combat. As a result, Bands rehearsed little, and performance quality declined. Hence, the distinctions that the Bands received accounted not solely for musical duties but also for the role the Bands played in combat and security during the Korean conflict.

In 1953, the British Government ordered deployment of its 1st Battalion of Northampton-shire Regiment and Royal Irish Fusiliers along with their Bands into the Korean War theatre. By the time the Bands reached, an armistice had taken effect. The Bands continued to play for the entertainment of United Nations troops. All members of both the Bands received United Nations Medal with Korean clasp (Curtis 2016).

The role of Bands cannot be complete without talking about the songs about the Korean War. These songs or their tunes were played by Pop Bands back home in the United States and other allied countries. The songs of Korean war are fairly rare, at least when compared to other modern Wars where the United States participated. The Korean war songs were dominated by four main themes: patriotism, the soldier in battle, faith, and emotional pain. A few songs expressed discontent about the war, but none of them opposed it outright. In this context, these songs represent a transitional phase between the patriotic and sometimes naive songs of World War II, and the anti-War songs of the Vietnam era. (Music about the Korean War 2012)

The jingoism reflected in the songs of previous wars slowly gave way to a more sobering account of the reality of combat toward the end of the WWII songs, and this trend continued during the Korean war. A number of songs touched upon the hardships of American soldiers on the front lines. *Rotation Blues*, for example, tells the story of a soldier who longs for his time on the front lines to end. Composed by a soldier named Stuart Powell, the song is about the American policy of rotating units in and out of combat zones. Powell's narrator longs for rotation to "set him free," and comments on how the Far East Command (abbreviated as F.E.C.) "is too far East for me." (Music about the Korean War 2012)

Most Korean War songs came from the country music genre, just a few years before the advent of rock 'n' roll. One of the earliest Korean War songs was also one of the most popular, Jimmie Osborne's *God, Please Protect America.* Osborne recorded the song on July 26, 1950, just a month after the UN Security Council passed Resolution 83, approving the use of force against North Korea. Osborne followed up the success of the song with *Thank God For Victory in Korea* recorded on October 2, 1950. He seems to have reacted to the successful Inchon landings in September, and the subsequent successful push-back of North Korean troops. This musical declaration of victory would prove to be premature, however, as Chinese forces entered the fray only three weeks later, fundamentally changing the character of the war. (Music about the Korean War 2012)

In *Good-bye Maria, I'm Off to Korea,* the narrator is a corn farmer from Iowa who had married an Italian girl during his first tour overseas, presumably during WWII. Now it's the "same old story" and he is back in the service to "win another fight for liberty." Another patriotic song addressing the Korean War was *Korea, Korea, Here We Come* by Harry Choates recognizing the sadness once again felt by American mothers as their sons go off to yet another war. Finally, Sister Rosetta Tharpe's upbeat song, *There's Peace in Korea,* celebrates the end of the war while giving credit to President Eisenhower for fulfilling his campaign promise to end the war (Music about the Korean War 2012).

The tone and tenor of War-generated Pop Music was to undergo a sea change by the following decade when the Vietnam war broke out. Coming back to Military Music, one must add that the US military Bands deployed in Korean War have become a permanent hallmark of US-South Korea friendship. The presence of permanent US bases in Korea had an impact on Korean military Band culture. Prior to the second World War, the Korean military Bands were raised on the pattern of Russian Bands in terms of their uniforms and marching styles. Since the Soviet Union had been on the side of the North Korea in the war, South Korean army Bands totally transformed their styles away from Russian-style as acts of patriotism. The present military Band structure in South Korea is heavily influenced by the American style of Bands. However, the Korean Army has retained a traditional Band playing in the *daechiwta* styles of ancient Korean kingdoms. The traditional army Band of South Korean Military uses Korean traditional musical instruments and dons traditional Korean imperial dress.

Across the border into North Korea, the Military Bands and Orchestras have totally adapted to the Soviet-Russian style of Military music. But for the musical repertoire, the Central Band of the North Korean Defense Forces is a striking replica, in form and style, of the Red Army Choir of the Russian Federation, a.k.a Alexandrov Band.

Military Music of the Vietnam War (1965-75)

As the situation in Vietnam became critical the presence of the US troops also increased. The US military Bands once again prepared for combat. By 1969, eight military Bands were stationed in Vietnam. The 266th Army Band was assigned to the military headquarters in Saigon while the remaining seven were Division Bands. These included the 1st, the 4th, the 9th, the 23rd and 25th Infantry Division Bands, the 101st Airborne Division Band and the 1st Cavalry Armored Division Band. The RVN Armed Force Band Headquarters and Band School at Thu Duc Marketplace oversaw the Band program in Vietnam including administration, budget, training and supply (Music 2005).

Bands in Vietnam, like those in Korea, often performed in combat areas. They flew in combat zones with instruments and weapons, prepared to play pop concerts or military ceremonies and to fight when needed. Bands gave powerful psychological support to the troops in conflicts. The appearance of military rock and jazz groups in remote areas assured combat soldiers they had not been forgotten (History of Army Music n.d.).

In Vietnam, Bandsmen built bunkers and served as guards for both inside and outside defensive perimeters, as well as being a vital part of pacification operations. While another unit screened people in a Vietnamese village for Viet Cong soldiers, the US Bands compensated through friendly vibes presenting concerts and entertainment to keep the non-combatant populace away from the screening unit. The local people enjoyed the concerts, and wherever Military Bands were present screening mission by other units would become easier and usually be completed without disturbance (Music 2005).

One notable example of the use of Bands in Vietnam was the "Thunder Road incident," which received national publicity. Major General John Hay, Commanding General of the First Infantry Division, ordered his Band to march down the Thunder Road for a distance of one mile while playing the tune *Colonel*

Bogey March. This road was critical to the US First Infantry Division, but was under control of a North Vietnamese Army (NVA) regiment located less than a mile away. The NVA, so confused by the impromptu parade, withdrew from the area allowing American infantry to seize the road without opposition (Music 2005). The Band fulfilled a remarkable combat mission without firing a shot, thereby saving human lives from both sides.

The discussion of musical legacy of Vietnam war cannot be complete without referring to the role music played in the soldiers' lives as well as the songs and music generated by the War. If by the time of WW II, Radio had become a household item, Vietnam war was being fought when the public had got near universal access to the television screens. The people could watch the misery and devastation caused by the War that ceased to remain fanciful and romantic. People came out on the streets against the war and rock and roll music was the quintessence of anti-war rallies.

Music enabled countless soldiers in Vietnam to connect with each other and to "the World" back home while helping them cope with the complexities of the war they had been sent to fight. Although many veterans never spoke about their experiences, even to their spouses and family, they could talk about songs like *Blood Sweat and Tears, And When I Die*; *Ring of Fire* by Johnny Cash and scores of others. And by remembering the music, they could begin to heal from the war's wounds.

A book explores the way Americans who served in the Vietnam War turned to music to cope with themselves and with the war experience. It is co-authored by Douglas Bradley, a veteran of the Vietnam War, and Craig Werner, a professor of music and literature in the Department of Afro-American Studies at the University of Wisconsin. Following are excerpts from Bradley (2015):[4]

> "In early February 1968 the CBS Evening News broadcast a segment from Khe Sanh, the outpost in northwest Quang Tri province where a US Marines base was under siege by the North Vietnamese Army (NVA). Vastly outnumbered and unsure of when or if a full-scale attack would begin, marines played cards, smoked, hunkered down at the sound of incoming artillery, and scrambled to pick up desperately needed supplies dropped by parachute.
>
> "Dirt, grime, and sweat caking their faces, to keep their spirits going, they relied on music. Half a dozen marines would sit on a bunker strumming guitars and singing "Where Have All the Flowers Gone?," a song written by the World War II veteran and pacifist Pete Seeger: Where have all the

soldiers gone?/Gone to graveyards every one./ When will they ever learn?/ When will they ever learn? For the marines at Khe Sanh and the more than three million other men and women who served in Vietnam, music provided release from the uncertainty, isolation, and sometimes stark terror that reached from the front lines to the relatively secure rear areas.

"But the sounds offered more than simple escape. Music was a lifeline connecting soldiers to their homes, families, and parts of themselves they felt slipping away. It was the glue that bound the communities they formed in their base camps, and lonely outposts from the Mekong Delta to the ravines of the demilitarized zone (DMZ). Both in-country and back in the United States, music helped them make sense of situations in which, as Bob Dylan put it in a song that meant something far more poignant and haunting in Vietnam than it did back in the US, they felt like they were on their own with no direction home. Music was the key to survival and a path to healing, the center of a human story that's too often been lost in the haze of politics and myth that surrounds Vietnam.

"With the crucial exception of combat situations, music was just about everywhere in Vietnam, reaching soldiers via albums, cassettes, and tapes of radio shows sent from home; on the Armed Forces Vietnam Network (AFVN); and on the legendary underground broadcasts of Radio First Termer. They played it in their hooches on top-of-the-line tape decks they purchased cheap at the PX and over headphones in helicopters and planes.

"Filipino Bands pounding out "Proud Mary" and "Soul Man" at EMCs and Saigon bars; touring acts from Bob Hope and Ann-Margret to Nancy Sinatra and James Brown granting momentary calm in the midst of the military storm. AFVN blanketed Vietnam with songs from stateside Top 40 stations. Soldiers in remote areas maneuvered their transistor radios in hopes of catching the week's countdown of stateside Top 40 hits.

"Like other members of their generation, those who served in Vietnam shaped the music they loved to fit their own needs, a process that continued after they returned to the United States. As Michael Kramer observes in The Republic of Rock, the music of the 1960's and early 1970's gave the younger generation "a sonic framework for thinking, feeling, discussing, and dancing out the vexing problems of democratic togetherness and individual liberation."

"Widespread availability of popular music, by way of soldiers' personal stereos made a year in Vietnam less isolating and more manageable." The soundscape of Vietnam unfolded in distinct movements, musical and military. As the war changed, the music changed with it. Or maybe, it was the other way around. Some of the songs show empathy with the enemy.

The Ballad of the Green Berets became a hit song, but others like *For What It's Worth* performed by Buffalo Springfield; *The Letter* performed by the Box Tops; *These Boots Are Made For Walking* performed by Nancy Sinatra; *Say It Loud I'm Black And I'm Proud* performed by James Brown; *We Gotta Get Out Of This Place* performed by Eric Burdon; *My Girl* performed by the Temptations; *Leaving On A Jet Plane* performed by Peter Paul and Mary; *Machine Gun* performed by Jimi Hendrix; *Chain Of Fools* performed by Aretha Franklin; and *What's Going On* performed by Marvin Gay are part of the musical legacy of the Cold War conflict in Vietnam.

On the Vietnamese side, the War and especially the fall of Saigon, and the plight of Vietnamese refugees gave rise to a collection of musical pieces that have become "classical" anthems for Vietnamese people both in Vietnam and abroad. Many of these composers, in the North, also contributed Vietnamese revolutionary songs, known as *Nh c đ* or "Red Music." The Military Bands of the Defence Forces of Vietnam have adopted these tunes for all military ceremonies and marches.

The Bands of the Communist Powers

Our discussion on the Military Bands of the Communist Powers during the Cold War is limited to the Military Bands of the Soviet Union till its disintegration in 1991 and on those of the Communist China till date.

Military Bands of the Soviet Union (1917-91)

Following the Communist revolution of 1917, the new Bolshevik leadership disBanded all the traditional military Bands, considering them as relics of imperial Czarist past. As in other countries, with similar revolutions, the necessity of reviving military Bands emerged pretty soon. A Military Band Bureau of the Red Army and the Navy was created in 1919 for centralised management of the military Bands.

The Defence Minister of Soviet Union Marshall Voroshilov ordered the raising of a Band ensemble out of the Frunze Red Army Central House in 1928. At that time, it had only twelve soldier-performers, a reciter and two dancers. As the story goes, dame luck smiled on the fate of the Band when Soviet strongman Joseph Stalin happened to attend a performance in St Petersburg. He ordered the Choir to be relocated to Moscow. It was named "Army Song Ensemble of the M. V. Frunze Red Army Central House," shortened to "*Frunze Red Army Choir.*"

The Frunze Red Army Choir made its debut performance in Moscow on October 12, 1928, being conducted by Alexander Alexandrov, who was made music professor at the Moscow Conservatory. The program, entitled *The 22nd Krasnodar Division in Song*, consisted mainly of short musical scenes of military life, including *Songs of the First Cavalry Army*, *The Special Far-Eastern Army*, and *Song about Magnitostroi*.[5]

As the process to colour all the tunes of the new military Band into "red" continued, the signature tune of the Band became the civil war song *White Army, Black Baron*. During the civil war of 1917-22, it was the theme song of the Bolshevik forces and has the same standing in Soviet military music as Communist China's *Eighth Army March* and American Civil War's *John Brown's body*.

In 1929, Stalin sent the ensemble to far eastern parts of the Soviet Union, to entertain and motivate the troops working on the Far Eastern Railway. Then on, its journey to all corners of the Soviet Union from the deserts of Tajikistan to the freezing shores of Northern Arctic, wherever the Soviet troops or workers were present, never stopped.

Increased staff of the Red Army in 1930s reinforced the need for more military musicians. That is why the network of military colleges increased significantly in those times, including the foundation of the Military Music Department of the Moscow State Conservatory. It was also then that military Bands were invited to work on the radio, make records and create music for movies.

The Frunze Red Army Ensemble could already safely count Joseph Stalin amongst its fans. Obviously, the Communist government started paying unusual attention to Ensemble which, within four years, grew to 300 performers comprising a male choir, an orchestra, and a dance troupe by 1933. Two years later, the choir was awarded the *Order of the Red Banner* and got renamed as the *Red Army Red-bannered Song and Dance Ensemble of the USSR*, dropping the name of M. V. Frunze from its official name. The renamed Red Army Choir became known as a propagator of Soviet songs within the Soviet Union and abroad, performing original compositions by composers such as Vasily Solovyov, Boris Mokrousov and Anatoli Novikov.

In August 1937, a group of 150 of its members was sent to Paris to perform at the International Exhibition of Art and Technology in Modern Life, where it won the G*rand Prix*, the highest honour bestowed by the jury. In 1939, before the start of the World War, the Ministry of Interior also raised a similar Band ensemble. Along with the Red Army Band, both had similar status as the four Special Bands of the United States Government.

As the Second World War started, the need for raising more Bands was irresistible being a military necessity and the rise of Bands followed. During the War, the Red Army Ensemble alone gave over 1500 performances at both Soviet fronts to the troops facing Germany in the far West to those fighting Japanese fourteen time zones away to the East. It entertained troops at gun emplacements, airfields, naval bases and those lying injured in military hospitals.

Alexandrov died right after the Second World War in 1946 and the choir leadership was inherited by his sons, Boris Alexandrov, who conducted it for almost forty years till 1986, and the younger Major Vladimir Alexandrov, who composed for the Ensemble. Boris's party trick was to position the members in a way that they could not all watch one orchestral leader. He would, at times, even leave the stage and allow the ensemble to perform alone. The idea was that the Ensemble members became so experienced and disciplined that they could feel the rhythm simultaneously, sing and play together automatically, without the conductor. During these decades, the Soviet Red Army Band performed in almost all the Soviet allied counties from Poland and Yugoslavia in Europe to Afghanistan and Syria in Asia.

Until 1969, the standard uniform for the ensemble choir, soloists and orchestra was the tunic and riding breeches. On 1 January 1970, this was changed to dress uniform till the end of the Soviet Union. Thus, from 1970s onwards all Band personnel were military officers on active duty, wore ranks and donned military uniforms while performing.

For decades, the Band remained known as an awe-inspiring entertainment machine whose renditions of military and patriotic songs as well as Russian folk opera were performed in concert halls, city squares and stadiums on all continents. During the Soviet Invasion of Afghanistan, the Band was a frequent visitor to Kabul to cheer up Soviet troops. At the end of the Cold War, and after the fall of the Berlin Wall, the Alexandrov Band performed at central Lustgarten in united Berlin to give the former Red Army's farewell to Berlin on a positive note and without any rancour from either side. This performance gave the whole of Germany an optimistic overtone.

Luckily, as the Alexandrov family eclipsed, the Defense Ministry at Moscow got the services of another great Khalilov family from the then Soviet Republic of Uzbekistan. After the fall of the Soviet Union, Red Army Band, along with the rest of the army, was in disarray. Colonel Valery Khalilov, as he then was, became the Conductor of the Central Defense Ministry Band of Moscow District and worked hard to reorganize and rebuild the Red Army Choir to the point that it had a more prominent feature than before in the Victory Day parades at Red Square. The fact that Khalilov was eventually promoted to the level of a three-star General through a Presidential decree of President Putin—the highest rank ever for a military musician in the world—evinces the importance even post-Soviet regimes give to military music. His brother Col. Alexander Khalilov was the author of the widely known song *We're leaving...*, famous with the veterans of Soviet forces engaged in Afghanistan war (1979-88). It is famous with military Bands in Russia today for official ceremonies.

Lieut General Khalilov was an accomplished music composer; whose work mainly being oriented towards brass music, wrote many pieces for the brass Band, including "Adagio" and "Elegy," marches such as "Cadet," "Rynda," "Ulan," "Youth," as well as patriotic and romantic songs. Many of these new military marches and songs were, and shall continue to be, used in the Victory Day parades conducted in Moscow.

In 1998, the Red Army Band was renamed after its first director, Alexander Alexandrov (1883–1946). Its formal name since then has been *Academic Ensemble of Song and Dance of the Russian Army named after A. V. Alexandrov*, shortened as Alexandrov Band. Despite the change in formal name to break with the Communist past, Alexandrov Band, remains one of the only two Bands of the 55 main Bands of the Russian government, allowed to use the term Red Army Band. The other one is of course the Ministry of Interior MVD Band. By 2000, Alexandrov Band had a 186-strong membership of an Orchestra, a Choir and a Dance troupe. It enlisted dancers and musicians playing classical and Russian folk instruments.

Tragically, the Choir of the Alexandrov Band died in a Tu-154 military airline crash in the Black Sea on Christmas Day of 2016. The Ensemble was on duty, en route to perform in the war torn Syria. Upon their death, political analyst Alexei Mukhin told Al Jazeera that Alexandrov Band [is], "An ensemble of victory, because many military and patriotic songs that were symbolic and sacred were performed by this ensemble." And not coincidentally, the last song that Alexandrov Band played publicly before the accident was no other than *White Army, Black Baron* on Moscow's Red Square the garrison orchestra—the one with which the Band had started its life almost a century earlier.

Military Bands of the Communist China (1949-)

The Band of the People's Liberation Army (PLA) was created in 1947, two years before the success of the Communist Revolution in China. In fact, it was the old

Eighth Army that was Christened as the PLA and its musical formations merged with the new PLA to form PLA Bands.

In 1950, on the eve of the first anniversary of the Chinese Red Revolution, Chairman Mao Zedong wanted to have the first-ever PLA military parade. It was realized that this was not possible without a Band. Plus, the Communist military leadership did not have experience of conducting a big parade. Zhou Enlai and five other military commanders who had a chance of witnessing Soviet military parade and Bands were tasked with choreography and arrangement of the Red China Military parade.

Chairman Mao also directed that a 1,800 strong military Band should be raised (at that time, the surviving contingent of PLA Band was less than 100-strong). Within the next ten weeks before the anniversary, the military committee was able to raise and train a 1,000-strong combined military Band that played at its first National Day parade in 1950 at Tiananmen Square (Lei 2015). The parade and therefore the Band became emblematic of the might of the Communist China. As Chinese military was a ragtag army in the first decade of the revolution, their parades saw Artillery pieces being towed by tractors and horses being displayed as transport arm of the army. Yet, the majesty that the Band created made the annual parade a truly remarkable and resilient affair.

In any case, during the initial years of Communist China, the Band was much more than motivator for troops. Unlike its Communist partner, the Soviet Union, which has stopped using military Bands for wartime signalling from the second half of the 19th century, the Chinese army used it well into the second half of the 20th century. In the Korean War (1950–53), the Chinese technical communication was so poor that they were still using drum beats and old style horns to give commands during the battles. And as a pleasant surprise for the Chinese, these horns had the unanticipated effect of terrorizing the American soldiers on the other side (Trotter 2005).

The Military Anthem of the Chinese People's Liberation Army is a patriotic song, originally titled *March of the Eighth Route Army*. This was one of the six songs in the *Chorus of Eighth Route Army*, all written by Gong Mu and composed by Zheng Lücheng. The song became known as the *March of the Liberation Army* during the second Chinese Civil War. This army, at one time commanded by Mao Zedong himself, fought against Japanese invasion and, as noted above, was renamed as PLA after the Second World War.

The lyrics were re-edited by the General Political Department in 1951 and the song renamed to *March of the Chinese PLA* in 1965. On July 25, 1988, the

Central Military Commission declared the song as the official anthem of the People's Liberation Army:

Ode to the Motherland
When the Motherland calls upon
Be a soldier, join the army, serve our motherland
March of the airman
March of the motorize troops
March of the rocket troops

Gradually, the Central Military Commission has shed away its reluctance to use patriotic songs from the last Qing imperial dynasty for the PLA Military Bands. In fact, the PLA has embraced many songs from original Qing lyrics that were commissioned by famous statesman General Zeng Guofan for the Xiang Army during 1860-64. Of course, the lyrics of various songs got changed whenever a word was found to be "counter revolutionary" and even music was recycled if it did not appear to be imbibing Communist spirit enough.

During the civil war, the Communists reworded the song titled *National Revolution Army* into the *Land Revolution Is Successful.* A further modification transformed the song into *Three Rules and Eight Notices*, which is the best known form today. The latest lyrics used by the present People's Liberation Army are an extension of Zeng Guofan's version of 1850s, and add additional rules to further inspire soldiers' discipline.

The Cold War has ended but a new USA-China military competition has emerged. The military Bands have become embedded in Communist China's military traditions. The Combined Band of the three services, Army, Navy and Air arms of the PLA, is brought out rarely. At the 60th anniversary parade of the revolution in 2009, for instance, it was only the fifteenth such Combined Band performance (1950 one included). Out of all the 55 Bands, 2,600 best musicians were selected for audition of whom 1,300 got selected to perform at the parade. The parade was led by Senior Colonel Liu Cheng, political commissar of the Band. The Band played 30 works, mostly instrumental but a few with songs, performed by the PLA Chorus. Most of the tunes and songs represent the classic wartime era while others being patriotic songs (Lei 2015).

"These works reflect the Chinese people's heroism and represent their aspirations for a strong nation and a mighty military," according to Major General Li Zhensheng, deputy head of the PLA General Political Department's publicity office (Lei 2015). For China and its military today, music is the weapon of choice.

Military Music of 20th century Regional Wars

In the contemporary world, there are a number of flash points in the world that have seen the outbreak of wars between traditional regional rivals. The Indians and Pakistani conflict, with three major and a number of minor wars, provides an interesting contrast with the Arab Israeli conflict, as far as war music is concerned.

Military Music of Indo-Pakistan Wars

Just like elsewhere in the world, the South Asian armies have deep-rooted martial music traditions. As early as 300 BC, the various kingdoms that existed where India and Pakistan are situated today, had Bands of primitive sort that actually moved with armies to play marching tunes. They were used to set order and discipline and to play motivational tunes to keep morale high. The tradition of War drums and bugles continued till the Sultanate of Delhi was established in 1206. The imperial armies of the great Mughal dynasty (1526-1857) had wartime drum rolls to order attack or retreat. It is interesting to note that when the British colonial administration expanded Westwards, musical instruments were well known to the mountainous tribes in North Western subcontinent, most of which is part of Pakistan's tribal belt, lying West of its province named Khyber-Pakhtunkhwa.

The Indo-Pakistani wars added a new dimension to the military music in both the countries. The two nations went to war within months of their independence and partition in August 1947. The events that led to the first Indo-Pakistan War of 1948, fought over the disputed State of Kashmir, apparently caught both countries by surprise. It was too early for the two nations to develop a distinct nationalistic music when they had been part of the same empire for millennia. At that time neither India nor Pakistan had established their Schools of Music, though, both did so shortly after this first war with each other. However, the cinema had a much greater impact on military and war music than the military schools of music in both the countries. Taking cue from the US Film Industry in Hollywood, Indian and Pakistani picture industry is called Bollywood and Lollywood, respectively, named after the name of the cities, Bombay (now called Mumbai) and Lahore, where the two industries are mostly concentrated. Bollywood has historically dominated the South Asian scene and screen for nearly a century, while the Lollywood pales in size before it. To study war music and war tunes, we need to understand the relationship of South Asian cinema with music.

Music and Songs in South Asian Box Office: Bollywood songs, along with dance, are a characteristic motif of Indian cinema which gives it enduring popular appeal, cultural value and context. The Bollywood movies are not musicals in the Western theatrical sense; the music aspect is an integral feature of the genre akin to plot, dialogue and other parameters. Bollywood cinema is unique in that the majority of songs are seen to be sung by the characters themselves rather than being played in the background. Hindi film songs form a predominant component of Indian pop music, and derive its inspiration from both classical and modern sources.

In Western films, a Music Director is responsible for selecting existing recorded music to add to the soundtrack, typically during opening and closing credits, whereas in Bollywood films, the head of Music has a much more critical role on which the success of the movie in box offices largely depends. He often has to go to great lengths to include lyrics of special significance and applicability to the film's plot and dialogue. Although sung by professional backstage singers, they are lip-synced by the actors to appear as they are singing. The songs usually advance the plot or develop the film's characters, though in some cases they serve merely as breaks in the storyline. Bollywood film songs have been described as eclectic both in instrumentation and style.

How did this unique musicality got embedded on the Indian silver screen is debatable. May be because most of the film producers in post-independence India of the 1950s, came from theatre-drama background. And having songs in theatres was a necessity to keep the spectators engaged during change of stage sets, etc. The musical film was a natural development of the stage musical after the emergence of sound film technology. Typically, the biggest difference between film and stage musicals is the use of lavish background scenery and locations that would be impractical in a theatre. In addition, music was so much embedded in Indian culture that an entertainment without songs woven into the narrative was inconceivable. The songs and dance in the backdrop of elaborate scenery also touched the dream chords of an average poor citizen whom it was appealing to see places and situations on the screen that are not possible in [his or her] real life. Since music also was a large economy with people's livelihood attached to music industry, the film industry found it convenient to use it as an additional revenue stream within the film business.

Be that as it may, Indian movie is the biggest producer of Indian music and songs. It is from Box Office screens that music is transmitted to the society and becomes a part of popular culture being commonly played in public transport, grocery stores, barber shops, clubs and homes. The Indian Military, like any Military, cannot remain immune from popular cultural or musical trends. In India, the patriotic and war songs also emanate from Bollywood as do the love songs. Indian Military Bands have developed the capacity to play any kind of tune from Mohammad Rafi to Lata Mangeshkar's songs with finesse. Pakistan's direction of music evolved differently. Here, the songs are usually created at Music Houses which then travel upwards to the Lollywood screens. However, there are exceptions to this general trend.

Military Music of 1965 War: During the second Indo-Pakistani war of September1965, Pakistan's music legend Noor Jahan dominated the television screens with her inspiring songs. Her songs had great impact on War spirit of the nation. Musical Legacy of 1965 war from Pakistani side include some very famous songs such as *Jaag utha hai sara watan* [The whole nation has risen up]; *Mera mahi Chhail chhabeela hai ni Karnail ni Jarnail* [My handsome beloved is a Colonel, a General]; *Ay putar hataan te nai wikday* [These sons of soil do not compromise] and *Ay Watan ke sajeelay jawano* [O bright young men of your homeland]. Today, the tunes of these songs dominate the ceremonies of the Defence Day, that Pakistan observes on 6th September each year, marking the day the second Indo-Pakistan war had started.

Interestingly enough, the marching tune of Indian army is a composition by South Asian poet-philosopher Allama Mohammad Iqbal (1877-1938) whose lyrics are *Sare jahan se accha Hindustan hamara* [tr: Our India is more beautiful than the whole world]. This song has the status of almost a second national anthem for India, after Tagore's *Jana Gana Mana.*

It is also pertinent to mention that when ceasefire resolution for the second Indo-Pakistan War was being debated in the United Nations Security Council in Sept 1965, Pakistani and Indian Foreign Ministers and diplomats repeatedly clashed over the status of Allama Iqbal as their national poet and criticized the other side for claiming so.

Military Music of 1971 War: In 1971, within six years that is, the Armed Forces of the two nations again confronted each other, which became the third Indo-Pakistan war. This time they fought over East Pakistan, the only time hostilities had broken out over an issue other than Kashmir. Musical Legacy of 1971 War includes two famous songs, the first of which is the standard marching tune of Pakistani army parades: *Ay mard e mujahid jaag zara* [Get up, O valiant soldier] and *Aye raah e haq ke shaheedo!* [O the martyrs of the right path]. Both were incidentally songs from the silver screen. The first one was sung by Inayat Hussain Bhatti in a movie *Changez Khan* [1958] and the second one was sung by Naseem Begum in a movie *Madar e Watan* [1966]. The latter singer died in her youth, a few months before the outbreak of the 1971 war but these songs became the theme songs of the war from Pakistani side.

The Pakistani musical onslaught was countered by the Indian movie onslaught. Bollywood—the Indian film industry—is the largest film producer after the American Hollywood. Over 50 Indian hit movies have war themes ranging from 1857 war with the British administration to various real and fictional Indo-Pakistani conflicts as well as the war against terrorism in India. Half of the songs in such movies are romantic and the other half are martial or patriotic in nature.

The first Indian movie made on 1971 Indo-Pakistani war was probably *Aakraman* released in 1975. All songs of the movie were patriotic songs but two of them by Kishore Kumar added to the musical legacy of 1971 from the Indian side. One was *Dekho Veer Jawanon* [tr. Look at our young soldiers] and *Fauji gaya jab gaon main* [tr. When the soldier went to the village]. Another movie on the same war titled *Border* in 1997 carried a conciliatory anti-war song "*Mere Dushman Mere Bhai*" [tr. My enemies are my brothers]. In yet another Bollywood production about the 1971 war, released in 2007, with the title "1971", that hit the box offices in 2007, there is a break from demonizing the enemy, especially in the song "*Sehlenge Hum Saare Sitam*" [tr. We will bear all the misery] composed by Shibani Kashyap that borrows from the American musical themes of WW-II era about loneliness and gloom brought about by the war.

Ab Tumhare Hawale Watan Sathiyo [tr. Whole country is now in your hands, comrades!] that hit box offices in 2004, has the title song of the same lyrics as the movie name. The movie is not based on any real event but broadly about India-Pakistan rivalry—especially Pakistan's purported support to militants working against India. Interestingly, there were two movies with the title *Hindustan ki qasam* [tr. Allegiance to India] one produced in 1973, which had a song with same title, and another in 1999. Although both were war movies but had different plots, casts, sound tracks and stories. The one released in 1973 is about the air battles between Indian and Pakistani Air Forces during 1971 war. The second one is about a fictional Indian-Pakistani conflict but has a conciliatory tone showing certain Indian operatives help abort a plan by terrorist to assassinate a Pakistani Prime Minister.

Military Music of Kargil War (1999): The Kargil conflict of 1999 did not escape the eyes of the media production world in India. Two famous movies titled *LOC Kargil* and *Lakshya* were released in 2003 and 2004, respectively. These obviously had their own soundtracks and, therefore, musical imprint on South Asia.

Pakistan Army also released a song and music titled *Yeh Ghazi for the Siachin* war—the highest battleground in the world since 1984 where Indian and Pakistani troops are pitched against each other for control of a high altitude glacier atop of the Himalayan mountain range. The tunes of all these songs are now title tunes of marches by various Pakistani military formations and branches

To conclude, the anniversaries of 1948 war, 1965 war and the 1999 conflict are observed in military cantonments in both countries religiously as both sides celebrate the "victory day". Their military Bands play their side of the musical legacy of the wars concerned. The only anniversary that passes quietly in Pakistan with no drums beating and no horns blowing is of the 1971 war.

Military Music of Arab Israel Wars

The Middle East conflict has two dimensions, one, the Israeli-Palestinian conflict over the (home) land, and the other is the broader political conflict between Israel and its Arab neighbours, mainly Egypt. The evolution of military music amongst the Palestinians, the Israelis and the Egyptians, had evolved through distinct routes: the Palestinian resistance music emerged as pop music, Israeli military music, and even cinema music for that matter, was mostly created by its Armed Forces, while for Egypt, the cinema took the lead role in creating military music.

Palestinian Military and Revolutionary Music: After the creation of Israel in 1948, large numbers of Arab Palestinians were forced to flee. They were housed in refugee camps in West Bank (then part of Jordan) and Gaza (then in Egypt). The Arab music was totally dominated by Egyptian voices. Composer Sayed Darwish (1892–1923)—the father of the Arabic pop music—still ruled the musical scene decades after his death well into the fifties and sixties when another superstar Umme Kulthum (1904–75) became a heartthrob of Arab masses including the Palestinians. However, musical influence of Darwish and Kulthum got absorbed by the centres for Palestinian music in the towns of Haifa and Nazareth. In time, a distinctively Palestinian musical identity emerged relating to their nationalist sentiments and dreams of statehood.

The history of songs dealing with the Palestinian struggle parallels in many ways the history of the Palestinian struggle itself. For instance, in the late 1950s/early 60s, the songs supporting Palestinian liberation expressed confidence in the Nasserist revolution. However, post-1967 songs expressed despair of defeat on the one hand, and hope in the Palestinian guerrilla movement then emerging, on the other. The Lebanese civil war and the ensuing Israeli invasions of Lebanon produced another crop of songs about the struggle, including the-then-still-recent loss of Jerusalem.

In the 1980s, many musical Bands including dance Bands or mix music-song-dance Bands emerged in the Palestinian communities with wholly political themes. The most influential pop Bands were the *Sabreen* Band and the *Al Ashiqeen* (Lovers) Bands. Following the first *Intifada* starting in 1987, not only more radical pop Bands emerged but existing ones' repertoire also became radicalized.

The Madrid Talks between Israeli and Palestinian representatives (1991) culminated in the Oslo Peace Accord of 1994. This has led to the establishment of a Palestinian Authority which gave limited autonomy to Palestinians and some degree of self-governance. The creation of quasi-State for Palestinians impacted their national life significantly. For one, their cultural expression began to stabilize. Wedding Bands, which had all but disappeared in the years following the formation of Palestine Liberation Organization (PLO) in 1965, right up to 1994, reappeared virtually all over the Palestinian areas. Initially they performed popular Egyptian and Lebanese songs but gradually compositions of Palestinian poets and musicians gave them a Palestinian character. The Band music soon became politically coloured.

Band Music also developed in the Palestinian Diaspora. The British-born Jazz Musician of Palestinian descent Reem Kelani is an obvious example. She has the backing of a 57-member Choir consisting of kids from almost as many nationalities. She has also performed with the Norwegian Philharmonic Orchestra based in the city of Bergen. She has led tours of Middle East to perform at Opera Houses with her troupe of British and Syrian instrumental musicians. In 2007, she got a commission from Manchester Music Festival to compose a 30-minutes piece for Beating Wings Orchestra, comprising 30 Syrian refugee musicians. Her music has a specifically Palestinian narrative and heritage. Her 2006 debut solo album *Sprinting Gazelle* had musical settings of popular and resistance poetry. All the songs on the album relate to "pre-1948 Palestine."

Music of Palestinian pop and youth Bands reflects Palestinian experiences such as the struggle of living under occupation, the longing for peace, and the craving for a Palestinian homeland. A typical example of such a song is *Baladi, Baladi* (My Country, My Country), which has become the unofficial Palestinian national anthem:

Palestine, Land of the fathers
To you, I do not doubt, I will return
Struggle, revolution, do not die,
For the storm is on the land.

During the occupation Palestinian classical music continued to rise, with new names in the realm of classical music along with the founding of many symphony orchestras, such as the Palestinian Youth Orchestra (PYO).

After the creation of Palestinian Authority, the PLO-led government was able to raise at least one Military Band. This Band's major public performance has been at the funeral of veteran Palestinian leader Yasser Arafat.

Israeli Military Music: It is said that the road to understand Israel goes through its military Bands. The history of Israel, its humour, its pain, its hope, and its evolution is all reflected in the Israeli army singing Bands whose genesis is traced to the period of the Second World War. These Bands performed for Jewish soldiers before the State of Israel existed. The popularity of the army's singing Bands reached its peak in the 1960s and 70s, when they dominated the Israeli music industry. Most of the top Israeli actors, singers, and musicians from that period, received their initial training in one of such army Bands. Even in Israel of today, many of the country's young performers get their early musical instruction from the military. However, they do not get the instant push to the top of music industry that their predecessors received in the earlier decades.

A discussion on Israeli military Bands cannot be complete without reference to *Lahakat HaNahal* (The Nahal Band). Nahal is acronym of Hebrew words *Noar Halutzi Lohem*, (literally: Fighting Pioneer Youth). The term refers to a paramilitary Israeli Defense Forces program that combines military service with the establishment of agricultural settlements, often in peripheral areas. In later years, the program expanded to volunteering for social welfare projects. Its soldiers formed the core of the Nahal Infantry Brigade. The Nahal Band, the military music troupe of the Brigade, is a prominent Band of Israeli military. The Band is known for its Eretz Yisrael (Land of Israel) Hebrew songs featured on Israeli television.

Nahal military Band produced or shaped other civil patriotic Bands; Kavaret being a prominent example. Danny Sanderson and his Bandmates first met during their army service in the Nahal Entertainment Troupe in 1968. During the military service, Sanderson operated a civil Band called *The Schnitzels* with a flexible line-up. During and after the third Arab Israeli War 1973, the Band was engaged to play as part of their reserve army duty, which in turn, led to the release of the Band's first album. For their post-war patriotic songs, the Band was voted "Band of the Year" by Israel Broadcasting Authority for next four consecutive years.

The military establishment in Israel, and the role of the military in Israeli culture, have been decisive influences on Israeli music. In the wake of decades of conflict with the Arabs, the themes of war and peace have become an integral part of Israeli music. From pre-state times until the present day, many songs deal with war, sacrifice, loss, heroism, and the longing for peace. Extremely militaristic songs that glorify triumph over the enemy are not the standard in the Israeli repertoire. Rather, most songs dealing with war are melancholy in tone.

The influence of the military on Israeli music, however, goes far beyond it being a source of inspiration for songs. The military establishment has been an active promoter of music, through its corps of military performance groups, and through its army-run radio station, Galei Tsahal. Since the 1950s, the Israel Defense Forces (IDF) has run performing groups called *Lehakot Tsva'iyot* (Army Ensembles). These groups, comprising enlisted soldiers with talent or performing experience, visit field formations and military bases to perform for the troops. Meticulously creating original materials, these groups became leaders in the Israeli music and entertainment field. Many of Israel's most popular songs were written for the Lehakot Tsva'iyot. These Army Ensembles, as noted at the outset, were incubators for performers and composers who, from the 1960s to the present, have become Israel's star artists, composers and lyricists.

The music of the Lehakot and of Galey Tsahal was not specifically military music; most of the songs produced and broadcast were general songs. However, the IDF did see music as an important propaganda tool, and actually sponsored the composition of songs on subjects it deemed important. For example, lyricist Haim Hefer was invited to spend a week accompanying the elite commando group "Haruv," and to base a song on his experience. The result was "Yesh Li Ahuv BeSayeret Haruv" (I have a lover in the Haruv commando unit).

Israeli Army has twelve military Bands. They have fairly simple uniforms. These Bands are the custodians of the tunes of Israeli military music and war songs. The Israeli military Bands are represented in various international Bands tattoos and competitions.

Egyptian Military Music: The Egyptian Military music is also a very interesting study. They had limited military music capacity at the time of first Arab-Israel war of 1948. But after the 1952 Nasser revolution, the military gave a lot of attention to revolutionary music.

"Patriotic Port Said" and other nationalist songs refer to the 1956 Suez war, when Israel, France and Great Britain attacked Egypt after President Gamal Abdel Nasser nationalized the Suez Canal. When war broke out on October 29, lightly armed civilians in Port Said were able to hold off the foreign forces in house-to-house combat. Local musical groups quickly composed songs, hailing the residents of Port Said as champions of Egypt's anti-imperialist struggle.

The second Arab-Israel War, also called the Six-days' War, took place in June 1967. Israel was not only able to capture Gaza and whole Sinai peninsula from Egypt, they also took Golan Heights from Syria and the whole area on West Bank of River Jordan, that included East Jerusalem, from Jordan. In the short run they had destroyed Arab capacity to fight back.

Heartthrob singer of the Arab world, Umme Kulthum's songs took on more a soul searching for Egyptians following the 1967 defeat. *Hadeeth el Rouh* ("The Talk ofThe Soul") is a translation from Pakistan's national poet-philosopher Allama Mohammad Iqbal's famous poem *Shikwa.* This set up a very reflective tone and even Egyptian military Generals in the audience are said to have been left in tears.

Not too many movies in Egypt dealt with the loss. However, a movie that was produced in 1972 dealt with the 1967 loss, and evoked many memories of unity and call to arms. The Arabic movie is titled on the opening lyrics of one of its songs which can be translated as "Song on the Passage." The movie tells the story of an Army unit that held their ground and refused to retreat even though the Egyptian Army has bailed out on them. But the song that immortalized the memory of 1967 war was another one from this movie titled "long lives your smile Egypt" (Shafiq 1998).

It was not only Egypt but the rest of the Arab nations, especially the Palestinians, who felt humiliated by this defeat. But Egypt went back to work and did take revenge by a counter-attack that triggered the third Arab-Israel war of 1973. Unfortunately, most of the songs and the movies created to commemorate the 1973 war were hastily done and thus are not too impressive. Yet, some of the songs that instilled enthusiasm and patriotism included one titled *Allah Akbar Besm Allah* which continued as theme song TV and radio for decades on the anniversary of the war every October 6. Another song titled "Mother of the hero," was by the singer Sherifa Fadel who has actually lost her son in the war and this song was dedicated to his memory. Another one by Abdel Halim Hafez was dedicated to eulogize the Egyptian leadership who took the decision to attack Israel.

During President Sisi's rule, the two Band fiascos where the Egyptian army Band literally butchered the tune of the Russian and then French national anthems, during welcome ceremonies at the State visits of President Putin and President Hollande, respectively, are obviously exceptions. Otherwise, compared to the rest of the Arab world, the Egyptian State has a very fine tradition of military, paramilitary and police Bands. On the occasions of the commemoration of 1948, 1956 and 1973 wars (they do not observe ceremonies to mark the 1967 war), the

Bands play these patriotic tunes. However, an Egyptian army officer right asked, "Are we going to defeat them [i.e. Israel] with a Song?"

Conclusion: "The Band's Visit"

The Military Music of the two World Wars was strikingly different from each other. There were also differences in the type of music in the initial and final years of each World War. And finally, due to different experiences in War, the music produced by various parties was also different. The United States, just like any other country, was able to utilize the exponential growth of the technological age, before the start of the World War up to the end of the Cold War, to compose music for various reasons.

Although during the World War, music was made popular because of the widely distributed radio, the number of concerts skyrocketed along with the incorporation of women and African-American musicians into the US military Bands and musical groups. Whether women were incorporated because of sexual attraction or actual acceptance by the institutions is still not very clear; what is clear is that groups were now mixed sexes and some even mixed races in an era of sexism and racism. This goes to show that the role of music not only had effects in the international sphere, but in the domestic one as well. Thus musical influence of war and war influence on music goes far beyond the battlefronts. The social transformations brought about by the wars are reflected in regional warfare also. The social and ethnic splits seen in Indo-Pakistani societies started dissipating during the wars. And patriotic music generated by the wars was one of the factors that fostered nationalistic spirit in both the countries above the parochial identities and differences.

The war songs of the primitive societies used to be sung by fighting members of a tribe in order to raise the morale of the comrade troops and to instil fear in the enemy lines. These roles somewhat continued during the modern warfare under review in this chapter, especially during the Cold War. The only function of Military Bands that has faded out is their role in wartime signalling due to availability of more effective and reliable means of communication available during the modern wars. But it does not mean that signalling use of Musical instruments totally ended during modern warfare. As recently as the second half of the 20th century, the Chinese troops in the Korean War and the Viet Cong Guerillas in the Vietnam War used Horns and other instruments for signalling. These sounds in the dead of the night in dark hills around would also unnerve the opponent armies. Nevertheless, the bulk of Cold War music from both sides of the fault lines was not to terrify the enemy, but as a conscious effort to keep the morale of the own troops high.

The Military Bands remain relevant in the remembrances of the World Wars, the conflicts of the Cold War and in memorial ceremonies of the regional wars in various parts of the world. The impact of the Band music extends beyond the troops to the general citizenry for raising the patriotic fervour on the one hand, and feeling of goodwill towards the adversaries on the other. This latter impact is capably depicted in an Israeli movie by Eran Kolirin entitled "The Band's Visit" (2007) that won eight Ophir Prizes awarded by the Israel Film Academy. The film portrays an Egyptian Police Band losing its way to reach a fictional Israeli town of Bet Hatikwa in Negev desert. This, according to the film's website www.theBandsvisitmusical.com celebrates the "deeply human ways music, longing and laughter can connect us all." The role of Bands in real life is not much different than this.

NOTES

1 Most of the discussion on the role of individual Military Bands during the World War II, except those referenced otherwise, is based on the official website of the British Ministry of Defence www.army.mod.uk/music

2 The discussion on Red Army Choir, later renamed as Alexandrov Band, is based on articles on www.revolvy.com and the websites of Al Jazeerah English and RT (Russia Today) television network website in the days following the death of 64 members of the Choir in a plane crash in the Black Sea near Sochi on X-mas day 2016.

3 It was even rumoured in the 1930s that Winifried Wagner, the composer's daughter-in-law, was destined to become Hitler's wife

4 Reprinted with permission of the publisher from We Gotta Get Out of This Place: The Soundtrack of the Vietnam War. Copyright © 2015 by University of Massachusetts Press.

5 Magnitostroi was a steel plant situated far away from any city, deficient in basic commodities and resources, and extreme housing shortages. Notwithstanding the extreme working conditions of -20 to -40 degrees, the Soviet recruitment strategies of extra pay and free transportation helped make it a modern industrial hub, showcasing Soviet successes in industrialisation

CHAPTER X

Third World War & Bands in Post-Modern Warfare

Be the light, in the dark,
Be the Calm in the storm, and
Be at Peace while in War

—Leo Tolstoy in *War and Peace*

The above words by the great Russian novelist fit very neatly to the military Bands. During the War, military Bands act as a light (hope) in the dark and somber atmosphere. They are like the calmness in the storm and are instruments of peace in the war.

The incidents of 9/11 and the ensuing War on Terror has brought us to a new generation of Warfare: the fourth generation. Today, the armies have to fight invisible enemies. They are tasked to patrol areas with the task to win over the local people where they have to coop with sniper fire, improvised explosive devices and guerilla tactics by terrorists. In the present day, the war is fought in the whole society rather than in any distant battlefields. Politics, electronic and social media, public opinion, cyberspace and many other factors have to be taken into account in developing the strategy.

Gone are the days when musical Bands could and were brought to the battlefronts during the First World War II to play tunes cleared by the military command for the troops. The Radio communication during the Second World War and the television programming during Vietnam war, for instance—of government choice, that is—could be transmitted to and from the battle fronts. In the present post-modern conflicts, however, the music accompanies soldiers from the recruiting office to the battlefield in their own iPods, laptops or mobile handsets.

What will be the role of uniformed military Bands in the new context? Can ways be improvised whereby the troops or the broader society be made to watch videos of performances of military Bands on their smart gadgets? Of course, not. Yet, there can be innovative nature of duties that Bands of the future may be required to perform. For instance, a time may come where the only military battles will be the Battles of the Bands. A musical competition determining the fate of disputes or disputed territories.

At present, the Bands themselves have landed into a global war, fighting invisible enemies on two fronts: in the form of terrorists killing them and in the form of politicians bent upon ensuring their demise through slicing their budgets. This is an existential threat that the Bands must win. This what I call the Third World War that the Military Bands are fighting against their own parent Military Forces.

This chapter will deal with the role of Bands in post-Modern warfare, from the Fourth Generation onwards. The War Against Bands is itself a post-Modern war which will be explored and examined below.

Military Music of the Global War on Terror

Military Bands had been playing a role in the wars against terrorists and insurgents much before the 9/11 and the US invasions of Afghanistan (2001-) and Iraq (2003-). Initially both these wars were initiated for regime change—Taliban regime had to be replaced in Afghanistan and President Saddam Hussain had to be ousted in Iraq. The new dispensations in Kabul and Baghdad proved to be the easy part. Soon the US-led coalition ended up fighting two formidable foes, the Taliban insurgents in Afghanistan and the so-called Islamic State in Iraq. This was a time when internet and smartphones changed the dynamics of war as well as information communication. Accordingly, the way military or war-related music would influence the conflicts was transformed.

On the other hand, information and communication technology has undergone such revolutionary changes that governmental control on media has virtually evaporated. The governments had a lot of control over the content of Radio during the World War and that of Television during the Vietnam war. It could and did do the sifting and filtering of what music soldiers should hear and what images the public should watch. But it's no longer so. In the US-led wars in Afghanistan and Iraq, a smartphone is in the pocket of every soldier and every citizen. The soldiers can upload whatever they like, they can hear whatever they prefer and they can broadcast as they please. No content can be blacked out from the soldiery or the citizenry by the State. The whole paradigm of music, patriotic and military music included, has therefore changed.

The Asian nations also had to face the menace of terrorism. The music of the war on terror and the role of military Bands in the war remains a relevant and important topic in its own right. India and Pakistan having the largest number of military Bands in their Armed Forces offer interesting insights into this under-studied and under-appreciated topic.

Hence, this section is divided into two sub-sections, one studying the role of Military Music in the US-led Western military operations in Asia, and the second on how music has influenced or is influenced by the home-grown terrorism within strong Asian military powers of India and Pakistan.

Military Music of US Wars in Iraq and Afghanistan

The reemergence of Western Military Bands in the Middle East started with the build up to the first Gulf War (Aug 1990 to Jan 1991). This operation, called Desert Storm, was authorized under a United Nations Security Council Resolution for the purpose of evicting Iraqi forces out of Kuwait. That mission was accomplished within 42 days (17 Jan- 28 Feb 1991) but the US and allied forces were in there for a long haul. In 2003, the second Gulf War started when on suspicion of Iraq having a clandestine weapons of mass destruction programme, the US and its allies invaded Iraq to dislodge the then President Saddam Hussain and his *Baath* Party regime from power. As hardly anyone could have foreseen at that time, the US forces were dragged into fighting a non-conventional war against guerilla forces for the next decade and a half.

The Operation Desert Storm was the first time, since the Second World War, when the Military Bands of Western Forces, saw duty in active combat in the Middle East. The Bands once again distinguished themselves through their devotion to duty. Eight Bands of the United States Army saw active duty in the first Gulf War. They were: Band of the 1st Cavalry Division, two Bands of the 1st and 3rd Armored Divisions, two Bands of the 1st and 24th Infantry Divisions, two Bands of the 82nd and 101st (Air Assault) Airborne Divisions, and finally, the 84th Army Band.

BandsDuties of the Bands were varied. The 3rd Armored Division Band provided music up to and including the start of the war. This was one of the Bands that performed direct military role as well. This Band performed on the enemy side of an earthen wall formed by the Iraqi Defense Forces while the 24th Infantry Division backed by the 3rd Armored Division advanced into Iraqi territory.

The Band of the 24th Infantry Division, however, provided little musical support. The Bandsmen were tasked with guarding the perimeter while their Division moved into Iraq, for which the Band spent countless hours.

During peacetime, the 101st Airborne Division (Air Assault) Band is located in Fort Campbell, Kentucky. When due to the exigencies of war, the Band was relocated to the Gulf region (inside a US army base in Saudi Arabia, two National Guard Bands, namely the 129th Army Band and the 151st Army Band, were activated to support Fort Campbell during the absence of 101st Division Band. The two National Guard Bands provided musical support to the families during the war. They also performed for troops returning from Desert Storm. And in a way, these two Bands performed for the war effort, while remaining within the United States, in addition to the eight Bands deployed in the Middle East.

The British Army was also part of the allied forces in the first Gulf War. The Band of Royal Anglian Regiment was initially sent to Saudi Arabia to be part of 5 Field Ambulance Unit. However, they decided to take their musical instruments along. This Band was the first to play in the liberated city of Kuwait after withdrawal of the Iraqi forces. Upon return to their Base back in the United Kingdom after the war, all members of the Band received the Gulf Medal with Gulf Clasp (Curtis 2016). In 2007, the 2nd Marine Aircraft Wing Band was deployed to Iraq to provide security at a tactical air control centre.

As noted above, the first Gulf War ended in 1991, but the US military commitment did not. The security situation became from bad to worse and ousting of Saddam Hussain by military means in the Second Gulf War did not help. On the contrary, the power vacuum was filled by non-State actors which started a war against the Western military presence and their own democratic governments accusing them of colluding with the West. So the United States found itself embroiled in a non-conventional war in Iraq since 2003.

Two years earlier, on 11th September 2001, nineteen hijackers had commandeered four passenger airliners to hit US landmarks including the World Trade Center twin-towers in New York and the Pentagon building in Washington DC. This was the first direct attack on the US soil since the Anglo-American war of 1812-14 nearly two centuries earlier. A noted terrorist Osama bin Laden, head of the Al-Qaeda—the network behind the attack—was enjoying shelter in the *Taliban*-controlled Afghanistan. The United States military moved to bomb the *Taliban* movement out of power from the national capital Kabul and the *Taliban* movement capital of Qandhar. Despite being swept out from their strongholds, *Taliban* proved to be far from being a spent force. They launched a guerilla movement against the US presence that continued for decades. It is the music, especially Band music, of these two engagements that concerns us.

The US wars in Iraq and Afghanistan have both lasted longer than the duration of US involvement in Korean and Vietnam Wars combined. The Vietnam and Korean wars were fought in the context of Cold War against a Communist enemy. The latter two conflicts are part of the Global War on Terror and the US forces are supporting the government forces of Iraq and Afghanistan against militant organizations, the so-called Islamic State and the Taliban movement, respectively.

The United States military Bands including those of the Army, the Marines and the Air Force were used repeatedly sent in operational areas in the Middle East. They made visible presence in US bases in Afghanistan also over the years, The U.S Bands played a part in these conflicts by increasing morale for Soldiers and providing music for military ceremonies as well as purely for entertainment of the troops.

Since, for the most part, the two wars went on simultaneously, the music that emerged from these is also overlapping. Most of the war music is that of frustration, fear, protest against government policies and a longing for home and family. In all, there have been 2.7 million US Servicemen and women who had at least one stint of duty in either of these two theatres.

Music is a form of soldier expression and in various ways the US soldiers fighting in the Iraq and Afghanistan Wars turn to music as a way to cope with and comment upon their experiences. The soldiers who returned from these theatres used music as an expression to vent their feelings about their war experience. The regular official military Bands would, of course, not play anti-war music, so people including veterans formed their own rock Bands. One revealing example is the small city of Khost in Eastern Afghanistan where coalition troops repeatedly faced *Taliban* fighters. Surprisingly, several rock Bands named "*Khost* Bands," unrelated to each other, emerged in such diverse places as Austin in Texas (USA), Birmingham in the United Kingdom and Brisbane in Australia, all by veterans of these countries who had served in Khost garrison of Afghanistan.

These private Bands created the repertory of anti-war pop music. The song *Wrong side of heaven, righteous side of hell* talks about the problems faced by veterans, claiming that 0.3 million veterans are homeless and another 1.4 million are at the risk of becoming so. The song titled *American Soldier* is about the pain of leaving home. The song titled *Arlington* talks about grave in a cemetery which for many of the servicemen becomes a new home, upon return from the war duty, i.e. those killed in action whose dead bodies are brought home. The song *I just came back from a war* complains that people do not care about the war or about the death of Americans. The song *21 Guns* is another protest song suggesting that what one was fighting for was not worth dying for. The song *Let Them Eat War* mocks democracy that the poor voted not for war which they cannot eat. Other songs *The Man I shot, B.O.B* (*Bombs Over Baghdad*), *To Washington* and *Dad's Gonna Kill Me* are about miseries brought by war. None of these songs are probably a great hit but the music being churned out from these wars is going to stay in national memory for times to come.

An important book written by Jonathan Pieslak for the first time explores in detail the role of music created and consumed by the American soldiers in both the Iraq wars. He did his research from US troops deployed for Operations *Desert Shield* and *Desert Storm* for liberating Kuwait from Iraqi occupation in 1990-91 and then the later phase of operation, starting 2003, aimed at overthrowing President Saddam Hussain's regime and finding any weapons of mass destruction that Iraq might have had (Pieslak 2009). Much of what he has said about the use of music in Iraq war is equally applicable on the war in Afghanistan.

It is a music of their choice in their laptops, smartphones and iPods and not the one that the Defence Ministry could choose to broadcast to them. Pieslak describes how American soldiers hear, share, use, and produce music both on and off duty. He studies the role of music from recruitment campaigns and basic training to its use "in country" before and during missions. Pieslak explores themes of power, chaos, violence, and survival in the metal and hip-hop music so popular among the troops (Pieslak 2009).

As for use of music in military recruitment advertising, he focuses his analysis on what he identifies as two recurrent musical themes: "honorable duty music" and music that "promotes action/excitement." Introduction of heavy metal music and rock music in more recent military recruitment advertisements is something that other military powers such as Russia and China are already doing (Pieslak 2009).

The important finding of the book is the fact that the music of rival sides has for recruitment videos has striking similarities in content and in dissemination techniques. In other words, the so-called Islamic State (in Northern Iraq and Syria), Gaza-based hardliner *Hamas* movement, and Iranian-backed Hezbollah (in Iraq) use such like inspirational content to motivate people to join as combatants.[1] Their songs highlight the duty of *Jihad* and love to the motherland on the one hand, and promote thrill and excitement of combat on the other.[2] Throwing out the Western troops is musically projected as a sacred and patriotic duty. And, given the total blackout of terrorists videos in cinema, television, radio and print, the medium of propagation remains social media, as the only, rather than the preferred, medium available to them. At the end of the day, it comes to smartphones, tablets and laptops where their fighters watch the war songs behind gory images of, say, slaughtering a Western or a Japanese hostage.

Pieslak explores music as an inspiration for combat and points out that same type of musical and psychological tactics are used in anti-America and anti-Israel videos created by a wide range of militant groups in the Middle East, that the US and Western militaries use for their troops. Pieslak usefully addresses the standardization found among such productions, noting, "the structure of most ISIL/ISIS videos is uniform, consisting of a slogan in an introductory graphic, an overdubbed war/jihad song, and images of an IED attack." He adds an informative discussion of the various similarities between these video productions and the US Armed Forces recruitment advertising (Pieslak 2009).

The employment of music in interrogation/torture is a rather unpleasant use of music both in Afghanistan and Iraq. While the debate as to what type of music use could aptly be defined as torture will go on amongst the legal minds, it is clear that troops used loud patriotic music on Iraqi and Afghan war prisoners, in an effort to frustrate, irritate, and sleep deprive them into answering questions.

Military Music in Pakistan and India during War on Terror

As peace remains elusive in South Asia, military and martial music continues to evolve. For example, the war on terror has deeply impacted Pakistani cinema and popular music. In turn, the incidents as well as the pop music of the War on Terror has greatly transformed Pakistani military music. As has been discussed in the context of Indo Pakistani wars, Indian cinema creates music that then permeates into the society as well as the military. In case of Pakistan, the direction is the reverse. The music is mostly created outside the film industry.

The media arm of the Pakistani Armed Forces is called the Inter Services Public Relations (ISPR). The ISPR is also the custodian of the musical legacy of military music that is continuously being created and updated as more and more conflicts make the army battle-hardened. In June 2014, the army launched a full-fledged Operation codenamed *Zarb e Azb* (lit. Hitting like a Sword) to flush out terrorists from tribal areas in the mountains bordering Afghanistan. A song titled *Qasam us waqt ki* (tr. I swear by that time) was released at the same to motivate and honour the troops that were being sent to the front lines.

A turning point in Pakistan's long running war on terror occurred when the terrorists attacked an Army Public School in Peshawar on 16 Dec 2014 and massacred school students studying there. Since the school mostly catered for children of military personnel, the massacre was, terrorist-sympathetic websites claimed, done to avenge for the Operation *Zarb e Azb*. A number of songs entered Pakistani national scene mourning the massacre of kids, such as the *Bara dushman bana phirta hai* (tr. The one who claims to be an enemy massacres innocent children) and *Mujhe dushman ke bacchon ko parhan hai* (tr. I have to make the children of my enemy to come to school/ I have to teach them).

At the first and second anniversary of the *Zarb e Azb* in June 2015 and June 2016, the following two motivational songs were released by ISPR which have become symbols of patriotism in Pakistani society: *Yeh Banday mitti ke Banday* (O these sons of soil!) and *Ay watan tera ishara aa gya* (O my homeland, you have beckoned me!). Today the music of such songs have become signature tunes of military Bands and have made a debut in Pakistan movies such as *Saya e Khuda e Zuljalal.*[3]

On the Indian side, terrorism has remained a hot topic for Bollywood film-makers. As highlighted elsewhere the Bollywood is the biggest single producer of songs and music in India. From 1995, the Bollywood war movies changed their focus from Indo-Pakistan wars to the war on terrorism. *Param Veer Chakra* (1995) had a playlist of six songs in all, of which "*Mere mehbub mere watan*" [tr. My love, my country!] became famous for its lyrics and has been played by military and police Bands since then.

Among the most famous movies on the fighting in Kashmir valley were *Mission Kashmir* (2000), *Yahaan* (2005), and *Shauria* (2008), all of whose musical playlists were instant hits. India was facing problems of armed insurgency elsewhere as well. Movies on issues other than Kashmir hit the box office too. In 1998, a movie *Dil Se* focused on rebellion in India's north east while the plot of 2005 movie *Tango Charlie* revolves around Naxalite rebellion. Needless to say that the repertoire of all these movies is a mix of patriotic and romantic songs and thus the two types become a must-play, respectively, for the military Bands and the marching wedding Bands.

Military Bands in the World War III

One must be forgiven to use a harsh term "World War III" for the global campaign against Bands. The military Bands face themselves being in a pincer movement where their own military commands as well as the terrorist movements are becoming increasingly intolerant at them. On the one hand, the terrorists and non State actors consider military music as the State's important weapon against them and target military Bands in a conscious manner. On the other hand, the State's own military authorities consider their own Bands as somewhat useless arm. Thus, it is not unusual for military top brass to start pandering to self-serving politicians who are bent upon eliminating the miliaty Bands. Thus, the taboo against targeting military Bands, that had held the field since the US Civil War, seems to be breaking apart on part of the State and Non-state actors, i.e. both the political/military leadership and the anti-State militants, alike.

As far as the terrorist element is concerned, this is a military conflict where Bands are being attacked by bombs and firepower worldwide. As for the political offensive, the conflict has all the trappings of the post-Modern warfare: concealment, psychological attacks, no direct enemy and the whole society ending up being the likely victim—hence, the label.

The terrorist strikes against Military Bands

It appears that the terrorists do consider the military Bands and Bandsmen as their enemies. Whether a lone wolf attack like the brutal murder of Lee Rigby, Drummer in the Band of Royal Regiment of Fusiliers on 22 May 2013 in London, or a well-coordinated bomb attack on the Royal Marines School of Music, Bands have remained on the hit-list of the non-State actors of various hues and ideologies. In the latter incident, the Irish Republican Army (IRA) attacked the Royal Deal Barracks, on 22 Sept 1989, in which 11 Musicians of Royal Marines Band got killed and another 22 injured

As for Drummer Rigby incident, he was off duty and was walking along Wellington Street when he was stabbed with knives and a cleaver by two Nigerian-born British citizens, Michael Adebolajo and Michael Adebowale, near the Royal Artillery Barracks in Woolwich, southeast London. The murderers remained at the scene until police arrived, telling passers-by that this killing of a soldier was to avenge the killing of Muslims by the British Armed Forces.[4]

As for the attack on Marine Band at Royal Deal Barracks in 1989, this was not the first incident of its kind. Seven years earlier, the twin bomb attacks by IRA earlier on 20 July 1982 in London also targeted Military Bands. The attack at the Hyde Park had killed four soldiers of the Royal Household Cavalry, known as Blues and Royals, while the one at the Regent Park in London claimed lives of seven Bandsmen of the Infantry Regiment called Royal Green Jackets. In the latter attack, the bomb was actually placed below the Bandstand where the 30-member Band was performing for the public on a bright summer afternoon.

Besides the 7 Bandsmen who lay dead, another 22 got injured. The twin bombings drew a lot of flak from all sides, since the IRA had chosen to target and massacre military Bands personnel whose only military training was that of saving lives.

A more recent loss to the Bands was the crash of a Russian Defense Ministry Tu-154 aircraft on Christmas Day 2016 in the Black Sea. The plane was carrying a 64-strong contingent of the famous Alexandrov Band to play for Russian and Syrian troops in the war torn Syria to mark the new year and the onset of a ceasefire. The so-called Islamic State (IS/ISIS)—a potent terrorist outfit—that the Russians had been bombing for months in Syria had pledged revenge for Russian backing of Assad regime. Months earlier the IS had claimed bombing of a Russian passenger aircraft killing all passengers over the Sinai desert. Although there is no evidence that the downing of the military Tu-154 aircraft was also a terrorist act but the fact remains that the Military Band died in the line of duty en route to performance in a warzone. Hence, there is no reason to question the fact that the 50-member Choir and the 14-member Dance ensemble were killed in the war on terror.[5]

When Pakistan joined the US-led War on Terror to exterminate terrorists within its territory after 9/11, one of the first operational decisions that the army took was to ban all military Band performances, public and private, outside military establishments of the country. The threat to the Bands was a real one and the army made sure that its drummers and pipers do not get killed in a suicide bomb attack that was signature *modus operandi* of several terrorist outfits in Pakistan.

The Political War against Military Bands

The political war against the Bands is not like the past wars where the States fought each other and the Military Bands from both sides played a role at or behind the battlefields. In this war, the States are pitted against their own Military Bands. This is, in fact, a global (political) war against the Military Bands. Institutions of the State had been instrumental in the rise of Bands. Today several of them are instrumental in a relentless campaign to portray Bands as relics of the past with little or no use.

Military Bands are a "wastage of State resources" is the battle cry by self-serving politicians. Even docile military commanders, pandering to the wishes of political bosses tend to agree. They would echo whatever will be "music to the ears" of the political bosses. Hence, we find certain forces bent upon reducing, merging and eliminating their own Military Bands.

This argument claiming financial cost of the Military Bands to be exorbitant has always been the primary assault weapon. In the United States, the cost for all the military Bands was US $437 million in the year 2016. This, the opponents of the Bands argue, although a fraction—less than 0.09 percent—of the US Military budget, is more than the total military budgets of at least four States amongst the 27 of its NATO Allies. It was also argued that slashing the funds for Bands to divert to defence-related heads may increase the security of the nation.

The second and obvious line of attack course, has been the human resource devoted to musical duties. "Drop the Tuba, pick up the Gun" was the headline of Daily *Fiscal Times* while covering a bill presented in the US Congress Bill to cut funding of military Bands, taking verbatim from the speech of Sponsoring Congresswoman Martha McSally, herself a former US Air Force Officer. The argument is that these men and women would serve the nation better if they were carrying weapons. "Doing that stuff in this day and age, when we don't have enough people for combat positions?" she said in a phone interview. "I just don't get it" (Philipps 2016).

The third main argument by President Houses, Parliaments and Cabinets to cut down the money on the military Bands is ostensible because they want the Armed Forces "to protect us, rather than entertain us." It is conveniently overlooked that Armed Forces Bands are much more than simple entertainment.

These or similar arguments have persistently been made in the United States over the past century and a half. It is neither inadvertent nor unintentional that the US army has reduced its Bands to 137 now down from a thousand Bands and 28,500 musicians during the same period. And the reverse counting on the number of Bands is still going on.

Admittedly, the trajectory of evolution of military Bands in different, far away and disconnected regions of the world had striking similarity. Such Military Bands in different cultural and historical contexts had remarkably matching formations and roles. It is no surprise, therefore, the degree to which arguments being made against Bands have so many common threads, in diverse and disconnected political environs.

In the continental Europe, Britain which had a pride of place in promotion of modern ceremonial style pipes and drum corps, progressively reduced the number of army Bands from 69 to 23 since the WW-II, while it is left with 13 Air Force and five Naval Bands. In the far South of the globe, New Zealand has merged all its 12 Bands into 3 for the whole country one each for Army, Navy and the Air Force. Situation in Germany, Belgium and many Nordic States is almost similar.

Here we shall only discuss three major political battles against the Bands: one waged by the Parliament (Sweden), another unleashed by the Government Auditors (United States) and the last one was a foray by the Treasury Department (United Kingdom) on payments to the Band Members. Sweden is distinguished by its rich history of Bands, the UK is credited with spreading military Bands around the world, while the United States has the highest military spending in the world but finds difficult to fund its Military Bands. Looking at how the Military Bands are getting treated in these two nations, it would be easy to guess the challenges the younger Military Bands are facing in the States with shorter Bands history.

Battle of the Parliament against Bands (Stockholm 1971)

The Swedish Armed Forces have regular Bands dating even before the era of the Great Northern War with the Russians to dominate the northern parts of the Globe. Like all other politicians of the world, the Swedish ones were no exception. Whenever there was a discussion on military spending, that on the Military Bands was considered as a low hanging fruit that would meet the eye of the Budget cutters. The argument goes like this, if we can do without something, we can go without Bands because it is a luxury. It is also politically safe to play with the Bands because a politician displays that he is doing something for austerity and since he is not cutting down on weapons, so at least he would not look unpatriotic to the voters.

In 1850, there were only 1,529 musicians left in all the military Bands of Sweden that are, thanks to persistent parliamentary oversight, left to 141 as of early 2018. Even this the Parliament finds "too many" and proposals are already afoot to reduce the number of total Bands members with the Armed Forces to 76 for the whole country. Can 76 men and women provide musical support to the royal palace ceremonies throughout the year, what to speak of that to the whole nation, is a moot point. What is important to note is that even these 141 (that is 76, if reduced to that figure) are civilians. Thus, the military does not consider the Band members as part of them and hence the latter have no lobbying power within military command structures.

All this started with the 1971 Music Regulation adopted by the Swedish Parliament which abolished 22 of the 25 army Bands at that time. Till then, Wind Music was entirely a military phenomenon and the new law totally divested the Armed Forces of the responsibility to provide patriotic music, transferring the 500 or so musicians to a civilian organization. In 1982, the Bands were regionalized and given to the 22 County Councils or Departments. The region had to fund the Band and the Band was to perform within the region. This hybrid model did not work and military music suffered a decline. But for the Territorial Home Guard, an entirely civilian auxiliary force, where people otherwise on civilian jobs, volunteer for fixed time a year, for defence and disaster management related duties, which owned the Bands, the Swedish nation would have found itself without the minimal number of military Bands required for the State to fulfil its ceremonial functions and duties. Thanks to the mess that the Swedish politicians have created!

Of the 26 Home Guard Bands, located across Sweden, three belong to Air Home Guard, three to the Naval Home Guard and one to the Amphibious Home Guard (aka Marine Band). As for the regular Armed Forces, there are just three Bands left: a Dragoon Guard of the King's Life Guards, a Central Band of the Army and another one of the Navy. Even the last Air Force Band was disBanded around 2002 making Sweden the only major Air Force in the world without a regular Band. For some time, the Swedish Air Force had an agreement with Wind Orchestra of the City of Vidsel for musical support but even that arrangement has not survived. Luckily, 17 of the 26 Bands of the Home Guard have been declared professionally qualified to perform at State ceremonies. It is this musical support by the civilian Home Guard that sustains Sweden's musical requirements including the daily change of guard ceremony at the royal palace.

Unpalatable as it may be for politicians, the Military Bands are a necessity. They represent exactly what the rest of the Armed Forces fight for. To fill the vacuum hundreds of amateur Bands have sprung up within the Federation of Swedish Amateur Orchestras and the Swedish Federation of Young Musicians, to which some 375 Bands are affiliated. This popular wisdom stands as a mockery of the collective elective wisdom represented by the parliament (Jansson 2018).

Battle of the Treasury against Bands (London 2011)

Barring the Air Force Bands, the United Kingdom's Armed Forces have 22 ensembles: eight symphonic wind Bands, one other wind Bands, six multi-capacity wind Bands, three brass Bands, three pop Bands and one string orchestra in all, in its Army, various Guards corps and the Royal Marine Band Corps combined, with a strength of nearly 2000 Musicians (Braw 2018). These Military Bands in toto perform at an average of 6000 events yearly; 85 per cent of the events utilize their services free of charge. In recent years, the Treasury "discovered" that the Band musicians were not entitled to remuneration for their concerts.

Since decades, and hardly anyone in the Department of Defence knew since when, there was a tradition that the Bandsmen and women were rewarded with a bonus of between £80 to £150 for each paid event. A total of 400 or so annual performances were commercially charged. Some Bands are so much in demand that the performance fee for the Band of the Grenadier Guards could reach up to £10,000 for a concert. Depending on the fee charged the per head bonus of the Band Members used to vary. The circa £1,000 bonus that the musicians made a year can hardly be said to compensate the long traveling, extra labour and many weekends that they spend away from their families to play for the public.

On 3 July 2011, Daily *Telegraph* reported that the Department of Defence had decided to do away with the Bonus saying that since the Bands were paid from the taxpayer money, they were not entitled to any bonus from performance fees. The Band bonuses came to around £2 million a year from the £40 million bonuses that the DoD used to pay to its employees. The level of disillusionment among the musicians can be guessed easily. The rationale of slashing only the Band Members honoraria represents a broader mindset of treating the Band Services as redundant. Situation had come to such a pass that a Musician of the Royal Marines Band, Arian Higginson, was caught having stolen GBP 19,000 of Saxophones and Clarinets to pay off his debts (Telegraph 2017).

Battle of the Auditors against Bands (Washington DC 2017)

The Government Accountability Office (GAO) in the United States is an equivalent of the office of the Auditor General in many states of the British Commonwealth. The Office conducts financial and performance audit of Government Departments and produces hundreds of reports annually. The number *GAO-17-657* of the 41-page report indicates that it was GAO's 657th Report in the year 2017. This one—as part of the *Total Army Analysis Process*—was about the Military Bands which, the Report claimed, could be "crowd-pleasers" but there was a need to assess the value of Bands "relative to resource demand from other priorities."

The Military Bands have been on the fire-line since the end of the Cold War when the Defense Secretary in the George W Bush administration raised fingers on the utility of the Military Bands. This negative view of Bands became more pronounced in all Republican administrations to date. James Mattis, the Defense Secretary under the Trump Administration, was unequivocal about his view of Bands no sooner had he taken office. "We are devoted to gaining full value from every taxpayer dollar spend on defense." Accordingly, amongst his first Directives was to realign military spending with an emphasis to "rebuild r*eadiness* and *lethality*" of the Armed Forces. [Emphasis added] Nobody could have counted Military

Bands as the *lethal* branch of the Armed Forces so justification for using tax-payers dollars on Bands was, by this logic, questionable.

Hence, the above discussed bill by Trump supporter, Congresswoman McSally, was neither surprising nor unique. It rather represents a mindset that has existed in the Capitol for decades at least. The same mindset that leads one to vote against regulatory mechanisms against greenhouse gas emissions, supporting indefinite detentions at Guantanamo Bay and increased spending on Tomahawk missiles. At least for Martha McSally, she has taken all these positions. If the press debates in her congressional district in Arizona are any guide, she is accused of the same attitude that other hardline conservative within the GOP are accused of. Taking alarmist positions, then evincing lack of transparency on data and facts, dodging pointed questions and eventually remaining vague on key parameters. Within her caucus in Congress, she has the third highest number of bills that made it through the House. Her proposal regarding squeezing public funds for Bands was just one of them.

The GAO Report must have come as a music to the ears of those who hate military music. But the Report itself had many surprises. First of all, the number of Bands and spending on it came out to be lower than earlier claimed by detractors. The Report noted that the expenditure on Bands was $303 million per annum (as against $437 million that the Defense Department keeps touting), of which $265 million were spent on account of salaries that the Military was to pay them, even if these officers and soldiers were not part of the Bands. The operational budget was a meagre $38 million for all 136 Bands put together. Again this figure was one less than the 137 that the Defense Department had thought it had. This was due to the latest merger of two US Air Force Bands reducing the USAF Bands to 14 from 15. And even before this GAO Report, five Bands and two musical detachments were already on their way out, under plans to further reduce the Bands' strength by 2019.

There was a continuous downward trend in the number of Bands since the previous plan in 2012 to downsize the military music corps. During the four years (2012–16), the number of Military Bands in US Armed Forces had already dropped from 150 with 7,196 musicians to 136 with 6,656 musicians. Thus there was a drop of 9.3 per cent in the number of Military Bands and nearly 7.5 per cent in the number of Musicians, all within the span of four years. The Air Force Bands reported a drop in annual expenditure by $1.6 million, the Navy Bands reported $4.1 million saving while the Army was still collecting data from its reserve Bands. Marines Bands reported a slight increase of $800,000 but this, they said, was due to underfunding of the previous years. This did not satisfy the

GAO which asked the Armed Forces to prove that the Military Bands increase patriotism through measurable and verifiable criteria. The two figures that the military keeps, i.e. number of Band performances (38,000/year) and the number of audience at each event (ranging between 75 to 81,000 per event) did not impress the GAO.

The Pentagon has agreed with the findings and announced to release a Plan by early 2018 to give *performance measures to Bands to better enable them to assess their mission objectives.* Placing value on arts and music and an attempt to measure impact on morale, in dollar terms, may itself be a unique endeavour in human and economic history.

Uniting for Peace: Stem the global tide against Bands

In Gospel of St Matthew, Jesus takes to task those who "strain at a gnat while swallowing a camel". There may be some element of hypocrisy when politicians want to save money from bugles and tubas which may cost as low as $70 apiece to a more sophisticated one still priced not exceeding three digits, in order to buy or build an aircraft career may well have a price tag of $27 billion.

Let us take all their arguments one by one. The primary concern about the cost of Bands, at first sight, appears to be poor mathematics. The price of modern Aircraft is astronomical, ranging from US $350 million apiece for F-22 Raptor fighter plane, to US $767 million apiece for B-2 Spirit Stealth Bomber. The programme cost of an advanced bomb such as the Massive Ordinance Air Blast (MOAB)—also called the Mother Of All Bombs—is a whopping US $314 million. None of this weaponry can conceivably be available cheaper on eBay or Alibaba.com. As for the trumpets and tubas priced at a few hundred dollars each, one can get them as cheap as US $70 apiece on such websites. Compared to this, a single military plane and sometimes a single non-nuclear explosive device costs more than the total annual cost of all Military Bands in the United States of all five branches of the Armed Forces combined. Selling off all musical instruments for good, will not get enough money to develop one MOAB. As one military musician wrote in his petition to the White House against McSally proposals:

> *We do much more for diplomacy and peace than McSally throwing away millions upon millions of dollars trying to upgrade something that won't be used and will become obsolete in a few years (Shappard 2016).*

The second argument of the diversion of human resource is also outlandish. Congresswoman McSally might know better that the US Air Force, the arm that she belonged to, has 308,600 active duty personnel, 177,221 civilian personnel,

69,200 Air Force Reserve personnel, and 105,500 Air National Guard personnel. From those, the personnel of the USAF performing duties in the 10 Bands are a mere 540 including 20 officers. There is a ratio of one airman performing in the Bands from every 1,223 uniformed men and women. It is that one person that the House Committee found to be a burden on the Air Force. And it is that person which if McSally succeeds in sending to combat will dramatically improve the combat effectiveness of the remaining thousand comrades. On the contrary, the one person remaining in the Bands contributes more in the battle-readiness of his thousand colleagues.

As for the third argument, the answer is Yes, the Military Bands do entertain but not as rock music Bands in commercial concerts but rather in concerts for fatigued soldiers on battlefronts, for patients in the hospitals and for peoples of the areas devastated by manmade or natural calamities. This is not a role that can or should be taken lightly.

And for every Bugle played in one such concert, there are seven, on an average played for military funerals for those who laid their life for the nation. Thus, so few Military Bands are left that they are not even enough for providing enough Buglers (Taps Players) to play at the number of military funerals that take place in any given year across the United States. Over the history, the United States has fought 42 wars. In some of the recent wars, there was very heavy deployment of the US servicemen and women. In all by 2017, around 1.5 million of the Korean war veterans, 6.9 million of the Vietnam war veterans and 4.4 million of the Iraq and Afghanistan war veterans were still alive and part of the 16-million strong war veteran community (DVA 2017). All veterans are entitled to a military funeral. Every year, there are up to half a million veterans who die.

In sharp contrast to the decorum expected of a veteran's funeral, for a nation that considers itself to be keeping veterans in high esteem, pre-recorded Bugle notes on portable stereos, devices like iPods and even mobile handsets, are played at up to 99 per cent of military funerals in the United States.

On top of it, the Military Bands are a customary component of the military's public affairs and community relations efforts. They are also designed to supplement a branch's community relations efforts by projecting a positive image of the US military through performances within the United States and abroad. This role adds to the security of that nation and ends up protecting lives in a much more cost-effective way. In any case, the non-Band budgets for such roles top $4.5 billion, ten times higher the amount annually spent on Bands. The

Military Bands provide free or low-cost support to community organizations by appearing at non-profit events, patriotic observances, and community festivals.

The Military Bands are the custodians of the national sound and costume heritage, that of historical and musical legacies and symbolize the best traits of a nation including discipline, courtesy and morals.

Finally, Bands contribute to troop esprit de corps which is absolutely essential for military training and discipline. Hence, defunding the Bands to spend this money on military training does not make sense.

Conclusion: Future of Bands in Fifth Generation Warfare and Beyond

If the Vietnam war is known as the first Rock-n-Roll war, in terms of musical legacy, both Iraq (2003-) and Afghanistan (2001-) Wars are the first of the iPod Wars. Today, every soldier has a smartphone or an iPod and a lot of music is generated and enjoyed through these hi-tech media. So nature and role of music is transforming and so is the role of Military Bands. But that does not justify the bills to cut military spending on Military Bands almost the world over.

We have discussed Congresswoman McSally's bill approved by the US House of Representatives in July 2016 in some detail above. However, as per George Washington University calculations of the operational price tag for a single Gerald R Ford Aircraft carrier (University 2017), is much higher than the running cost of all 137 Bands of US Military even if their annual funding continues at present level for next half a century. True, the number of military Bands is already shrinking at an alarming rate. But that has to do with political point scoring by defeatist minds, who lack a better agenda. So using military Bands as a punching bag, they show that sometimes there is *no method* in a madness.

In case, one slashes the amount of money to be spent on a Tuba and rather spends it for a gun, one ends up playing in the hands of the terrorists. This is exactly what they want done. The military Bands are the peace-loving face of the military forces and of the States. Far from increasing the number of guns, one must be aiming at increasing the number of tubas.

In his epic novel *War and Peace*, Nobel laureate Leo Tolstoy observed that the effectiveness of an army is the product of the mass multiplied by something else; by an unknown "X"—the spirit of the army. Throughout history, music has had the effect of raising that unknown "X" by a considerable measure. That is why each War has led to creation of countless number of Bands. Just like the Bands played on the sinking *Titanic*, the world's military Bands are determined to play till the end. If they have to go down, they will go down playing!

If the Bands win this Third World War being fought against them, we may well see an "nth" Generation of Warfare, it does not matter whether it is labelled as the fifth, the sixth of tenth Generation, where the most relevant military arm shall be the musical corps. The only military battles fought shall be the Battles of Bands. And the victory or defeat in a Tattoo between the Military Bands of enemy nations shall determine the fate of a disputed territory, property or issue between States. And if we do not find a number good enough to describe this future generation of Warfare, we may call it the Xth Generation after Tolstoy's factor X or the Mth Generation where M stands for Military Music or Military Bands.

NOTES

1 Though Pieslak's work focusses on Iraq, but by extension, similar tactics are used by many anti-US fighting forces in Afghanistan such as the *Taliban* movement and the ISIS-inspired rebel group—self-styled as the Islamic State in Khorasan. The latter group operates mainly in the inaccessible mountain ranges between Pakistan's tribal belt and Afghanistan. The *Taliban* Islamic movement which had, in its early years in power (1996-98), started a campaign to wipe out all kinds of music from Afghanistan by banishing artists and blowing up music shops, and by the third year in power introduced a marching band with their annual parade in Kabul. They now rely heavily on motivational songs to attract and retain recruits in their fight against the government in Afghanistan as well as the US forces.

2 The only movement that has rolled back on religiously motivated lyrics is the Palestine Liberation Organization (PLO), popularly known by its Arabic acronym *Al Fatah*. Its discourse now relies on secular nationalist ideology based primarily on love for the motherland.

3 Literally translated as the "Shadow of the Glorious God" is the last line of Pakistan's national anthem. The movie is one of the many sponsored by ISPR. This one was about the terrorists trying to destabilize Pakistan and the efforts by military and police officers to lay down their lives for glory of the motherland.

4 The Police was able to shoot and arrest the injured assailants who were recent converts to Islam, being born and raised as Christians. Both have been sentenced to life imprisonment.

5 That these were non-combatant deaths cannot denigrate the value of the sacrifice of Alexandrov Band. Even for the US casualties in their war on terror, every fifth fatality of their troops fighting the insurgents in Iraq and Afghanistan, is a non-combat death, such as helicopter crash, disease and accident.

CHAPTER XI

Modern Role of Bands: Statecraft

If one desires to know if a kingdom is well governed, if its morals are good or bad, the quality of the music will furnish the answer.

—Confucius

The State-owned Bands are an important tool at the disposal of the States for use in governance. There exists a small amount of literature studying the role of Bands in the wars; the study of their role in diplomacy is fairly limited. It is the role of Bands in the statecraft that scholarly work is conspicuous by its absence.

The modern state uses its Military and Police Bands for many more purposes than the State ceremonial. Bands have been used to pacify the public, for riot control, to divert public attention from something awkward or tricky, as a diversion for terrorists before an anti-terrorist operation, as a tool for psychological warfare in a security-related operation where use of direct force could be deemed as diplomatically or morally unfeasible. What is important is that the impact of the use of Bands has invariably been positive. In some cases, the very use of Bands has avoided bloodshed which could have otherwise ensued. In others, the use of Band or music has tempered the bluntness of the operation. Yet in others, the needful has been achieved in a manner that would appear politically softer.

A few examples would suffice to show the diverse ways in which Bands have been employed in pursuance of State objectives from the broad strategic to the immediate tactical ones.

Employing Military Bands in civil war and counter insurgency ops

The States have used Military Bands in many innovative ways in the fight against terrorist and insurgent forces, both on the home ground and abroad. Sometimes the Bands have been used to boost morale of troops, at other times to irritate or annoy the terrorists and sometimes as a direct military tactic.

Role of Military Band in Civil War in Dominican Republic

A prominent example of the use of Military Bands in aid of a foreign state or its government, for political purposes, is the deployment of United States Military Bands in the Dominican Republic during its political turmoil (April 24 to Sept. 3, 1965). The conflict started when supporters of constitutionally elected ousted President Juan Bosch re-captured Presidential Palace overthrowing military-backed acting President Donald Reid. This prompted the military chief General Elías Wessin y Wessin to organize elements of the military loyal to President Reid, known as loyalists, initiating an armed campaign against the so-called constitutionalists (Bosch supporters).

The US Government feared that the Dominican Republic could likely become a "second Cuba" unless the US Forces intervened to restore order. In the spring of 1965, US President Lyndon Johnson, ordered US troops into the Dominican Republic ostensibly "to protect lives of the US citizens" but also to restore order. As the 82nd Airborne Division troops landed in the capital, Santo Domingo, the Band of the Division was also entrusted with certain duties.

The capital city was divided by a corridor into regions held by the loyalists and the constitutionalists. In May, at the risk of their lives, the Band of the 82nd Airborne Division Band was ordered to parade in the sniper-infested corridor, as a demonstration of goodwill to the people of the city and to develop espirit de corps with the citizens fighting for democracy. Besides, boosting morale of the citizens of the battle ravaged city, the Band parade was designed to convey a message to the rebels that Americans were not to be intimidated. The Band members had their rifles strapped to their backs as they marched. The Band Parades concluded without any untoward incident. The role of Military Bands reassured the citizenry that armed conflict had all but ended. This, in turn, restored an air of normalcy to the city before the US forces were withdrawn.

Role of Military Bands in Japan Embassy Hostage Crisis in Peru

The most obvious example of employing Bands and military music directing into counter-terrorism operation is provided by the 127-day long Japanese Embassy hostage crisis in Lima (Peru) during 17 Dec 1996-22 April 1997.[1] The terrorists belonging to a socialist militant organization called the Tupac Amaru Revolutionary Movement, named after an 18th century Inca leader of the same name, took a number of hostages to force the government to accept its demands. Commonly known by its Spanish acronym as MRTA, this armed organization was founded somewhere in the early 1980s, with the prime objective of establishing a Socialist state in Peru. The most spectacular terrorist activity that MRTA ever carried out was this incident which is erroneously known as the Japan Embassy hostage crisis. In fact, it was the residence of the then Japanese Ambassador to Lima where the hostage drama unfolded.

On 17 Dec 1996, fourteen MRTA guerillas blasted their way into the heavily guarded residence of the Japanese Ambassador to Peru, while a lavish dinner function to mark the 63rd birthday of Emperor Akihito was in progress. The terrorists took all 600 attendees, including ministers, military commanders, foreign diplomats and top businessmen, as hostages. The mother and brother of the President Alberto Fujimori, himself of Japanese descent, were among the hostages. The MRTA had a number of demands that included, among others, release of 471 of their comrades held in prisons.

Despite Japanese and international pressure for a "peaceful solution" to the crisis, President Fujimori rejected all the MRTA demands outright. Through diplomatic and Church mediation, gradually all but 72 high-profile hostages were released from the compound by MRTA. The latter thought it was easy to guard and manage 72 hostages, rather than hundreds. The crisis lingered on for over four months.

Apparently, President Fujimori had made up his mind for a military solution to the problem, right from the beginning. Initially the government used tank manoeuvres near the compound to intimidate the rebels but this did not irritate them enough. The Government then decided on playing loud military music towards the compound from across the roads. The terrorists were so incensed by the patriotic music that they would start firing as soon as the music began. This made the situation so critical that even the Prime Minister of Japan personally called President Fujimori not to take any measures that could endanger the lives of the hostages including 24 Japanese nationals.

The Peruvian Government had meanwhile decided to dig three tunnels from nearby houses into the Ambassador's compound to facilitate a commando operation. Thirty-two miners were hired to do the drilling and though it took two months to complete the tunnel, it was kept top secret even from the Government of Japan. Since drilling sounds could have alarmed the terrorists, the government again relied on military music to be played on amplifiers in order to suppress any noise from the drilling operation going on underneath. The rebels were fed up with military music but did not want to compromise their ammunition by firing at the sound of military marching tunes each time.

When all tunnels were dug, the Government decided to launch a rescue operation. Although the Band used to play different tunes, the message was somehow conveyed to 72 remaining hostages inside that when they heard the Band playing the Naval March tune, it would be a signal that the rescue operation was about to begin. At that tune, they should not only mentally prepare for storming out of the compound but also keep a considerable distance from the MRTA terrorists.

The MRTA terrorists used to be on high alert during nights and early dawn when counter-insurgency operations usually took place. It was in the afternoons, however, they would have their daily half-an-hour session of indoor football to keep them physically fit. On the afternoon of 22 April 1997, when 8 of the 14 terrorists were playing football, two were taking rest as per their shift, and only four were on guard duty, the Military Band outside switched tune from Army march tune to the Naval march tune. Hardly did the hostage-takers know that this tune was a coded message or an indication of something. The military stormed through the three tunnels and blasted their way in, killing all 14 MRTA terrorists and releasing 71 of the hostages. The only hostage fatality due to a heart attack was that of a Supreme Court judge with preexisting cardiac problem history. The forces lost two of their officers including a Lieutenant Colonel and a Lieutenant. This 140-member commando unit that conducted the rescue later used to lead the Peruvian Republic Day military parade each year.

The Band had been used thrice in the 127 days standoff—firstly, to confuse and irritate the terrorists, secondly, as a ruse to cover sound from drilling the tunnels, and finally as a signal to the hostages that the rescue operation was about to begin.

Deployment of Military Bands in anti-Narcotics Operation

In contemporary history, the case of Manuel Noriega, provides one of the most dramatic and startling examples of anti-Drugs operation for law enforcement. The account of "Operation Just Cause" (Dec 1989) is important not only because the notion of Presidential immunity was thrown to the winds when for the first and the last time in contemporary history, a serving President of a country was arrested for leading a drug smuggling cartel. From our perspective, nabbing the President-turned-Drug Baron through military force, is relevant because the diplomatic delicacies precluded the option of using force against the diplomatic mission of the Holy See where Noriega was sheltering. So the weapon of choice was military music!

Use of Military Music for Operation Just Cause in Panama[2]

The use of Military Music in the operation to arrest President Noriega of Panama, codenamed "Operation Just Cause" has drawn attention to scholars and students of Music and War. The Music Historian of the US wars in Iraq, Jonathan Pieslak also calls the operation a "seminal event in the practice of utilizing music as a distinct psychological tactic" (Pieslak 2009).

The capturing of Manuel Noriega in Panama brought not one or two but four US Military Bands into operation: The 79th Army Band, the 5th Infantry Division Band, the 7th Infantry Division Band and the ever-famous 82nd Airborne Division Band. The 79th Army Band was directly part of the operation "Just Cause" inside Panama, guarding the command post and Tactical Operations Center. Even as the rest of the command returned to normal duties, the Band still performed a security mission. The only musical mission that this Band performed was its Buglers performing memorial services for the US troops killed in action—40 US servicemen lost their lives in the initial phase of the operation.

The background of the operation is that in February 1989, a US Court had indicted Panama's then President General Manuel Noriega for Drugs smuggling and laundering of money from drug proceeds. Before his arrest warrants were issued, Gen Noriega, a ruthless military dictator, along with his military Generals, had been minting money through illicit drug business and racketeering for over half a decade. On 20 Dec 1989, the United States President George W Bush approved plans for a military invasion in Panama to topple him and bring him to face trial in the United States.

On the fifth day of the US invasion, President Noriega felt his end was imminent. He phoned the Ambassador of the Holy See, to allow him to come to the *Apostolic Nunciature*, as the diplomatic missions of the Vatican are known, in Panama. Otherwise he threatened to flee to the countryside to wage a guerilla war against the US troops. Given that the *Papal Nuncio* (i.e. Vatican ambassador) Monsignor Laboa had only ten minutes to decide, he could not consult Vatican and allowed the President to enter his diplomatic compound. While allowing Noriega to enter, the Papal diplomat had hoped to convince the President to surrender to the US authorities. He was obviously frustrated and dismayed when the Panama's embattled President and his four close confidantesefused to leave the compound and claimed to have taken asylum with the Church.[3]

Gen Noriega knew very well that the US forces whose task was to arrest him could not violate the sanctity of the diplomatic mission as it would have been a breach of international law and would have offended Roman Catholics worldwide. The asylum seekers turned over the weapons to the *de facto* Vatican Embassy. The besieged President spent his time in a stark room with no air conditioning or television, reading the Bible for the duration of his stay. Although, it had none of the regal comforts that he, as President, had been accustomed to, but was definitely better than a prison in California.

Noriega thought that he could prolong his stay in the diplomatic mission so that the US would lose the will to arrest him due to international pressure. The Americans lost patience earlier than Noriega could have anticipated. The US soldiers set up a perimeter outside this building and chose a novel method to harass Noriega to exit and surrender himself, i.e. deafening Band music.

During the following ten days of crisis, strong diplomatic communication ensued between the US Secretary of State James Baker and the Papal authorities in Vatican. While the Americans asked the Vatican to revoke the sanctuary status, the latter insisted on stopping the metal Bands music, which according to the Church was a harassment. While Pope John Paul II did not speak on the issue except to lament the deaths in the military operation, the Vatican spokesman, Jaoquin Navarro-Valls, initially denied that Noriega would be handed over to the American forces, despite the fact that in the first place he had not taken asylum with Vatican's consent. In fact, when his personal plane and helicopters were disabled by the US Seals by shooting T4 rockets, precluding any chance of aerial escape, Noriega rather tricked his way into the Vatican's diplomatic compound in Panama.

The psychological warfare tactics, as the US would call it, led Vatican Ambassador Labao to decide that if Noriega did not surrender to the law enforcement, the Papal staff would evacuate the building, move into a Catholic high school and declare it the new embassy—leaving Noriega alone in the aBandoned building to face the Americans without any benefit of Vatican sanctuary.

On Jan 3, 1990, Noriega asked permission to phone his wife and three daughters, who had taken refuge in the Cuban embassy nearby and sought assurances that they would be flown to exile in the Dominican Republic if he surrendered. The same, mediated by the Vatican authorities, were given. Noriega surrendered, was arrested and taken to the United States to face trials in the US Courts of Law. Getting sentenced to 40 years in jail, he became the first foreign head of state to be sentenced in the United States on drug charges.

Although there had been loss of life in the initial phase of the invasion but the operation for arrest was successful without firing a single shot. How could the US fire on Vatican embassy or allow its troops to storm it? But did loud music violate the diplomatic immunity and sanctity of the compound? The US National Security Advisor Brent Scowcroft would later assert that it did. Pointing to the psychological harassment of the Vatican Embassy [called *Papal Nuncio*], he called it a "low moment in US Army history." He criticized the US decision noting that this approach had been "silly, reproachable and undignified."

The 82nd Airborne Division Band, the 5th Infantry Division Band and the 7th Infantry Division Band remained in the continental United States (CONUS) while being part of the operation. They were tasked to provide musical support to returning troops which they did with devotion and finesse.

Military Music & Band Music as an interrogation technique

Military and Band Music has been used in psychological operations. The term "musical torture" is used by critics of the practice of playing loud music incessantly to prisoners or people besieged.

The debate between policy and academic circles as well as among psychologists and medical practitioners continues whether musical interrogation is a "torture" at all, and if so, what amount of Band music will cross the threshold of being labelled torture. However, the United Nations condemns the practice.

In January 1998, the Supreme Court of Israel declined to outlaw the use of loud music as an interrogation technique which was allegedly being used against Palestinians prisoners. The known systematic use of music for interrogation, however, was during the military rule in Greece in the 1970s and during US invasions of Iraq and Afghanistan since 2003 and 2001, respectively.

Use of Music by Greek Military Police on political detainees

First confirmed use of music as interrogation technique on political opponents is reported against the Greek military Junta (1967–74) in the headquarters of the Special Interrogation Unit of Greek Military Police (ESA), Athens, against political opponents. Interviews with survivors point at the use of songs, popular hits of the time, played loudly and repeatedly from loudspeakers as the detainee had to stand without rest, food or drink.

The European Court of Human Rights has banned the use of loud music in interrogations and since Greece is a member of the European Union since 1981, the practice no longer exists there.

Use of Band Music by US Army on prisoners at Guantanamo Bay, Abu Ghuraib and other detention centres

Such techniques were used subsequently by US troops on "non-cooperating" Prisoners of War both in Iraq and Afghanistan. Music by the American heavy metal Band *Metallica* as well as that of children's television programs *Barney* and *Sesame Street*, was used for sleep deprivation and to culturally offend the Iraqi and Afghan detainees.

While it is acknowledged by the US interrogation experts that sleep deprivation interviews with loud music would cause enough discomfort in four days [using cycles of 16 hours with strong lights and loud music and four hours off] to break someone undergoing an interrogation but insist that it causes no long-term effects.

Set up by legal charity *Reprieve*, which represented over 30 prisoners in Guantanamo Bay, Zero dB was an initiative against music torture. Under this initiative, various musicians were coordinating their objections to the use of their music as a technique for softening up captives by calling on governments to uphold and enforce the Convention Against Torture.[4] The initiative was backed by the British Musicians Union which kept calling on British musicians to voice their outrage against the use of music to torture by British and their American coalition partners in Iraq and Afghanistan.

Role of Bands in managing riots

Military Bands have been used during urban riots in the past over half a century. During the 1968 inner city riots in the United States, for instance, various Bands of the National Guard performed in the inner cities to calm the populace. The legendary 82nd Airborne Division Band assisted the Police in controlling civil disturbances around Washington DC by performing musical duties in riot hit areas.

Police Bands perform similar functions. According to an Inspector General of Police of Ghana, David Asante Apeatu, the Police Band was the "ideal tool to be used in forging these good relations [with public], because music was one medium, which forged unity by destroying inner turmoil, which in the long term, minimised external conflict" (Fiabu 2017). Another example is from Pakistan during the first stint of Prime Minister Benazir Bhutto.

Use of Police Band during anti-government demonstration in Lahore, Pakistan

During the first tenure (1988–90) of Pakistan's first female Prime Minister Benazir

Bhutto, an anti-government demonstration was taking place in the second largest city of Pakistan, Lahore. There was a foreign delegation from China that was holding a meeting with the officials of the Government in the Government House (old Freemason Lodge), located at *Sharae Quaid-e-Azam*—an expressway which is the nerve centre of the city of Lahore. The famous Lahore Police Band was available on the premises to give backdrop music during the luncheon hosted for the distinguished guests (Chaudry 2011).

The protestors were marching towards the Government Lodge raising loud slogans. They had already vastly outnumbered the anti-riot police contingents that had been deployed to tackle any untoward situation. Police officers on duty felt that it would not be possible for them to stop the procession to reach near the Government House without use of force. On its part, the Government did not want the guests to be embarrassed by hearing anti-government slogans or by the sound of gunfire or that of the tear gas shelling, were that to be used to counter the mob (Chaudry 2011).

The civil servants at the scene thought of a different idea. Instead of summoning more anti-riot units of the Lahore Police, they called two more companies of Lahore Police Band. The idea was that the three companies would play together and the sound will be loud enough to suppress any noise being made by the mob through sloganeering. The Bands continued to play inside the House as long as the tumult outside did not subside. The Band music amused the demonstrators and the mob eventually dispersed late in the afternoon.

Conclusion: Confucian understanding of State

> *Music is to the military what broken windows are to crime: if you let standards slip, the whole ship sinks.*
>
> Elisabeth Braw

The use of music for any political purpose has never been free of controversies. The use of Bands in Dominican Republic was criticized by the US lawmakers who accused the President of risking the lives of the Bandsmen. The use of Military Music in the Peru hostage crisis left President Fujimori in hot waters as the Governments from Japan to Canada put pressure on him not to do anything that could agitate the terrorists and thus endanger the lives of the hostages. The use of Bands in Panama was virtually ridiculed as being "silly, reproachable and undignified."

The most debated conundrums revolve round the practicability, reliability, efficacy and permissibility of musical torture. The legal debate aside, the question arises that whether the detainees in Abu Ghuraib prison or Athens ETA-HQs avoided Musical interrogation, whether they would have evaded torture at all, or might have faced fiercer forms of torture such as water boarding and dogs let loose on them?

Same question can be asked about the siege of Vatican Embassy in Panama City. Had music not been used, what alternative means could be employed to force Noriega out, that would have been less harmful than loud music? Be that as it may, the Military and Police Bands are instruments that the States use at their convenience. Mostly, their use is much less lethal and much more humane than any other option available for the State to exercise.

This chapter was started with a Confucian quote about the quality of music being reflective of the quality of governance of a State. Similar arguments have been made to this day. Regarding Defence spending cuts on British Military Bands, Elisabeth Braw argued in Financial Times that, "Military Bands trumpet the might and status of their nation ...Spending cuts to [Bands treating them as] non-essential armed services, *undermine international standing*" of a nation. Not disputing that combat soldiers are more essential to defence than trumpeters, yet she argues that military musicians represent a country's face to the world (Braw 2018).

NOTES

1 The account of the so-called Japan Embassy Hostage Crisis [Actually it was the residence of the Japanese Ambassador to Peru, has been prepared from online encyclopedia http://encyclopedia.thefreedictionary.com/Japanese+embassy+hostage+crisis , Website of the Association for Diplomatic Studies and Training http://adst.org/2013/12/the-dramatic-hostage-crisis-and-daring-rescue-at-the-japanese-embassy-in-peru/ and the websites of daily Guardian and daily New York Times http://www.nytimes.com/1997/04/26/world/how-peruvian-hostage-crisis-became-trip-into-the-surreal.html>

2 The account of the Operation Just Cause has mainly been prepared from the Council on Hemispheric Affairs website http://www.coha.org/operation-just-cause-a-historical-analysis/ , Al Jazeera New Website http://www.aljazeera.com/indepth/opinion/2016/01/truth-operation-panama-160131085323562.html and the Global Security Website http://www.globalsecurity.org/military/ops/just_cause.htm all accessed between November and December 2016.

3 Besides the President Noriega himself, Lieut. Colonel Nivaldo Madrinan, head of Panama's secret police; Captain Eliecer Gaitan, chief of special force charged with protecting the President; Belgica de Castillo, the former head of the immigration department, and her husband Carlos Castillo, had taken refuge in the Papal Nuncio, as Vatican's *de facto* Embassies are called worldwide.

4 Reported by *Associated Press (AP)* on 9 December 2008

CHAPTER XII

Modern Role of Bands: State Ceremonial

Of all of the arts, music is the perfect art, because it strikes the soul without the aid of the intellect.

—William Kindler (Philosopher and poet)

Along with national flags, national anthems, and national costumes the military Bands are identity of nations—colours, tunes, and clothes—all in one! That is why there is no concept of a State ceremony, of festivity or of mourning, today without Bands giving the backdrop. A national day, a State event, an inauguration, a coronation, opening of Parliamentary session, a funeral, a memorial, a parade, there is hardly any event conceivable that will be worthwhile without Bands. Where there was no Band, it means it was not a national event, let alone an important event at all.

The tradition of inviting military Bands to give pubic performances is dated to Napoleonic period in France. The origin of "massed Band" can also be traced to this period when loudness of music had to be ensured to drown the ambient noise levels of large audience which gathered near parade grounds or city squares. The military regalia or mass pipes and drums could have either type of objective: to sway the subjects or citizens of one's State of the glory of the sovereign or to impress or intimidate a foreign State, especially when represented by the Head of State or other high dignitaries, of the might of the host nation. In fact, the concept of giving a 21-Gun Salute to a visiting foreign head of state or government or inviting him to inspect an honour guard of the army of the host nation also have similar interesting origins but are out of the scope of this work. As for the State ceremonial of international nature, the next chapter will deal with the topic.

At the national level, we shall explore six types of ceremonies where Military Band is almost universally essential, namely, National or Republic Days, Royal coronations in the Monarchies, the Presidential Swearing-in in the Republics,

State Opening of the Parliament or Legislative Body, Days associated with the Defence organizations, and the State or royal funerals.

Bands at National Day Ceremonies and Parades

The most important National Day of a country in each calendar year can be the anniversary of the founding of a modern State. For countries, which had been under colonial administration within past few centuries, the *Independence Day* is marked with a lot of fun and fanfare. The States that had remained under foreign military occupation and had got liberation after an armed struggle usually call it a *Liberation Day*. In the monarchies like Japan, Thailand or the United Kingdom, with no recent history of being colonized, the red letter day usually is the Monarch's Birthday.

In many democracies, however, the most important national day can be the Constitution Day (called Republic Day in some countries) which is usually the anniversary of the Constitution or of the day when an absolute monarchy was replaced by a democratic order. Bastille Day of France is the most obvious example. Although monarchy later made comebacks in France again and again till the Fifth Republic—when the nation bid adieu to the monarchial system for good—the Bastille Day fanfare and parades celebrate the first time, monarchy was overthrown. The United States, for one, is amongst those few big states that do not have military parades as a regular annual feature. President Donald Trump made the first serious effort to introduce the tradition. One of the few military parades in the US History include the National Victory Parade in Washington in June 1991 to mark the victory in Operation Desert Storm earlier that year, that led to Kuwaiti liberation through Iraqi defeat. President George W. Bush took the salute as various Bands including the President's Own Marine Band marched past him.

In many ideological States, the biggest annual event observed at the State level can be the Revolution Day. This is mostly true for ex-Communist and most Socialist States like the former Soviet Union, China, Cuba and North Korea. It is also true for the Islamic Republic of Iran which celebrates the anniversary of the 1979 Islamic revolution with great ballyhoo. The Revolution Day usually celebrates a replacement or overthrow of the monarchy, but in case of Communist States, it can mark the overthrow of a democratic or republican civilian government as well. The *Baath* regimes in Iraq and Syria would observe the anniversary of *Baath* revolution with great pomp while Egypt and Yemen would observe the military take-over by the Socialist-leaning military officers (1952 and 1979, respectively) with great pageantry.

Depending on the historical context, the Unity Day, the Reunification Day, commemoration of a civil war, sometimes that of an abortive revolutionary war, a cultural diversity day, or birth anniversary of the founder of the nation, are many such occasions which are celebrated as a State function with military parades and military Bands.

In most nations, there would be more than one national day, but only one in a year would be observed with a military parade. And the Parade is not possible without military Bands. All other national occasions may have flag hoisting ceremonies at State mansions, grand public meetings addressed by the political leaders, fireworks or festivities of other kind. And yet again, none of the events are likely to be without the display of Bands at some level.

Apart from the military parades backed by Bands music, in many countries, the massed Bands display is a separate event in addition to, in replacement of, or, preceded by, the grand annual military parade. In the United Kingdom, "trooping the colour" is a Bands-backed pageantry to mark the sovereign's birthday, as is the "Beating the Retreat" in India on its Republic Day (January 26).

The Military Bands tattoos are not necessarily held on the annual or recurring national days alone. Many countries choose Military Bands tattoo to celebrate a one-off event or an anniversary, such as the Tripoli International Military Music held in September 2009 to celebrate 40th anniversary of the Libyan revolution of 1969 (by the then President Col Qaddafi), the Hong Kong International Military Tattoo in July 2017 to celebrate the 20th anniversary of the establishment of the Hong Kong Special Administrative Region, or the centennial anniversary tattoos planned for the Armistice Day of World War I in November 2018.

Apart from playing at home nation's national days, it is a common practice for military Bands to be invited to perform at national days and other occasions in friendly countries.

Bands at Royal Coronations and events related to Royalty

In the monarchies, the Bands play at the royal coronations and the birth of a prince or a princess and also at royal weddings. The Military Bands were a standard feature in the imperial courts of China, Turkey, Vietnam and various African monarchies for hundreds of years. The Bands would play at the coronation, the royal birthdays and other important events and dates associated with the royalty. The theme of these Bands used to be wishing long life, health and happiness to the monarch and his family. The music, dance and songs of the Courts were often a celebration of, or prayers for, victory and national progress.

Modern developments in healthcare have led to average life span rising for all human beings, no less for the Kings and Queens. And being a monarch is a life-long position. The long life of the Queen of England, the King of Thailand and the Emperor of Japan have shown that coronation Bands are not likely to be played more than twice or thrice in a century in the same country.

Of the nearly 200 states and territories in the world, around one-eighth are Monarchies. Besides the British Crown there are 25 other monarchies in the world. The British Crown is most famous since the monarch is not only for the United Kingdom but 16 other territories, dominions, states or statelets, as well. Hence, the coronation of British monarch is a much more elaborate affair as the Military or Police Bands from all the dominions also take part. The last British coronation ceremony took place in 1952 when Queen Elizabeth II was crowned. At that time, Bands from various Commonwealth counties took part. India had become a Republic in 1950 while Pakistan became one in 1956. Hence, Pakistan was a dominion of the British Crown at the time of the last coronation and it was represented by the City of Jacobabad Police Band at the coronation of Queen Elizabeth.

The Military Bands in the monarchies also play when a new prince or princess arrives, i.e. at a birth in the royal household, at royal all the royal weddings, at the birthday of the ruling sovereign each year, and also at each anniversary of the coronation of the monarch.

The monarchies in Europe (UK, Spain, Benelux and the Scandinavian states) are mostly ceremonial. The monarchies in East Asia (Japan, Cambodia, Thailand and Malaysia), however, command religious sanctity and respect, but have hardly any role in day to day running of the State. The administrative authority in both the regions rests with the elected governments but the pomp and glory is mostly associated with the royal households and their ceremonies.

In contrast, however, the Middle Eastern and African monarchs are mostly direct rulers of their kingdoms where parliaments, even if existing, have limited consultative role. Still, there is little pomp and ceremony attached to the royal households in many cases. Saudi Arabia, for instance, has one of the most powerful monarchies in the world but there is no pomp involved with royal coronation or funeral, neither is the King's birthday or anniversary celebrated at State level. However, the anniversary of the founding of the dynasty of nearly a century ago is celebrated with Military pomp and military Bands.

Every Kingdom has historic tunes that its military Bands play during the coronations and these tunes have a history behind them. Even the arrival of a monarch at a function is usually heralded by brass music. In the United Kingdom and most of Commonwealth, a tune called "fanfare" is played by trumpeters as soon as a King or a Queen arrive at any function or venue. This is a roughly equivalent of the tune "Hail to the Chief" and "Hail Columbia" for the President and Vice President of USA (see next section). For other royal functions including royal weddings, royal birthdays, announcement of a baby born in the royal household, the military Bands of every nation has a different and unique repertoire for each occasion.

Bands at Presidential Swearing In

Most of the world's states and territories are now republics, where being the President or the Prime Minister is usually a tenured position. It is common for the military and marching Bands to play at presidential inaugurations. Playing at the swearing in of the Prime Ministers is, however, a rarer spectacle.

Every country has unique historic tunes that are usually repeated each time a new President is sworn in. The inauguration of the President of the United States is probably the largest such ceremony in the world. Hence, a look at the Bands' traditions at US inauguration may act as a case study. A number of Military Bands and non-Military Marching Bands are involved in each Inauguration. The number of Bands attending the ceremony is taken very seriously as a token of prestige of the office and that of the incoming incumbent.

Military Bands at US Presidential Inauguration

For the United States military Bands, in addition to the national anthem, there are standard tunes that they play at such ceremonies, including standard patriotic notes such as "Yankee Doodle," Battle Hymn of the Republic," "Hail America" and "Chimes of Liberty" among others. The tradition started on March 4, 1801, when the President's Own Marine Band performed for Thomas Jefferson's inaugural and has performed for each of the 55 Presidential inaugural since that time, including all four inaugurations of Franklin D. Roosevelt. Every President added his bit like President Madison, in 1809, added the concept of Ball after the inauguration while President Adams, in 1828, was responsible for another major change in White House social customs when he brought dancing to the White House. Of course, the music for these activities was to be provided by the President's Own Marine Band. (Fettig 2016) The inauguration of President Donald Trump was the 58th inaugural event in US history, and the 55th in which the President's Own Marine Band provided the musical accompaniment.

The Military Bands perform ruffles and flourishes prior to the entrance march of a dignitary. Four ruffles played by the Drum and four flourishes by the Bugles are authorized for the President and Vice President of the United States, at the time of their inauguration or otherwise at their arrival. Following ruffles and flourishes a pause is observed to allow the announcement of the dignitary. The appropriate entrance march is then performed. The tune of "Hail to the Chief" is entitled to the President of the United States.

"Hail to the Chief," written by James Sanderson as incidental music to a dramatic adaptation of Sir Walter Scott's epic poem *The Lady of the Lake* is possibly derived from an old Gaelic air. It appears in a gallant boating scene honouring the highland chieftain, Sir Roderick Dhu. The song was already very popular by 1829 when the Marine Band played it at the laying of the cornerstone of the first lock of the Chesapeake and Ohio Canal for President Andrew Jackson. However, its association with the Presidents of the United States is credited to two successive First Ladies. Julia Tyler, the young second wife of President John Tyler (1845–49), was an amateur musician and composer. President Tyler entertained frequently at the White House. Some scholars believe Julia Tyler would always ask the Marine Band to play "Hail to the Chief," so much so that this became a signature tune of Presidential receptions. Tyler's successor as the US President was James K. Polk (1845–49)—an "unassuming man of slight stature"—so much so that his arrival at events, including those within White House—sometimes went unnoticed. First Lady Sarah Polk reportedly ordered the performance of "Hail to the Chief" to announce the president's arrival in order to avoid his embarrassment. Many attempts to change this tune, one by none other than John Philip Sousa, who composed "Presidential Polonaise" for indoor affairs and "Semper Fidelis" for outdoor events, on the orders of President Chester Arthur (1881–85) proved abortive. The tune survived well into the 21st century.

However, the date of the earliest use of ruffles and flourishes as musical honours for the president of the United States is not known. A Navy regulation of 1876 stipulated that a ruffle of drums would be used to signal the arrival of the president. In 1893, a regulation stated that the President would receive four ruffles and flourishes. The practice of preceding "Hail to Chief" with four ruffles and flourishes became firmly entrenched by the time of US President William McKinley (1897–1901).

The tune for "Hail Columbia" is authorized to the Vice President of the United States. The last 32 bars of "Stars and Stripes Forever" are performed as a generic entrance march for American civilian officials below the rank of Vice

President. One example of the latter is the Salute by Military Bands offered to each new Secretary of the Army and Secretary of the Navy upon their inaugurations. In case, there are foreign civilian dignitaries, then this tune is replaced by the tune "Hands across the Sea".

Non-Military Bands at US President's inauguration parade

Military Bands play in the White House as part of their official duty. However, outside the White House, a grand inauguration parade takes place which is attended by a large number of Marching Bands including those from Police and Fire services, schools and colleges and some community marching Bands. Except for Bands of the government agencies such as the Police, the participation of Bands in the parade is voluntary. As the inauguration debate of US President Donald Trump in January 2017 has shown that the presence of Bands is much more than an entertainment. It is more of a political statement.

It was most apparent in the debate about the participation of the historical black BandTalladega College Marching Band, Tornadoes, in President Trump's inauguration parade. Despite opposition by College members due to—what they believed were—President Trump's deriding comments about the African–American community, the Band eventually decided to participate in Trump's inauguration. This, they said, was to demonstrate African–American support to the new President by rising above the racial debate.

Non-participation in parade, however, was the decision of a number of school marching Bands, both inside and outside of Washington DC area. Many of the ones that had participated in one or both of President Obama's inauguration parades (2009 and 2013) decided to stay away from Trump's. As per a news report by *NBC Washington's* Andrea Swalec, the interest in playing the 2017 inauguration appeared lower than normal, as most Bands in DC area did not even apply to participate, including one DC public school marching Band that has participated in all the five immediate past inaugural parades since President Clinton's 1997 inauguration.

Ballou High School's Majestic Marching Knights had performed Destiny's Child's "Lose My Breath" at George W. Bush's second inaugural parade in 2005, and stepped along Pennsylvania Avenue as they played James Brown's "I Got You (I Feel Good)" at Barack Obama's second inaugural parade eight years later. For President Trump's inauguration in 2017, it likewise had not even applied for consideration. This absence was explained by the Principal that the Band "wanted to take rest, after many recent performances." As for Dunbar High School's Band that had also marched in Obama's first inauguration in 2009, but decided to stay out from Trump's, it was because, its Principal said, they were rebuilding the Band. Eastern High School also chose not to participate, and their Principal declined to elaborate. Band Director of Howard University Marching Band, John Newton, suspected that many political beliefs of Band directors and school administrators affect their decision. "I think everybody knows why and no one wants to say and lose their job."[1]

Trump's inauguration parade drew 1,60,000 people and a total of 41 equestrians, drill or Band teams, nine of them were School or College Marching Bands. However, it paled before the his predecessor Obama's first inauguration (2009) which was attended by around 1.8 million people and around 9,00,000 attended his second inauguration (2013). The number of drill and Band teams in Obama's first inauguration was 103 and roughly half of them were school, college or community Marching Bands.

In other words, the number of attendees and the number of participating marching Bands is important as a measure of popularity and support for the Presidents. Joining or abstaining from an inauguration parade by a Band is a political statement on behalf of the institution or the community. The Bands add to the prestige and importance of the event for the whole nation. The tunes played at Presidential inaugurations have immense historical and ceremonial significance.

Bands at State Opening of Parliaments

Opening a session of the Parliament with a military Band is increasingly becoming common in countries and traditions as diverse as United Kingdom and China, for example. The Dutch Defence Ministry rates Prinsjesdag (the State Opening of Parliament) as the number one event where military Bands are played, placing it higher than the coronation or royal weddings, meaning that performance at an elected body, as far as the Dutch Government is concerned, is more important than that for a hereditary office.

The spectre of military Bands performing at occasions related to parliaments or legislative bodies are gradually but consistently becoming entrenched in the parliamentary traditions in Europe, Asia-Pacific, Africa and the Americas in recent decades.

The British parliament is called the mother of all Parliaments. The State Opening of parliamentary year at Westminster in London traditionally accompanies a lot of pageantry. The Monarch comes to the Parliament House in a State Coach escorted by mounted ceremonial guard and preceded by a number of military Bands. In 2016, the royal cavalcade was led by the Band of Irish Guards and the Irish Guards Corps of Drums.

On the far end of the democratic spectrum is China. It is a one-party state and its 5000-strong National People's Congress (the closest body to a parliament) meets twice a year for a week each. Unlike, the tradition of long debate and free speech in Westminster, the People's Congress merely affixes stamp of approval whatever the Politburo has decided. What is common with British parliament, however, is the presence of Bands. Military Bands playing during the opening meeting of the China's National People's Congress (NPC) at the Great Hall of the People in Beijing, China, are a regular feature for the first day of the session.

The lawns and halls of legislative buildings now resound with military and police Bands. In Canada, for instance, Fortissimo is a military and musical spectacular created for the lawns of Parliament Hill featuring massed military Bands, pipes and drums, guest performers and the soldiers of the Ceremonial Guard. It is a showcase event in the Ottawa since it began in 1997.

Similarly, in Italy, Military Band concert is performed every first Sunday of a month in front of Italian Parliament on Piazza Montecitorio. The concert starts at 11:00 a.m. and lasts about an hour.

Many of the island states in the Pacific had British colonial ancestry. One of the small states is Fiji. State opening of the parliament in Fiji is done with Army and Navy Bands at the maiden session, each time a new Parliament is elected.

Coming to Africa, South Africa is one of the countries where since the stint of Nelson Mandela, democratic traditions are catching roots. State of the Union address by President of South Africa accompanies five or six military and police Bands in the lawns of the parliament in Cape Town each year at the beginning of each new parliamentary year.

The Bands reflect the sanctity and prestige of the elected houses and embody their status as people's representative institutions.

Bands at State or Royal Funerals

State funeral ceremony, observing the strict rules of protocol, are held to honour people of national significance. State funerals usually include much pomp and ceremony as well as religious overtones and distinctive elements of military tradition. Generally, state funerals are held in order to involve the general public in a national day of mourning usually after seeking consent of the family of the deceased. A state funeral will often generate mass publicity from both national and global media outlets.

Which category of persons or holders of high offices are entitled to State Funerals differs from State to State. The universal common thread is that without a Band or an instrumental accompaniment, there is no concept of a ceremonial funeral. A formal state funeral takes place upon the death of a monarch. Not all the countries entitle the Head of Government to a State funeral as they do for a head of state. In United Kingdom and the Netherlands, State funerals are the norm for monarchs but Prime Ministers or heads of government are not so entitled as a matter of course. Thailand is the only monarchy where the Prime Minister is also entitled to a State Funeral.

In some countries, only the head of state dying in office is entitled to a State Funeral while a retired or former head of state is not. In other countries, such as the United States, every serving or former President is entitled to a State Funeral. In Canada and Australia, all serving and former Governor Generals and Prime Ministers are equally entitled to State funerals. Similarly, in Ireland and Lebanon, both the President and Prime Minister are identically entitled. In Italy, a President is entitled regardless of whether he did in office or otherwise, while Prime Minister is so entitled only if he dies in office.

In India, serving and retired Presidents are equally entitled while in Pakistan only a serving President dying in office is entitled. Prime Ministers in both India and Pakistan, as per British tradition are not ordinarily entitled. Exceptions have been made in both the countries for Prime Ministers who died in office (four in case of India and one in case of Pakistan).

Some of the Heads of State attain international fame so State funerals of South African President Nelson Mandela, Indian Prime Minister Indira Gandhi, Egyptian leader Gamal Abdul Nasser and many others became international events. In Communist nations like Soviet Union, China and especially North Korea, a lot of pomp goes with funerals for former heads of State.

In rare cases, a civil official lower than a Head of State may get a State funeral such as Lakshman Kardigamar, the then Foreign Minister of Sri Lanka. Assassinated on 12 Aug 2005, he got a State funeral with military Bands playing at his funeral in recognition of his political contribution for racial tolerance and the promotion of peace in the conflict-ridden island nation.

Military Bands are indispensable for State and Royal funerals. The difference between the two is that State funeral is allowed to a Head of State, whether he is an elected President or a hereditary monarch, while Royal funeral is for persons of the royal family lesser in status than the sovereign. In the British context, former crown princess Diana and the Queen-mother of the present Queen would ordinarily fall in the latter category. Ordinarily, a State funeral for the reigning monarch is paid for the by the taxpayer while for a royal funeral it is the royal family that foots the bill. The two funerals referred above had trappings fairly, closer to a State funeral though they were not.

In democracies, the term Head of State may have an expansive definition, for such ceremonials entitlements to State funeral, such as noted above for the United States of America, where the serving President, any former President and a President-elect is equally entitled to a State funeral. Of the 44 past President, five were still alive at the time of inauguration of Donald Trump as the 45th President in January 2017. Seven had died in office and got a State Funeral. The remaining 32 who had died after retiring were also given the same protocol as for those who died in office. None of the President-elect has died before reaching office. The Vice President of the United States is not entitled to a State Funeral.

However, the United States Government—like any other government, for that matter—may direct any person to be entitled to a State Funeral, that may include a Vice President or any other distinguished American. Some of the examples include the constitutionalist founding father Benjamin Franklin and the World War-era Chief of the American Army General Pershing who were given State Funerals in the US. The importance of Bands at State Funerals can be gauged from the fact that Jacqueline Kennedy, widow of President John F Kennedy personally requested for President's Own Marine Band to perform funeral music at her husBand's State honours.

In the United Kingdom, where the monarch is entitled to a state funeral but the Prime Minister is usually not, has also seen such exceptions. In the past century, two of the Prime Ministers were given this honour, Winston Churchill and Margaret Thatcher. Other people honoured in this way in the United Kingdom in previous centuries include the Duke of Wellington (1852)—a former prime minister who was victorious in the battle of Waterloo, and Admiral Lord Nelson (1806), after his death in the Battle of Trafalgar. Former prime ministers Lord Palmerston and William Gladstone were also deemed worthy of state funerals. Benjamin Disraeli was offered one, but declined in his will.

In South Asian tradition, a State funeral would usually entail the following: A national period of mourning (usually lasting 3 to 10 days) is officially declared; the national flag is flown at half-mast during the mourning period; first day of mourning is usually declared a public holiday; the deceased person's bier or coffin is draped with the national flag (which should not be lowered into the grave or burnt in the pyre); and finally he/she is honoured with a gun salute. The salute is ordinarily preceded by prayers as per rituals of his/her religion and burial or cremation is followed by Military or Police buglers performing appropriate mourning tunes. In almost all of the Commonwealth countries, this mourning tune is the one called "Last Post" while America follows a different tune called "Taps". The number of days of mourning and the number of volleys to be fired are decided by the government in each case.

In Pakistan, two heads of State died in office (its founding father Mohammad Ali Jinnah and General Zia ul Haq). Both were honoured with State funerals. Although Prime Ministers are not so entitled but exception was made for the only Prime Minister Liaqat Ali Khan who was assassinated while in office in 1951.

In India, serving and former Presidents are equally entitled to a State funeral. However, four of India's Prime Ministers died in office including Jawaharlal Nehru, Lal Bahadur Shastri, Indira Gandhi and her son Rajiv Gandhi. Military Bands came to perform at the last rites of all four of them in State funerals. Two other ex-Prime Ministers, two famous Chief Ministers and Mr Sarabjeet Singh,[2] a person accused and then convicted of espionage and sabotage in Pakistan, were given State funerals.

Exercising the State power to authorize any person to receive a State funeral, India also bestowed Nobel Laureate-Philanthropist Mother Teresa with this honour. Pakistan allowed State funeral to philanthropist and social activist Abdul Sattar Edhi, also called Pakistan's Father Theresa.

In Egypt, other than the Head of the State, any person awarded the highest medal of Order of the Nile is automatically entitled to State Funeral like the Head of the State. In Egypt, there is also a convention that any Egyptian who wins a Nobel Prize is given the Order of the Nile as well. Of the four Nobel Laureates of Egyptian descent; President Sadat was already a head of state when he was assassinated. The remaining three Nobel laureates included Najib Mahfouz, Ahmad Zuwail and Mohammad Al Baradei who got Nobel Prize for Literature, Chemistry and Peace, respectively. All three were decorated with Order of the Nile. The first two have died and military Bands led their processions at the State funerals.

All serving or former military personnel in most countries are entitled to "military funerals" which are different from State or Royal funerals. Military Funerals come in the category of military ceremonies.

Bands at Military Ceremonies

The images of the President's Own Marine Band at such noteworthy military events as the ground-breaking ceremony for the Korean War Memorial and the National Guadalcanal Commemoration Ceremony, celebrating the 50th anniversary of the Battle of Guadalcanal, along with US President George Bush are already embedded in public memory. We shall deal with the Bands at Military Ceremonies in two sub-heads, military ceremonial events and the military funerals.

Military Ceremonial Events

Military Bands are considered a traditional component of military culture. They provide the required musical accompaniment to the military in its important professional events. The public duties of military Bands include performances at guard mounting, change-of-command ceremonies, ship christenings as well as the commissioning, promotions and medal ceremonies of the military officers. Most great powers maintain robust Bands' programs within their national military establishment to support these missions.

The military ceremonies where the Military Bands are needed may include Armed Forces Day in some countries and Defense Day or Veterans Day in others. The Bands come to play war and memorial tunes at such days. Most States also observe Victory Day Parades for past wars. There are also commemoration day parades of important military events such as the Armistice Day related to the First World War, or the D-Day Landing during the Second World War. The Military Bands have a role at the Heroes Day (Rwanda), Martyrs day (Iran) and Veterans Day (United States). No need to say, virtually all of them are marked by military music. They also play at the raising or revival of a regiment, foundation day of the regiment or the army as a whole and at commissioning of a ship or an air fleet. The Military Bands play at events such as military tattoos, concerts for military families and, where military wedding is entitled, weddings of military officers.

The Military Bands also play at the change-of-command ceremonies when a new Army, Navy or Air Force Chief takes command. The arrival of the military chiefs or military officers of senior ranks is also marked by musical announcements through military buglers or trumpeters whenever they participate in any of the military ceremonies noted above. In the United States, the four-star General, Admiral or Air Marshal is entitled to four ruffles and four flourishes, just like the President and the Vice President, although the subsequent tunes are different for the military. After the ruffles and flourishes, the tune of "General's March" is played for Army and Air Force generals and that of the "Flag Officer's March" is played for four-star Admirals of Navy and equivalent Officers from the Corps of Marines. For the three, two, and one-star military officers the welcome is reduced correspondingly to three, two or one ruffle and flourish each. Other countries have their own standard tunes to herald the arrival of their military commanders.

Military Funerals

In almost every country, military veterans are entitled to a military funeral. In United States, every active duty and honourably discharged military veteran is entitled to a military funeral, if so requested by his family. For a military funeral, a minimum of three persons are required. This is so because the minimum honour guard is that of two uniformed persons, at least one of whom should be from the same branch of military that the deceased belonged to. In addition, at least, one Bugler is needed to play the "Taps".

Every country has distinct tunes to be played at military funerals. The tune may differ depending on the branch of the army to which the deceased belonged to, may vary as per the denomination of the deceased, may be different if a person died on duty or after retirement, and tune may also depend on whether the funeral is of a single soldier or a whole unit killed in action. The tunes may also vary for a remembrance day of past military deaths or for the funeral of a just-died soldier, sailor or airman.

The "Last Post" is the most recognizable bugle sound in the United Kingdom and all Commonwealth nations both at the funeral of fallen military personnel and on remembrance days in subsequent years. This Bugle tone was invented in the early days of the invention of modern brass instruments, around 1790s or so. It was initially one of the 24 or so Bugle calls for British soldiers to issue commands like "wake up," "assemble," "to the bed," etc. Wrist watches had not been invented yet, so Bugle calls were the only way to regularize the disciplined lives of the soldiery. In the days when most Bandsmen were civilians and did not necessarily go overseas with the units on military assignments, the soldiers were at a loss on how to honour a fallen comrade. In the absence of the Band, one of the soldiers would first play "Last Post" to signify, not the end of the day but end of the life for the dead colleague, and then after a few moments of silence, play the wake-up Bugle tune of *Reveille*—the first Bugle call of the day—to signify his rebirth in the eternal life of the hereafter. It was the "Last Post" whose tradition has continued to this day and adopted by military traditions in scores of countries. It was standardized in 1873 for military funerals and memorials in the British military to a 75-second long notes, from the original 45 second ones. There is no song attached to the Last Post.

The equivalent tune in the American context is the "taps" which originated during the Civil War (1861-65) to mourn the fallen comrades. In the anti-colonial spirit, the Americans did not want to adopt a British tune. During the Civil War, the ceremonial three volleys of fire to honor the dead could have been misconstrued by the opposite side as an attack, and hence was not practicable. Brigadier Gen Daniel Butterfield, a Union General during the Civil War, is credited with tasking musician Oliver Norton to compose a mourning tune. By July 1862, Norton was able to arrange a French tune which got modified and adopted to become what is known as "Taps" today. Originally called Butterfield's lullaby it was formally recognized by the US Military in 1874 as the official tune to mark the death of a soldier.

Taps was originally composed for the modern bugle which, unlike the trumpet, does not have any keys or valves. And "Taps," unlike the Last Post, does have lyrics to accompany its ceremonial melody. The lyrics for the "Taps" were composed by Horace Lorenzo Trim. The call also goes by the first line of Trim's lyrics, "Day is Done." There are many other lyrical adaptations of the call, but Trim's is the most famous.

By the time of the First World War, when the British and American troops were fighting on the same side against the Ottoman, German and Austro-Hungarian armies, the rival sides had also developed funeral music. The Ottoman music historically relies on drum beats, rather than wind sounds, for everything musically important, including death of a military officer in the line of duty. The Germans and the Austro-Hungarians, however, had a great affection for wind music. In fact, many of the greatest European composers had been Germans or Austrians. The lyrics of the song *Ich hatt' einen Kameraden* ("I had a comrade") is a traditional lament for the Armed Forces in Austria, Hungary and Prussia (modern-day German). Its opening notes are played on bugles at military funerals. This tune has the same (emotional) connotation as Last Post in British and the Taps in the American military forces.

The moving poem was composed by German poet Ludwig Uhland in 1809. Its immediate inspiration was the deployment of Badener troops against the Tyrolean Rebellion. In 1825, the composer Friedrich Silcher set it to music, based on the tune of a Swiss folk song. The lyrics are about the immediate experience of a soldier losing a comrade in battle, detached from all political or national ideology. As a result, its use was never limited to one particular faction, so was sung or cited by representatives of all political backgrounds throughout the 19th and 20th centuries. Apart from Germany and Austro-Hungarian regions, the lyrics got translated for use in numerous fighting forces and various variants of tune were used by French, Dutch, Spanish, Japanese and others.

Using a British tune for the military heroes was also an anathema for the Irish military. They use the tune of "Oft to the stilly night" by their national poet Thomas Moore, who wrote this poem as a lament to the lives of his friends who died in the 1798 Irish uprising against the British. Sir John Stevenson arranged this poem and set to music. Moore's influence on Irish military music is unmatched by any other poet. One will rarely listen, if at all, an Irish military Band or an Irish Pipes and Drums Corps, without a composition from this poet laureate. His influence is so strong that even all the Irish regiments of the British military, at one time or the other, marched to Moore's song "St Patrick's Day."

However, the military funeral music is not limited to a single tune. For instance, in the United States, if a single bugler is available he will play the Taps through his Bugle to give graveside honours to the deceased. However, if a whole Band is available, then it will play the specific hymn prescribed by the branch concerned. For instance, the US Air Force prescribes that if the deceased officer was a Roman Catholic then tune of "Faith of Our Fathers" be performed but at Protestant burials, "Amazing Grace" tune is to be played. A specific funeral tune for Muslim Servicemen and Women within the United States Armed Forces who die in duty is yet to be decided. At the moment, "Taps" suffice. If, however, the remembrance ceremony is for a whole military unit, rather than an individual, then the Band shall play the tune of "Battle Hymn of the Republic" immediately following the homily recite by the priest.

There are so many entitled funerals (averaging over half a million a year across the United States) and so few military Bands left across the United States that giving funeral military honours to all most deceased veterans is becoming difficult. The Pershing's Own Army Bands supports up to 2000 military funerals each year (almost six-a-day) in Arlington military cemetery alone. In the rest of the country, the situation is not too bright.

In the state of New Jersey alone, there are 400,000 veterans living. Each year around 3,800 military funerals take place which is more than ten a day. So they often depend on volunteers or on pre-recorded "taps" on iPods, tablets or stereos to play funeral music. *Bugles Across America*, with 8,000 buglers and horn players on its roll, sends its civilian volunteers mostly as patriotic duty, free of charge along a 100-mile radius of his home to play at a military funeral.

The practice of Military Funeral for the unknown soldier started in UK and France after the first World War and it was emulated in the United States as well.

Conclusion

Some governments have assigned codified rules for the Bands performance. The Government of Netherlands is one such example. The website of the Defence Ministry of the Netherlands spells out that Military music is played *during ceremonies and special occasions involving the Royal House and the Defecse organization.* Examples given for such ceremonies and occasions are given in this order: *Prinsjesdag* (the State Opening of Parliament), state visits, the presentation of credentials to dignitaries, Royal weddings, state funerals, swearing-in ceremonies, commemorations, change-of-command ceremonies, medal award ceremonies, events such as military tattoos, Veterans Day and concerts (including Liberation Day concerts).[3]

These rules and roles pretty much apply to the military Bands in the whole world. In countries, where the responsibilities for military Bands are clearly delineated, they are worded in more or less similar terms. Even the States having no codified rules about the events where Military Bands are supposed to play, follow unwritten conventions which boil down to more or less similar terms.

NOTES

1 https://www.digitalmusicnews.com/2016/12/16/washington-dc-marching-band-donald-trump/

2 Mr Sarabjit Singh was sentenced to death in Pakistan in 1991 for his alleged role in a bomb blast in the city of Faisalabad (Pakistan) claiming 14 lives a year earlier. Execution of his death sentence was postponed sine die by Pakistan government. He ended up spending the next 22 years in jail in Pakistan. When, in 2013, the Indian government decided to execute a Kashmiri citizen Afzal Guru, on charges of being behind the Indian Parliament attack of 2001, enraged fellow Pakistani prisoners attacked and clubbed Sarabjit to death. In a tit-for-tat killing in an Indian prison, a Pakistani prisoner named Sanauallah who was member of the Jammu Prison Band was lynched to death by fellow Indian prisoners.

3 Quoted from the official website of the Royal Dutch Ministry of Defense https://www.defensie.nl/english/topics/music/during-ceremonies Page: Military Music During Ceremonies, accessed on 7 March 2017

CHAPTER XIII

Modern Role of Bands: Inter-State Relations

We provide connection between cultures, we set stage for strategic talks, we provide context, we bridge the gap, we help celebrate, we help mourn.

—Lt Col Domingos Robinson (Commander of US 8th Army Band)

In her confirmation hearings before the US Senate before becoming Secretary of State under President George W Bush, Jr.'s administration, Condoleezza Rice, pointed out that there were almost as many Diplomats working for the Government of the United States as were US Military Bands' members. She was slightly off the mark in figures—the US had 6,200 diplomats and around 8,000 Military Bands personnel in 2001 when the hearing took place. By late 2016, with Military Bands getting on the chopping block, the equation reversed when number of diplomats swelled to 8,100 in its 294 embassies, consulates and diplomatic missions abroad, as against military musicians reduced to 6,500 in 137 military Bands. But the relationship between the two jobs is hard to miss. In fact, defence forces and diplomatic corps perform the same function, defending the state interests overseas, but in different ways. Thus, diplomats are called a nation's first line of defence and the defence forces more often conduct what is nowadays known as "Defense Diplomacy."

The role Military Bands play as any country's peace ambassadors is only second to its diplomats. In the United States, the diplomats outnumber the military Bands personnel by a meagre 1,600. This ratio between the two may well be comparable in other nations too. The role of military and diplomacy converges to the extent of defending the nation's interests against external threats. Diplomacy after all, to quote Clauzwitz, is, "War by other means." Only that the diplomats do not fight with arms. Military Bands do not fight at all. Neither do they cause violence, nor bring any direct harm to the enemy troops. This type of soft power is a tool with which to rebuild the confidence and coherence of a community at home and the international community abroad.

Marcy A. Sudock, the head of MSLM, quoting some British paper in her blog, explains the phrase Soft Power as one that, "has long been used to describe a situation where you can influence, reassure and win hearts and minds to maintain and build long *lasting diplomatic relationships* without the use of force. Music is a proven tool that can be used as an enabler to to bridge language and cultural barriers to best *influence both friendly and enemy forces.*"[1] [Emphasis added]

Apart from peace-building, there are State Ceremonials at international level where role of military Bands is pivotal. Examples may include ceremonial occasions related to Diplomacy such as a State Visit (official visit by a foreign head of state), presentation of credentials by a foreign Ambassador or sending a country's Military Band to perform at the national day of another State, etc. This role of Bands in Diplomacy cements relations with friends, improve relations with adversaries and leaves an indelible positive mark on communities and third parties. Thus, the Military Bands are cornerstones of the above referred "Defence Diplomacy."

We will discuss the Diplomatic role of Military Bands under four heads, Bands at international Peace conferences, Bands at State Visits, Military Bands in friendly countries and Military Bands in unfriendly states.

Practice of playing Bands during peace treaties and peace anniversaries

After silence, that which comes closest to expressing the inexpressible is music.

—Aldous Huxley

There are a number of ways of creating, facilitating or celebrating peace through Military Bands. The task of creating peace is discussed later in this chapter, however, the first two roles are the topic of this section. Celebrating peace means celebrating a peace treaty through military Bands and facilitating peace means creating an environment where peace may succeed.

Celebrating Peace through Military Bands

The first known example of the use of Military Bands to celebrate a Peace Treaty comes from the Treaty of Karlowitz in 1699. Despite the failure of second siege of Vienna in 1683 by the Ottoman army, their war with the European empires lasted another 14 years (1683–97) to no avail. Ultimately, the diplomatic representatives from the Ottoman empire and various European monarchs signed the Treaty, ending the Turco–European Wars and dividing eastern Europe into respective spheres of influence. To mark the occasion, the Ottomans sent a Mehter Band to perform in city of Karlowitz for several days. The daily Band display not only softened the tensions but provided a relaxed ambience for the logical culmination of the peace negotiations. The Military Band was, in fact, a celebration of Peace after decades of bloodshed.

Czarina Anna Ivanova, the Duchess of Courland in Baltic Region (near present day Lithuania) obtained her own *Mehter* Band from Turkey in 1725 to upstage the Kingdom of Poland which had got a *Mehter* Band as a gift from the Ottoman Caliph five years earlier. When Anna became Czarina (Empress of Russia) in 1730, she brought her Band with her to the Russian imperial capital of St Petersburg. In the last year of her reign, when the Russo–Turkish Peace Treaty of Belgrade was being signed in 1739, it was the *Mehter* Band brought by Empress Anna, rather than any accompanied by the Turkish side, that played music for many days to celebrate the signing of the peace treaty between the Russian and Turkish empires.

Within the United States, Peace has been celebrated again and again through Military Bands shows. As early as 1869, the famous composer and conductor, Patrick Gilmore was allowed by US Government to go ahead with his celebration for peace through a *National Peace Jubilee* in Boston on June 15, 1869. As the Bands' Jubilee celebrated the end of civil war and advent of an era of peace, Dr. Oliver W Holmes was commissioned to write the "Hymn of Peace," set to the music from "American Hymn" by Matthais Keller. The Jubilee featured 486 musicians with various military wind Bands, a 525-member orchestra as well as around one hundred choral groups totalling 10,926 singers, making the it become the "high-water mark in the influence of the Band in American life."

Three years later, an International Peace Jubilee was also organized to celebrate the end of Franco-Prussian War in 1872, in the city of Boston. The peace was marked by a great military Bands show where the Band of the Grenadier Guards, from UK, the Band of the Republican Guard of France, Band of the Kaiser Franz regiment, from Prussia (Germany), and a Band from Dublin (Ireland) performed for tens of thousands of spectators. Most of these foreign Bands had performed for the first time in the United States. And again, they were there for a celebration of peace. One concert had the performance of Verdi's Il Trovatore by a 2,000-member orchestra, conducted by Johann Strauss, Jr., and 100 assistants, accompanied by a 20,000-voice chorus coming from all parts of the United States. A new piece, titled *Festival Hymn: Peace and Music,* was composed for this Jubilee by American composer, Dudley Buck.

In 1898-99 three more National Peace Jubilees were organized in Chicago, Atlanta and Philadelphia, during the tenure of President McKinley, to mark the end of American–Spanish War. The advent of peace was again symbolized by performances of military Bands at all these places.

More recently, the founding President of South Sudan, Gen John Garang, the youngest republic on earth, also called Military Band of Sudan People's Liberation Movement (SPLM) to celebrate Peace Treaty with the Khartoum Government in 2005, allowing for a referendum within six years to decide the fate of South Sudan. In his congratulatory speech to his nation on the occasion, Garang highlighted his decision to include Military Band in order to celebrate the Peace Treaty. His successor President Salva Kiir has also upheld the tradition of display SPLM Band at the anniversary celebrations of the treaty and of independence.

In recent years, the date of end of a particular war has gradually started replacing the date of initiation of hostilities as a cause of celebration. Pakistan used to observe September 6, Egypt would honour October 6 and Iran used to glorify September 22 as the Armed Forces Day. The three days, respectively, mark the start of second Indo-Pakistan War of 1965, the third Arab-Israel War of 1973, and the Iran-Iraq war of 1980-88. The day of the start of active hostilities symbolizes valour, victory and defiance in the face of an enemy. Times have changed. More countries now consider the day a war ended as more important day for celebration. Almost the whole world observes Armistice Day on November 11, the day when the hostilities ended and peace was restored, after the First World War. Even North Korea, not known as the friendliest of States, observes June 27—the day ceasefire came into effect in the Korean war in 1953—as the day of military pageantry rather the day the war started. Peace appears to triumph on war jingoism when nations start observing the ending of a war as their national day of celebration.

Facilitating Peace through Military Bands

The Military Bands are said to help set the stage for Strategic Talks. The official website of British Military Music rightly points out that the military Bands, in themselves, do not resolve the disputes but help create a cordial atmosphere where disputes could be resolved.

A pertinent example is the Band music performed in Portsmouth in 1905 during the negotiations to end the Russo-Japanese War (1904-05), sometime termed as "World War Zero" to distinguish the conflict from the two World Wars that ensued in which both Russia and Japan fought on opposite sides. The concerts by local town Bands and military Bands brought to Portsmouth for the occasion helped create the atmosphere for peace that resulted in the Treaty of Portsmouth signed on September 5, 1905.

The military music setting tone for tense talks or softening the atmosphere to a level that the negotiations are more likely to be successful is seldom appreciated. There are many stories of military musicians alleviating tension in the room whenever talks are about resolving a military dispute. It is not unusual for a Defence Minister or a four-star general hosts to have a Military Band to perform at a dinner hosted for his counterpart from opposite side. The Band performance helps set the mood.

Bands may be required to perform at State Banquets hosted by the heads of state too. And if it is a meeting or a banquet for the head of the nation, one recently had a war with, it is all the more important that the impact of Band is evaluated at the tone of the meeting. Most political memoirs somehow take Military Music as a given, as much as the air or weather at the venue, and seldom mention its influence separately.

The Indian military Bands are said to have welcomed Pakistani President Zulfikar Ali Bhutto in his first post-1971 war State visit to India. This gratified Mr Bhutto whose penchant for military pomp and show was no secret. Barely seven months earlier, as Pakistan's Deputy Prime Minister and Foreign Minister, Mr Bhutto had promised to fight a thousand years' war with India, in his emotional speech before the United Nations Security Council. This visit was marked by the historic Simla conference of July 1972 that culminated in the Simla Peace Accord between Pakistan and India. How much was the contribution of the goodwill generated by welcoming music to the atmosphere is hard to guess.

The Israeli military Bands played a role during Egyptian President Sadaat's official visit to Israel in November 1977 by playing tunes from Arab heartthrob singer Umm Kulthum to soften their Egyptian guest. The US Marines Band marked the signing of Camp David Peace accord in March 1979 when President Carter hosted the Egyptian and Israeli leaders to the White House reception. Again the impact can never be quantified. But this does not mean that it can be discounted either.

That is why, in Washington, DC, the military musicians are often utilized at the White House—as a show of precision, like during an arrival ceremony or when the Army Chorus performs a visitor's favourite tune from the visitor's country, putting them in a certain frame of mind before discussions getting rid of the tension in the room.

Use of Bands for Friendly Relations between States

Music and rhythm find their way into the secret places of the soul.

—Plato

The Military Bands are a very important feature of friendly relations between the States. There are a number of ways through which Bands play a role in strengthening friendly relations between States such as playing to welcome a foreign Head of State at a State Visit and military Bands being sent to each other country's national day parades. Even without a national day in another country, the gesture of sending Bands and Orchestras to another country to forge friendly relations has become a default use of Military Bands outside the home country. The Bands also take part and play at Military tattoos, displays and Military Band competitions abroad.

While all military forces in the world use terminology such as "defending the state," "destroying the enemy" and "laying down life for the motherland," etc., in the role and duties of the Military forces, the same is not true for the objectives laid down for the military Bands services. The Band units of the military are treated as a diplomatic strength. In fact, how many times the word "ambassadors" is used for the role and duties of Military Bands in diverse countries and cultures of the world is in itself striking.

For instance, one of the Objectives of the US Military Corps of Music is to "*advance international relationships*, using music to bridge language, cultural, societal, and socio-economic differences."[2] The Website of the United States Air Force Band announces that it [USAF Band], "Conceived and pioneered the concept that a musical organization can be a *nation's most effective goodwill ambassador*".[3] Then, the Mission statement of the West Point Military Academy Band, which is one of the four Special Bands of the US Armed Forces obliges the Band Members to "to act as *Ambassadors* of the United States ... to the local, national and international communities".[4] [All emphases added]

Bands at Ambassadorial credentials ceremonies since Ottoman era

Use of military Bands for diplomatic ceremonies is rooted to the Ottoman time. The Ottoman ambassadors, appointed to western capitals, brought *Mehter* Bands along to play not only at the time of presenting the credentials but also at important occasions subsequently. This practice continues to the present day when diplomatic credentials are received at a formal ceremony by the head of state of the host country The Ambassador-designate is no longer required to bring his country's

Military Band with him. In fact, it is the host nation's military Band that plays the national anthems of both the host nation and the one that Ambassador is representing. The Band also plays at the reception that usually follows the credential ceremonies. One can assume that European travellers heard the Janissary Bands during the ambassadorial receptions when their delegates were received in Istanbul. They took these nice ideas back home until the practice became universally institutionalized in diplomatic norms.

Today, this usage of Military Bands is much more entrenched than yesteryears. For instance, the military Bands of Singapore and Indonesia took six months to prepare for a ceremony of 30 minutes to mark the 50th anniversary of establishment of diplomatic relations between the two nations. The ceremony was held on 5th September2017.

Soft Power in World War: Military Bands for Allied States

During the World War I, the Triple Entente countries showed their friendship through Bands. In 1916, on the request of the French Government, King of England agreed to send the Band of Coldstream Guards to go and play for the troops and civilians in France. At the height of the War, the *Festival des Trois Gardes* (Festival of Three Guard Bands) took place in Paris that included the Band of the British Coldstream Guards, Band of the Republican Guard of France and the Band of the Royal Carabinieri from Italy. The Band Shows showed the power music to "influence minds of civilians, to stimulate ardour, to energize resolution and fortify coherence" (Dean 2016).

In 1917, the King of Italy requested similar concerts by the Military Bands of Italy's allies in Rome, Milan and Florence. The Band of the 18th Army Regiment of USA, the Band of French Republican Guard and the Band of Irish Guards from the United Kingdom arrived in Rome and gave concerts in all these cities. The British Ambassador to Italy wrote that, "*No better propaganda work has been done for the allied cause than the visit of the Guards Bands to Rome*" (Dean 2016).

This sort of role continued into the Second World War. For instance, the President's Own Marine Band performed a special concert on May 20, 1943, at the White House Franklin D. Roosevelt hosted his ally British Prime Minister Winston Churchill for the war conference. Despite a pouring rain, Roosevelt and Churchill sat through the concert, and Churchill sang "The Battle Hymn of the Republic" with the Band (Fettig 2016).

Military Bands Diplomacy by United States

The United States' Air Force Band website proclaims the Band to be "a musical organization that merits its reputation as *America's International Musical Ambassadors*, for it is one of the potent instruments of goodwill at the command of the American people. This concept has been proven through twelve international concert tours, covering 48 countries and 40 world capitals on five continents." The United States Air Force Band and its components have performed live for over 60,000,000 people of every race, colour, creed, religion and ideology. Additional millions have heard them through numerous radio and television appearances. By giving a first-hand insight into American culture, the musicians have created a better understanding among the peoples of the world.[5] The Army, Navy and Marine Bands of the United States too believe their roles to be similarly *ambassadorial*, but it would be repetitive and superfluous to cite from all their official websites. It would Suffice to mention that the United States treats its Bands as its messengers of goodwill.

Military Bands Diplomacy by Russian Federation

Military Bands are called modern Russia's "singing weapon." The Alexandrov Ensemble played in all friendly countries of the Soviet Union including Poland Yugoslavia, Afghanistan, North Korea and multiple times in Syria. In post-Soviet period, the Band was used as a diplomatic weapon to mend fences with erstwhile friends and strengthen friendship with existing ones. In 1993, it became an item of pop culture by performing with the Finnish Band named *Leningrad Cowboys* on the Senate Square in Helsinki, the capital of Finland, before an ecstatic audience of seventy-thousand. In a visit to Syria in 2016, the whole Choir died in a plane crash in the Black Sea.

Military Bands Diplomacy by Communist China

China's use of Military Bands in diplomacy is being called China's "musical approach to image building." In its dispute on new manmade islands in South China Sea, instead of having military parades to show muscle, China sent military Bands. The recent shows by Navy Band is not only to perform and entertain construction workers but also to project a peace loving image to the rest of the world.

Military Bands Diplomacy by United Kingdom

According to the website of the British Defence Ministry, the Government employs military Bands to "*achieve influence in order to further Defence and National interests* of the United Kingdom."[6] The Royal Marines Bands of the United Kingdom continue to fly the flag abroad with many prestigious engagements undertaken, including many in continental Europe such as those marking the 60th Anniversary of D-Day landing, and others at Gibraltar, the USA, and Australia, for instance.

Custom of Bands in ceremonies in connection with foreign State Visits

With Music you often don't have to translate it.

—David Byrne

At her State visit to China in May 2010, Pratibha Patel, the President of India was expecting a tough talk from her hosts. One thing she and her entourage might not have been expecting was the tunes of golden oldies of Bollywood like *mera naam chin chin chu,* and *bar bar dekho hazar bar dekho* from the military Band of China. The Chinese had touched an emotional chord not only with their surprised guests, but also millions of Indians watching the ceremony live on their television sets.

The relations between two Asian giants, namely, India and China, have remained uneasy since the Indo-China war of 1962. The irritants between the two nations span over a wide range of issues that both want to resolve. At the formal State banquet held by President Hu Jintao for his Indian counterpart, before the formal round of talks, the Band of People's Liberation Army (PLA) went on to play *gore gore o banke chore* and *Roja jaaaneman.* Indian delegates were pleasantly surprised by the selection of songs by the Band, whose music conductor Zhang Haifeng also played five non-Indian numbers. This is not the only incident of its kind where Military Bands have strategically been used to improve the outcomes from a State Visit.

This tradition of welcoming foreign Heads of State with Military Bands that was started by the Ottoman Turks permeated all over Europe and got introduced eventually in the United States too. The first time, a US Military Bands performed for a Head of State was during President Grant's administration at the visit of King Kalakaua of Hawaii (now a State within USA) on 12 December 1874.

Military Bands at State Visits

How much musical tunes effect the mood and how much they influence the outcome of talks is difficult to quantify or measure. Nevertheless, the military music remains a major factor in outcomes from the Summit level diplomacy. And the tunes selected for a reception remain a serious policy choice. The background music at the official luncheon or dinner hosted to honour the foreign guest is not the only occasion that the Bands play during a State visit.

The role of military Bands starts the moment a foreign head of state alights from his aircraft in a foreign country for a State visit. This may include a welcome music or trumpets playing "fanfare" or appropriate welcome tune of the country. The formal welcome ceremony for any foreign Head of State or Head of Government that takes place right at the airport or at a State House or the residence of the host head of state, involves military Bands. The Military Bands then play the national anthems of the two countries, first that of the guest State then that of the host State. The Military Band then plays background music at the inspection of Guard of Honor or the military parade. Any welcome without a Military Band at the formal ceremony may be treated as a diplomatic affront. The other occasions for Bands to play during the visit of a foreign Head of State include, but are not limited to, inauguration of a project, floral wreath laying at the host country's military or heroes' memorial, or his visits, if scheduled, to military facilities or some Ministry, etc.

The Ottoman Caliphs used to take their *Mehter* Bands with them at State visits abroad. But that was the time when most of their host nations did not sport military Bands. Following on the Ottoman footsteps, the US President Richard Nixon took his Marine Band, at least, twice during two of his most important State visits. In 1970, Nixon had the Marine Chamber Orchestra to Yugoslavia to provide music during a dinner and reception given for Yugoslav President Tito. And in 1974 a string ensemble from the Marine Band accompanied him to the Soviet Union to provide music for a dinner hosted by President Nixon for his Soviet counterparts (Fettig 2016).

Bands at Dignitaries' reception other than Heads of State or Government

The Military Bands may also be used to play at the arrival of distinguished foreign guest of a lesser status than the head of State or Government like Speaker of the Parliament, a Foreign Minister, a Defence Minister or even an Ambassador. But here conventions differ from country to country. It may also depend on how close the relations are between the two nations. It may also sometimes depend on the depth of personal relationship between the visiting dignitary and his host. And this is also related to military and ceremonial traditions of the host country which may vary across regions and across times.

Specific Band Tunes for Foreign Dignitaries

Again, United States is an example which, despite being a new nation (compared, for instance, to China, England, France, India or Turkey) has developed broader canons for military music for all occasions. The welcome tunes at the White House, the official residence of the President of the United States are different for their own President or Vice President than for visiting statesmen and women of equal ranks. Likewise, not only the tunes to herald the arrival of a military and a civil official of the United States are different from each other, but also welcome tunes for the dignitaries from foreign states are different from those for local ones.

Foreign heads of state and heads of government arriving at the White House are welcomed with the tune of "Call to Statesmanship." If the official is a foreign dignitary lower in rank than the President or the Prime Minister, the last 16 bars of "Hands Across the Sea" is used instead.

Just as appropriate tunes are important for relations between two nations during a state visit, any musical fiasco or wrong tune can be embarrassing for both sides. The way the Egypt military Band played the Russian national anthem during the State visit of President Vladimir Putin (Feb 2015) and that of France during the visit of President Francois Hollande (April 2016) embarrassed not only the host President Sisi, but also the media in France and Russia, calling it a "butchery" of their anthems. Daily *Telegraph* of the UK called the latter incident as a "massacre of French anthem."

Egyptian army was not the only one to play the Anthem notes of foreign countries poorly. In a 2010 State visit to Norway, President Doris Leuthard of Switzerland and her entourage were surprised when the Norwegian Military Band started playing what was supposed to be Swiss national anthem. Nobody knew that song but it was definitely not the national anthem of Switzerland. Likewise, in his 2014 State visit to Venezuela, Chinese President Xi Jinping had only to listen to the poorly played Chinese national anthem on arrival, to gauge the strength of the Venezeulan polity which could not produce a rendition properly. Similarly, when US President Donald Trump landed in Saudi Arabia on a State visit in 2017, the way Saudi Army Band played the *Star-Spangled Banner*, there was no further evidence needed on how much the Saudis had enhanced their fighting clout through large defence purchases.

Bands in Adversary States: Building bridges between nations

> *The regular rhythm and upbeat tunes of military music or marching Bands positively affect your mood even if you don't actually 'enjoy' listening to it.*
>
> —Liz Miller

"When music speaks, everybody understands". The EMMA for Peace tagline is a simple but powerful mantra. Music, it suggests, can succeed *where language simply cannot.*[7] [Emphasis added] Sometimes, the Military Bands perform as ambassadors or representatives of the local field commanders towards the other side. At other times, they act as representatives of their governments to perform at an unfriendly country or an opposite military alliance. Instances are legion.

Military Band as interlocutor at a local theatre

An example of this is provided from the time of stationing of both American and Russian troops in the war-torn Bosnia and Herzegovina right after its civil war (1992–95) ended with the signing of Dayton Peace Accord. It was the use of "Mo Better Blues," a blues rock Band composed of musicians from the 1st Armored Division Band, to soften up the Russians with whom a number of operational disagreements had arisen. The Band was sent to entertain Russian Army soldiers during a contentious joint deployment to Bosnia in 1996. At the time, a US State Department liaison officer claimed the Band did "more for U.S.-Russian relations in 90 minutes" than he had been able to do in 30 days.

The military Bands set the stage for strategic talks, mainly by reducing tensions. All countries utilize military Bands when high ranking officials host a foreign counterpart. The Band will play at arrival ceremony for a high official, provide entertainment after the dinner and before the meetings for the next day. Military Bands are a potent instrument for human beings to relax, connect and have meaningful interactions. Hence, a military Band playing in for officials from an unfriendly country or before an audience from such a country also helps in building goodwill for each other.

Military Bands as Goodwill Ambassadors between USSR and NATO

In case, a Military Band is sent to a hostile country, or one with which hostilities had taken place in the past, they would act as a softener for normalization of relations. The Military Bands do not resolve disputes but at least they set a stage or create an environment where disputes could be resolved.

Instances of Bands easing tensions were witnessed during the height of the

Cold War between the Western and Eastern Powers as well as subsequently. As early as in 1948, much of Berlin was still in ruins after the World War II, and the city was divided into four occupation zones, controlled by the USSR, France, the UK and the United States. This was before the raising of Berlin Wall when it was still possible to travel between zones. An American officer suggested a concert in the *Gerndarmenmarkt* (in the Soviet zone at the time), and the French zone commander supported the suggestion. The musicians were to be provided by the USSR, and the famous Alexandrov Ensemble was chosen. A temporary stage was set up in the square, with flowers all along the front. The 1948 peace concert was to consist of German folk songs and opera extracts and Russian folk songs (*Nightingales*, *Zemlyanka* and *Roads*). The same two nations had fought till three years earlier, having killed 26 million of each other's people. But music has no religion, no race and no nationality. Some 30,000 people joined in from all four Zones to sing German lyrics of *Heidenröslein*. Then, it was the turn of Victor Nikitin, the famous tenor soloist of Alexandrov Band, to sing Russian folk song *Kalinka* three times in a row, The crowd, from five distinct nationalities—the Germans and four occupying powers—kept standing and watching for hours. In 1994, towards the end of his life, Boris Alexandrov, the head of Alexandrov Band, said:

> *The visit to Germany was unforgettable. It is dominant in the history of the ensemble. It was necessary to make a new creative leap – from wartime military music to post-war relaxing harmony.*

Forty-two years later, the Cold War ended and Berlin wall had fallen. Once again in 1990, the Alexandrov Band participated in Roger Waters' concert, again in Berlin, celebrating the fall of the Berlin Wall. They performed an anti-war song, *Bring the Boys Back Home*

In 2007, seventeen years after the end of the Cold War, the situation had improved to the extent that Russian Federation's Alexadrov Military Band performed at the NATO headquarters in Brussels, the first-ever Soviet-Russian Band to have played at NATO premises. They performed the song "The Sacred War."

Conclusion: Military Bands as Unifiers

The Military Bands present a soft image of their country abroad as well as soft image of the Armed Forces both within the country and outside. From times immemorial there has been a tradition not to shoot at Military Bands during battles. The concept of bright prominent uniforms is based on the logic that they should be clearly recognizable from a distance so may not be shot at. Thus, the Military Bands have become a strong element of goodwill between opposing military forces, a potent form of cultural diplomacy between the adversary governments and a valuable asset to help strengthen relations with allies.

Colonel Robinson, an ex-Conductor of US 8th Army Band stationed in South Korea, is vocal in his blog about the significance of Bands in bringing about harmonious relations between the nations. This chapter begins with a quote from his blog. The US and Republic of Korea's army Bands playing together is a spectre that both nations have been witnessing since the end of the Korean war when the two armies became comrades-in-arms in warding off the North Korean attack. On the north side of the 38th parallel De Militarized Zone (DMZ), the Russian and former Soviet Military Bands have remained a familiar guest of the DPRK's government and the military. In fact, the Central Band of the North Korean Defense Forces is exactly modelled on the Alexandrov Band of Russia. The performances together over the previous decades has cemented the relations between Russia and North Korea. In the wake of "fire and fury" threats by US President Trump, North Korean leader Kim Jong Unh showed softening of his stance with South Korea, sending his real sister and the North Korean female military Band, as his charm offensive. The goodwill resulted in North Korea taking part in Winter Olympics in South Korea during January 2018.

The Global Peace Song Awards believes that, "Music has the power to speak directly to the heart. It can inspire enlightened awareness and lovingly empower us to see and treat each other as brother and sister. When our souls know such liberation, *War as we know it will end and peace on earth will prevail.*" The truth of such optimist assumptions shall be put to test one day if and when Military Bands from Republic of Korea and DPRK (North Korea) play together in each other's territory or, may be, remaining within their side of De-Militarized Zone (DMZ) on the 38th parallel but performing face to face.

After all, this is exactly what happened around the German reunification. Sweden was the last overseas trip by the Central Military Bands of the German Democratic Republic, the GDR, as the Communist East Germany was then known, before German unification at the end of the Cold War. Upon unification of Germany, the military forces of the two parts also merged, and so did their Military Bands. The Conductor of the GDR Military Band became the second-in-command of the unified German Military Band. So, besides German unification, there was a musical unification too.

NOTES

1 Quoted from the Blog of Musique Sur La Mer (MSLM) at http://www.mslmorchestra.com/connect/blog/ accessed on June 23, 2017.

2 Quoted from the official website of the United States Air Force Band http://www.bands.af.mil/main/welcome.asp, accessed on 07 November 2016.

3 Ibid.

4 United States Military Academy (USMA) Band Mission Statement cited from Official Website of West Point Military Academy www.usm.edu and article on bicentennial celebrations of the Band at https://www.army.mil/article/187505/service, both accessed on 22 May 2017.

5 Words quoted from the US Air Force Band Official Website < http://www.usafband.af.mil/ >, accessed on 3 October 2016

6 Quoted from the British Army Official Website http://www.army.mod.uk/music/33204.aspx Page: Corps of Army Music, accessed on 15 Jan 2017

7 The Euro Mediterranean Music Academy for Peace—shortened as EMMA for Peace—is a musical initiative for peace on the rim of Mediterranean Sea in nations of Middle East, North Africa and Southern Europe. Tagline is taken from their website http://www.emmaforpeace.org, accessed on 22 March 2017.

CHAPTER XIV

Bands at the Service of the People

In ancient times music was the foundation of all the sciences. Education was begun with music... with the persuasion that nothing could be expected of a man who was ignorant of music.

—Marcus Tullius Cicero (106-43 BC), Roman Philosopher, Statesman, Writer and Orator

Being part of the Band is also a tryst with history and a good education to begin with, for an individual, for a group and for a nation. That is one reason to be optimistic that the Bands phenomenon shall not go down easily despite the global war that was discussed in earlier chapters. The mushrooming of Bands in the civilian domain, offers a silver lining under the clouds. But for this latter phenomenon, the musical Bands could well have been declared as "endangered species" already.

As the number of Military Bands in the United States, for instance, which now stand at 137 for all four arms put together, are down manifold since the time of the civil war of 1861–65. During the same one and a half century, private, civilian and non-government Bands rose in that country from a mere 300 or so to a whooping 30,000 or so, presently. Thus, an over 90% fall in the number of regular military Bands has been met with a 10,000 per cent increase in the number of civilian Bands (many of which operate in military style), in the same country during the same period.

This phenomenon is neither by some grand design, nor purely accidental. The roles that Bands play in human lives, wittingly or unwittingly, in a myriad of positive ways, the ordinary citizens continue raising Bands of their own while the governments and politicians continue to guillotine State-controlled military and civilian Bands. In this chapter, we shall analyze how do Bands impact human life at an individual level, at group level, at community level and at the national level.

Benefit of Bands at Individual level

Without music life is a journey through desert

—Pat Conroy

Bands have a positive impact on human health and learning. First of all, the Harris Poll that found that 73 per cent of CEOs from Fortune 1000 companies were involved in music programs in high school. It may be instructive to note how many celebrities in so many diverse fields of life had been Band members in their student lives: Former US President Bill Clinton; Banker Alan Greenspan, the long serving Chairman of the Federal Reserve; Astronaut Neil Armstrong, the first human to set foot on the moon; Actress Gwen Stefani, also famous singer and fashion designer; Athlete Vince Carter, the Basketball star; Actress Julia Roberts and Filmmaker Steven Spielberg are just among the few names who were musicians in marching Bands during their youth. Here we list a few individual benefits for being part of a Bands (Ray 2011).

Personal grooming and character building

Music programs are important because they give students practice and experience in skills that reach far beyond musical notes and instruments. This experience in so many non-musical life-skills has positive impacts on kids as they become adults. First of all, marching Band is also a crash course in *time management.* Balancing school, homework and practice can be quite the challenge. But again, this is a skill that one appreciates more and more as one gets older.

Learning Music makes one better at *multitasking* as the neurological benefits of music are long proven and well documented. Marching Bands make one a better all-round musician. Plus, Marching Band directors are some of the most dedicated educators around and are awesome people to know. Their love of music and learning is infectious. It is no small feat to take 50 to 150 diverse students and turn them into a well-oiled marching machine (and make sure they sound good doing it).

Marching and playing at the same time is challenging, and marching Band members meet the challenge of marching on one tempo while playing on another. The neuronal connections grown in marching Band will benefit the students throughout their lives, for multi-tasking through the workplace, and for them as parent, when they become one. The kids applaud other Bands at competitions which is an act of *generosity* that they inculcate in their personality for good.

Resilience is another important benefit. Students mess up. They keep going. Judges make mistakes or make calls we do not agree with. The Band members keep going. Students learn that a defeat during a competition is not the end of the world. Resilience is a hot topic in psychology today, and being able to bounce back after a setback is an important skill throughout life. *Flexibility* combined with *creative problem solving* is another important learning outcome. The Band members embrace feedback from judges' commentaries. Instead of rigidly insisting that the show they put together is perfect, they take constructive criticism seriously and make adjustments where needed.

Marching Band is also a hard physical *exercise.* Walking miles, carrying along a 7 kg Piccolo or a 22 kg Bass Drum holding one's breath along the way, makes one's muscles stronger. Marching Band requires *discipline* and *dedication.* Long rehearsals are not for the faint hearted. To work strenuous hours through tough conditions instills a mental fortitude and ethic that serve the student throughout their life. *Teamwork* is a necessity when one is part of a marching Band, so that no one gets left behind. And finally, the Band members imbibe *manners* and *respect.* Students represent both school and community when at a performance or competition. The Band members on the field remain perfectly still in situations where we all know they wanted to dance and scream. Marching Band teach students to *grow from adversity.* One cannot win every competition. They learn to take critical feedback, be it from judges or from the Band instructor & use it as lessons to perform better the next time.

Besides, the foregoing general benefits, there can be countless examples of Band experience helping a person in specific circumstances. One illustrative example is about five women who said their Band experience helped them heal from the trauma of sexual assaults. One wrote in the Stanford Daily:[1]

> *And I can say that Band helped me become myself again. Over time, Band helped me separate what happened to me from who I am, and live without feeling every moment like my life had been commandeered by someone whose identity, to this day, I still don't know. Because of Band's culture, I was able to shake the feelings of anxiety and shame that had consumed me and remember how to be happy. My life was my own again, and I had Band to thank for that.* (Anonymous 2016)

Band encourages and helps its members to become their truest selves as the Bands help people figure out who they really are. Bands help them reconnect with themselves especially after any trauma such as a social break up from a loved one, recouping from a serious disease or recovering from an incarceration or torture.

Bands as Musical Therapy

Every sickness is a musical problem, the healing therefore, is a musical resolution.

—Georg Philipp Friedrich von Hardenberg (1772-1801), 18th century German mystic poet

Music is used for medical treatment. In fact, Musical Therapy is now a recognized and scientifically proven method of treatment for a wide range of ailments including war injuries. There are 6,000 professional music therapists in 30 countries of the world today.

The United States Army extensively used music therapy as a form of treatment. At least 80,000 war veterans have benefited from music therapy programs in United States. No less than 7.538 veterans were advised by medical authorities to undergo music therapy.

Nowadays, Indian fusion style music has become famous outside South Asia for this very purpose. The soothing sound of these instruments is used to heal and cure even severely ailing people. It has brought the revolution in the history of music. People are taking more interest to learn these instruments. This has brought a new taste of music in human life.

Bands for Individual recognition

"Music is your own experience, your own thoughts, your wisdom. If you don't live it, it won't come out of your horn" Charlie Parker had aptly noted. The more one lives one's musical experience, the more would be the chance to win a recognition. It will be instructive to mention the awards instituted by the John Philip Sousa Foundation for promotion of Bands and Band Music. The *Star of the Order* is the highest award that recognizes outstanding contribution to the excellence of Bands internationally while the *Medal of the Order*, also called Medal of Honor, is the equivalent that recognizes laureates for their services within the country (i.e. the United States). The Sousa Foundation also administers the *Legion of Honor* that recognizes an individual Bandleader for outstanding leadership over the course of two decades or more.

There are a few recognitions outside the Sousa Foundation for individual recognition of Band Music. Fairly recently, since 2010 to be precise, the United States Armed Forces have instituted *Col Finley R. Hamilton Military Outstanding Musician Award* which is reserved for non-commissioned officers (ranks E4 upto E6) in all five branches of the US Military. The Best Musicians, from the US military Bands, are shortlisted for the Award for their outstanding achievement in solo and ensemble performance, displaying exceptional leadership quality and for the potential of future service.

Benefit of Bands at Group level

Good Music Comes out of People playing together

—Keith Richards

Music can excite, thrill, console and comfort without the need for words, and it has the ultimate ability to unite disparate and even opposing communities. The most common use of Bands for benefit of a whole group is provided by institutional Bands. The Band can be the most recognizable face of a military unit, of a city police, of a University, College or School, or of any particular institution. The Bands foment camaraderie in the members of the institution, provide opportunity for team recognition, inculcate discipline and boost morale in the uniformed forces, and alleviate levels of fear or stress for people in a common trauma such as a hurricane hit community or people in a sinking ship. The Band aboard the famous *Titanic* more than a century ago epitomizes this role and hence merits a separate discussion below.

Bands for Group Identity and Camaraderie

Is Music *per se* a sport? It probably is not. But being a part of a marching Band is indeed a team sport that too, it can be argued, very different from ordinary sports. In an ordinary sports team, where the goal is to defeat opponents in games, teams try to go after an opponent's weakness and to shut down an opponent's strong scorer. On the other hand, the teamwork in marching Band is of a more positive nature, about individual and group self-improvement, competing with self, comparing results with self over time. This is regardless of whether one is a member of a Band in a uniformed force, in a community or in a school.

The students learn *trust*, for instance, when one is marching backwards, or sideways, one must trust that his Bandmates are doing what they are supposed to do so that one does not crash into them on a trek across the field during precision marching. For a school or college Band, the members get an opportunity to see the benefits of *sacrificing* what one would want to do (computer gaming, online chatting or missing favourite TV show) for the good of the team. All this holds equally good for the military Bands.

This is recognized by the United States Military Corps of Music which, on its website, requires the Military Bands to, "Foster, enhance and lift the morale and esprit de corps of the United States forces especially forward deployed locations" (USAF-Website n.d.) This type of trust, sacrificing and team spirit is absolutely essential for all uniformed forces. The *espirit de corps* that the Marching Bands bring to the disciplined agencies and forces has no parallel in classroom style instruction. The Bands develop camaraderie in the troops within a regiment or the sailors on a ship or the police officers of a particular city or formation.

Bands for Team recognition

Just like Sports teams can win world cup or national cups and individually or collectively earn gold, silver or bronze medals, there are a number of recognitions for the best performing Bands as well. They can be trophies, shields, medals or Flags of Honor.

In the United States, John Philip Sousa Foundation has taken the lead in instituting recognitions for excellence in Band music. Starting from early 1980s, the Foundation recognizes the best Concert Band though the *Col George S Howard Citation*—the highest award for a military or concert Band. The Award does not recognize winning a particular competition but recognizes outstanding performance by a Band over the course of several years. A *Sudler Silver Scroll* is similarly awarded to the best community Band in the United States by the Foundation.

There are a number of recognitions for School, College and University Marching Bands. The Sudler Trophy is for the best University or College Marching Band

For the Schools, the recognitions include Sudler *Flag of Honor*, an award to recognize the best High School Band anywhere in the world; the *Sudler Shield* recognizes the most outstanding high school marching Bands within the United States and the *Sudler Cup* for the best junior or middle school marching Band. There are a number of other competitions that take place in the United States where Band Teams may win laurels for themselves as well as the institution and community they represent.

In India, there is an annual All-India Police Bands competition which recognize the best amongst the Bands of Police, Militias, Border Guards and other law enforcement agencies. In Pakistan, there is a tradition of annual Military Bands competition that takes place yearly in Fortress Stadium, Lahore. These competitions recognize and reward best amongst marching Bands. The largest Marching Bands competitions in Pakistan so far, bringing together both the Military and the Civilian Marching Bands include the Lahore Festival of Marching Bands (2013) which awarded Flags of Honor to winner Bands and the Gilgit Tattoo of Marching

Bands (2012) that awarded Trophies to winner teams and gold, silver and bronze medals to each musician of the winning teams.

Bands for Morale Boosting and Training for Soldier community

The Military Bands boost the morale of the troops in war and peace times. As the only uninterrupted living tradition for centuries they provide continuity to the forces and are indispensable for the drill and training of the troops. Hence, the official job responsibilities of the British Military Corps of Music include the following:[2]

- Sustain and develop the moral component of fighting power
- Represent the professionalism of Service personnel
- Represent the broader attributes for which Britain is admired

Visit of Bands at bases outside the parent country are a spirit booster for the men. They provide entertainment to the troops at special occasions as well as provide honour to the fallen men. The importance of Military Bands for the morale of the troops in a war theatre is also unfathomable. Throughout the American Civil War, military Bands were well thought of by the soldiers. A soldier of the 24th Massachusetts Regiment wrote in a letter home in 1862: "Dear Fanny, I don't know what we should have done without our Band. It is acknowledged by everyone to be the best in the division" (Snell 2004). Similar stories of the role of Bands in soldiers' lives have been related elsewhere in this work.

Bands to relieve stress, trauma and pain

The effect of Bands to relieve stress or trauma is so well established that the Governments take conscious decision to deploy Bands specifically in conflict-ridden or disaster-hit areas. A prominent example is furnished by Hurricane Andrew. But perhaps the most iconic example of music Soothing the heart and easing the pain is furnished by the Band on the famous ship *Titanic* immortalized by the famous eponymous movie and other books and films in popular culture.

Books written specifically about the Titanic's musicians include Steve Turner's work titled, *The Band that Played On: The Extraordinary Story of the 8 Musicians Who Went Down with the Titanic* (2011) and Christopher Ward's non-fiction, *The Titanic Violinist and the Glovemaker: A True Story of Love, Loss and Betrayal* (2011). Ward is the grandson of Titanic Band member Jock Hume. The book became a Sunday Times bestseller and was made into a documentary for the Discovery Channel titled *Titanic: The Aftermath* (2012). Two other documentary films have been made about the Titanic's Band; the British film *Titanic: The Band Played On* (completed in 2012) and the American documentary film *Titanic–*

Band of Courage (2014). Hence, a detailed look on the role of Bands for Syrian refugees in Australia, that during Hurricanes Andrews and Charley in the USA and the background of the Band on *Titanic* during its fateful journey across Atlantic Ocean, is in order.

Syrian Refugees Marching Band: Before the tragic civil war in Syria, before 2011, almost every Christian Church in the country used to have a Band. The war devastated the country and most Bands were dissolved as fear of bomb blasts precluded any chance of public performance. But their ranks were diluted due to mass immigration and internal displacement.[3]

In Australia, Syrian-born Father Samir Haddad of St Joseph's Melkite Catholic Church in Fairfield, decided in 2015 to unite his flock from far-flung suburbs. He thought that instead of the kids, he should focus on Syrian youth, staying at home crying, missing their country, that they can do something good. While their parents learn English with other volunteers, the Band recruited music teacher volunteers to train them in music and marching in a Brunswick community centre. They assemble in their elaborate uniforms to play Syrian folk tunes which is has a positive impact on relieving the stress and reintegrates the society as people are encouraged to become healthy active members of the community.

Bands in Hurricane Andrews and Hurricane Charley: The Hurricane Andrews struck southern Florida in 1992. Damages and casualties were catastrophic. The US Federal Government helped the recovery with the operation titled "Provide Comfort" dispatching two Bands as part of the effort. The 10th Mountain Division Band, and the 13th Army Band (Florida National Guard) reached the area to provide support. They performed concerts for refugees and relief workers, and provided other valuable assistance. These concerts boosted morale and provided authorities an effective means to gather people and disseminate supplies and information.

Stories of Bands playing to reduce pain and trauma are legion even within the United States where even School and College Marching Bands volunteered to go and perform in flood or earthquake hit, or any other natural calamity hit area. One such example is also provided by Venice High School Band, from Albertsons, USA, participated in the relief effort to help the victims of Hurricane Charley in August 2004, that hit South Eastern coasts of the United States.

Bands aboard Titanic: Operated by White Star Lines, and built by Harland & Wolff Shipyard in Belfast, the *Titanic* was a British passenger liner—largest ship afloat at the time with a passenger capacity of above 2,200—that sank in its maiden voyage in the North Atlantic Ocean. It started its journey from Southampton in Britain, carrying some of the wealthiest persons of its time as well as hundreds of immigrants from England, Ireland and Scandinavia. She collided with an iceberg on 14 April 1912, causing the hull plates to buckle inwards, gradually filling the ship with ice-cold water. As the ship did not have enough life boats, death for most of the passengers and crew became imminent.

As fate would have it, the luxury liner had eight musicians aboard, members of a three-piece ensemble and a five-piece ensemble. Both ensembles were booked through C.W.& F.N. Black in Liverpool, by the White Star Line, for entertainment of its rich passengers. This Liverpool firm used to place musicians on almost all British liners who themselves travelled as second class passengers but played for first class ones. Until the night of the sinking, the orchestra performed as two separate entities: a quintet led by violinist and official Bandmaster Wallace Hartley, that played at teatime, after-dinner concerts, and Sunday services, among other occasions. The remaining four members of the Band included John Wesley Woodward (cello) John Frederick Preston Clarke (string bass and viola) John Law Hume (violin) and Percy Cornelius Taylor (piano). The other three-member ensemble was the Cello, Piano and Violin trio, played respectively, by Roger Marie Bricoux, George Alexander Krins, and Theodore Ronald Brailey, at the À La Carte Restaurant and the Café Parisien.

As *Titanic* began to sink, on the fateful night between 14–15 April 1912, the Bandsmen faced death as much as most other passengers. But as an act of ultimate heroism, which is recognized to this day, Hartley started conducting both ensembles with the intent of calming the passengers facing imminent and immediate death. As the crew loaded life boats, these eight men aged between 21 and 32 played on for as long as the musicians possibly could. Gradually the ship submerged and all went down with the ship. Many of the survivors said that Hartley and the Band continued to play until the very end. One second-class passenger said:

> *Many brave things were done that night, but none were more brave than those done by men playing minute after minute as the ship settled quietly lower and lower in the sea. The music they played served alike as their own immortal requiem and their right to be recalled on the scrolls of undying fame.* (Vollbretch 2012)

The disaster in the wee hours of 15 April 1912 led to the death of 1,500 passengers making it the greatest commercial liner maritime tragedy in peacetime. Although all the musicians of the RMS *Titanic* perished with the ship but their heroism immortalized their names. Their paid-duty to play music was as long as the ship was afloat. When it was sinking, they took upon themselves a new duty to soothe the passengers by deciding to play on. They could have made a beeline towards the lifeboats available but they did not. The valour that the Bands have shown in history is thus not limited to military Bands alone.

Titanic Band also influences Music of the world. Harry Chapin's album *Dance Band on the* Titanic (1977) is dedicated to the *Titanic's* ensembles and contains a song titled "Dance Band on the Titanic." The album *Titanic: Music As Heard On The Fateful Voyage* (1997), by Ian Whitcomb and the White Star Orchestra, recreates songs played aboard the *Titanic* the night the ship foundered, and includes detailed notes about the music and excursion

Benefit of Bands at Community Level

> *Music expresses that which cannot be said and on which it is impossible to be silent.*
>
> —Victor Hugo (1802-1885)

The type of functions that Military Bands perform at community level include their role as the bridge between the military and the general population. The Bands remain the public face (and sound) of the military and police forces. This they perform in a number of ways including, but not limited to, acting as medical personnel, fire fighters and humanitarian relief workers.

Military and Police rapport with public

Save for active war zones, for most of the population, military Bands are the only interaction with the military that they have. Service Bands are tasked to engage the local population in operational theatres, paving the way for co-operation and communication. The Military Bands remain amongst the most respected, versatile and accomplished musical organizations in the world. The tradition of representing the country to local and global audiences develops rapport with the people at large. Jonathan Ward, conductor of a US Military Band, aptly points out, "Our job is to tell the army's story...[and] music is our most lethal weapon in telling that story."

The Objectives of the US Corps of Music highlight the following roles for Military-Citizen relations:[4]

- Increase public understanding of the importance of military, their mission, policies, and programs and the bravery, sacrifice and dedication of troops.

- Inspire patriotism and encourage young men and women to serve in various branches of the military.
- Foster a deep appreciation of the rich history and legacy of the Armed Forces.
- Strengthen relationships with a variety of publics to enhance the reputation of the Armed Forces as a respected professional organization charged with an integral role in maintaining the U.S. national security.

Two interesting examples of all the above roles being fulfilled by the military Bands in real life situation are provided by the political crises in Hungary in 1956 and in the Caribbean nation of Haiti in 1995.

Hungarian Military Bands during the Uprising 1956: The Hungarian military Bands already had a proud history of 200 years by the time of the outbreak of the Second World War in which so many Bandsmen were killed in action, injured or went missing that, much like elsewhere in Europe, a reorganization of Military Bands was called for. The number of military Bands was reduced to eight, and unlike Regiment based, as they were before the War, they became city-based. Also to survive the War all four were civilian Bands, under the control of the Government, those of the Police, Fire Services, Customs and the Finance Ministry.

The role of military Bands to soothe their own people came sooner than later. The Hungarian uprising of 1956 was suppressed brutally by the Soviet troops and the Hungarian army under the so-called dictatorship of the Proletariat in Budapest. The prestige, repute and support of the army was at its lowest ebb. To build rapport with the public, the government decided to use Military Bands. Garrison Clubs were established where the Military and amateur civilian Bands were tasked to play together to promote cultural life and promote social and civic activities. The Bands were used as a State policy to build a new public relationship between the State and the Society (White 2015).

Military Bands Role in Haiti Crisis: In October 1995, the US troops intervened in another Caribbean nation of Haiti to restore democracy. Sanctioned by the United Nations Security Council under its resolution 940. (Sept. 1994–March 1995), the Operation "Uphold Democracy" was an intervention designed to remove the military regime installed by the 1991 Haitian coup d'état that overthrew the elected President Jean-Bertrand Aristide.

The US Government ordered the 82nd Airborne Division and the 10th Mountain Division to launch operation from the nearby base on Guantanamo Bay. While the lead units of both Divisions were already in the air, a diplomatic channel led by former US President Jimmy Carter, U.S. Senator Sam Nunn and retired Chairman of the Joint Chiefs of Staff General Colin Powell persuaded General Joseph Raoul Cédras and other military leaders of the military regime in Haiti to step down and return power to the elected government.

Since no combat took place so the armed units of the Division had no great role to play. It was the Bands of the two Divisions that had the lead role thereafter. The 82nd Airborne Division Band performed numerous concerts for US and NATO troops as well as the Haitian people. In addition to a musical mission, the Band also went on patrols. The 10th Mountain Division Band also participated in *Operation Uphold Democracy* by entertaining troops, dignitaries at the US Ambassador's residence, and the Haitian people. When not playing music, the Band guarded points within their area of responsibility (AoR).

Ghana Police Centennial Celebrations: Thus, renowned Police Forces use their Bands in a conscious effort to build rapport with the public. The Inspector General of Police (IGP), Mr. David Asante Apeatu, was of the view that for the Police Force to perform to the best of its abilities, it needed the goodwill and support of the citizenry. Through the unifying strength of music, he argued, the Police Bands had the ability to draw the public closer to the Police for better understanding and collaboration. Thus, launching year-long public collaboration activities throughout the country to mark its Centenary Anniversary of the Ghana Police, a theme of "Impacting Lives through Music" was adopted. The anniversary activities, according to Ghana Police Spokesperson, mainly sought "to educate the public on police work, as well as the responsibilities of each citizen towards crime prevention." The activities also aimed to "draw the citizenry closer to the Police through musical performances laced with the education of the people" by the Public Affairs Department of the Police (Fiabu 2017).

Bands as Medics

The Military Bands have performed as medical units since as early as they became a regular feature in the Armed Forces. Since as early as 1788, the Military Bands in Australia, and sometime later in New Zealand, doubled as Medics. This role spread to other nations in time.

In the United Kingdom, the Band Units of all three branches of the Defence Forces have played their role as medics and rescue handlers. The Infantry units of the British Army used to have a Band Company, for at least as far back as the Crimean War, whose primary duty was that of stretcher bearers in order to remove the sick and wounded in the battlefields. The Pipe Band phenomenon increased by the end of the 19th century when around 60 Infantry Units could be counted as having such Bands. Other units overseas had non-combatant Drummer Boys with similar duties.

The Royal Air Force musicians of the United Kingdom are also trained to provide medical support in times of war. During the Gulf conflict musicians were deployed to various locations in the Middle East, where they undertook a variety of tasks, ranging from being medical orderlies to guards at hospital sites.

Royal Marines Bands also were involved in both the Falklands conflict and *Operation Granby* (Gulf War 1) as casualty handlers on various hospital ships. In 2000, RM Band Service ranks were deployed to Kosovo for six months during *Operation Agricola* supporting the 3rd Commando Brigade of Royal Marines. In the early part of 2003, 39 Band Service ranks deployed with the Primary Casualty Receiving Facility on RFA Argus, which is a sort of floating Ocean Hospital. It is a casualty handling ship in the fleet of Royal Navy, providing casualty handlers and a further 26 ranks deployed with 3rd Commando Brigade as Decontamination teams during *Operation Telic* (Gulf War 2). Also in 2007, a number of the Bands took part in operations in Afghanistan with 3rd Commando Brigade where they assisted the Medical Squadron and the Commando Logistic Regiment, as well as providing musical entertainment. Another 38 Royal Marine Band personnel deployed to Afghanistan again in 2008-9 with the same 3rd Commando Brigade as ambulance and general duties drivers.

Germany also has a very strong tradition of military Bands. The medical role of Military Bands continues there too as the German Government explained to the European Court of Justice that, "[As} far as the military-music services are concerned, in the event of hostilities, those services are disBanded and *their members assigned to medical units as nursing or auxiliary nursing staff*"(musicians belonging to military Bands are given the requisite training during peacetime).[5]

Bands in Fire Services and Social and Relief Work

The Military Bands and civilian Bands have been used for fire services, at least in the United Kingdom. They have also contributed to relief operations indirectly by raising funds through concerts.

Bands as Fire Brigades during Operation Fresco: It was the in United Kingdom during the second firemen's strike) in 2002-03 that *Operation Fresco* was initiated. From the UK Military, 150 Band Service ranks were deployed with "Green Goddesses" to various Temporary Service Fire Stations around the UK. The Green Goddess is the colloquial name for the Bedford RLHZ Self Propelled Pump, a fire engine used originally by the Auxiliary Fire Service (AFS), and latterly held in reserve by the Home Office until 2004. This was the second time the military Bands had been used as Fire Service personnel. Earlier in 1977, first major strike of the firemen across the United Kingdom took place. Then too, the military Bands had been deputed to take over the fire services for the duration.

Bands for fundraising during Hurricane Katrina: A pertinent example of Rock Bands performing concert for hurricane relief is provided by NBC Universal Television Group. The purpose of this hour-long, celebrity-driven benefit concert broadcasted live on September 2, 2005, from NBC Studios in New York was to raise money, relief, and awareness in response to the loss of life and human suffering that resulted from Hurricane Katrina in five southeastern States in the United States. Hosted by Matt Lauer, it was simultaneously telecasted on many televisions channels, watched live by approximately 8.5 million viewers who were encouraged to donate to the American Red Cross Disaster Relief Fund. The benefit generated within one hour was $50 million. All thanks to the Bands!

Benefit of Bands at National level

Music is a way to dream together.

—Cecilia Bartoli

The military Bands, being the culture beams, preserve and multiply the glorious traditions of music, dress and drill of every nation throughout history. Military Band is the only living tradition common between the national heritage and military history.

Legatees of Musical Heritage

The Bands have contributed to conservation of music in a number of ways that have made them the legatees of musical heritage of humankind. Military Bands had immense long-term impact on the development of music in the world. Firstly, Military Bands had direct influence in invention and development of most musical instruments for centuries. Secondly, they are largest patrons of musical training. Thirdly, the Military Bands contributed to music by becoming the largest singular employers for the vocation of musicians.

Many of the national anthems, for instance, emanated from the Military Bands repertoire. Accounts on Jefferson's stint at the White House—and his penchant for the Marines Band performance—talk of "exquisite Band of music played at intervals martial, patriotic, and enlivening airs, which reverberated through the spacious dome." One of such enlivening tune was "To Anacreon in Heaven," first sung at the White House on 4 July, 1806, by someone named Mr.

Cutting. Exactly eight years later, this well-known melody was given new words by Francis Scott Key. And yes, this is the same hymn that became very popular as "The Star-Spangled Banner" (Fettig 2016).

The concept of Musical Patriotism is symbolized and personified by Military Bands. Some of the most obvious types of musical propaganda are found in patriotic songs, national anthems, and military music. The social necessity of having a national anthem began with England in the mid-1700s, followed by Spain and France later in the century.

In 1845, the Bolivian president commissioned a composer to create a national anthem, which premiered that year at a state celebration commemorating a battle that led to the first well-defined boundary between Bolivia and Peru. The anthem was proudly performed by a military Band in front of the governmental palace. On that same evening, in order to effectively reach the citizens with this message of musical nationalism, the anthem was performed in the municipal theatre where it was sung by a five-part choral arrangement accompanied by an orchestra. These carefully orchestrated events served the government's purpose by proclaiming the sense of nationalism espoused in the anthem.

Today, there is perhaps no country in the world without a national anthem and there is no military Band in the world that cannot or does not play the national anthem of the country at important State occasions and State mansions. Yet, the military Bands are the custodians of national music in a much broader way. The repertoire of the Swedish Armed Forces Bands, for instance, includes 17 per cent Marches or other military tunes, 25 per cent opera and ballet, 15 per cent local and folk music and 17 per cent dances. It leaves only a quarter of the repertoire for national anthem and patriotic songs.

Legatees of Drill and Dance Heritage

The military dance, i.e. any movement acknowledged as such within a culture, has aesthetic and symbolic value. Dance can be categorized and described by its choreography, by its repertoire of movements, or by its place of origin or historical period. The use of Dance may be social, ceremonial, competitive, erotic, martial or sacred/liturgical. Other forms of human movement are sometimes said to have a dance-like quality, including martial arts, gymnastics, figure skating, synchronized swimming and many other forms of athletics.

The military drills, dances, parades and other movements have preserved the physical and performance history of humankind. Elsewhere in the present work the tribal dances have been talked about that have been preserved by the Armed Forces Bands from Russia to Fiji and from New Zealand to Kenya.

Legatees of Dress Heritage

A military Band plays tunes, dons exotic uniforms and makes marching formations, thus displaying visual, aural and performance art, all in one. Part of the reason Military or Marching Bands highlight and increase aesthetics to any ceremony or function where it performs is that they wear the most beautiful of dresses reflecting centuries of tradition of the country, the society and its military.

As a thumb rule, the uniforms of Band soldiers are as elaborate as the Officers on non-musical duties. Similarly, the uniform of a Band Major can be more elaborate than even officers of the Regiment. When the Bandmaster himself is of the rank of a Commissioned Officer his accruements may make his uniform as elaborate as that of a monarch or a scion of the royal family. Such uniforms of royal guards or royal Bands sometimes irked even the monarchs. King Carl of Sweden was so incensed by the uniform of the Coachman of his royal carriage that he ordered him to be mounted on a horse rather than front of the carriage in royal processions. This way, he thought the royal couple would get more public attention than his elaborately dressed coachman.

The uniforms of the Military Bands are at the same time characterized by the height of their paradoxical uniformity and non-uniformity. At the one extreme, the level of uniformity is to the extent that until recently the Musicians of the Spanish Military were barred from wearing glasses or sporting beards in the interest of visual uniformity on top of their dress uniformity. This was not expected of any military personnel other than the Band members. On the other hand, the Military Bands of different regiments may be starkly different, to represent the regimental colours (i.e. flags) even when the base uniform of those regiments may be nearly identical save for a small regimental logo or insignia on the berets or shoulders.

The Band of the Grenadier Guards of the United Kingdom, the Old Fifes and Drums Band of the United States, the traditional military Bands of Mongolia, South Korea, Kenya, and several other countries sport dresses, that but for these Bands, could have been erased from national memory or consigned to the dustbin of cultural history.

The challenge today is that there are not as many Military Bands as are the number of dresses and costumes to be preserved. The Danish Museum of Arsenal in Copenhagen, for example, showcases around 90 different helmets, hats and headgears that the royalty or military of Denmark had used over its history. Even if each Military Band uses three different uniforms with different headgears, one each for Summer, Winter and ceremonial, it would require 30 military Bands to be uniformed in these 90 headgears to keep them alive in use and in public memory. Thus, it is not only that Bands need historic uniforms to be relevant—rather history and uniforms need Bands to keep them from extinction.

It is also important to note that Military Bands are perhaps the only major and noticeable military formation that reflect national colours. It is not for nothing that the base colour theme of the Royal Uniform donned by the Kings of Sweden, that of the King's Own Life Guard regiment and the Royal Dragoon Mounted Band uniform is the same as the colour of the flag of the Kingdom of Sweden. Denmark's royal family, royal palace guards and even the iconic Tivoli guard boys and girls wear red jackets and white trousers to symbolize the colours of the Danish Flag. Pakistan's Army, Navy and Air Force have distinctive uniforms but whenever a Tri-Services Band, consisting of musicians from all three arms, goes abroad to represent Pakistan in any tattoo or event, it dons the flag-coloured Green-jacket and white trousers.

Conclusion: *Bandonomics* or the Economy of Bands

It was a Russian saying that the, "Military Band is the signature card of the regiment." It was when there used to be hardly any military Bands outside the infantry regiments. Today, the Military and other Marching Bands are the signature cards of the State as a whole. Because, the Bands have led to preservation of tunes, of dances, of traditional marching formations and historical dressings. Thus, they contributed to audial and visual continuum for the humankind of their cultural heritage. They may remain at the centre of art and aesthetics of the humankind.

Bands have a number of benefits at individual, group, community and national level. At personal level, the Bands influence each member in grooming his personality and can be a big stress-reliever. That Music soothes the heart and eases the pain could hardly be epitomized to any greater degree than what the Band did on the sinking *RMS Titanic*. At the group level, the Bands promote camaraderie, team spirit and sense of ownership. At the community level, the Bands have acted as medics, as fire service personnel or as relief workers. Finally, at the national level, they are Custodians of Cultural and Historic traditions.

One under-explored area is the economics of Bands; let's call it Bandonomics. Admittedly, the music is much more than the Bands. If we consider all allied professions and retail sales of everything from music CD's to online streaming, the figures for the music economy are staggering. According to one estimate, the annual revenue of entertainment industry in California State alone has reached US $47 billion, in some counties it is close to 8.4 per cent of the GDP, in late

2012. In addition, every thirtieth person's profession and livelihood is linked directly or indirectly to this industry. It is not easy to separate music revenues from other forms of entertainment and to single out the economics of Band Music from all other types of music. There is hardly any work done on it and reliability of data is another serious issue for want of an accepted definition of what music is and there being no organization representing all type of musicians or music-related professions.

Yet, there is a possibility to segregate some data about maintenance of Bands. Though this does not cater for all Band-related costs to the economy from Band Tourism, or broadly music tourism, the manufacturing and retail of Band instruments, the cost of tickets of all Band concerts and Band tattoos and retail of streaming of Band videos. Leaving all of them aside, there is some data about the operating costs of Military and Marching Bands, at least for the United States.

The 137 or so military Bands in the country cost less than half a billion per annum to the taxpayer, which comes to around US $3 million per Military Band per year. The operational price tag of 30,000 or so institutional marching Bands in the country must be around US $ 3-4 billion because a School Band may cost up to a US $100,000 as running expenditure per year while much larger University and College Marching Bands may cost up to four times that much. The cost of University Bands is higher than Schools as the former are more mobile and may go out of the town to perform. The military Bands cost much more because 90 per cent of this cost is on account of their salaries—the military Band members are regular military personnel, while school, college and university Bands are volunteer-driven. Secondly, the transport costs are higher as the military Bands perform out of the country as well.

NOTES

1 Being a rape victim, the writer decided to remain anonymous and the *Stanford Daily* respected her choice by not publishing the name of the author.

2 Cited from official website of the Defense Ministry of the United Kingdom (Page: Corps of Music), http://www.army.mod.uk/music/33204.aspx, accessed on 7 March 2017

3 Online edition of Daily The Age, (Victoria), 26 June 2017 http://www.theage.com.au/victoria/20170626-gwyryn.html accessed on 1 July 2017.

4 Cited from official website of the United States Air Force Band, http://www.bands.af.mil/, accessed on 7 March 2017

5 Opinion of Advocate General La Pergola (26 October 1999) delivered before the European Court of Justice in case titled Tanja Kreil v Bundesrepublik Deutschland(Case C-285/98) is reproduced in preliminary ruling (2000 Page I-00069As)

CHAPTER XV

Future Role of Bands: Instruments of Creative Diplomacy

Where I cannot go with a F-16 squadron, if I can, I will go with the Band.
—Gen. Frank Gorenc, Commander of U.S. Air Forces in Europe

What is the future of Bands? As their critical role in signalling during wars has ended, is there a chance that their role in Statecraft, State ceremonials and inter-State relations (Diplomacy), may also be dispensed with? If history is any guide, the Military Bands are there to stay. In fact, far from becoming extinct, they may well be at the centre of "War And Peace"—not as a Novel of Tolstoy—but may have a real role in "[avoiding] War And [building] Peace." In both the future roles, they will be at the centre of Creative Diplomacy.

It is high time that a people's movement is launched in support of military Bands. Each dollar spent on a tuba or trombone in the military budget reduces a dollar from bullets and explosives from the Armed Forces arsenal. If for every $10,000 dollars spent on military, only $9 dollars are spent on Bands, it means for every 10,000 persons killed in war, 9 are saved by the Military Bands. In other words, 2.7 million of the 3 billion or so war-related deaths in human history might have been saved by the Bands. By this measure, nearly 200,000 lives might have been saved by the Bands, in the 20th century alone.

There are five major initiatives that the Marching Bands for Peace, formerly the Cosmopolitan Alliance for Drummers and Pipers for Peace, launched since 2001 that merit the consideration of the decision makers.

Proposal for a four-yearly Olympics for Military Bands

Marching Band, the sport for intelligent people.
—Anonymous

It has been argued elsewhere that Music promotes peace. By observing April 6 as the "World Day of Sports for Development of Peace," UNESCO tells us that Sports also promote peace. Besides being musical ensembles, the Military Bands of all kind are in nature of a Sports team. Marching Bands have multiple attributes of being a field sport. Hence, an argument can be made that Military Bands competitions can be helpful in promotion of peace much more than musical contests and sports competitions alone.

The recorded origin of Olympics from 776 BC was also to celebrate peace when the Olive Tree, as a symbol of Peace, was instituted. The victors in games' competitions were donned with wreaths of that Olive tree. Fast forward by 27 centuries to 1896. Baron Coubertin, the founder of modern Olympics, also believed that worldwide games would be a harbinger for world peace. And the Olive wreaths graduated to become medals of Gold, Silver and Bronze. In order to argue our case for a Military Bands Olympics, we need to establish a linkage between the Military and the Olympic Games and between the Games and the objective of Peace. In addition to the Olympics of three kinds (Summer, Winter and Paralympics), International Sports Competitions for military personnel and ones for Police and Fire personnel are also held, all of which can contribute their bit to the proposed Band Olympics. But first let us look at the international Bands tattoos already taking place

Modern Military Bands Tattoos

The modern day concept of Military Bands tattoos is a form of global musical friendship and partnership. The Concept of an international assortment of military Bands is nothing new, though. During the Tang Dynasty rule in China, the imperial palace used to have ten ensembles of musicians and dancers, two from China (one folk and one classical Band troupe) and the remaining eight in attendance for imperial ceremonies were Foreign Bands from the empires and kingdoms known to the Chinese including from India, Central Asia and the defeated Korean Kingdoms of Goguryeo and Baekje. Thus, an international tattoo was in daily attendance at the imperial court.

The modern day military Bands tattoos are musical performances, with or without competitions. The term *tattoo* comes from the early 17th century Dutch phrase *doe den tap toe* ("turn off the tap"), a signal sounded by drummers or trumpeters to instruct inn-keepers near military garrisons to stop serving beer and for soldiers to return to their barracks. The tattoo was originally a form of military music, but the practice has evolved into more elaborate shows involving theatrics and musical performances.

The *Edinburgh Tattoo of Military Bands* started in 1949, is held at the Edinburgh Fort in the capital of Scotland each Summer bringing together Military and Police Bands from around 40 countries. The *Basel Tattoo*, established in 2006 in Switzerland, has emerged to be the second biggest military music tattoo in terms of budget and participation. It attracts only the very best Bands from across the globe and thus covers all music genres, from march to rock, folk to classical music. This shows the diversity of top international Bands, but also produces a great military show. Another prominent tattoo is the *Royal Nova Scotia Bands Tattoo* held annually since 1979, in Halifax, the capital of Nova Scotia province of Canada. It is the largest military Bands tattoo in the world that is *held indoors*.

From 2007 the Russian musical diplomacy touched new heights when the Government founded the Spasskaya Tower International Military Music Festival which has since become a regular annual event with up to a thousand musicians from Military Bands from as many as fifteen countries outside Russia each year.

Not all the Military Bands tattoos have the same frequency. The *Oslo Tattoo of Military Bands* founded in 1996 and the *Virginia Tattoo of Military Bands* beginning from 1997, are held every second year. The latter one, held in port city of Norfolk, is held in cooperation with the NATO. The German Music Tattoo and Festival is held every six years in Germany, and the next one is expected in 2019 at Osnabruck.

Most of the above tattoos are for Concert and Military Bands. The American Championship of Pipe Bands takes place in Fairfax Virginia, before the biennial international military Bands tattoo. However, what was, to all intents and purposes, the first World Pipe Band Championship, was held at Cowal in 1906. It came about following a suggestion from a committee member that such a contest be held. Fittingly, Queen Victoria's daughter, Princess Louise, Duchess of Argyll, was instrumental in the production of what was named the "Argyll Shield" to be presented to the champion Band. This shield is still presented today at Cowal, though the contest there is no longer considered an RSPBA pipe Band championship. The RSPBA, or the Royal Scottish Pipe Bands Association, was established in 1930. It tried to clear the mess that was there in the formation, composition and repertory of the Pipe Bands in the world at that time. It also laid the foundation of the World Pipe Bands Championship.

The only major World Pipe Bands Competition today is the one held by RSPBA at Glasgow Greens in Scotland biennially. The first Championships were held at Murrayfield, Edinburgh, in 1947. The event was first held in Glasgow in 1948 but was discontinued time and again. Finally, it has been staged in the city of Glasgow uninterruptedly since 1986.

At the 2017 World Pipe Band Championships, 219 Pipe Bands brought around 8000 pipers and drummers to Glasgow Green to compete at the Show. Approximately 35,000 people attended the event over the two days. Bands from 15 nations including USA, Canada, Northern Ireland, France, England, Australia, New Zealand, Belgium, Austria, Netherlands, Republic of Ireland, Switzerland, Denmark, Argentina and Scotland took part. The RSPBA Website claims this annual championship to be the flagship event of, what it calls, the Twenty-First Century Pipe Band movement

Paradoxically, all the major military Band tattoos of the present time have started, with some degree of regularity, after the World War II; many being instituted after the end of the Cold War. Anywhere between 10 to 300 Bands attend each event Bandsfrom up to 40 countries and involve as many as 3000 Band members (up to 8000 musicians for the Pipe Band competition). These militaries facing each other in healthy musical competitions indicate towards the peace that the world is enjoying compared to the times of the two world wars. This friendly foray by Military Bands, which are after all part and parcel of the Military Forces symbolizes peace. So, greater the peace, the more the number of military Bands tattoos worldwide. It follows that reverse flow of peace may not only be possible but also desirable. If we try to have more Military Bands competitions, we are more likely to move closer to World peace. Thus, there is a dire need to have a world Olympics of Military Bands comprising all the nations of the world, rather than between 10 to 40 per show.

The Military Origins of International Sports Competitions and all kinds of Olympics

The close relation between war and sports is manifest by the marathon race, covering 26 miles 385 yards. This race honours the ancient Greek soldier–messenger, Pheidippides (or Philippides, i.e. modern-day Philip, according to some historians), who ran from Marathon to Athens to announce the Greek victory against the Persians in the Battle of Marathon in September 490 BC. Having fought in the battle himself, when Philippides reached Athens, he was so exhausted that immediately after announcing the victory, he collapsed, and died. Needless to say, the distance between Marathon to Athens is exactly 26.219 miles or 42.195 kilometres.

Marathon is a road race and today more than 500 Marathon races are held every year across the world. Marathon race was also the main sports event when modern Olympic games were revived in 1896. Men's Marathon is usually the last Athletic event of the Olympics, usually held on the last day of the Summer games.

Since the Los Angeles Olympics (1984), Women Marathon race has also been included.

In fact, the earliest games were all war-like games including firstly, the combative games such as wrestling, boxing and fencing; Secondly, the equestrian games such as horse racing and finally, the Pentathlon. This last game was based upon five military skills—fencing, riding, running, shooting, and swimming—in one go. Although Pentathlon was discontinued after 1928 Olympics, it was revived in 1948 London Olympics as the modern pentathlon, which is less dangerous and more audience-friendly than the ancient Pentathlon.

For centuries, when City States, i.e. *Polis*, were formed in what is modern-day Greece, they often found themselves at war with each other. The Greeks believed that a healthy body was essential for healthy life. Sport was viewed as good preparation for war. After all, the Greek armies had to be fit enough to march long distances, carrying all their heavy equipment, and then begin the fight with the enemy. It was not coincidental, therefore, that most Athletes used to be soldiers and vice versa.

It is instructive to note that all three types of existing Olympics as well as disjointed Military Bands tattoos held worldwide have military origins but paradoxically they were all aimed at strengthening Peace. And we find traces of primitive Bands playing at the earliest of Olympic games as early as 8th century BC.

Origins of Olympics, its relation to Peace and to Marching Bands

Although the first recorded Olympic games are dated to 776 BC but some scholars speculate that games might have been held from as early as in the 14th century BC. What happened in 776 BC was the peace agreement between the city-states of Elis and Pisa after a long period of warfare. As a result of that, it became possible to hold games every four years. The Eleans traced the founding of the Olympic games to their King Iphitos, who was told by the Delphi Oracle to plant the olive tree, symbolizing Peace. Since then it was from this Olive tree that the wreaths for winners of various competitions were made.

These wreaths from sacred Olive Tree were, as noted above, the precursors of modern-day gold, silver and bronze medals. The winners of the matches marched around the grove to the accompaniment of a flutes played by Pipers, while the fans sang songs written by prominent poets. Again this march of Bands and singing of songs has now been replaced with playing for formal national anthems of the winners' countries.

Over the centuries, the Greeks established a truce for each Olympics. No matter how long, bloody or fierce the war had been, the soldiers were permitted to leave the military to participate in the Games and were guaranteed safe passage through enemy territory. For seven days before and seven days after the Olympic Games and during the period of games, fighting was outlawed. No attack on fans and players going to and from the Olympiad was permissible. Attack on the sacred venue was prohibited with the belief that any such sacrilege could bring the wrath of gods. Olympic festivals were a peaceful influence on the warlike city-states and brought about first-ever recognized ceasefire periods, sanctioned by law, in human history.

The French Historian and Educationist, Baron Pierre de Coubertin (1863–1937) is widely recognized as the founder of founder modern Olympics Games revived since 1896. It is revealing that Coubertin had firm belief that worldwide Games would become the impetus for peace. Although his assertions were questioned for decades by scholars, but today Olympics Games of all three kinds testify to the truth in his belief.

Military Origins of Winter Olympics

Coming to the Winter Olympics, that too have military origins. Roots of the Winter Olympics are traced to the Swedish Central Association for the Promotion of Sports [SCFIF], which was founded by high ranking military officers of Sweden in 1897. Games like Military Patrol, consisting of four-member military units (as teams), including an officer, a non-commissioned officer and two soldiers, combined military skills of cross country skiing, snow mountaineering and rifle shooting, used to be the highlight of the sporting event of the Winter Olympics. Today, it has been replaced by *Biathlon* which is a developed form of military patrol. Another event is the *Patrouille des Glaciers* that has similar competitions and rankings but for civilian competitors.

Military Origins of Paralympics

Paralympics— Olympics for the physically challenged—also have military origins. Right after the Second World War, sixteen British War veterans, disabled due to war injuries, took part in the 1948 London Olympics. Since the Seoul Olympics 1988, the Paralympics are held after every regular Olympic games.

Outside the Olympics, there are international non-Band Sports events restricted to Military and Police/Fire forces.

Military Sports Competitions by Conseil International du Sport Militaire

Few people know that CISM, established 1948, is the second largest multi-sport discipline organization after the IOC. It holds over 20 competitions annually, including the Military World Games and World Military Cup for the Armed Forces of 134 member countries.

The declared mission of CISM is to promote sports activity between Armed Forces The CISM motto of "Friendship through Sport" brings together soldiers in friendly sports competitions, who may have previously met on the battlefield in not-too-friendly an encounter. The CISM, may in coordination with International Olympics Committee, or on its own, consider merging all existing world military Bands tattoos into a world Olympics of Military Bands to further its aims of promoting peace through healthy activities between Armed Forces.

World Police and Fire Games

The World Police and Fire Games (WPFG) is a biennial athletic event, open to active and retired law enforcement and fire service personnel throughout the world. The Games are held under the auspices of World Police & Fire Games Federation—a non-profit organization, run by the Californian Police Athletics Federation.

California Police Olympics were first held in 1967. The concept evolved over the years and led to the creation of the Federation in 1983. Two years later, in 1985, the first World Police & Fire Games were held in San Jose, California. Since then, the Games have been held every second year at a different venue. With anywhere between 5,000 and 10,000 competitors, it is the largest sports event in the world after the Summer Olympics, relegating the Commonwealth Games to the third place. In 2012, the Summer Olympics were held in London, followed by World Faire and Police Games in 2013 in Belfast, Northern Ireland and then Commonwealth Games in Glasgow, Scotland in 2014. That was the only time in human history that the three biggest sports events of the world were held in the same country consecutively.

Otherwise, United States has remained host to the Games almost half the times since 1985. The 2011 Games were held in New York, the 2015 ones in Fairfax Virginia and 2017 Games in Los Angeles. However, the next three World Police and Fire Games are scheduled for China (2019), Netherlands (2021) and Canada (2023). The Games have the potential to become forerunner of Word Police and Fire Bands Tattoos and competitions. The Bands have to be more visible than just at the opening and closing ceremonies of the Games.

Case for four-yearly Band Olympics

It is high time now to institute an International Band Olympics for which an International Bands Olympics Committee (IBOC) can be constituted as a subcommittee of the existing IOC. The proposed IBOC will not only organise a world Military Bands competition but will try to foster peace between Armed Forces Bands of warring nations to face each other in peaceful matches.

At present, there are three type of Olympic Games: the Summer Olympics, the Winter Olympics and the Paralympics. The Summer Olympics are held every four years since their revival in 1896. The Winter Olympics that started in 1924, are also held in four yearly cycles but since 1994; they are held every even year between the two Summer Games. Thus, they follow their own four-year cycle two years after each Summer Olympics. At present, the Paralympics follow the main Olympic Games (both summer and winter) at the same venues.

The idea to amalgamate all Tattoos into a World Military Bands Olympics would mean that we may end up having four types of Olympics in four-year cycles but in four separate years. So each year, we may have one type of Olympics, the Summer Olympics in Year 1 (Even/Leap Year), Paralympics in Year 2 (Odd year/instead of being held along with main Olympics), Winter Olympics in Year 3 (Non-leap Even Year) and the proposed Military Bands Olympics in Year 4 (Odd year preceding the year of Summer Olympics). If the Military Bands Olympics are instituted, they may eclipse the pageantry of the remaining three types of Olympics Games.

If IOC does not agree to institute an Olympics of Bands , the mission may be owned and adopted to the International Military Sports Council, known by its French acronym, CISM, to merge all Military Bands tattoos into a global military (and police) Bands competition where all nations of the world are represented. They may also coordinate with World Police and Fire Games organizers (CPAF) to also merge the police and fire Bands competitions into the proposed World Olympics of Bands for all kinds of uniformed forces internationally.

Proposal for a Geneva Convention on protection of Bandsmen

Music is the moral law,

—Plato

The present day International Humanitarian Law is largely based on the four Geneva Conventions of 1949, which in turn, were built upon the customary law as well as certain codified instruments including the international treaties that held the field at that time. The four Geneva conventions, respectively, relate to the war on land; the war on sea; sick, wounded and POWs during the war; and the protection of the civilian population. There are at least two branches of the military, the medics and the chaplains of the fighting units, to whom the protections are specifically extended. Then, there is the International Hague convention of 1954 which declares any destruction of cultural heritage a war crime and so does the Statute of the International Criminal Court (2002).

At present, none of the laws specifically gives protection to the Bandsmen. However, the same is not only available in the customary law but a close reading of all the documents also hints at implied protection to the Bands by virtue of their incidental duties and non-combatant role. This does not dispense with the need for a clear unequivocal instrument extending protection to the military Bands personnel in time of war. Let's start with a look at the customary law and then we shall deal with implied protections in existing humanitarian framework.

Protection of Bands under Customary Law

However, the protection of military musicians *per se* has been observed as a customary law in fiercest of wars such as the American Civil War. The military Bands are unarmed part of the army, just like the medical and religious services, and are innocuous for both sides. Hence, not shooting at them always made logical sense. A fortiori, even at the height of hostilities, Union and Confederate forces did not target each other's Bandsmen. In fact, Brent Becker, a renowned Stanbury Band Uniform Designer, argues that the origin of bright colours for uniforms of military Bands owes to the need for them to be distantly recognizable so the enemy does not and would not shoot them.

Implied Protection from Harm due to duties incidental to Band duties

As of now, there is no separate protection for members of Armed Forces Bands during war and peace. However, a careful reading of all the instruments makes it clear that protection of Bandsmen and women stands covered protection under multiple clauses. The protection accorded does not necessarily owe to their non-lethal musical duties, but under the general principle that non-combatants cannot ordinarily be targeted in a war, except when they pose a direct threat. In addition, their protection comes because of other tasks entrusted to the Bands such as paramedical duties, causing "spiritual peace" and protection of Prisoners of War. During these three types of duties, the protection given respectively to the medical personnel, to the clergy and to the POWs, whom they are protecting gets impliedly extended to the Band Members.

Protection to Band Members on Medical duties

It may also be highlighted that Bands Companies were basically stretcher-bearers of Infantry Units. And protection of medical personnel and facilities, stretcher bearers included, has always been at the core of international humanitarian law. State practices had already established this rule as a norm of customary international law applicable in both international and non-international armed conflicts.

Since its inception in 1864 Geneva Convention, it has been repeated, expanded and reinforced in the subsequent Conventions such as *Geneva Convention for the Amelioration of the Condition of Wounded, Sick and Shipwrecked Members of Armed Forces at Sea* (1906) and the Convention relative to the Treatment of Prisoners of War (1929). This protection to medics finally got enshrined in the First, Second and Fourth Geneva Conventions of 1949 as well that have replaced and updated the earlier conventions.

Article 27 of the 1899 Hague Regulations states that:

> *In sieges and bombardments, all necessary steps should be taken to spare as far as possible ... hospitals, and places where the sick and wounded are collected, provided they are not used at the same time for military purposes. The besieged should indicate these buildings or places by some particular and visible signs, which should previously be notified to the assailants.*

Art 27 of Hague Regulations (1907) is a verbatim reproduction of the above clause for the land forces while Article 5 of Hague Convention (IX) of 1907 says the same thing with respect to Naval forces. Finally, Art 19 of the 1949 Geneva Convention I provides:

> *Fixed establishments and mobile medical units of the Medical Service may in no circumstances be attacked, but shall at all times be respected and protected by the Parties to the conflict. Should they fall into the hands of the adverse Party, their personnel shall be free to pursue their duties.*

Art 18 of Geneva Convention IV extended "respect and protection" to civilian hospital. The scope of this immunity was further extended by the Two Additional Protocols of 1977. Art. 15 of the Protocol-I covered civilian medical personnel into the protection while Art 11 of Protocol II covered the civilian medical transport (i.e. Ambulances, etc.).

Under the Statute of the International Criminal Court, "Intentionally directing attacks against ... hospitals and places where the sick and the wounded are collected, provided they are not military objectives" constitutes a "war crime in both international and non-international armed conflicts."

Other Instruments that give protection to medical units include Article 17 of the Brussels International Declaration concerning the Laws and Customs of War (1874), the Oxford Manual on Land Warfare (1880), Rule 25 of Hague Rules of Air Warfare (1923), Paragraph 2.2 of the Agreement on the Application of International Humanitarian Law between the Parties to the Conflict in Bosnia and Herzegovina (1992), and the UN Secretary-General's Bulletin on Observance of IHL by UN Forces (1999), not to mention Military Manuals of all civilized nations of the world.

The protection of medical services in war zones is also part of International Humanitarian Customary Rules and is reflected in the domestic law and military manuals and codes of all countries around the world, without exception. This extension was also supported in State practice, which generally refers to medical personnel without distinguishing between military or civilian medical units, or between stationary and mobile ones, even by those States that were not, at the time, party to either Protocol.

Protection to Band Members for Spiritual duties

Another customary protection available through most of the international conventions and legal instruments is that to the military and civilian "religious personnel" exclusively assigned to religious duties. As they bring "spiritual comfort" to the troops, hence their entitlement to, what Geneva convention refers to, as "respect in all circumstances". It may be argued that the Military Bands perform roles that may not necessarily be spiritual in the religious sense but their duties have a soothing effect on the troops both friends and foes. And they deserve not only the protection but also the respect that the Law demands for the clerical establishment.

Protection to Band Members being Cultural Heritage of Nations

Finally, the *protection of cultural property* is granted by both The Hague Convention on Protection of Cultural Heritage during Armed Conflict (1954) and the ICC Statute. It is based on the principle that damage to the cultural property of any people means, in the words of the 1954 Convention, "Damage to the cultural heritage of all mankind." It covers "immovable and movable cultural heritage ... [in order] to ensure the cultural legacy and, by extension, the cultural property of nations, groups and distinct members of a society worldwide facing armed conflict" remains safe. The emblem of Blue Shield has been granted to cultural properties by this Convention which, one would argue, must be worn by Military Bands in war zones, as well as their establishments and mobile vans must carry this emblem.

Protection to Band Members due to distinctive emblem

Another provision of the ICC Statute extends the definition of war crimes to intentional targeting of "personnel using the distinctive emblems... in conformity with international law" An expansive interpretation of this very clause would seem to extend the protection available with medical personnel to the cultural units of the Armed Forces like their Military Band companies and the Band Centers as well. Both, after all, are entitled to use the distinctive emblems under international law. It is well known that Red Cross, Red Crescent [and lately] Red Crystal are authorized for the medical personnel and establishments, while it is little known that the Blue Shield has been recognized as an Emblem for Cultural Property. It is another matter that hardly any Military Bands ever uses Blue Shield emblem on their uniforms or on their transport vehicles or fixed establishments.

Exceptions to the Protection

The only situation in which this protection will not be available would be if the medical, religious or cultural property is used for military purposes or for any act harmful to the enemy. Even then a warning to desist from using the property as such has to be given. An attack would only be justified if such a warning remains unheeded for a reasonable time. The Geneva Conventions clearly spell out that possessing small arms by the medics for self-defence or having pickets or sentries outside medical establishment, does not constitute acts "harmful to the enemy." By analogy, Band members cannot be targeted only if their placement is in guarded parameter or they carry some weapons for self-defence.

Case for Additional Protocol-III to Geneva Convention 1949 for Protection of Military Bands during armed conflicts

It has been argued in this work that the non-musical duties of Bandsmen were primarily medical. Before battles, Bandsmen gathered wood for splints and helped set up field hospitals. During and after the fighting, they carried the wounded to hospitals, helped surgeons perform amputations, and discarded limbs. Hence, Bandsmen are entitled to above mentioned protection.

In other countries Military Bandsmen are used for protecting POWs or preparing food when playing becomes impractical due to intensity of conflict. Again, any attack on establishment where Prisoners of War are kept is illegal since it may endanger the lives of the POWs. Here again, by default Band Members are protected.

Hence, there is strong case that an effort is made to draft and agree on a third

Additional Protocol to the four Geneva Conventions to consolidate and codify all protections available to Bandsmen into a legally binding separate instrument.

Proposal for UNESCO declaring Military Bands as a common and endangered heritage of Humankind

Music is the universal language of mankind.

—Henry Longfellow

In the early periods of the modern Turkish Kemalist Republic, the Ankara Government sent its Mehter Band to give various concerts in Europe as part of its charm offensive. The impact the Turkish Bands had on European streets, especially the craze in the people to rush to watch the display was summarized by some newspapers with headlines commenting that, "Ottomans conquered Europe again." Military Bands symbolize the identity of the nation much more than the national flag or national anthem or the national dress would do individually. All we need today is to formally declare this to be the case. If the United Nations Educational, Scientific and Cultural Organization (UNESCO) can list world's cultural heritage sites, it can also make listings of world's traditional Military Bands and try to ensure that none of them gets in danger of extinction.

Need for a UNESCO Declaration on Military Bands

The Ottoman example is enough to show that a Military Band is that part of a national heritage that has the greatest capacity to connect with other cultures. Hence, expectation on the UNESCO to play its role for the preservation of military Bands is not misplaced.

After all, UNESCO website declares its conviction that, "no development can be sustainable without a strong culture component. Indeed, only a human-centered approach to development based on mutual respect and open dialogue among cultures can lead to lasting, inclusive and equitable results. Yet until recently, culture has been missing from the development equation."[1] There is a strong case for the UNESCO to declare Military Bands heritage as common international heritage of humankind. The UNESCO may also like to take the Military Bands as endangered intangible cultural heritage.

Doing so may well be within the UNESCO mandate. The UNESCO website proclaims that:

> *"in today's interconnected world, culture's power to transform societies is clear. Its diverse manifestations ... [like] traditional practices and contemporary art*

> *forms enrich our everyday lives in countless ways. Heritage constitutes a source of identity and cohesion for communities disrupted by bewildering change and ... instability.... Both heritage and creativity lay the foundations for vibrant, innovative and prosperous knowledge societies".*[2]

The time is running out fast and with the global offensive to do away with military Bands continues with the present momentum, our posterity may never forgive us for sitting aside when Military Bands were being wiped away from the society. On 27 September 2016, Trial Chamber VIII of the International Criminal Court (ICC) delivered its landmark judgment in the famous Al Mehdi Case. In the case titled *The Prosecutor vs Ahmed Al Faqi al Mehdi,* the Chamber unanimously found Mr Al-Mahdi guilty beyond reasonable doubt as a co-perpetrator of the war crime consisting in intentionally directing attacks against religious and historic buildings in Timbuktu, Mali, in June and July 2012 during the civil war. The Chamber sentenced Mr Al Mahdi to nine years' imprisonment and substantial fine. Can the likes of Congresswoman Martha McSally be the next in line to be tried for attempted destruction of cultural heritage by defunding the historic military Bands of the United States? But a timely action by the UNESCO may make it difficult for politicians to play around with any form of cultural heritage related to military music.

Case for declaring September 21 as World Day of Military Bands for strengthening Peace

Can Music promote peace? For many, the answer is a strong affirmative. There are many initiatives in the world today that believe in the power of Music to bring about world peace such as the World Peace Song Award, *Musique Sur La Mer* (MSLM) and the Euro Mediterranean Musical Academy (EMMA-for-Peace). There are other global drives that believe in the power or music for the promotion of peace and harmony that are acknowledged elsewhere in the present work.

There are many stories from the United States Civil war about Bands representing the softer face of enemy forces. During the American civil war, from behind earthworks, Bands often played concerts, including the other side's favourite songs. On occasions, Confederate and Union Bands would join in concerts when camped close together. A Union Band gave a concert for their own troops stationed at Fredericksburg, Virginia. After all, the sound of music was being heard on the opposite side of the trenches. Once a few favourite selections of the Union troops had been played, a voice called from the Confederate positions across the river, "Now give us some of ours." The Band played "Dixie," a favourite of both sides, My Maryland" and "Bonnie Blue Flag." (Maddock 2015)

The idea of the World Music Day started from France as *Fête de la Musique*. It was the brainchild of the then French Minister of Culture, Jack Lang. It was first celebrated on the 21st of June, the midsummer solstice, in 1982. Since then, it has spread to over 120 countries where free public events are held in 700 cities around the world on this day, not including France, where there were too many events to count!

There are two pillars of this celebration. One, that all amateur musicians should come out and sing and play music on the streets, not indoors. Two, concerts are arranged for the pubic by the professionals but neither a fee can be charged to the public nor a remuneration on this day is paid to the musicians. All genres of music must be accessible to public, for free, on this day.

A day has come where we may argue for a World Day for Military Bands where all Military Bands will come out and play out on the streets, for the general public, and for free. And UNESCO is the best forum to declare a particular day as the World Day of Military Bands.

Today, there are 134 days celebrated by the United Nations and its Agencies, out of which 51 days have been declared by the UNESCO alone. Although the World Music Day is a people's initiative and has nothing to do with the United Nations or any of its bodies but some of UNESCO's World Days do have something to do with music, with literature or with peace. For example, April 30 is the day of Jazz Music, March 21, is the World Poetry Day, and finally, Sept 21 is the World Day of Peace, Ceasefire and Non-violence. It is this latter Day, which can be linked to the Military Bands as well, as a celebration, as a recognition and as an appreciation of their role in peace-building.

September 21, is the world day of Peace since 1981. It was the effort of one man, singer Jeremy Gilley, who started to make the Peace One Day documentary in 1998, eventually deciding to aim for a UN resolution formalizing the idea. This goal was achieved in 2001 when the UN General Assembly adopted the resolution to observe September 21 as the World Day of Non-Violence and Ceasefire. One man can achieve so much!

So this work aims at influencing UNESCO to declare September 21, the World Day of Peace, as World Day of Military Bands for Promotion of Peace, as well. Why UNESCO? Because the Organization provides, as proclaimed by its own website, a "global platform for international cooperation and cultural governance system based on human rights and shared values, ...for the emergence of dynamic cultural sectors".[3] To ensure that "culture takes it rightful place...[UNESCO] support[s] governments and local stakeholders to safeguard heritage, ...and encourage cultural pluralism."

The idea is that on the World Day of ceasefire, military Bands will visit and play in their own and in enemy territory without fear of attack. The Military Bands will carry the message of peace and solidarity.

All Military Bands that day will also play, for free, out on the streets, in all major cities of the world. People may get to know all genres and styles of military music. The public may get an understanding of the role Military Bands play for world peace.

Recommendation for the United Nations Secretary General's Own Military Band

The United Nations has started tacitly accepting the linkage between International Day and the Military Bands. The UN Day of Peacekeepers observed on May 29 each year, is now accompanied by glorious tunes played by a military Band. When the ceremony takes place at Vienna, Military Band of the Austrian Armed Forces plays the musical notes. How about the United Nations having its own Concert Band to play at UN-related events and to celebrate peace and peacekeeping?

The trend is already set by the initiative called World Orchestra for Peace having musical fusion from 40 different nations. [See the next Section] This Orchestra, as the name indicates, aims at promoting peace through Music.

The United Nation's Secretary General's Own Band needs to be created to play once in a year to celebrate peace wherever the UN efforts result in peace. This may be a 1,000 to 1,500-member ensemble with representation from all 193 UN Member States. This may involve a fusion of uniforms, a collection of instruments and a new repertory of global tunes. Going by the Russian saying of a Band being *Signature Card of Nation,* this Band may become the *Signature Card* of the United Nations.

Proposal for Battle of Bands to be a UN-recognized dispute resolution mechanism

> *The true beauty of music is that it connects the people, it carries the message and musicians are the messengers.*
>
> —Roy Ayers

Military Bands can be used as an instrument and as a method for peace building. Along with negotiation, good officers, medication, conciliation, arbitration and

ICJ litigation, there can be a battle of Bands as a recognized available method of pacific resolution of disputes.

Pacific Dispute Settlement Mechanisms available with the United Nations

Chapter VI of the Charter of the United Nations deals with the pacific settlement of disputes. Its opening Article 33 reads:

1. The parties to any dispute, the continuance of which is likely to endanger the maintenance of international peace and security, shall, first of all, seek a solution by negotiation, enquiry, mediation, conciliation, arbitration, judicial settlement, resort to regional agencies or arrangements, or other peaceful means of their own choice.
2. The Security Council shall, when it deems necessary, call upon the parties to settle their dispute by such means.

Although the Charter does not refer to music as a means of settlement of disputes but today there are voices emerging who believe that this is possible. Most creative use of military Bands can be in future Dispute Resolution. The concept of peace through music was unheard of till, say, a decade ago but now it is resonating almost everywhere. Before making our case to introduce Military Bands Displays or Battle of Bands to be used for peace-building it is instructive to have a look at a number of global initiatives, one founded by no less than the living Nobel Peace Laureates, that believe in the Music's power for world peace.

Existing Musical Initiatives for World Peace

One recent example is *Euro Mediterranean Music Academy (EMMA) for Peace* which was launched at the 13th World Summit of Nobel Peace Laureates in October 2013. The objective of EMMA for Peace, according to its founder, a young Italian called Paolo Petrocelli, is to have a "positive impact" on young people throughout the religiously and politically diverse Middle East and Mediterranean regions through, according to its website, "a network of music institutions... brought together in the shared interest of *music and the promotion of peace.*"[4] [Emphasis added]

EMMA for Peace joins several other individuals and institutions who, over the years, have harnessed music for the fostering of peace. For example, the World Orchestra for Peace, set up in 1995 by conductor Sir Georg Solti to commemorate the 50th anniversary of the United Nations, brings together more than 90 of the finest players from the world's top orchestras. Its aim is to show that, through music, people of different beliefs, cultures and backgrounds can unite as a global family. "If we poor musicians from 35 different countries can get together on a stage and talk the same language," said Charles Kaye, the World Orchestra for Peace's general manager and Solti's right-hand man for over 20 years, "why can't the politicians?" In 2009, the Orchestra, under its conductor Valery Gergiev, performed Mahler's Symphony No. 5 in Krakow to mark 70 years since the start of World War II.[5]

Another similar initiative is the World Peace Orchestra (not to be confused with the World Orchestra for Peace) set up in 2013.[6] Its mission is "to promote peace and understanding through the unifying power of music. We strive to cultivate a new, compassionate generation of leaders who understand that borders, oceans, languages, and cultures cannot break the fundamental bonds of humanity." The youth orchestra combines players of Western and folk instruments, and held its inaugural concert in New York's Avery Fisher Hall back in September 2013, under the baton of Lithuanian conductor Gintaras Rinkevièius.

Project Peace On Earth (PPOE) organizes international peace initiatives that consist of developing and producing inspirationally transformational music concerts and workshops, medical missions, aerial art and fine art events/exhibits, and engagement activities towards the end goals of empowering inner peace through sacred music, fostering the process of forgiveness and compassion; inspiring the recognition of shared interests, commonalities of goodness and the message of love and producing worldwide events that humanitarian, political and spiritual realization that, "All Are One and Lovingly Connected."[7] Peace Song Awards website proclaims that it serves as a search for our world's most enlightened "musicians and songs that can guide the way to peace on earth."[8]

The purpose of above-mentioned famous initiatives is to underscore that the proposal in this book is not something new, unique or unheard of. There are persons (no less than most living Nobel Peace laureates), groups and initiatives already in this world that believe in the power of music to bring peace. There is a need to channelize these initiatives under the United Nations umbrella to bring in the nation-states as end-users of this mechanism for peace.

Introducing Battle Of Bands as a means to end violent conflicts

The *Battle of Bands* can be a solution where other peaceful means such as negotiation, mediation, conciliation, arbitration or litigation, etc., fail and military forces of the two sides are still facing each other. There can be a situation where neither side has a further appetite for bloodshed. Subject to concurrence by both sides, the United Nations or any regional agency may arrange a Battle of the Military Bands to decide the outcome.

Imagine Syrian troops and Free Syrian Army fighters locked in fight for Aleppo city causing bloodshed but military scene remains a stalemate. Imagine the UN convinces both sides to withdraw all forces from the conflict zone except their Corps of Music. The Bands of two sides compete by playing patriotic tunes and the UN Moderators [Band Majors from some neutral Scandinavian States, agreed to by both sides] declare one side to be winner in the battle and allows their troops to retain the area.

This may not need an amendment to the UN Charter. The Article 38 of Chapter VI of the UN Charter gives wide latitude to the UN Security Council to suggest any recommendation to the parties for settlement of disputes if they so request. Any innovative idea today or in future may catch the eyes of the Council.

A recent example of a military standoff between two Military Giants, India and China, over the Doklam Plateau, West of Bhutan at the tri-junction between the three nations, provides an interesting example. This was in July 2017. Neither of the two nuclear armed powers wanted to escalate the conflict by firing at each other. While the Indian troops were ordered to stop the Chinese from building a road which India thinks threatens its slim land corridor to its seven Eastern States, they were not allowed to open fire. Fortunately, the orders to Chinese forces appear also to have been to keep the conflict level low. In the initial days of the standoff, soldiers of the two sides exchanged harsh words. Then they tried to physically push each other away from the disputed area. The most serious incident involved a slapping of Indian solider by a Chinese. Days later even stone pelting started but not a shot was fired in seven weeks.

States, thus, are seeing the futility of using weaponry against each other. This conflict cannot go on like this indefinitely. Either a road will be built as the Chinese want or the project may be aBandoned as the Indians want. If the conflict is allowed to simmer like this, it may flare up someday with dangerous consequences for the two sides. In such a conflict, the State Parties can be convinced to use other non-lethal means such as a Battle of Military Bands between the Border Security Force of India and the Armed Border Police of China.

This may seem bizarre or outlandish at first. But many ideas appeared so in the beginning, including one to revive Olympic games in 1896 for world peace after a gap of twenty-seven centuries or the one to work for global conventions to regulate use of force in warfare that led to the four Geneva Conventions of 1949. Many of the innovative ideas that challenge the inertia are initially ignored, then ridiculed, then vehemently opposed and ultimately adopted as that were the most logical positions. This idea of *Battle of Bands* may well pass through all the phases in order to become a recognized international practice within the coming decades.

Proposal for a Nobel Prize for Peace for all Marching Bands

Where Words Fail, Music Speaks.

—Hans Christian Anderson

"I see us as another branch of the service – a peace keeping and peace enabling force." So believes Marcy Sudock, who is the musical director and conductor of Musique Sur La Mer [tr. Music on the Sea] Chamber Orchestra, a California-based Orchestra of youth and professional musicians with the slogan "Peace through the international language of music."[9] As a Peacekeeping and Peace-enabling arm of the Military Forces, the Military Bands may well be the next candidate for Nobel Prize for Peace. The United Nations own Peacekeeping Forces have already got the Nobel Peace Prize in 1988.

The First-ever Nobel Peace Prize in 1901

Henry Dunant (1828–1910) was the brain behind the 1864 Geneva Convention and was acknowledged for this as first recipient of the Nobel Peace Prize in 1901 (jointly with compatriot social activist Frédéric Passy).

Dunant was a Swiss businessman and social activist. During a business trip in 1859, he was witness to the aftermath of the Battle of Solferino in modern-day Italy. The Battle of Solferino on 24 June 1859 that resulted in the victory of the allied French Army under Napoleon III and Sardinian Army under Victor Emmanuel II (together known as the Franco-Sardinian Alliance) against the Austrian Army under Emperor Franz Joseph I, was the last major battle in world history where all the armies were under the personal command of their monarchs. Perhaps 300,000 soldiers fought in the important battle, the largest since the Battle of Leipzig in 1813. Dunant arrived in Solferino on the evening of the battle where 23,000 wounded, dying and dead remained on the battlefield, and there appeared to be little attempt to provide care. Shocked, Dunant himself took the initiative to organize the civilian population, especially the women and girls, to provide assistance to the injured and sick soldiers.

After returning to Geneva early in July, Dunant decided to write a book recording his memories and experiences which he titled *Un Souvenir de Solferino* (A Memory of Solferino). It was printed in 1862 at Dunant's own expense in an edition of 1,600 copies that he distributed to many leading political and military figures in Europe. Within the book, he described the battle, its costs, and the chaotic circumstances afterwards. He also developed the idea that in the future a neutral organization should exist to provide care to wounded soldiers that inspired the creation of the International Committee of the Red Cross (ICRC) in 1863. Many of his ideas contributed to the signing of the Geneva Convention in 1864. His contribution to the ideas of peace not only made him the first Nobel Laureate but also saved countless lives in human history and reduced miseries for war victims.

The present work has been inspired by Henry Dunant and the successful realization of his ideas. It is a humble attempt not only to propound innovative ideas for world peace but also to develop a framework which may one day help the Military Bands of the World win a Nobel Prize for Peace.

Criterion for Nobel Peace Prize and its Award to Ideas and Institutions

Since December 1901 the Nobel Prize has been awarded (with some exceptions) annually, to those who have "done the most or the best work for fraternity between nations, for the abolition or reduction of standing armies and for the holding and promotion of peace congresses." The recipients have been persons, organizations and even ideas embodied by a person or an organization.

Between 1901 and 2016, the Nobel Peace Prize has been awarded 26 times to organizations, instead of individuals. The Office of the United Nations High Commissioner for Refugees (UNHCR) has received the Nobel Peace Prize twice, in 1954 and 1981, and the work of International Committee of the Red Cross (ICRC) has been honoured three times, in 1917, 1944 and 1963. The other 21 organizations and institutions that have won the Nobel Prize include the European Union, the Organization for Prevention of Chemical Weapons (OPCW), the Doctors Without Borders (*Medicin Sans Frontiers)*, the Amnesty International, the United Nations itself, as well as some of its agencies (UNICEF, ILO, and IAEA), among others.

Military Band as an Institution as Candidate for Nobel Peace Prize

This monograph has made a point that Military Bands have done a lot in all three criteria set by the Nobel Committee. One, the Military Bands have contributed to fraternity between nations. Two, they have contributed to reduction in offensive wings of the Armed Forces. Every soldier, sailor or airman who has been given a Tuba, this is at the cost of replacement of the gun that has been taken away from him. And finally, the Military Bands have performed their role in world's peace congresses since 1699. Hence, they fulfil all three criteria that the Nobel Foundation has set for the Peace Prize.

In recent years, the Nobel Committee has been awarding Peace Prizes for works ranging from protection of forests, ending child labor, promoting female education, working for democracy and attempting to eradicate poverty through micro-finance loans, for instance. There is no gainsaying that these initiatives do contribute to peace. However, not so as envisaged by Alfred Nobel himself! The proposed Nobel Peace Prize to military Bands would neither require an expansive definition of "peace", nor need the stretching of criteria that Nobel had envisaged.

Even when the Military forces are waging war, their Bands are busy waging Peace. For instance, the Military Bands are the only institution that brought Unionist and Confederate Forces closer in peaceful encounters during the US Civil War and the German and British forces closer during the Christmas of 1917 at the height of the First World War (Maddock 2015). There are many more examples from the contemporary world. For instance, Military Bands are the only institution that brought the Militaries of Pakistan and India together under the UN Flag during Peacekeeping operations in Congo. Since then, proposals have been floated for exchange of Military Bands between the two hostile nations

Another example is provided by the Military Bands of Ireland and United Kingdom that played together in Ulster in 2016 at the centennial memorial ceremony for the Battle of Somme that took place in 1916. Otherwise, the two militaries had Ulster's memories only as battlefield against each other for more than a century.

Yet another instance of this was witnessed at the 1984 Summer Olympics in Los Angeles, USA. The Chinese military music—the Military Anthem of China—was played in the presence of representatives from both the People's Republic of China and the Republic of China. But for military music, the two nation's representatives might not have acquiesced to any other form of a political statement without one side walking out of the arena.

The Military Bands are the only institution that bring enemies together under one music—the Music of Peace. The role of Military Bands in Peace Missions, the Military Bands giving a message of Peace at the Armed Forces Days, the Military Bands bringing foes together in Peace or Armistice Memorial Days and the Military Bands Tattoos promoting Peace are some of the notable roles of Military Bands for promotion of Peace.

Military Bands in Peace Missions

Military Bands have been performing in Peace Missions also. One such example is the involvement of the United States in peace mission in Bosnia and Herzegovina after the Dayton Peace Accord of 1995. The 1st Armored Division Band, the 33rd Army Band and the 76th Army Band were deployed for the peace mission. Although the duties varied but the latter two Bands mostly concentrated on musical missions. The Armored Division Bands performed both security and musical assignments with one week on and one week off. When performing guard duty, the Band split in half and part of the Band would perform guard duty and part remained available for musical commitments. The British Military Bands played their role when the Band of the 1st Battalion Welsh Guards in Banja Luka, Northern Bosnia, made a huge impact wearing scarlet tunics and bearskins in what was still a war zone, and helped the British to win over the hearts and minds of the local population.

Several other examples of Military Bands being used to maintain or strengthen peace have been provided elsewhere in this book including those of Haiti, Dominican Republic, Hungary and elsewhere.

Military Bands as a Message for Peace at Armed Forces Days

All over the world, the display of "hard power" at the Military Day celebrations are being replaced, or at least complemented, by demonstration of "soft power" of the Armed Forces. In other words, the exclusive display of tanks and missiles is being complimented by a greater space being given to Military Bands. The end message is usually "peace." In countries as diverse and distant as France and India, for example, the annual national day military parades displaying tanks, guns and missiles are softened by the *Beating the Retreat*-type military Bands musical display.

In 1995, the German Defense Forces observed their 40th anniversary, attended, among others, by the Chancellor Helmut Kohl, President Roman Herzog and Defense Minister Volker Ruehe, through a "Grand Tattoo" featuring soldiers and Bands. At an earlier reception, the chancellor thanked the eight million Germans who have served in the army, called the *Bundeswehr*, since it was founded 10 years after the end of World War II. The message from the army day was that of "Peace." "We can be proud of this *army of peace and freedom*," Kohl said. "Fifty years ago, the longest *era of peace* in modern German history began, and the Bundeswehr had a considerable role in this." [Emphasis added] Message was loud and clear that the German Army stood for "Peace," that they have and shall continue to play their role for Peace.

Now such messages are heard across the political spectrum. As of 2017, the

Army Day in the biggest democracy, named India, and the Armed Forces day in Myanmar—a country traditionally ruled by the military—had an identical message, that is Peace. In two unrelated events, as the Indian military Bands played, the Chief of India Army addressed his troops reaffirming Indian commitment to peace. In Myanmar, the Commander-in-Chief of Defence Services pledged that the Myanmar Armed Forces (called *Tatmadaw*) will "participate in *establishing everlasting peace* using the six peace principles laid down by the Defense Forces under supervision of the government." [Emphasis added]

Military Bands Tattoos as Instruments of Peace

There is a growing realization in recent decades that Military Bands tattoos and shows are held as a means to promote peace. South Korea founded the Wonju International Tattoo where up to 14 military and civilian Bands from 8 countries, including France, Japan, Mongolia, Spain and the United States, other than many Korean Bands have participated in the biennial event. It was originally named *World Peace Fanfare* at its debut in 2000. It has since evolved from a local music festival into a national event that seeks to bring together music from the best military and brass Bands from all over the world. The theme for the biennial event has also revolved around Peace with titles such as "Music for the Peace, Marching for the Future."

One of the biggest annual tattoos is the Spasskaya Towers Military Bands Tattoo at Kremlin, Moscow. There is hardly any doubt in the minds of the participant military and police forces that the aim to bring together military Bands is "Peace." In an interview, head of the Abu Dhabi Police Band (UAE), Fahed al-Hammadi, said that his country was "expecting an atmosphere of celebration and peace that will allow us to proudly represent our country while coming together with other cultures to mark this prestigious event in Russia. For us, the music festival is a great platform to display our pride in the culture and heritage of the United Arab Emirates, while also being able to experience and appreciate the national, artistic and military traditions of all participating countries, *in the spirit of peace.*" [Emphasis added]

Tetsuji Nozaka, head of the Sansa Odori Folk Band from Japan, participating at Moscow Tattoo opined, "We think attending this event gives us more mutual understanding and more communication. But it also *creates real peace and real respect* between ... our countries." [Emphasis added]

Military Bands at War Commemorations: Mourning for enemy troops

The military Bands are a standard way to pay tribute to fallen heroes even of the opposite side. It is no longer rare for leaders of erstwhile forces to come together to observe anniversary of a war or a battle. In 2016, the British Prime Minister David Cameroon and the German President Joachim Gauck, jointly attended a memorial service at St Magnus Cathedral in Kirkwall, Orkney, to honour the 8,645 men who were killed in the Battle of Jutland-the largest naval battle of the First World War. Nothing more can highlight the military Bands' role for peace when they play mourning tunes jointly to remember those who were killed by each other's military forces in some past war.

Such-like ceremonies take place not only with respect to major battles or landings of the two world wars but in commemoration of many regional or local wars as well. The ceremony to commemorate the massacre of Muslims in Srebrenica is now attended by both Bosnian and Serb Presidents. Peace commemorations of Rwandan civil war and the genocide of Tutsis and moderate Hutus is likewise supported by military Band music.

Another similar instance was witnessed on 1 July 2016, on the centennial anniversary of the Battle of Somme when the Bands of the 36th Ulster Division (former UVF) and 36th Irish Division (rival Irish Volunteers) performed together at Enniskillen Castle. One million casualties had been suffered from both sides during the 141-day standoff in Northern France a hundred years ago. The Irish Defense Forces Army Band no. 1 from the Republic of Ireland and the Royal Irish Regiment Band from the United Kingdom performed mourning tunes for the dead—one of the rarest spectacles for the two nations' Armed Forces.

Another recurring anniversary of a peace treaty is celebrated locally in Portsmouth for the Portsmouth Treaty of 1905 that ended the Russio-Japan War. Thanks to intensive historical research in period newspapers, local library collections and musical archives throughout the country, Sea-coast Wind Ensemble conductor Richard C. Spicer has assembled a collection of Band music that was played in the days leading to the treaty. The same repertoire is used for the peace treaty commemoration in Portsmouth each year when Marching Bands march through the streets of Portsmouth remembering the peace treaty.

In short, the military Bands herald and symbolize peace. For example, when a US military Band could pass through the streets of Dominican Republic after the war, there was no further proof necessary to convince the people that peace had returned. The day a US Military Band would be able to play through the streets of Baghdad or Kabul, no announcement from White House would be able to substitute this act, to announce the return of peace.

Conclusion

The website of the British Ministry of Defence sanguinely proclaims that Music does not resolve disputes it creates a climate in which disputes can be resolved. There is no reason why Military Bands may not act as a dispute resolution mechanism. Though true for the moment, one may not lose hope that in the future, the Military Bands may have a direct role in the resolution of military conflicts. It may be one day be recognized as mechanism of pacific settlement of disputes. As a starting point, there must be an additional protocol to the Geneva Conventions of 1949, specifically for protection of Military Bands affording them the same protection as medics and chaplains have.

Moreover, one may be forgiven for believing that the Military Bands have already contributed so much for Peace, that they merit consideration for Nobel Peace Prize as an institution. In any case, in terms of academic disciplines that are entitled to a Nobel Prize, the Peace Prize is one for "International Relations" (IR), albeit for its practitioners, not researchers and writers on IR, as is the case with Economics or Literature, for instance. Being diplomats, the Military Band members are IR practitioners, practicing Peace.

Coming to the status of Military Bands as a field sports, case has been made for the institution of an international Olympics of Bands. It is evident that all three existing types of Olympics have, to some varying extent, military pedigree. The declared mission of promoting peace remained at the foundation from ancient to the modern Olympics. The nexus between Peace and Olympics is so symbiotic that in ancient Greece, when four yearly Olympics had to take place, no war could continue. In modern day, both the times the world was at war, Olympics could not be held. The international military Bands Olympics may go a long way in creating an air of cordiality between rival fighting forces. Broadly speaking, the culture of the people must lead to a culture of peace and non-violence [which] the United Nations specialized agency, UNESCO, avers, "is a commitment to peace-building, mediation, conflict prevention and resolution, intercultural and interfaith reconciliation." If so, then there is no harm in declaring the World Day of Peace and Non-violence as the World Day of Military Bands as well.

Epilogue

Music is shorthand of emotion.

—Leo Tolstoy

In an article in Scientific American, the Nobel-Prize-winning quantum physicist Brian Josephson theorized that, "Music stems less from superficial cultural influences than from timeless universal 'structures' of the mind." By probing the human response to music, Josephson stated, "Researchers may discern these structures." This is indubitably an area that tantalizingly demands further scientific inquiry. In music then, the significance of Bands can scarcely be overstated.

Probably for the reason mentioned by Josephson, if there is one institution in the growth of which the whole world has contributed, it is that of music, song and dance. As a corollary, if there is one institution in the development of which the whole humankind has contributed, it is that of the Military Band. Turkey is credited with being the first to raise regular Army Bands; Russia took lead in creating Navy Bands; the United States founded the Marine Bands and the first Air Force Bands were born in the United Kingdom.

In the civilian domain, China took pride in laying the foundation of Palace Bands; the Latin Americans oversaw the origin of dedicated Parliament Bands; the Vietnamese kingdoms could boast of Civil Service Bands; the first Police Bands sprang up in the Caribbean nation of Barbados and those in Militia forces probably in France. Among the mounted Bands, the Indo-Pakistan region has traces of horse-mounted Bands spanning centuries ago; the Persians (modern-day Iran) had elephant-mounted Bands in ancient times; Namibia in South West Africa saw camel-mounted Bands during its colonial history while the Netherlands has maintained its bicycle-mounted Bands.

The oldest continuing fanfare Band is traced to Belgium, the flag throwing Bands to Tuscany in Italy, the signalling Bands to the Saracens (early Arabs) and the oldest funeral Bands can be traced to central Africa. The Dance Bands existed and independently emerged in opposite corners of the world such as New Zealand, South and East of Africa and the Siberian region of Northern Russia. Wedding

Bands of different types emerged in different parts of the world—such as the wedding marching Bands in Indo-Pakistan, Wedding Jazz Bands in North America, wedding orchestras in Western Europe and wedding dance troupes in whole of Eastern and South Eastern Europe.

Coming back to the Military Bands, they are the Custodian of historical and cultural legacies of all nations on earth. Other than the institution of the monarch which survives in few countries, it is the military Band that have preserved costumes, sounds, marches and traditions of yesteryears. This, the Bands could not have done, without the patronage of the monarchy. In fact, all enduring pieces of fine arts owe a lot to royal or elitist backing. Without the patronage, financial sponsorship and encouragement of the centres of power, individual or institutional, big works of art and culture could neither be created, nor be preserved. Like all other facets of art and culture, the Military Bands reflected the political standing, social status and personal or institutional ambitions of its patrons. The patronage came from the royal court, the Church, the nobility and the military at different times and at different places.

The Military Bands shared, traded, exchanged, adopted and adapted musical and formational traditions as much from friendly nations and troops as from the adversary nations and enemy forces. The human history is replete with romantic stories of Band members as an integral part of the military formations during the wars and their unique role in peacetime ceremonials.

In spite of that, there has been a global crusade against Military Bands in recent decades, considering them as a useless branch of army and a waste of public money. The question is that of the relative value of martial music in "inspiring the existing troops" to that of "providing additional troops" at the cost of Music. The Government Accountancy Agency (GAO), at least in the United States, asks the Armed Forces to calculate both the costs and come up with objectively measurable performance objectives for the military and for the Bands. It remains to be seen whether the true worth of priceless arts, and of Bands, is calculable!

ANNEX–A

Organizations Promoting Military & Marching Bands

Bands World
407 Terrace St.
Ashland, OR 97520, U.S.A
Phone: +1 541 778 3161
Email: support@bandworld.org

International Association of Bands Tattoos
Mailing address: PL 70, FI-49401 Hamina, FINLAND
Street address: Raatihuoneentori 16, 49400 Hamina, FINLAND
Phone: +35 840 199 1426
Email: tattoo@hamina.fi

International Military Music Society
9 Hirst Grove, Darlington DL1 4NX, UNITED KINGDOM
Phone: +44 1325 352862
Online Contact: http://imms-online.org/contact-membership/

Marching Bands for Peace
395, Shaheed Rd Corner, Sector-I, Airport Housing Society,
Airport Link Road, Islamabad, RWP- 46200, PAKISTAN
Phone: +92 302 8555073
Email: *Info@marchingbands.band*

Royal Edinburgh Military Tattoo
1-3 Cockburn St, Edinburgh EH1 1QB, (UK) SCOTLAND
Phone: +44 131 225 1188
Email: administration@edintattoo.co.uk

World Association of Marching Show Bands
World Championships Palm Springs,
PO Box 4983, Palm Springs,
CA 92263, U.S.A
Phone: +1 760 409-6531
Email: wamsb@wamsb.org

ANNEX–B

Official members of the International Association of Tattoo Organizers (IATO)

The Edinburgh Military Tattoo *www.edintattoo.co.uk*
Established 1950, annually

Basel Tattoo *www.baseltattoo.ch*
Established 2005, annually

The Swedish Military Tattoo
Established 1986, biennial

The Berlin Military Music Festival *musikfest@dbwv.de*
Established 1995, annually

The NATO Music Festival (NATO Musikfest Mönchengladbach)
www.airn.nato.int/nmf/NMFDEU/
Established 1960, biennial (1965 in Kaiserslautern)

Kremlin Military Tattoo (Spasskaya Bashnya) *www.kremlin-military-tattoo.ru*
General Director Sergey Smirnov Established 2006 as Shows of State Honour Guards units on Poklonnaya Hill, annually

International Military Music Event Hamina Tattoo *www.haminatattoo.com*
Established 1990, biennial

Musikschau der Nationen *www.volksbund-bremen.de*
Established 1965 as "Militärmusikschau", annually

The Netherlands Military Tattoo *www.nationaletaptoe.nl*
Established 1954 as "Tattoo Delft", annually

International Tattoo Heerlen (Internationale Taptoe Heerlen)
www.taptoeheerlen.nl
Established 1996 as minor music festival, annually

Virginia International Tattoo *www.vafest.org*
Producer and Director J. Scott Jackson, Established 1997, annually

Wonju Tattoo International *www.wonjutattoo.com*
Established 2000 as "World Peace Fanfare" at Chiak Gymnasium, biennial – annually from 2006

Québec City International Festival of Military Bands *www.fimmq.com*
Established 1999, annually, chief instigator of the Festival, Jacques Du Sault,

Royal Nova Scotia International Tattoo *www.nstattoo.ca*
CEO and Executive Producer Ann Montague Established 1979, annually

Herning Indoor Tattoo (Danish Military Tattoo) *www.herningindoortattoo.dk*
Established 2004, annually (no show since 2007)

Norwegian Military Tattoo (NMT) *www.normiltattoo.no*
Chief Executive and Producer Col Christer Johannesen Established 1994, biennial

Canadian International Military Tattoo (Hamilton International Tattoo)
www.canadianmilitarytattoo.ca
Established 1992 as Greater Hamilton Tattoo, annually

Windsor Castle Royal Tattoo *www.windsortattoo.com*
Established 2008, annually

Luxembourg International Military Tattoo *www.militarytattoo.lu*
Established 2007, annually

South African Tattoo *www.satattoo.co.za*
Executive Producer Simon Carter Established 2008, annually

ANNEX-C

Instrumental Composition of Military Bands

1. Composition of Pipe Bands in South Asian military

S.No.	*Instrument Name*	*Number of players*
1	Bagpipes	Thirteen (13)
2	*Shehnai*/ Flute.	Two (02)
3	Tambourine/ Dafli	One (01)
4	Maracus	One Pair (01)
5	Tenor Drums.	Two (02)
6	Marching Snare Drums	Six (06)
7	Bass Drum Marching.	One (01)
	Total:	Twenty Six (26) Instruments

2. Brass Band Composition in European tradition

S.No	*Instrument Name*	*Number of players*
1	Eb Soprano Cornet	One (01)
2	Solo Bb Cornet	Four (04)
3	Repiano Bb Cornet	One (01)
4	2nd Bb Cornet	Two (02)
5	3rd Bb Cornet	Two (02)
6	Bb Flugelhorn	One (01)
7	Solo Eb Tenor Horn	One (01)
8	1st Eb Tenor Horn	One (01)
9	2nd Eb Tenor Horn	One (01)
10	1st Bb Baritone	One (01)
11	2nd Bb Baritone	One (01)
12	1st Bb Tenor Trombone	One (01)
13	2nd Bb Tenor Trombone	One (01)
14	Bass Trombone	One (01)

S.No	Instrument Name	Number of players
15	Bb Euphonium	Two (02)
16	Eb Bass	Two (02)
17	Bb Bass	Two (02)
18	Percussion	Upto Four (2-4)
	Total:	Twenty Seven (27-31) Instruments

3 (a). Concert Band Composition in South Asian tradition

S.No.	Instrument Name	Number of players
1	Concert Piccolo.	One (01)
2	Concert Flute.	One (01)
3	Eb Clarinet.	Two (02)
4	Bb Clarinet.	Fourteen (14)
5	Bb Cornet.	Five (05)
6	Bb Trumpet.	Five (05)
7	Eb Alto Sarophone.	Two (02)
8	Bb Tenor Sarophone.	Two (02)
9	Bb Tenor Tiombone.	Three (03)
10	Eb Alto Horn.	Four (04)
11	Bb Euphonium.	Two (02)
12	Eb Bass.	Two (02)
13	Bb Bass.	Two (02)
14	Side Drum Marching.	Two (02)
15	Bass Drum Marching.	One (01)
	Total:	Forty-Four (44) Instruments

3 (b). Concert Bands Composition in European Tradition

S.No.	Instrument Name	Number of players
1	Piccolo	One (01)
2	1st & 2nd Flutes	Two (02)
3	1st & 2nd Oboes	Two (02)
4	Eb Clarinet	One (01)
5	1st Bb Clarinet	Six (06)
6	2nd Bb Clarinet	Six (0)6

S.No.	*Instrument Name*	*Number of players*
7	3rd Bb Clarinet	Six (06)
8	Bb Bass Clarinet	One (01)
9	1st Eb Alto Saxophone	One (01)
10	2nd Eb Alto Saxophone	One (01)
11	Bb Tenor Saxophone	One (01)
12	Eb Baritone Saxophone	One (01)
13	1st & 2nd Bassoon	Two (02)
14	1st & 2nd Horn in F	Two (02)
15	3rd & 4th Horn in F	Two (02)
16	1st Bb Trumpet	Two (02)
17	2nd Bb Trumpet	Two (02)
18	3rd Bb Trumpet	Two (02)
19	1st Tenor Trombone	One (01)
20	2nd Tenor Trombone	One (01)
21	Bass Trombone	One (01)
22	Euphonium	One (01)
23	Basses	Four (04)
24	Percussion	Up to Six (2-6)
25	Double Bass	One (01)
	Total	Fifty Five (55-60) Instruments

4. (a). Instrumental Composition of a Classical Orchestra

S.No.	*Instrument Name*	*Number of players*
Wooodwinds		
1	Western concert flutes	Two (02)
2	Oboes	Two (02)
3	Clarinets(Bb, C, or A)	Two (02)
4	Bassoons	Two (02)
Brass		
5	Natural horns	Two (02)
6	Natural trumpets	Two (02)
Percussion		
7	Timpani	Two (02) but performed by a singly Timpanist

4 (b). Standard Instrumentation of Modern Philharmonic Orchestra

S.No.	*Instrument Name*	*No. of players*
Woodwinds		
1	Western concert flute (1 doubling piccolo)	2-4
2	Oboes (1 doubling cor Anglais)	2-4
3	Clarinets (1-2 doubling bass clarinet and/or Em& Clarinet)	2-4
4	Bassoons (1 doubling contrabassoon)	2-4
5	Contrabassoon	One (01)
6	Saxaphone of various types	One or more
Brass		
7	German(usually double) horns in F/Bm& (in France: French horns; in Vienna: Vienna horns)	4-8
8	Trumpets in Bm&	3-6
9	Trombones (1–2 bass trombones)	3-6
10	Tubas	1-2
11	Baritone horns/euphoniums	One (01) or more
12	Wagner tubas	One (01) or more
Keyboards		
13	Piano	One (01)
14	Celesta (Pipe organ in some works)	One (01)
15	Harps	1-2
Strings		
16	Violins-1	Sixteen (16)
17	Violins-2	Fourteen (14)
18	Violas	Twelve (12)
19	Cellos	Ten (10)
20	Double basses	Eight (08)
Percussion and others		
21	Drum Kit plus Two Timpani (played by one timpanist), Snare drum, Tenor drum, Bass drum, Cymbals, Tam-tam, Triangle, Wood block, Tambourine, Glockenspiel, Xylophone, Vibraphone, Tubular bells, Marimba	As per requirement

Bibliography

Adams, Micheal C. C. *Echoes of War: A thousand years of military history in popular culture.* Lexington (USA): University Press of Kentucky, 2002.

Akkus, Ceylan. "Role of Music in World War II." *prezi.com.* February 25, 2015. https://prezi.com/8cg0gmxo3ke4/role-of-music-in-world-war-ii/ (accessed May 01, 2017).

Anonymous. "As a rape survivor, Band was my healing space." *The Stanford Daily*, Dec 14, 2016.

BMB. *History of Bursa Mehter Band.* Brochure, Bursa: Bursa Mehter Band Inc, 2017.

Booth, Gregory D. *Brass Baja: Stories from the World of Indian Wedding Bands.* New Delhi: Oxford University Press, 2006.

Bowen, C. "Adult Community Bands in the Southeastern United States: An Investigation of Current Activity and Background Profiles of the Participants." *PhD Dissertation.* Florida: Florida State University, 1995.

Bradley, Craig Werner & Douglas. *We Gotta Get Out of This Place: The Soundtrack of the Vietnam War.* Amherst, MA (USA): University of Massachusetts Press, 2015.

Braw, Elisabeth. "Military Bands Trumpet the Might and Status of a Nation." *Daily Financial Times.* https://www.ft.com/content/0d614e8e-e0ea-11e7-a0d4-0944c5f49e46 (accessed 01 03, 2018).

Brayton, Ed. "Army Launches Investigation of MRFF Complaint on Band at Mormon Event." *Patheos.* Dec 27, 2017. http://www.patheos.com/blogs/dispatches/2017/12/27/ (accessed 27 December 2017).

Campbell, Kay Hardy. "Mehter Music Echoes Down the Centuries." *Aramco World*, Sept-Oct 2012: 2.

Chakravarti, P. C. *The Art of War in Ancient India.* New Delhi: Low Price Publications, 2011.

Chaudry, Aminullah. *Political Administrators: The Story of the CIvil Service of Pakistan.* Karachi: Oxford University Press, 2011.

Ching-chih, Liu. *Critical History of New Music in China.* Translated by Caroline Mason. Hong Kong: Chinese University Press, 2010.

Churchill, Winston. *The Story of the Malakand Field Force.* London: Thomas Nelson and Sons, 1916.

Cousins, Sgt F. A. M. "Military Music in South Africa: A critical study of its use in time of peace and its potential in times of War." *South African Journal of Miitary Affairs* 11, no. 3 (1981): 1–8.

Curtis, John. "Soldiers First: Bands in the World War Two and Since." *Bands International* 38, no. 2 (2016): 73–76.

Dahle, Jan Magnus. "Wind Music in Norway." *World Association of Symbhonic Bands and Ensembles.* 2017. http://www.wasbe.org/resource-details.php?id=4 (accessed 02 February 2018).

Dean, Colin. "The Power of Music: Bands of the Brigades of Guards during the First World War." *Band International* 38, no. 3 (2016): 114–21.

Dobney, Jayson Kerr. "Military Music in European and American Traditions." *Metropolitan Museum of Arts.* October 2004. http://www.metmuseum.org/toah/hd/ammu/hd_ammu.htm (accessed 2 Dec 2016).

DVA, Department of Veteran Affairs. *Factsheet on America's Wars.* 2017. https://www.va.gov/opa/publications/factsheets/fs_americas_wars.pdf (accessed 13 March 2017).

Farmer, Henry George. "Crusading Martial Music." *Music Lett* (Oxford University Press) XXX, no. 3 (1949): 243–49.

Fauser, Annegret. *Sounds of War: Music in the United States during World War II.* New York: Oxford University Press, 2013.

Fettig, Colonel Jason K. "The President's Own: Marine Band and the US Pesidents." *United States Marine Corps Official Website.* 2016. http://www.marineband.marines.mil/About/Marine-Band-and-the-Presidents (accessed 12 February 2018).

Fiabu, Anane. "Police Band Centenary." *Ghana News Agency.* 28 December 2017. http://www.ghananewsagency.org/social/police-band-s-centenary to draw civilians-closer-for-effective-policing-126913 (accessed 28 December 2017).

History of Army Music. n.d. http://www.goarmy.com/band/about-army-bands/history.html (accessed 30 September 2016).

Howard, Philip. *The Black Warch (Royal Highland Regiment).* London: Hamish Hamilton, 1968.

Jansson, Leif A. "Wind Band and the History of Swedish Music." *World Association of Symphonic Bands & Ensembles.* 2018. http://www.wasbe.org/resource-details.php?id=7 (accessed 02 February 2018).

Khan, Saad S. "Red Band and Black Sea: Obituary of a Musical Legacy." *Global Age*, March 2017: 48–50.

Kingston, Geoff, interview by Author. *Chairman, International Military Music Society* (12 March 2016).

Knight, Ian. *British Battles.com/Battle of Isandlwana.* 2004. http://www.britishbattles.com/zulu-war/isandlwana.htm (accessed 3 October 2017).

Lei, Zhao. "Thousand Musicians Help Parade Keep in Step." *China Daily*, 09 April, 2015.

Maddock, Sally S. "Music and Combat Motivation." *Defense Technical Information Center.* 1 April 2015. www.dtic.mil/get-tr-doc/pdf?AD=ADA635065 (accessed Aug 28, 2017).

McNeill, William H. *Keeping Together in Time: Dance and Drill in Human History.* Cambridge, MA: Harvard University Press, 1995.

Mehter Army Band. n.d. http://www.ottomansouvenir.com/Music/Mehter_Army_Band.htm (accessed 04 April 2017).

"Military Music." *Norway Armed Forces Official Website.* July 15, 2015. https://forsvaret.no/en/facts/culture/music (accessed 02 February 2018).

Morris Jastrow, Jr. *The Civilization of Baylonia and Assyria.* Philadelphia, USA: J. B. Lippincott Co., 1915.

Music about the Korean War. July 18, 2012. http://www.historyonthenet.com/authentichistory/1946-1960/2-korea/3-music/ (accessed 10 October 2016).

Music, US Army Elementary School of. "History of US Army Bands." *Federaton of American Scientists.* October 2005. http://docshare.tips/army-bands_58958ad3b6d87f8e868b4ef7.html (accessed 07 April 2017).

Philipps, Dave. "Military Is Asked to March to a Less Expensive Tune." *Daily "New York Times"*, 1 July 2016.

—. "Military is asked to march to less expensive tunes." *Daily New York Times*, 1 July 2016.

Pieslak, Jonathan. *Sound Targets: American Soldiers and Music in the Iraq War.* Bloomington: Indiana University Press, 2009.

Rager, Daniel. *In Search of Wind Band: An International Expedition.* Chardon, Ohio: Wind-Band Music, 2013.

Ray, Penny. *18 Lessons Marching Band Teaches Our Kids: A Parent's Perspective.* Nov 29, 2011. http://www.amparents.org/a-parents-perspective-18-lessons-marching-band-teaches-our-kids/#comment-344610 (accessed 22 April 2017).

Reed, Col Joseph. "Letter from Colonel Reed to Mrs. Reed: Account of the engagement on the plains of Harlem." *Northern Illinois University (Online Library Archives)*. 22 September 1776. (accessed 8 April 2017).

Saoud, Rabah. "The Arab Contribution to the Music of the Western World." *Muslim World Music Day.* Edited by Salim al Hassani. Foundation for Science Technology and Civilization. March 2004. http://muslimworldmusicday.com/files/music.pdf (accessed 25 January 2017).

Shafiq, Viola. *Arab Cinema: History and Cultural Identity.* Cairo: American University of Cairo Press, 1998.

Shansky, Albert. *A Trio of Zen Buddhist Stories: The Roshi, The Japanese Castaway, Escape from Exile Island.* Bloomington, IN: iUniverse Inc, 2011.

Shappard, Rebecca. *DoD Spending Budget and Military Bands: That is not how it works Congresswoman!* June 25, 2016. https://www.benzinga.com/general/politics/16/06/8122699/ (accessed 10 February 2017).

Snell, Bruce C. Kelly and Mark A. *Music Resounding: Music and Musicians of the Cold War Era.* Edited by Mark A. Snell Bruce C. Kelly. Columbia: University of Missouri Press, 2004.

Telegraph, Daily. *News Item on Stolen instruments.* London, 06 September 2017.

Trotter, William R. "The Music of War." *HistoryNet.com.* 2005. http://www.historynet.com/the-music-of-war.htm (accessed 31 January 2017).

University, George Washington Center for Innovative Media— a Project of George Washington. *Face the Facts/ Facts.* February 02, 2017. http://www.facethefactsusa.org/facts/New-Aircraft-Carrier-Does-More-with-Less-Crew.

USAF-Website. *Official Website of the United States Air Force.* n.d. http://www.bands.af.mil/main/welcome.asp (accessed 02 February 2017).

Vollbretch, Matthew. *Titanic: The Most Complete Story Ever Told.* Open Book Audio, 2012.

Watson, Frederick. *The Story of Highland Regiments.* London: A&C Black, 1915.

Werner, Eric. *The Sacred Bridge.* New York: Columbia University Press, 1984.

White, Nigel Lilly. "A History of Hungarian Military Music." *Band International* 37, no. 3

(December 2015): 102–3.

Yang, Hsüan-chih. *A Record of Buddhist Monastries in Lo-Yang.* Princeton, NJ: Princeton University Press, 2014.

Younghusband, Captain G. J. Younghusband and Col Sir Francis E. *Tho Relief of Chitral.* London: Macmillan and Co., 1910.

Index